LITERACY IN AMERICA

LITERACY IN AMERICA

Historic Journey and Contemporary Solutions

Edward E. Gordon and Elaine H. Gordon
Foreword by Gerald Gutek

 PRAEGER

Westport, Connecticut
London

Library of Congress Cataloging-in-Publication Data

Gordon, Edward E.
    Literacy in America : historic journey and contemporary solutions / Edward E.
Gordon and Elaine H. Gordon ; foreword by Gerald Gutek.
        p.   cm.
    Includes bibliographical references and index.
    ISBN 0–275–95524–9 (alk. paper)—ISBN 0–275–97864–8 (pbk. : alk. paper)
    1. Literacy—United States—History.   2. Educational sociology—United States.
I. Gordon, Elaine H.   II. Title.
LC151.G68   2003
302.2'242—dc21   2002068609

British Library Cataloguing in Publication Data is available.

Library of Congress Catalog Card Number: 2002068609
ISBN: 0–275–95524–9
        0–275–97864–8 (pbk.)

First published in 2003

Praeger Publishers, 88 Post Road West, Westport, CT 06881
An imprint of Greenwood Publishing Group, Inc.
www.praeger.com

Printed in the United States of America

The paper used in this book complies with the
Permanent Paper Standard issued by the National
Information Standards Organization (Z39.48–1984).

10 9 8 7 6 5 4 3 2 1

*To our mothers, who guided our first steps on the road to literacy
and nurtured our love of reading*

Contents

List of Figures

Foreword

Abraham Lincoln attended school for less than a year. In many respects, he was his own teacher. Borrowing books whenever he could and reading them in whatever time was available, Lincoln mastered the English language, practiced as a highly skilled lawyer, and became one of the nation's greatest presidents. Though unschooled, Lincoln valued the written word and his own oratory established him as a truly literate person and a great communicator. In their new book, *Literacy in America: Historic Journey and Contemporary Solutions*, Edward and Elaine Gordon research and analyze the process of how a person such as Lincoln achieved the literacy that enabled him to rise to the pinnacle of American political life. While we can marvel at how Lincoln attained literacy on the Kentucky, Indiana, and Illinois frontier in the early nineteenth century, he was not alone in his achievement. Becoming literate outside of school was not limited to exceptional people like Lincoln but was a process going on in the lives of ordinary people throughout the United States. Edward and Elaine Gordon engagingly craft the story of how many Americans became literate in the period before the establishment of public education, either without schooling or with only the meager kind of schooling that Lincoln had.

To bring a focus to their study, the Gordons begin by stipulating a definition of literacy "as the degree of interaction with written text that enables any person to be a functioning, contributing member of the society in which that person lives and works." They then examine the various means that Americans used to become literate, such as domestic education, dame schools, subscription schools, moving schools, self-study, and tutoring.

Many historians of education have customarily equated education with schooling and viewed literacy as a consequence of being instructed in a school. Lawrence Cremin in *The Wonderful World of Ellwood Paterson Cubberley*

(1965) and Bernard Bailyn in *Education in the Forming of American Society* (1960) challenged the then standard interpretation that education is the same as schooling. They called for a larger and more comprehensive analysis of education that encompassed informal and nonformal as well as formal kinds of learning. Informal education occurs when a person learns through everyday interaction with his or her social milieu and environment. Here, the educational process is more or less accidental and unstructured. The opportunities for learning depend upon the person's own curiosity and motivation and on the variety and richness of the environment in which he or she lives. Some aspects of literacy learning that result from random encounters with the written word are informal, as when people work to decode broadsides, placards, and signs. Nonformal education is the learning that takes place when instruction is given to a learner but not in an institutionalized setting. For literacy learning, subscription society clubs and libraries and instruction by tutors were forms of nonformal education. Formal education, or schooling, is the deliberate instruction of individuals, typically children or adolescents, in an institution expressly established for that purpose. In their book, the Gordons examine dame, subscription, and moving schools, which provided literacy instruction before the advent of the common schools. It is within this broadened context of education—as informal, nonformal, and formal processes of learning—that the attainment of literacy needs to be considered.

In *Literacy in America: Historic Journey and Contemporary Solutions*, Edward and Elaine Gordon proceed with the challenge of examining how people became literate in America. The book, a carefully researched and well-crafted narrative history, provides an enriched and finely contextualized examination of education that results in the forming of literate women and men. Their effort adds to and helps to redefine the history of American education.

The Gordons' writing of history does not follow the usual pattern of literacy studies that focus on statistical analysis or examinations of the acquisition of literacy as a function of schooling. Rather, they set out to document that the attainment of literacy, like education, is a much broader and more complex task than being instructed in reading and writing by a teacher in a school classroom. Rather than focus on statistical data relating to the number of literates at a given time, the Gordons weave a narrative that recounts how people struggled to achieve literacy.

To create their narrative, the Gordons used extensive primary sources, especially the autobiographies of those who attained literacy, often against compelling odds, to find the processes used to become literate. What events and situations provoked people's desire for literacy? What methods and materials did they use to accomplish their goal? To answer these questions, the authors examined how Americans, through the colonial, early national, and frontier eras, became literate in a variety of changing geographical, social, and economic contexts. They also examine how African Americans often defied the antebellum laws that forbade them to learn to write and how Native Americans succeeded in becoming literate while facing the threat of cultural extinction.

The Gordons in their conclusion argue that literacy education cannot be left to schools alone. Just as they examined the variety of ways that Americans used to attain literacy in the past, they point to a variety of ways that can be used to enhance the development of literacy in the contemporary American situation. They offer specific recommendations for enhancing parent involvement and parent-school collaboration to promote higher levels of reading fluency.

Building on the work they began in *Centuries of Tutoring: A History of Alternative Education in America and Western Europe* (1990), Edward and Elaine Gordon's *Literacy in America: Historic Journey and Contemporary Solutions* enlarges our perspectives on the social, political, economic, religious, and intellectual contexts in which educational developments occur. Their new book is a welcome addition to studies of literacy and educational history.

Gerald Gutek
Professor Emeritus
Loyola University

Introduction

Americans have always been a people on the move. Across 300 years of history their quest for a new life included many different ways of attaining literacy. At the beginning of the twenty-first century, literacy in the United States is treated almost as a birthright. Yet until the last few decades its history has received scant attention. One reason may be that so few Americans are totally illiterate. Another factor may be that literacy theory is full of too many abstractions, making even the simplest ideas difficult to understand if not downright incomprehensible. The important human story of how past generations of Americans became literate is the focus of this book.[1]

In today's world, the word *literacy* is used in a wide variety of contexts, such as computer literacy, cultural literacy, or numeral literacy, which serves to create controversy about its basic meaning. Here, the authors define literacy as the degree of interaction with written text that enables a person to be a functioning, contributing member of the society in which that person lives and works. That definition assumes no single fixed standard for literacy. Instead, we believe that literacy is constantly being shaped by the social, economic, and technical demands of particular times and places. We see literacy as a lifelong process by which each person learns a set of skills that gradually builds reading fluency and thinking abilities. We agree with many other historians that literacy standards in America have changed substantially over the past 300 years.[2]

In the early American colonial era the ability to read at least parts of the Bible was the common definition of literacy. This is a far cry from today's high-tech world. A literate person must now possess a much higher degree of fluency in reading, writing and math, up to the 12th- or 13th-grade level (U.S. Departments of Labor and Education), for many technical and professional occupations.[3]

HOW MANY PEOPLE WERE LITERATE?

Before the availability of modern census data, historians attempted to determine how many people were literate in a specific place and time by counting signatures on documents. They consulted church registers for married couples or civil court records such as land titles, wills, or deeds of sale. These historians broadly used one's ability to sign one's name as a determinant of literacy. Using this data, historians estimated what proportion of the entire population was literate.

Before the twentieth century, only a small fraction of all children went to school. Many were taught at home. In the eighteenth and nineteenth centuries, women were considered literate if they could read. It was then thought essential that women read the Bible and other religious books because of their future role in child rearing. Writing was thought to be a useless and dangerous skill for women, since it was then considered necessary only for business. Society prohibited women from the world of commerce and industry. Since women did not sign documents, but many were able to read, how accurate are the historians' literacy estimates from these early time periods? Another troubling fact in interpreting the historical record is that many male signers of documents never went beyond learning how to sign their names. In many cases, a signature was the mark of a population that knew how to sign but not always how to read or write. Critics charge that the relationship between the learning of writing and reading skills varied enormously from place to place, from time to time or from group to group.

Keeping all of these possible exceptions in mind, we find that after 1600, the percentage of signers rose sharply in Europe and America. Based on the ability to sign a parish register, male literacy in New England was estimated to be 60 percent, as compared with 40 percent in England. The passage of school attendance laws in New England was a primary reason for this great disparity. Male literacy based on signatures on New England wills showed a steady rise throughout the seventeenth and eighteenth centuries (1650, 60%; 1705, 70%; 1758, 80%; 1795, 90%). These rates compared favorably with those of Europe in 1800 (France 54%, England 62%, Scotland 88%).

Beginning with the 1840 U.S. Census, literacy figures were based on asking heads of families how many persons in the family over age 20 had the ability to read and write. However, this form of "self-reported literacy" contained many accuracy problems. What it meant to read and write was self-defined and self-assessed by each adult. Sometimes illiterate adults reported themselves as being illiterate in writing but not in reading (thinking this the lesser evil), thereby further distorting the census numbers.

These problems were partially corrected by the 1870 U.S. Census. For the first time, literacy information was gathered on children between the ages of 10 and 19. More important, for the first time a distinction was made between reading literacy and writing literacy. As a result, the 1870 census showed a 25 percent decline in U.S. literacy since 1860. By 1900 the U.S. Census Bureau defined an "illiterate" as a person 10 years of age or older unable to read and write in a native language.[4]

Other historians have attempted to use more indirect methods to determine literacy rates. One approach is to relate the number of schools in existence to the number of literate people. However, this link is neither precise nor consistent over time or between countries or even between regions in the same country. Sweden is a good example of a country with high levels of reading ability and very few schools until the nineteenth century. An additional problem with this approach is that educational advances such as schools, tutors, or governesses were not equally available to all classes of people or even to male and female students.

A second approach to measuring the number of literate people examines the production and sale of books, the argument being, "The more books purchased, the more people are literate." The major problems of interpretation posed by this argument include: Who bought the books? Who read the books? How much did they understand?

The third means of measuring literacy in a society is to consult estate inventories that show how many people possessed books at their death. Such a literacy measurement taken from estate records has several drawbacks. If an individual possessed books that were valuable, they may have been given away before or immediately after a person's death and thus been omitted by such an estate inventory. Books can be borrowed and therefore not represent the true level of someone's literacy abilities or be bought for show rather than for reading.[5]

More historians are becoming skeptical of the literacy-illiteracy dichotomy and the equation of signing abilities or census responses with actual reading ability. What is important is a history of literacy whose central theme is how people became literate and used literacy in their daily lives, rather than a fixation on trying to calculate theoretical literacy rates.[6]

HOW AMERICANS BECAME LITERATE

Unlike many previous historical studies of literacy in America, our aim is not be to determine what percentage of the population was literate in specific regions of America during a certain time period. Instead, we examine the variety of ways in which people became literate. What methods and materials were used in basic literacy instruction? How has American society defined literacy in various geographic regions and at different times? Who became literate and why? Why did some individuals strive to become literate while others were disinterested? When and how did literacy become a universal need of all Americans? What influences did literacy have on the lives of individual Americans, and how would literacy help define America's emergence into the modern era? These are some of the important literacy issues we will consider.

The authors contend that literacy and education are not synonymous with schooling, a viewpoint shared by much historical and educational scholarship.[7] Much of our analysis will concentrate on America prior to 1900, before compulsory schooling laws were either enacted or effectively enforced throughout the nation.

This book examines common patterns in literacy development through autobiographical materials that reveal how people learned to read and what literacy meant to them and their community. A diary is the best record of an individual's literacy as well as of his or her immediate family. While it is impossible to estimate how many people kept a diary or personal journal, they were apparently distributed widely throughout American society from colonial times to the early modern period. The authors show how we can learn much from this archival material about the role of reading in individual lives, personal motivation, and literacy's wider social and economic context. These factors are critical to better understanding how literacy developed throughout American history to our own time. In reviewing 300 years of how literacy developed throughout America, the authors do not attempt a detailed account of the history of literacy in every state. Instead, we hope to give readers an accurate overview of major literacy developments for specific geographic regions during the different historical eras of the United States.[8]

BOOK OVERVIEW

Literacy in America begins with Part I, "Literacy and Religion in Colonial America (1620–1789)." Chapter 1 examines the literacy education of the New England Puritans and how they were influenced by practices in Europe. Though the frontier forced many instructional adaptations, literacy continued to grow across that society throughout the American revolutionary period. Chapter 2 then shifts our focus to the middle colonies. Except for a few large cities, the greater diversity of ethnic groups in New York, Pennsylvania, and New Jersey prevented a more unified community literacy response. Chapter 3 moves us to the colonial South, where a very dispersed population and a plantation-based class system severely limited literacy opportunities for almost everyone. Also, in the original thirteen American colonies, only a minority of children progressed beyond the most basic literacy fluency levels. Fewer literacy opportunities were usually offered to women and girls than to men and boys, and this unfortunate social condition persisted for the next 100 years.

In Part II, "Literacy in the Young Republic (1790–1860)," Chapter 4 explores how literacy increased in the early northeastern United States. This increase was the result of the continued growth of education at home, private schools, and the initial stirrings of the first meaningful system of state-funded common schools. The antebellum South portrayed in Chapter 5 sharply differs with these practices. There, individuals and small groups struggled to increase the spread of literacy, working against a general social ambivalence toward literacy that pervaded much of the pre–Civil War agricultural southland.

Part III, "Literacy and the Frontier Experience (1790–1900)," moves us first, in Chapter 6, to the American Midwest. There we learn how early settlers adapted Eastern literacy practices, leaning heavily on subscription schools and domestic education. Chapter 7 travels farther west to show us the effects of both vast distances and a sparse population on the struggle to achieve literacy. Yet literacy was among the first thoughts of these western settlers as "a life essential." Their little one-room subscription schools dotting the plains and mountains helped them to overcome an often harsh physical environment. Through myriad means including self-education, circuit-riding schoolmarms, and church missionary activities, western literacy activities can be viewed as adding a new dimension to how the West was really won.

In Part IV, "Literacy Outside the Mainstream (1620–1900)," we turn to those Americans who had very limited literacy opportunities. American Indian literacy education, reviewed in Chapter 8, was used as a part of a broader attempt to acculturate Native Americans into white Western society. From colonial times to the twentieth century the results of these educational programs were often devastating to the general Indian population. This bleak picture was at times relieved by the literacy efforts of a number of Indian tribes. In Chapter 9, we discover how the long, torturous struggle for African-American literacy was far more important than just acquiring a personal basic education. Literacy became a critical personal first step on an individual's road to freedom and human dignity.

In the book's last section, Part V, "Literacy in the Modern Age (1870–)," Chapter 10 examines the impact of the Industrial Revolution and urbanization on the drive for literacy education. During the early twentieth century's Progressive Era these critical forces helped fashion America's first literacy revolution. By 1920 universal, tax-supported, compulsory (to age 16–18), public schools (first to twelfth grade) had been mandated in all the states. We also discover how the literacy demands of a modern global-tech society are raising the personal literacy bar even higher. Unfortunately far too many Americans are being left behind both socially and economically by failing to attain these accelerating standards.

The book concludes with the authors' contention that the job of literacy education cannot be done by the schools alone. During past eras in the literacy journey of America many parents were more personally involved in each phase of their children's development as readers. Family literacy was essential to awaken and support the personal responsibility that all students must ultimately assume for their own literacy. Though the state has a legal obligation for schooling, the family has a "higher responsibility" for literacy. Unfortunately, far too many Americans today are experiencing the social and economic consequences of falling short of an accelerating global literacy standard. The authors offer specific suggestions for better parent-school collaboration that will promote higher levels of personal reading fluency. What the authors make clear is that how the American people became literate is a compelling, intricate human struggle that does not fit into any one neat academic theory. It is a journey that is far from over.

ACKNOWLEDGMENTS

Over the past 10 years the authors have had the opportunity to work with many libraries, archives, and literacy research institutions, which have provided invaluable primary source documents, diaries, letters, published materials, and professional advice. In particular we wish to thank the following individuals and institutions: Henry E. Huntington Library, San Marino, California; Loyola University Library, Chicago; the Nebraska State Historical Society, Lincoln, Nebraska; the Newberry Library, Chicago; the Northwest Museum of Arts & Culture/Eastern Washington State Historical Society, Spokane, Washington; the Panhandle-Plains Museum Library, Canyon, Texas; the Rutgers University Library, New Brunswick, New Jersey; the University of North Carolina Library, Chapel Hill, North Carolina; the University of Texas Library, Austin, Texas; Suzanne Knell, Executive Director, Illinois Literacy Resources Development Center, Champaign, Illinois; and Eunice Askov, Executive Director, Institute for the Study of Adult Literacy, the Pennsylvania State University, University Park, Pennsylvania.

The authors deeply appreciate the steadfast patience and excellent advice of Lynn Taylor, assistant vice president at the Greenwood Publishing Group.

Finally, we wish to acknowledge Sandra Gula Gleason, who continues to employ her great expertise in preparing our manuscripts for publication. She has made many invaluable contributions to the text, charts, and figures through our many, many revisions of this book. However, for any factual errors contained herein the authors take sole responsibility.

NOTES

1. Carl F. Kaestle, "The History of Literacy and the History of Readers," *Review of Research in Education* 12 (1985): 11; R. A. Houston, *Literacy in Early Modern Europe* (New York: Longman, 1988), 130.

2. Daniel P. Resnick and Lauren B. Resnick, "The Nature of Literacy: An Historical Exploration," *Harvard Educational Review* 47 (Fall 1977): 370–385; Harvey J. Graff, *The Legacies of Literacy* (Bloomington: Indiana University Press, 1987), 388–389; Marie Costa, *Adult Literacy/Illiteracy in the United States: A Handbook for Reference and Research* (Santa Barbara, California: ABC-Clio, 1988), 46–47.

3. Edward E. Gordon, Judith A. Ponticell, and Ronald R. Morgan, *Closing the Literacy Gap in American Business* (New York: Quorum Books, 1991), 17–18; Edward E. Gordon,

Skill Wars, Winning the Battle for Productivity and Profit (Boston: Butterworth/Heinemann, 2000), 140.

4. Philippe Aries and Georges Duby, *A History of Private Life: Passions of the Renaissance* (Cambridge: Harvard University Press, 1989), 111–115; Graff, *Legacies*, 163–65, 173–174, 260–262, 343–344, 351, 375; Carl F. Kaestle, "Literacy and Diversity: Themes from a Social History of the American Reading Public," *History of Education Quarterly* 28 (Winter 1988): 523–549; Houston, *Literacy*, 120–127; Kenneth A. Lockridge, *Literacy in Colonial New England: An Enquiry into the Social Context of Literacy in the Early Modern West* (New York: W. W. Norton, 1974), 517–521; F. W. Brubb, "Growth of Literacy in Colonial America: Longitudinal Patterns, Economic Models, and the Direction of Future Research," *Social Science History* 14 (Winter 1990): 451–482.

5. Houston, *Literacy*, 117–118.

6. Carl F. Kaestle et al., *Literacy in the United States: Readers and Reading Since 1880* (New Haven: Yale University Press, 1991), 31–32.

7. Kaestle, *Literacy in the United States*, 6, 22–23, 30–31; Kaestle, "Literacy and Diversity," 544; M. Spufford, "First Steps in Literacy: The Reading and Writing Experiences of the Humblest Seventeenth-Century Spiritual Autobiographers," *Social History* 4 (1979): 409; Lawrence A. Cremin, *American Education: The Colonial Experience, 1607–1786* (New York: Harper & Row, 1970), 78; Edward E. Gordon and Elaine H. Gordon, *Centuries of Tutoring: A History of Alternative Education in American and Western Europe* (Lanham, Maryland: University Press of America, 1990), 6, 245–246, 266, 280, 285.

8. Houston, *Literacy*, 127–128; Kaestle, "History of Literacy," 45.

Part I

Literacy and Religion in Colonial America
(1620–1789)

Chapter 1

A Light in the Forest: Colonial New England

EUROPEAN ROOTS

The Puritans stepped upon Plymouth Rock (1620) with a literacy heritage shaped by events in Europe. The printing press, the Renaissance, and the Reformation planted the seeds for the democratization of reading in America.[1]

The economic changes that swept Europe during the Renaissance were powerful forces for the spread of learning and literacy. As trade grew between Europe and the East, Italian merchants in Venice and Florence needed a greater understanding of the marketplace. German and French farmers, with an eye on profits, required account books to follow prices and agricultural developments. With each passing European generation, literacy became a more important means for the upward social mobility of individuals and families.[2] However, it is important to note that education in a school was only part of a much wider process of literacy in Europe, which encompassed the home, peer groups, and work experience.[3]

Historians agree that literacy was promulgated in many ways that may seem strange to us in the twenty-first century. During the Renaissance, "the gap between the tutor at home and the master in the school was one of degree rather than kind, since most modern techniques of group instruction had not been invented and scholars were still dealt with one by one."[4] The concept of teaching groups in classes divided according to age and ability was an eighteenth-century invention.

Many teachers worked in the homes of their pupils. They taught in barns, humble dwellings, or manors. Often teachers went to their pupils rather than the students going to a building designated as a school. Even more often, children were taught at home by their parents, older children, or relatives. Between

1500 and 1900 the family throughout Europe was far more important in the literacy-education process than it is today.

European education in the home was not the exclusive preserve of the upper classes. Beginning in the sixteenth century and culminating in the nineteenth century, the use of tutors and governesses spread rapidly down the social ladder: first from the aristocratic upper classes into the homes of the professional classes, then to the newly expanding merchant classes, and finally to the expanding middle class. These educators were employed to provide children basic literacy and an elementary education. Before the twentieth century, domestic education was a stepping stone to the university for many boys, and the entire education received by most girls.[5] Many of Renaissance Europe's most influential educational treatises were written by individuals who were schoolmasters and tutors. Roger Ascham is a good example. Ascham, a Cambridge University scholar, generally educated a few children at a time within a family setting. His most interesting pupil was England's Queen Elizabeth I, whom he taught during her adolescence and well into adulthood.

From these experiences Ascham wrote *The School Master* (1552). Ascham advised parents to individualize the learning of each child. Teaching should be paced to the student's rate of learning. Though many of his ideas were not new, Ascham's thoughtful review of instructional methods made *The School Master* a significant influence on parents in England and later in Colonial America. Ascham is considered by many a pioneer in modern educational methods that helped increase the spread of literacy.[6]

The principal result of this English educational revolution was an increase in the ways to acquire literacy in early seventeenth-century England. Of course, no real "school system" existed in any modern sense. But "petty" schools which concentrated on basic reading, writing, and arithmetic proliferated. Grammar schools offering more advanced instruction in the previously mentioned subjects plus Latin, Greek, and Hebrew became common.

During this schooling process there was considerable blurring in the agencies of literacy. Households, churches, and schools were all in use. Petty schools and grammar schools could be found in private homes, shops, and churches as well as in school buildings. The American colonists were the heirs to English literacy traditions that stressed the central role of the household as the primary agency of human association and literacy.[7]

Protestantism was also a powerful factor in the spread of literacy. In northern Europe the Protestant tradition of family home education and personal religious involvement through reading the Bible produced the ability to sign one's name one and a half times greater than in the Catholic areas of Europe. The Reformation seemed to encourage literacy both through the advocacy of personal education and the desire of individuals to have direct access to the Bible. God's people were to be literate people, taking in God's word from the printed page. With these strong literacy traditions the Pilgrims crossed the Atlantic to the New World.[8] America's Puritans were instructed, even harangued, by sermons that proclaimed the correctness of these traditions. The Puritans came to America to worship as they pleased and to see that others did the same. They became one of literacy's strongest advocates in the American colonies.[9]

LITERACY IN THE WILDERNESS

Upon their arrival in the New England wilderness the first colonists had to overcome a daunting series of novel problems if they were to transplant the literacy revolution from Europe. Aside from struggling to provide the basic necessities of life—food, shelter, protection from Indian attack—the distances between settlements and difficulty of travel on the frontier meant that there were simply not enough schoolmasters to meet the educational needs of this isolated population.

Historians seem to agree that there was a blurring of lines between institutions that supported literacy and the "schooling" that went on here, there, and everywhere, in schoolrooms, kitchens, shops in towns, barns on farms, mansions, meetinghouses, churches, and even taverns and inns. Students were taught by one and all—schoolmasters, parents, relatives, tutors, governesses, clergymen, physicians, artisans, shopkeepers, lawyers, and even indentured servants. Most of the teaching was done on an individual basis.[10]

In the New World the role of the family in providing literacy to the young became even more important than in England. This happened partly out of necessity, as other social institutions such as the school and the church were often inaccessible. These colonists had come from the largely rural population of England, where most people lived in villages and the family was the basic unit of society. The home was both the locus of family life and the place of employment: farming, textile work, milling, or baking. Parents in New England had to bear even a greater responsibility for education. The colonial family wore many and varied hats.[11] The Massachusetts Bay Colony was first in importance for the development of literacy throughout New England. The Puritan migration to Massachusetts included a higher proportion of educated leaders than any other colony, including before 1650 over one hundred Oxford and Cambridge University graduates. Most of these men were pastors of churches. These intellectual leaders, such as John Winthrop, Nathaniel Ward, John Cotton, and John Harvard, gave the community its literacy ideals. The presence of such leaders explains why a public school, a printing press, and a college were established in the wilderness of Massachusetts before 1640.[12]

These men viewed their world through a religious framework. Their world was a Christian world. In seventeenth-century Europe, religion (Protestant or Catholic) was one of the most dominant features of everyday life. Given the unique intellectual character of early New England, it is not surprising that the church became the chief agency of deliberate systematic teaching. What the English Puritan family had wanted but had been unable to do, the New England family was forced to do. In the face of a scarcity of ministers and wilderness demands for everyday survival, the family assumed the educational role assigned to it by the Puritan church.[13]

It was the Puritans' firm belief that the ultimate purpose of education was salvation. Achievement of that purpose, from the Puritan perspective, was complicated by the fact that children were born evil as well as ignorant. The main purpose of literacy was to prepare children for conversion by teaching them the doctrines and moral precepts of Christianity.[14]

The Puritans considered each child's mind an empty receptacle, one that had to be infused with knowledge by careful instruction. They believed that children developed intellectually more rapidly than we expect most young children to develop today.[15]

In early New England the teaching of the catechism in the home rather than in the church became the norm. As we shall see, a great number of early literacy laws were passed that required the heads of families to catechize their children or any servants in the household.[16]

The father assumed the role of primary educator in the Puritan household. The mother often assisted him in this task. A reason for this arrangement was that men might have been more literate than women. One study estimates that 60 percent of men among the early settlers could sign their wills, while only about 30 percent of women were able to do so.[17]

Once a week the father was legally bound to teach his children from a catechism. There were a great variety of such books, which summarized in the form of questions and answers the Puritan system of Christian beliefs. These "how to" religious manuals were all designed for the instruction of young children. It was each child's responsibility to study the book and learn the answers by heart. This rote-learning method often meant that children began memorizing their catechism before they could possibly understand its meaning. Therefore, parents were instructed to ask their children questions as they grew older, to help them understand the true meaning of the catechism.[18]

Books on familial education, often written in England, were widely used in the colonies. Two of the best known were *A Godly Form of Household Government* (1598) by Robert Cleaver and *Of Domestical Duties* (1622) by William George. These books portray the family as a mini-state with the father at its head. Education was a primary duty that parents owed their children. One of the first New England treatises on child-rearing that continued these ideals was Thomas Cobbett's *A Fruitfull and Usefull Discourse Touching the Honour Due from Children to Parents and the Duty of Parents Towards Their Children* (1656). It is interesting to note that in all his extensive and detailed advice for parents on the "good and godly education of their children," schools are never mentioned. This omission perhaps shows how few schools existed at that time and the relative importance of home schooling.[19]

For at least the next one hundred years the Puritan home remained the institution most responsible for teaching children to read and to lead pious lives. New England journals are replete with references to this dimension of family life. The diary of Samuel Sewall, who recorded the daily educational progress of his eight-year-old daughter Elizabeth, clearly illustrates his belief that this parental educational duty was a sacred obligation.[20] Another example is the education of the famous colonial poet Anne Bradstreet (1612–1672), who came to Massachusetts in 1630. As a child she had up to eight tutors at one time, and all of her tutors may not have been family members.[21] We know that private teachers first appeared in Boston in 1630, shortly after the town was settled.[22]

LEGISLATING LITERACY

The Puritans did not rely solely on their ministers to exhort parents regarding their spiritual and literacy duty toward their children. In 1642 Massachusetts enacted the first law that required heads of families to teach their children and apprentices to read. This reaffirmed the earlier English tradition of domestic education under the various Royal Injunctions begun by Queen Elizabeth I.[23]

By the time this first literacy act was passed, 21 towns existed in Massachusetts, with a combined population of about 9,000. Most of them had a church and a university-educated minister. Harvard College had been founded in 1636 to help ensure an adequate supply of New England clergymen. This very close connection between literacy education and religious faith was well expressed in the following thoughts inscribed on the west gateway of Harvard Yard:

> After God had carried us safe to New England
> And we had builded our houses
> Provided necessaries for our livelihood
> Reared convenient places for God's worship
> And settled the civil government
> One of the next things we longed for
> And looked after was to advance learning
> And perpetuate it to posterity
> Dreading to leave an illiterate ministry
> To the churches when our present ministers
> Shall lie in dust.[24]

The rationale behind the 1642 law is clear: The Puritans insisted upon education in order to ensure the religious welfare of their children, requiring "that all masters of families do once a week (at least) catechize their children and servants in the grounds and principles of Religion."[25]

The colony ordered local town officials, "selectmen," to have "a vigilant eye" to make certain that parents were teaching their children reading. They put some teeth into this enforcement by giving the selectmen the authority to issue a 20-shilling penalty for each infraction.[26]

However, enacting compulsory education should not be confused with compulsory schooling. As we will see again and again, they existed independently of the other during the next several hundred years, both in the literacy history of the original colonies and in the later United States. Today we take for granted compulsory school attendance by all children between certain ages, supported by public taxation and state regulation. However, the first literacy legislation of 1642 did not even mention schools. Instead, parents or the "master" or "governor" of a family or "guardian" were to act as the teacher. At that time the word "master" was usually applied to someone who held a child as an apprentice and was acting in place of a parent. Though the principal reason for this law's passage was to promote religion, it also included instruction in a trade and the rudiments of general literacy.[27]

By 1647, even though Massachusetts had tried to place sole responsibility for education on the family, at least nine schools were open in the colony. Boston, Charlestown, Dedham, Dorchester, and Ipswich operated town-initiated grammar schools. The town of Salem ran a petty school.[28] The householders in Roxbury sponsored a quasi-public grammar school in contrast to the private schools managed by individual teachers in Cambridge and Newbury. However, it should not be of any surprise that the majority of the colony's townships had not yet taken any action to provide children with formal schooling. Most town's citizens simply assumed that the parents would teach their children enough reading and writing to satisfy their religious obligations.[29]

Some families, however, failed to educate their children, and many communities refused to establish either petty or grammar schools. In 1647, to remedy these failures, the General Court of Massachusetts enacted a law requiring the establishment of schools because it was "one chief project of that old deluder Satan to keep men from the knowledge of the Scriptures."[30]

Known today as the "Deluder Satan Act," it had a decisive influence on the spread of literacy for the rest of the colonial period in New England. Families were still expected to introduce basic literacy at home. However, the Deluder Satan Act also called for communities of one hundred or more households to establish a grammar school and those with 50 or more households to maintain a petty school.[31] Similar literacy education laws were adopted by other colonies such as Connecticut (1650), Plymouth (1658 and 1677), and Pennsylvania (1683).[32] However, domestic education's continuing importance was shown in specific instances of court orders (1670, 1674, and 1676) that enforced their literacy obligation upon negligent parents.[33]

On the other hand, these laws were never vigorously enforced on townships. In Massachusetts, during the decade following 1647, only a third of all towns large enough to meet the requirement for establishing reading-and-writing schools obeyed the law. The rest just ignored it.[34] Thus, in some larger communities, parents had the option of sending their children to one of the petty schools, but in most towns they were still forced to teach their children themselves.[35]

The varying degree of public enthusiasm for a comprehensive system of schools rested upon at least one factor that has persisted to our own time—cost.

Many colonial taxpayers were reluctant to assume the expense of elementary education, particularly of someone else's child. Town meetings frequently reaffirmed the responsibility of parents alone for educating their own children. The cost of sending a child to a seventeenth-century grammar school tended to restrict attendance to the children of the moderately prosperous families in a community. Even so-called public education was not free. Most schools levied fees for entrance, candles, books, ink, quills, paper, and—often most expensive of all—firewood. Usually tuition was also charged in addition to the town taxes already paid by all the members of the community to at least partially support a schoolmaster and sometimes the construction and maintenance of a proper schoolhouse. Thus, there is every indication that the colonial household was an even more important agency of literacy than the schools.[36]

Josiah Cotton (1680–1756) of Massachusetts noted in his diary, "My younger days were attended with the follies and vanities incident to youth howsoever I quickly learned to read, without going to any school I remember."[37]

Many historians now agree that in colonial America it was the family that was the cornerstone for literacy. As we will see, the letters and diaries of that time record that a broad formal education could sometimes be given by a parent making extensive use of the family library. Two generations of the Mather family in Boston illustrate how extensive domestic education could be offered at home.[38]

THE EDUCATION OF A SAINT

Cotton Mather (1639–1723) grew up under the careful tutelage of his father, Increase, and his mother, Maria. "I learned to read of my mother. I learned to write of Father, who also instructed me in grammar learning, both in the Latin and the Greek tongues."[39] Increase Mather was an austere Puritan divine who for 16 years served as president of Harvard College. He spent up to 16 hours a day in his study. It was left to Maria Mather to play her part in helping Cotton and his sibling learn to read the Bible and memorize their catechism thoroughly.

Cotton Mather taught himself to write before ever attending a writing school. When Cotton began attending Boston's grammar school, his father's concern for his health caused him to be tutored at home during the winter months. In his library Increase tutored Cotton in church history and Latin. By the age of 11, Cotton was so fluent in Latin that he took Latin notes on sermons that were delivered in English. Cotton was the youngest student ever admitted to Harvard, beginning to attend the college at age 11½ and graduating at the age of 15. He was ordained as a minister seven years later at Boston's North Church. Until his death Cotton Mather was the preeminent Puritan minister of Boston.[40]

Continuing a tradition maintained by his father and grandfather, Cotton kept a personal diary (1663–1728) that offers a detailed picture of literacy education in a family setting. His personal participation in the education of his children, nine of whom were born to Abigail, his first wife, during a 16-year time span, can be best understood in the context of his own literacy.

Cotton read a great deal and speedily. He was highly skilled at skimming. A very high value was placed upon the reading activity itself, since Cotton used books as a means for personally addressing the spiritual and emotional needs of himself and others. Writing was also a high priority in Mather's life. Cotton was expert at summarizing and paraphrasing. He also composed as rapidly as he read. The very act of composition and the physical result, published books, were used as an aid to his own spiritual development and in his work with others. All of these personal literary habits were used as the basis of the education of his nine children by Abigail and later, after Abigail's death, of another six children from his marriage to Elizabeth.

Mather's purpose in writing these diaries was not publication, but his own spiritual improvement and in later years the benefit of his children. We are fortunate that over these years of writing the journal entries become longer and sometimes more detailed regarding plans for his children's specific educational activities. This increases their value to us as a historical record of early colonial literacy practices.[41]

Through one such entry in Cotton's diary (1706), under the heading "SOME SPECIAL POINTS RELATING TO THE EDUCATION OF MY CHILDREN," we can learn how he used tutoring at home and teaching at school to educate all his children. Cotton often employed his own books as models in instructing his children. He then gave them specific writing or reading assignments that followed these models.

In addition, he had the children learn the catechism by heart and copy these texts. Cotton also taught his children reading comprehension, but had them use textual interpretations that were not intended to be challenged. He occasionally required them to summarize and encouraged them to look for the main idea in a story. On several occasions he set them to write the equivalent of essays. On at least one occasion, Mather insisted that the children be able to justify their statements by using relevant verses from the Scriptures to support the tenets of the catechism. Besides these individual educational activities, father and children shared books in common through oral reading. Cotton sat with his children while they read aloud in turn.

Home education was combined with formal schooling. Mather's son Sammy, when he was under five years of age, was sent off to the wife of a grammar-school master to learn to read. Both Sammy and his sister Liza attended writing school.

Cotton's diary also indicates that he secured literacy instruction for his servants and African-American slaves. Although it is not clear whether this instruction took place in his household or in a school, these dependents were instructed in reading, scripture, and the catechism.[42]

Although Cotton Mather's family was not typical of that period, his diaries give significant insight into how one colonial family developed their own children's literacy. Certainly many other New England families would follow his example of domestic education to some degree.

WHAT IS A SCHOOL?

During the 1600s and 1700s a confusing array of schooling institutions dotted the New England landscape. These ranged from the literate but relatively untutored housewives who offered "dame schools" in their kitchens and parlors to the cultured university graduates who presided over the more elaborate "grammar schools."[43]

Other "petty schools" or "reading schools" were almost all private-venture schools supported by private benefactors or supported through tuition. Most were found in rural parishes, though some existed in cities and towns. Children usually entered them from age five to seven and often already had learned the alphabet at home or in a dame school. Some petty schools were located in an individual school building, but most were in the teacher's own home or a parish church. Children usually attended for between two and three years, learning reading, writing, and their catechism.[44]

Though grammar schools offered a classical curriculum, the so-called academies were the least well defined of these provincial school types. An academy prepared students for Harvard or Yale and faced competition from private secondary schools. They offered what the master was prepared to teach or what the pupils were prepared to learn or, perhaps more important, what the academy's sponsors were prepared to support. In some ways the academy expressed the fluid, flexible nature that literacy seemed to take during much of the colonial schooling experience.

Josiah Quincy, later in life the president of Harvard College, was sent at age six to Phillips Academy in Andover, Massachusetts (1778). In his class by his side sat a man of 30. Both began to memorize pages of a book, which the younger child certainly could never have understood.[45]

Still the list is not complete. "Summer schools" and "moving schools" further blurred the lines between the exact purpose and nature of all these educational institutions. However, we do know that the vast majority of all these schools remained ungraded, and most instruction was individualized. Students approached the master's desk one at a time to recite or display their work. Instruction was by a rote catechetical mode not only in religion but also for reading and arithmetic.

This confusing arrangement of schools makes it almost impossible to assess their number and overall impact on literacy. At the same time, because of the unusual nature of early New England society, it was almost universally true that the church was the chief social agency that influenced these many educational offshoots. The churches continued to serve as literacy centers throughout the colonial period. They offered both informal and formal instruction, with the ministers catechizing, teaching, and tutoring in church or in the schoolrooms or visiting the homes of parishioners.[46]

Yet the church underwent certain fundamental changes in the eighteenth century that markedly transformed the character of education in New England. The increasingly scattered population, a drop in the perceived need for literacy in farming areas, and the disruption of the French and Indian Wars led to a decline of religious motives for education. These social forces greatly lowered the public's interest in schools. Many parents became content with their children receiving only short periods of instruction and achieving meager personal literacy abilities. This fragmentation of education led in the towns as well as on the frontier to the creation of a variety of improvised institutions for literacy.[47]

Dame Schools

In seventeenth- and eighteenth-century England the dame school is a well-documented source of literacy. A woman took small boys and girls into her own home for a few hours a day to introduce her charges to reading. Without doubt another major contribution of such schools was early child care, giving an overworked mother a few hours' respite from her three- and four-year-olds.[48]

In New England, if a child grew up in a home of non-readers, neighbors often offered to tutor the child. When a mother decided to tutor outsiders in reading on a regular basis, usually in her kitchen, for a modest fee, she became a dame school. In Virginia the same activity was called a "petty school."[49]

The idea that the family was itself a "school" was clearly tied to the Puritan sense of purpose. The dame school was part of this expression of New England domestic education. Often starting with a woman's own children, then taking in others as young as two years of age, the dame school continued to flourish throughout most of New England until 1776 and even after.[50]

Dame schools must have been near to the homes of the children, for the pupils were very young. Teachers were expected to teach young children to stay out of mischief, to mind their manners, and to learn their catechism. The curriculum was basic literacy: learning the alphabet, a little spelling, mastering a few simple religious texts, knitting and sewing for the girls, sometimes writing for the boys, and perhaps a little oral arithmetic illustrated by numbers scratched on the floor with a stick. Dame schools were often very small, with from three to ten or fifteen children. The quality of the dame school varied widely with the personality and talents of the teacher. But there is extensive personal testimony from former pupils about the excellence of many of the women who taught them.[51]

Lydia and Convers Francis began their formal education by attending a Medford, Massachusetts, dame school taught by a woman known affectionately by her pupils as Ma'am Betty. For 12 cents a week this elderly spinster taught school in her bedroom with an abundance of motherly care, useful knowledge, and salutary discipline. Ma'am Betty was a somewhat odd teacher who chewed tobacco and drank water out of the spout of her tea kettle. However, Convers remembered what a great friend she became and how often during long winter evenings the old woman and young boy sat together while he read aloud books she liked.[52]

Many dame schools taught a substantial amount of reading, sometimes using students to tutor their peers. John Barnard recalled that when he was less than six years old (1686), the dame-school mistress made him a sort of usher to tutor reading to both older and younger children.[53]

During the early colonial period the dame school was seldom funded by the town; it was usually a private venture, representing a most useful source of income for many women. There are recorded instances where colonial women taught for almost their entire adult lives. When Abigail Fowler of Salem died in 1771, the local newspaper's obituary recorded how this noted dame-school teacher began teaching children before she was 18 and continued until her 68th year, with the exception of a few years after her marriage.[54]

The first dame school in Oxford, Massachusetts, was taught in the home of Miss Betty Jermer, who lived about one mile east of the old north common. There was no road, only a bridle path passed her house. A heavy stone chimney and a deep cavern-like fireplace presented a cheerful log fireside in the winter. The floor was scoured to whiteness and covered with the finest sand so that Miss Betty could teach arithmetic by making figures on the sanded floor with her rod. Her pupils copied the sums she gave them on their square pieces of birch bark with bits of charcoal.[55]

These schoolmistresses were often women of great energy and versatility. During an Indian attack on Deerfield, Massachusetts, in September 1694, Mrs. Hannah Beaman led her young flock from her home to the fort. It was a race for their lives, with the dame charging up the street and the Indians running up the swamp parallel to the town to intercept them. Fear gave wings to the children's feet, and Hannah safely shepherded them into the fort and shut the gate.[56]

Individual towns tried a variety of options to encourage attendance at local dame schools. In 1707 Haverhill, Massachusetts, voted to set up a house near the town meeting hall so that a local wife would be better accommodated for keeping a school to teach children reading. Concord, New Hampshire, in 1744 noted that anyone who hired a private schoolmistress could use the local schoolhouse as their schoolroom until such future time that the town offered a public education program. Other towns voted funds to hire women to teach children to read in their homes. Still others built little houses to accommodate the dame school.

Though New England towns inaugurated a variety of these halfway measures to assist the spread of dame schools, the general public sentiment for much of the seventeenth and eighteenth centuries was that parents should furnish this elementary form of literacy. Poorer children suffered the most neglect under this ad hoc educational arrangement. Occasionally, such children were aided by some philanthropic citizen. For example, Samuel Brown at Salem in 1729 donated funds for a dame school to teach six very poor children for six or seven months a year. Individual towns sometimes took action on their behalf. Charlestown in 1712 and Marblehead about 1700 voted funds for poor children to attend dame schools.[57]

The dame school existed in three forms. In the early colonial period the private neighborhood dame school seemed to be present in every town. A later development was the semi-public dame school started by a local town with some slight assistance from its treasury. But it remained heavily dependent on the pupils' tuition. The final evolution into a real public dame school occurred when male masters were hired during the winter to conduct reading and writing schools and women still conducted regular summer schools. Both of these finally merged into the public primary school.[58]

Thus by the beginning of the 1700s New England children were being educated in a variety of venues by those towns that maintained schools: by the family, the dame school, and the town school. Some of these were "grammar schools," a combination of grammar, reading, and writing. Others were simply "writing schools" that offered only writing instruction.

A common pattern in the evolution of education was that the dame school furnished basic literacy education as an admission ticket for the town school. As the dame schools became more public, cities and towns began paying teachers a small salary. As salaries increased, public control did as well; by 1789 Massachusetts required dame school teachers to be licensed.[59]

The fitting epitaph given to Miriam Wood of Dorchester when she was buried in 1706 could be given to many other colonial dames:

A Woman well beloved of all her neighbors for her care of small Folks education, their number being great, that when she dyed she scarcely left her mate.
So Wise, Discreet was her behaviour that she was well esteemed by neighbours.
She lived in love with all to dy'd, So let her rest to Eternity.[60]

Moving Schools/Summer Schools

The growth of New England towns into outlying precincts presented a new challenge to literacy education. One response to this educational demand was the "moving school," in which the town schoolmaster traveled from parish to parish in the town, teaching in each area for varying time periods. Financial support for the moving school was dependent on the amount paid by each individual settlement. The length of instruction was determined by the monetary support of each local community. The moving school system became quite prevalent in New England after 1725.[61]

Across much of New England grammar schools operating in town centers, moving schools functioning in the outer locales during the winter, and dame schools providing summer instruction became a common pattern. This arrangement led to many very curious divisions of instructional time. Individual children could have short school terms and very long vacations. Such was the case for Gloucester in 1734 with its seven moving school districts. The schoolmaster took three years to make the entire circuit. Another report in 1725 by Harvard's overseeing selectmen reported that the local moving schoolmaster had conducted school on the Neck for 150 days, but at Still River for only 75 days.[62]

Over time the dame school was transformed into an official public summer school in which women taught young boys and girls of various ages. As early as the 1760s school districts began this practice by hiring young unmarried daughters of farm families. Ruth Henshaw left her family farm in Leicester, Massachusetts, to teach school in nearby Spencer or Brookfield every summer between 1791 and 1801. Elizabeth Bancroft of Pepperell, a contemporary, boarded out and taught summer school in the mid-1790s. Both Ruth and Elizabeth taught from 20 to 45 students, but the attendance numbers varied greatly from day to day.

To our modern eyes these schools seemed to operate on an irregular, loosely organized basis. The duration of the summer–school term varied from two months to as much as six months (April to October). They seemed to teach reading but not writing. In the 1760s Hannah Adams remembered attending such a school in Medfield, Massachusetts, in which her female teacher instructed her in reading, sewing, and other domestic kinds of work. The limited quality of this curriculum should come as little surprise. For example, the town of Manchester, Massachusetts, in 1763 allocated half of the school budget in the winter to employ a male schoolmaster to teach Latin. However, the rest of the funds hired four school dames to run summer schools.[63]

Domestic Literacy

In addition to this multitude of schools outside the home, the enterprising colonial parent in search of literacy for himself or his children could often arrange for systematic instruction at home or nearby from professional private tutors. Numerous colonial newspaper advertisements by tutors and governesses in Boston and other larger cities provide evidence that enough children or adults paid for tutoring to keep a large number of these private entrepreneurial teachers in business.

Even before 1689, Boston had at least eight private tutors who taught writing or account keeping. Adults could be tutored in a fascinating variety of subjects including surveying, navigation, and commerce, or even fencing. Women could learn dancing or needlework. Between 1709 and 1775 some 200 teachers were thus employed in the colonies.

1720

At the house formerly Sir Charles Hobby's are
taught Grammar, Writing and a free and easy
manner, in all the hands usually practiced,
Arithmetick Vulgar and Decimal in a concise and
practical Method, Merchants Accompts, Geometry,
Algebra, Mensuration, Geography, Trigonometry,

Astronomy, Navigation and other parts of the
Mathematicks, with the use of the Globes and other
Mathematical Instruments, by Samuel Grainger.

They whose Business won't permit 'em to attend the
usual School Hours, shall be carefully attended and
instructed in the Evenings.

1716

This is to give Notice, That at the House of Mr.
George Brownell, late School Master in Hanover
Street Boston, are all sorts of Millinary Works and
Write English, and his Wife for teaching Needle
Work, any Person that wants such may be informed
at the Post-Office in Boston.[64]

In some instances day-school masters supplemented their meager salaries by accommodating students in the evening. In other cases other professionals such as accountants taught certain aspects of their trade during the evening hours. Some of these private teacher-tutors such as George Brownwell, who taught Benjamin Franklin, traveled throughout the colonies. Brownwell taught for a period of almost a quarter-century in Boston, New York, and Philadelphia. He may well have been one of the most versatile private schoolmasters in the colonies, offering instruction that ranged from arithmetic to embroidery.[65]

Another well-used alternative was self-instruction. One multi-volume educational tool enlisted for that purpose was *The American Instructor*. Used by the aspiring young adolescent or adult, these books were encyclopedias that were filled with useful career information. Instruction in English was offered first, since fluency in language was understood to be "a necessary and principal qualification in business." Also advice was offered on personal writing skills to attain "a good, fair, free and commendable hand." The student became familiar with various business-related form letters, including a server of handy legal forms (deeds, wills, etc.). Some elements of arithmetic, bookkeeping, and geographical observations regarding North America and the British Isles were given with the principles of measurement for carpentry and bricklaying. This eighteenth-century potpourri of the world's knowledge was designed to provide self-help to eager young New England Yankees.[66]

With all this private instructional activity for adults, it should come as little surprise that the colonial New England child who became literate was as likely to be taught at home as in any school. Hannah Adams (1755–1831) was born into a farming family in Medfield, about eighteen miles from Boston. "My health did not even admit to attending school." Her father failed as a farmer and opened a store for the sale of "English goods" and books. He was such a greedy devourer of books that he was nicknamed "Book Adams." He was much better than any index, since he could tell you where to find any fact in the multitude of books he stocked.

Hannah became an eager reader in her father's library. "I read with avidity a variety of books." A gentleman who boarded at their home also tutored her in Latin, Greek, geography, and logic. She must have been an apt pupil, for as a young woman Hannah tutored three local gentlemen in the rudiments of Latin and Greek.

Her own attendance at any school was limited not only by her frail health but also by her low opinion of the county village schools, "since even the elementary parts of education are much neglected in them." "I never," Hannah lamented, "was taught how to hold my pen." However, this does not seem to have held her back in life.

Hannah was probably the first woman in colonial America to make writing her profession. In 1784 she authored *The Alphabetical Compendium of the Various Sects Which Have Appeared from the Beginning of the Christian Era to the Present*. This was followed by five other books, including a *History of New England* (1749), a *History of the Jews* (1812), and *Letters on the Gospel* (1826).[67]

Another equally fascinating account of domestic education and parental concern over childhood literacy can be found in the correspondence between John Adams and his wife Abigail. John often wrote to Abigail (1774–1818) during his long absences while serving in the Continental Congress and later as an American diplomat in France. They frequently discussed Abigail's education of their four children.[68] Adams assured Abigail that she was well qualified for the role of "school mistress." He encouraged her to elevate the minds of their children by cultivating the habits of thinking and study. But their bodies also needed exercise since, "Without strength and activity and rigor of body, the brightest mental excellencies will be eclipsed and obscured."

Adams took great care in outlining the content and method for his wife's instruction of their children. He wanted them to learn a concern for "great and solid objects," a sense of moral purpose, and useful skills, such as writing and French. Why did John take the time to scrupulously outline this teaching program?

I never had a regular Tutor, I never studied anything methodically, and consequently never was completely accomplished in any thing. But as I am conscious of my own deficiency, in the respects, I should be the less pardonable, if I neglected the education of my children.[69]

Early youth was the best time to begin formal education, John wrote his wife, before a child forms his tastes and judgments. "The Faculty of Writing is attainable, by Art, Practice, and Habit only. The sooner the practice begins the more likely it will be to succeed."

Adams also wrote his children to encourage their studies. John told Tommy (then three years old) to mind his books because "it is only from books and the kind instructions of your parents that you can expect to be useful in the World."

As his sons entered their later childhood, Adams shared with Abigail his ambitions for their later education. "My sons ought to study mathematics and philosophy, geography, national history, naval architecture, navigation, commerce, and agriculture, in order to give their children a right to study painting, poetry, music, architecture, statuary, tapestry and porcelain."[70]

These designs for a "liberal education" for his family and their progeny excluded any schooling in Europe or the "Grand Tour." "Upon no consideration whatever, would I have any of my children educated in Europe."[71] This was perhaps the reaction of his American patriotism and his disgust after prolonged exposure as a diplomat to the dissipated French court life of Versailles.

Abigail Adams' response to her husband's educational counseling was tempered by some feelings of inadequacy. She wrote to a friend, Mercy Warren of Plymouth, that "I am sensible I have an important trust committed to me and tho I feel myself unequal to it, tis still incumbent upon me to discharge it in the best manner I am capable of." Abigail's own education seems to have been a combination of home instruction and local dame schools. Her ambition for a better education and her disappointment at its unavailability led her to lament the lack of training she received in the care and early instruction of children.[72]

Faced with the education of her four children, Abigail told her friend how she had read with great interest *On the Management and Education of Children*, by the English writer Juliana Seymour. This book was one of the many such works written for parents in the eighteenth century to guide them in the "domestic education" or "fireside" education of their offspring. From the tone of Abigail's letter we can deduce that educating her children was not only an important intellectual task but also a role that fulfilled her as a parent. In part, this daily forced intimacy with her children compensated for dreadful months of lonely separation from her husband. Over these circumstances she was not bitter. In a 1773 letter Abigail included a poem that described her conception of a parent's duties in a child's "fireside education."

> Parent who vast pleasure find's
> In forming of her childrens minds
> In midst of whom with vast delight
> She passes many a winters Night
> Mingles in every play to find
> What Bias Nature gave the mind
> Resolving thence to take her aim
> To guide them to the realms of fame
> And wisely make those realms the way
> To those of everlasting day.
>
> Each Boisterous passion to controul
> And early Humanize the Soul
> In simple tales beside the fire,
> The noblest Notions to inspire.

> Her offspring conscious of her care
> Transported hang around her chair.[73]

It was obvious that not every mother in colonial America agreed with this idyllic portrayal of "domestic education." Mercy Warren wrote Abigail from Plymouth and bemoaned the fact that the tutoring of their children was left wholly up to them for so many years. It appeared that parental separation notwithstanding, a great deal of colonial domestic education was left exclusively in the hands of the mother.[74]

Her friend's complaints had little effect upon Abigail's educational philosophy. Many years later she wrote her daughter, Abigail Adams Smith, instructions on how to teach her son, Johnny. Without hesitation she counseled that a child's education would occupy much of a mother's day. Education must begin early and continue in earnest. "You will always keep in mind the great importance of first principles and the necessity of instilling the precepts of morality very early into their minds."[75]

We know that in America's colonial period a broad formal education was given in many households by a tutor or parent. Through the extensive use of the family library, individual reading, responsive reading, and communal reading were daily literacy activities in many colonial households. Reading was often taught on an each-one-teach-one basis by parents or other elders or by siblings or peers.[76]

This combination of parents, tutors, and governesses educated many children at home. America's colonial era is replete with examples of how the practice of one-to-one instruction became an integral component of existing literacy practices.

A School Is Where You Find It

Throughout the 1700s New England communities continued to struggle with the responsibility of literacy and how to provide it. Financial support for the schools was squeezed out of the town budget, for this was largely a cashless agricultural society. Parents found it more convenient to pay teachers or family tutors in commodities rather than money.[77] The life of John Cleaveland and the schools of Chebacco, Massachusetts, offers a good example of the ongoing evolution of New England literacy.

John was born in 1722 near rural Canterbury, Massachusetts. His mother taught him how to read at home. Cleaveland described his mother as "a woman of experimental piety," who "took considerable pains not only to teach us to read but also, to show us the danger of an unconverted state."

John's formal education was limited to three winter months a year. The local minister taught him Latin to prepare him for Yale College, which he entered in 1741. He was expelled from Yale because of his unorthodox religious views, which did not prevent his ordination in 1747 as an evangelical pastor of a New Light congregation in Chebacco (today the town of Essex, Massachusetts).[78]

Public education began in Chebacco in 1695 with the appointment of Nathaniel Rust, Jr., an innkeeper, as the first schoolmaster. He taught in a room in his house, which also happened to be the village tavern. In 1702 the first schoolhouse for a reading-and-writing school was built on six acres of common land near the center of the village.[79]

By the mid-1750s the town had grown enough that moving schools had to be established for its outlying residents. District schools were built in these parishes in 1757 and 1761. Private proprietors (householders) were hired to build, administer, and maintain these schoolhouses. They hired the teachers, collected the town's school tax, assessed tuition, and sometimes even provided the schoolmaster room and board. The town provided the land for each schoolhouse and assessed the "school rate." Otherwise, the town gave over most of its authority to these semi-autonomous groups of householders, who acted as the schools' proprietors.

After 1740 these schools were open only during the four winter months. Of the 12 teachers whose names are known, only four were college graduates. Most teachers were local residents. In addition to the innkeeper, there was a doctor, a parish church deacon, a county lawyer, and a farmer.[80]

School attendance was not required by law since parents could provide basic literacy education themselves to their children at home. Sending a child to school meant that a family lost the child's labor, as well as paid tuition over and above local school taxes.

In 1760 it has been estimated that 24 families in Chebacco, about 16 percent of all households, paid tuition to send 36 boys and girls to school. This represented about 10 percent of all Chebacco's children under age 16. During the same time period, roughly the same proportion of the under-16 population also attended schools in Boston.[81]

It can be understood from these figures that, even though most of New England's colonies enacted compulsory education legislation, enforcing attendance remained a major problem during the 1600s and 1700s. In particular many towns neglected establishing grammar schools since reading-and-writing schools usually provided the basic literacy that most parents saw as adequate.[82]

Another factor that supported this trend was the grammar schools' emphasis on classical learning (i.e., Latin and Greek). These schools prepared a select number of boys for potential careers as ministers or in the professions after attending Harvard, Yale, or Princeton (then the College of New Jersey). In the minds of most parents this intellectual option was superseded by the need to emphasize more practical vocational education through the reading-and-writing schools or by attending private vocational schools.

For instance, by 1727 in Boston there were 210 scholars in grammar schools and 220 in writing schools. However, over the subsequent 40 years overall grammar school enrollment dropped 16 percent, while reading-writing school enrollment rose 241 percent.[83]

Yet despite these evident shortcomings, New England's district school system remained a fixed educational institution that fostered widespread basic societal literacy until long after the American Revolution (1776–1783). As we have already pointed out, it is difficult to accurately measure the extent of the enforcement of these literacy laws or the validity of contemporary statistical evidence. However, analysis of colonial records of that time points to a higher degree of very basic adult literacy in New England (95 percent) than in other regions such as Virginia (54–60 percent).[84]

This whole process of early literacy in New England and elsewhere took place in the glow cast by the reassuring image of both women and men surrounded at home and elsewhere by small children. The history of literacy blurred two societal institutions, the family and the schools, into a common alliance that persisted until the early twentieth century.[85]

WOMEN'S LITERACY

A gap existed between male and female literacy throughout the colonial period. Studies that measure literacy by the ability to sign one's name have shown that in many New England communities in 1750, only half as many women as men were literate. However, at that time many women were taught to read, but not to write. This improved with almost each passing decade, to 60 percent by the 1760s and to 80 percent in the 1790s. By 1850, when the first U.S. Census measured literacy by gender, both women and men in New England were almost universally literate. What caused the eighteenth-century disparity in literacy and how it was eliminated are critical questions for our understanding of early New England literacy.[86]

In the seventeenth century girls were allowed to attend dame schools. However, education in the common schools was generally withheld from girls during the seventeenth century and most of the eighteenth century. The popular culture of the time ridiculed anyone educating a woman. One Connecticut town voted not to "waste" any of its money in educating girls. Mrs. John Adams (wife of President Adams) wrote, "It was fashionable to ridicule female learning. . . . Female education in the best families went no further than writing and arithmetic; in some few and rare instances, music and dancing."[87]

Women were only to be taught what was absolutely necessary to help raise a family, and nothing more. Any departure from this male perspective on women's education was seen as highly undesirable. In fact, a woman who became better educated was branded with the contemptuous name "bluestocking," as a revolutionary no longer fit to be anyone's mother.[88]

When Massachusetts Governor Winthrop's wife lost her mind, even her Puritan women friends attributed it to too much book learning. Likewise, it was commonly believed that the young wife of the governor of Connecticut had gone insane "by occasion of giving herself wholly to reading and writing."[89]

However, a shift in attitudes toward female education occurred in mid-seventeenth-century New England that can be at least partially traced to a growing unwillingness of adult males to join the church. Thereafter, church membership became increasingly feminized, but with male elders and deacons retaining control of the congregation. As a result, many male heads of households were unwilling, incapable, or even unreliable in fulfilling their legal responsibility to educate and catechize their children and servants. This social trend led in the long term to a greater reliance on mothers as teachers, since they continued to join the church in larger proportions than their husbands. If women had to do the catechizing and provide for the general education role in the family, they had to become literate beyond the simple ability to read the Bible by themselves.[90]

Although they originally did not teach in the town primary school, young women gained teaching experience in their own home and as we have seen as dame-school teachers. A Northampton, Massachusetts, resident described his experience being taught by women in this way. "When four or five years old I went to school one summer to Hannah Parsons, daughter of Jacob, at his house; one summer to Rachel Parsons, daughter of Isaac, at his house. After this I went several years to Prudence Parsons, daughter of Josiah, at his house. Prudence kept school 10 or 12 summers, not in winter. She had 20 or 30 scholars."[91]

These "summer schools" began to appear as early as the 1760s in many New England communities. They began to admit two categories of students that had been almost totally excluded from regular town schools or grammar schools during the winter term, older girls and younger children of both sexes between the ages of three and six. These summer schools were also often called "women's schools" because of their practice of employing women as teachers. They provided an important historic precedent.

Though women's schools had all the characteristics of the earlier informal dame schools, the students now met in the town's school buildings and the teachers were paid from public funds. From that moment the literacy of girls gradually became a recognized public responsibility throughout New England.[92]

Employing women teachers in these publicly funded summer schools also was a demonstration of New England frugality. As we have already seen, a woman who could teach basic reading could be hired at almost a third the salary of a male schoolmaster. However, even opening a summer school signaled a desire by these communities to teach at least introductory literacy skills to a broader spectrum of both male and female students.[93] Though the overall motivation behind New England's school laws may have been religious, the resulting broadening of literacy operated on a societal rather than a strictly religious basis. The education of the daughters of Timothy Edwards, a minister in East Windsor, Connecticut, shows this changing public attitude toward female literacy.

Edwards's family included 10 daughters in addition to his famous son Jonathan. His wife, Esther, had also been a minister's daughter. Esther went to Boston to complete her education and had the local reputation of being brighter than her husband. Her mother had also been highly literate and led book discussion groups into her nineties. As was a common practice for ministers of that time, Timothy Edwards tutored local male students preparing for college. His household normally included several boarding students. Edwards tutored his own daughters so well that they in turn were able to tutor his students in the classics during his frequent absences from home. Although he was unable to provide them all with suitable marriage dowries, he had trained them to become teachers or governesses.[94]

If a father died leaving an unmarried, ill-provided-for daughter, there were few other careers open to her other than teaching. Beginning in the mid-1700s this option opened to increasing numbers of middle-class women. Timothy Edwards gave his daughters and son a tutorial education at home that prepared them all for college, the final goal actually realized only by their brother Jonathan.[95] Nor were his daughters the only example of parents who advanced their daughters' literacy.

Jane Colden was educated by her father, Cadwallader Colden, an American scientist in natural history. He tutored her at home with an emphasis on science, particularly botany. Jane was also taught Latin for scientific use. Her education was so advanced that Jane ultimately assumed the responsibility of filling the European botanical requests addressed to her father.[96]

Mercy Otis Warren, as we have seen was a personal friend of Abigail Adams. She received an advanced literacy education with her brothers James and Joseph from an uncle, the Reverend Jonathan Russell, a religious and educational leader of the Cape Cod region.

James, the family's official candidate for Harvard, was Russell's star pupil. However, the pastor admitted Mercy to her brothers' lessons. In time James, three years older than she, also took on the role of tutor and advisor in her studies. They became inseparable companions. James went on to Harvard and became a successful lawyer and pamphleteer in the early struggle for American independence.

Mercy continued her own education based on books borrowed from her uncle's library on such subjects as theology, history, philosophy, and poetry. Later her *History of the Rise, Progress and Termination of the American Revolution* (1805) assisted in inspiring the patriotism of the early United States.

As an adult Mercy, in turn, tutored her three sons. Abigail Adams and Mercy constantly exchanged books on education to help each other. Mercy was not completely tied down by their education; she also had some assistance in her task from the local dame schools that flourished near her home town in Plymouth, an option unavailable to Abigail, who lived on a rural farm. Mercy continued to train them in literacy, composition and moral principles on many winter evenings with the logs blazing brightly on the hearth.[97]

The gradual increase in schooling opportunities for females facilitated important social changes throughout the New England colonial era. However, the parallel common practice of domestic education for both boys and particularly girls offers a far more complete explanation for the gradual rise in female literacy.

APPRENTICESHIP AND LITERACY

In colonial New England a three-tier apprenticeship system mandated by law also made important contributions to overall societal literacy. The basic divisions of this apprenticeship system included:

1. *Upper Level*—Parents of teenage sons paid fees to have them apprenticed with qualified lawyers, doctors, or silversmiths.
2. *Mid Level*—Parents voluntarily indentured a child as a craft apprentice or servant.
3. *Basic Level*—Poor children were indentured out by the overseers of a town or a parish as apprentices.[98]

These laws covered three essential points: first, bringing up a child to work at some employment or trade; second, supporting the child, so that he or she would not become a charge on the town; and third, seeing that the child was taught to read. It is significant to note that in all these colonial apprenticeship laws the agency for educating the child is the parent or master. No mention is made of schools or schoolmasters. The reason was that the system of home manufacturing that existed in colonial times precluded compulsory education through school attendance, as this would seriously interfere with the normal economic conditions of life for a large proportion of the population. New England also emphasized apprenticeship education to help solve two social issues that have persisted to this day, unemployment and "pauperism" and meeting labor-market needs by ensuring an adequate number of entry-level skilled workers.[99]

The apprenticeship system was controlled through voluntary or compulsory written indenture contracts recorded in town, county, or colony records. These indentures were enforceable in the courts. The general term of apprenticeships for males was to the age of 21 and girls to 18. Children could be bound out by voluntary action of the parents at any time.

Indenturement got its name because it was originally written in duplicate on one sheet of paper and then cut apart, forming indentations. One half was given to the master, the other to the apprentice or his family. The two parts would thus fit together perfectly, indicating who was apprenticed to whom.

Such was the case of the indenturement of eight-year-old Isaiah Thomas to Zachariah Fowle on July 7, 1756, by the Boston overseers of the poor. Bound out at the age of eight, upon reaching 21 his indenture was inscribed on its face "Free January 8th, 1769." Apprenticed as a printer, Isaiah Fowle grew up to become one of colonial America's most notable journalists.

The entire 1600s and 1700s apprenticeship system presumed that literate parents, masters, or the local town would provide or pay for vocational and literacy education. Such a conception of compulsory education to attain public literacy is very different from our twentieth-century conception of compulsory attendance in organized schools at public expense. However, modern readers cannot but marvel at the high ideals of these New England farmers, craftsmen, and clergy who wrote laws for a frontier society that was often in its earliest days still struggling for survival. This idealism perhaps inspired them to use apprenticeships for literacy education to help build their conception of a better world freed from the poverty and ignorance many of them had fled in contemporary England.[100]

A 1703 Massachusetts supplement to earlier literacy acts reaffirmed the need to provide apprentices with an education by stipulating that the masters should provide "for the instruction of children so bounded out, to read and write, if they be capable." However, in 1710 an amendment altered the order to "males to read and write, females to read." "Cyphering" was added for males in 1741. This is important because the whole purpose of apprenticeship was to give children enough skills for a lifetime of gainful employment. Boys needed to be able to write; girls did not.

In the contemporary viewpoint, writing was a job-related skill. Girls were not being educated to hold jobs, but to become successful homemakers. Therefore, penmanship was an irrelevant educational activity for them. A study of 267 apprentices in seventeenth-century Massachusetts, including 32 girls, identified 40 different crafts and trades for boys. However, the girls were limited to learning "housewifery," though in two cases this also included sewing or knitting and spinning. Between 1743 and 1760 in the town of Newbury, Massachusetts, 60 poor children were put out for apprenticeship indentures. Forty-nine boys were apprenticed to learn a broad range of skills, from blacksmithing to wig making. However, the 11 girls only learned "women's work" or "housewifery." All the apprentices were promised reading instruction, but only the boys were to be taught both reading and arithmetic.[101]

Apprenticeship was common and widely practiced throughout colonial New England. Thus it provides an additional component of our overall understanding of early literacy practices.

THE PRACTICE OF LITERACY

How did literacy instruction happen on a day-to-day basis? Under what conditions did schoolmasters teach? How were they paid? What did they teach and how did they teach it? Finally, what teaching materials and books were used in a "typical school"?

Schoolmasters hired by a town did not require the community to build a proper schoolhouse. As we have already noted, "school" was held in the schoolmaster's or dame-school teacher's home, the child's home, rented rooms, barns, inns, taverns, or almost anywhere. "School" was a generic term used in colonial America to designate an instructional concept, not an actual building. If a colonial town did build a schoolhouse, it did so for the sake of convenience, tradition, or civic pride, not because of any legal obligation. As one would expect, these tiny wilderness communities built small, mean, primitive schools. A typical building was often only 20 feet long, 18 feet wide, with only a six- or seven-foot-high ceiling. Most schoolhouses were of frame and clapboard construction. Such schools had two or three stationary windows, with lime-plastered walls to help brighten the room. The flickering flames of a large fireplace and later the Franklin stove near the door of the room also provided light for reading. Long plank desks with backless plank seats lined three sides of the room. Near the door stood the schoolmaster's large table, the symbol and seat of learning.

This crackerbox schoolroom had poor ventilation and often became either a learning "hothouse" or "icebox." Warren Burton, who attended such a school recalled how in winter "every cold afternoon, the old fireplace, wide and deep, kept a roaring furnance of flame, for the benefit of blue noses, chattering jaws, and aching toes, in the more distant regions (of the room). It was a toil to exist much less to learn."[102]

Classes met all year, but the length of day and who attended varied with the season. In 1700 Salem's town school followed this schedule: March 1 to November 1, 7:00 A.M. to 5:00 P.M.; November 1 to March (shorter daylight hours), 8:00 A.M. to 4:00 P.M. Vacations were few: election day, Thanksgiving, and Wednesday and Saturday afternoons. Sunday was for church service attendance in both the morning and the afternoon.[103]

Town land was often set aside to address another major problem: paying the schoolmaster. Sometimes called the "school-meadows" or "school-fields," this income supplemented the "town rate." This principle of taxation seemed to be adopted only for the education of the children whose parents were too poor to pay tuition themselves. Though the schools were public they were not free, and parents had to pay tuition for children to attend. Not until after the American Revolution were schools paid for entirely by general town taxes in Massachusetts.[104]

In Chester, New Hampshire, Dr. Samuel Moores was paid 108 pounds in 1749 "for schooling." Schoolmasters in general were poorly paid. Some towns combined the post of schoolmaster with being the "first physician." The Massachusetts town of Braintree required Mr. Thompson "In urgent cases to close his school to attend to his professional duties." Malden gave its schoolmaster/physician sixpence a visit and 16 pounds for six-month schoolmaster engagement. Yet other doctors were paid only three pounds or even less for keeping school.

This combining of professional duties was a common practice during this era. In 1661 the duties of a schoolmaster could also include any one of the following tasks: acting as a court messenger, serving a summons, leading the Sunday choir, ringing the bell for public worship, and serving as a gravedigger.

Next in importance to hiring a minister who could teach was hiring a teacher who could preach. Such schoolmasters could supplement meager salaries through the congregation's free contributions.[105]

Because this was a largely cashless economy, schoolmasters were often paid in a wide variety of commodities, including beaver skins, wheat, peas, corn, beans, wampum, or any agricultural product simply known as "truck." Logs for the school fireplace were furnished by some parents as part of their child's tuition. In one colonial Salem schoolhouse, a student was always seated by the window who, while attending class, could also be on the lookout to hail perspective passers-by and sell them the accumulation of barter crops and goods given in payment to the teacher. The stereotypical picture of an ultra-frugal New England Yankee society certainly applies to the financing and pay of its colonial schoolmasters.[106]

Though a wide spectrum of people, duties and modes of payment typified early New England literacy, the same instructional materials were typically used by everyone. Direct references to the exact method of teaching reading are extremely rare. But the arrangement of materials and the books used by the colonists are well known, and they bear further witness to the assumption that the literacy methods practiced in the England of that day were commonly followed across the Atlantic in America.[107]

Though there are gaps in our exact knowledge of literacy instruction, we do know about its sequence. Reading was taught before writing. In fact, instruction in writing presumed instruction had already occurred in reading, just as instruction in mathematics presupposed the acquisition of writing. Reading instruction was conducted orally using an alphabet method.[108]

The advice of famous English philosopher, economist, and tutor-educator John Locke in his *Thoughts Concerning Education* (1690) was followed by many parents and schoolmasters alike on both sides of the Atlantic. His recommended method of teaching children to read was always "the ordinary road of Hornbook, Primer, Psalter, Testament and Bible." The child was to begin by learning to read and write as painlessly as possible in his native language by first mastering the alphabet and syllables, progressing from hornbook upward.[109]

The "hornbook" was undoubtedly the first link in the chain of childhood literacy. Hornbooks were made from a wide variety of materials, including wood, iron, pewter, ivory, silver, and even gingerbread! Since gingerbread was then such a childhood treat, someone conceived the idea of simple behavior reinforcement by bribing children to engage in the task of learning by eating their way through the alphabet. They could eat each gingerbread letter as they learned to name it.[110]

Unfortunately, the typical hornbook for most children was far less palatable, consisting of a sheet of paper about three by four inches square fastened to a thin paddle-shaped book. The name "hornbook" came from the translucent sheet of horn that covered the paper and was fastened around three sides of the horn by a narrow metal strip. The fourth side was left open to allow the insertion of instructional sheets of paper. The board was held by its handle, and a string through the handle could suspend the hornbook around the child's neck. This early teaching device often contained only the alphabet, but later hornbooks also offered syllables and Bible selections.[111]

By far the most common basic literacy text was *The New England Primer*. There will never be any accurate way to determine the exact numbers of American colonial children and adults who used these primers to become literate on their own, with the help of relatives or friends, or in the first schools. However, given the extraordinary circulation of primers, both American and foreign, the number of people who achieved some degree of literacy through them must have been considerable.

The New England Primer's first edition appears to have been compiled by Benjamin Harris, a London printer who immigrated to Boston (1685). There he set up a printing business with John Allen. Although no copy exists of the first edition, it was probably published between 1687 and 1690. (Harris later returned to London and also published *The New England Primer* in that city.) For one hundred years the *Primer* was the schoolbook of the Puritan dissenters of America, and for another hundred it was frequently reprinted.[112]

The reasons behind its long-lived popularity was that *The New England Primer* introduced the important innovation of combining into a single volume the substance of the traditional hornbook (the alphabet and syllabication drills) with the substance of the traditional primer (the Lord's Prayer, Bible selections, and an authorized dissenter catechism). Some earlier editions also contained the Ten Commandments, the names and order of the books of the Old and New Testaments, Arabic and Roman numerals and words, and helpful advice on locating specific chapters and verses in the Bible. Another famous part was the poem of John Rogers (burned as the first Puritan martyr in England during Queen Mary's Catholic reign), with a picture of him burning at the stake with his wife and children looking on. The poem was written as an exhortation to his children. By 1700 editions also included either the *Westminster Assembly's Shorter Catechism* or John Cotton's *Spiritual Milk for Babes.*

By the later nineteenth century the anti-Catholic nature of *The New England Primer* was one of the motivators for Irish and other non-dissenting immigrants to abandon the public schools of New England. These churches established their own parochial-educational institutions.[113]

In seventeenth- and eighteenth-century America a preschool child probably would have first been introduced to *The New England Primer* at home. The alphabet instructional method was the sole teaching method used. Many a colonial child learned to read by first mastering the letters and syllables phonetically and then hearing scripture passages again and again with the reader pointing to each word. Children were taught to parse words out in syllables to pronounce them. As part of this learning process, students were made to memorize lists of syllables that in themselves had no meaning.[114] Such was the experience of Jane Turell, who was born in Boston in 1708. Before she was three years old, Jane could speak distinctly, knew her letters, and placed on a table to show off her learning, could relate many stories out of the "Scriptures to the satisfaction and pleasure of the most judicious." When Jane was three years old, she could recite the greater part of the Assembly's Catechism, psalms, and lines of poetry and was a good reader. By the age of four she "asked many astonishing questions about divine mysteries." In some New England Puritan homes, very young children often developed a detailed knowledge of their religion, which would seem unusual today, but was then part of the popular culture.[115]

After the primer the next book used in literacy instruction was the Psalter (the Book of Psalms). Its purpose was not only instruction in reading but also the training of children, particularly in the reading of the holy scriptures.[116] In fact it has been estimated that over 40 percent of all the books printed in England between 1480 and 1640 were religious in theme. In the colonies the number was even higher, over 50 percent between 1639 and 1689. No phase of Christian living for child or adult was left untouched. But this resulted in a dire scarcity of anything approaching what we today would consider "children's literature." Twenty-first-century young children would hardly like to read such books as *The Prodigal Daughter* or the *Disobedient Lady Reclaimed*.[117]

In the teaching of reading there were other non-religious books that parents might also turn to as self-help textbooks such as Edmund Coote's *The English Schoole-Maister* (1596), which went systematically from letters, syllables, and words to sentences, paragraphs, and short essays. Writing and ciphering were taught from Lewis Hughes' text *Plain and Easy Directions to Faire Writing* (c. 1650) or Edward Cocker's *The Tutor to Writing and Arithmetic* (1664).[118]

After about 1760, children attending school most likely received spelling books for their first text. Their function was not just to teach spelling, but also reading, morals, and religion. Perhaps the most popular speller of this period was Thomas Dilworth's *A New Guide to the English Tongue* (1740). First published in England, later reprinted in America by Benjamin Franklin (1747), it had fourteen additional reprints by the time of the American Revolution (1778). It contained several pages on spelling rules and the writing of English and featured 12 fables in a high moral tone. The remaining pages of the speller were devoted to religious materials.[119]

The path to literacy in colonial New England dame schools or reading schools might begin for boys and, as the 1700s progressed, growing numbers of girls before the age of five. These petty schools were expected to make children proficient in reading in two to three years. After children had mastered their hornbook and speller and the *New England Primer*, they could go on to a writing school. For a boy, the next step was grammar school to study the classics of Rome and Greece. If the child was intelligent and the family wealthy, he might next attend Harvard College and study the seven liberal arts. If he chose, he might then study theology with the goal of entering the ministry.[120]

THE FRUITS OF LITERACY

One day each year, most Americans gather around the family table to remember the Pilgrims and give them thanks for America's bounty. Perhaps we should also thank them for planting and nurturing the first important sprouts of American literacy.

The New England literacy experience provided ample evidence of how European literacy practices (particularly from England) often paralleled developments in the American colonies. It is now apparent that during this early period (1620–1790) sundry sources of literacy instruction were open to children.

The diverse world of colonial New England literacy contained widespread examples of domestic education from the famous Cotton Mather and John and Abigail Adams to the most obscure farmer. There was schooling of every conceivable variety: grammar, petty, dame, summer, moving, reading, writing, academy, and primary. Apprenticeship education was also important, particularly for indentured servants. (We will later see them acting as tutors themselves.)

This literacy process was driven by a common curriculum that started and ended with the Bible and also included such literacy tools as the hornbook, speller, primer, and Psalter. The chronicle of New England literacy education helps form a basis of comparison for the other thirteen original colonies. It also underscores the family as an essential component of basic literacy for the future United States.

NOTES

1. Carl F. Kaestle et al. *Literacy in the United States: Readers and Reading Since 1880* (New Haven: Yale University Press, 1991), 19.

2. R. A. Houston, *Literacy in Early Modern Europe: Culture and Education 1500–1800* (London: Longman, 1988), 98–99, 103.

3. Ibid., 91.

4. Laurence A. Cremin, *American Education: The Colonial Experience, 1607–1786* (New York: Harper & Row, 1970), 78; Houston, *Literacy*, 62.

5. Ibid., 5, 92; Edward E. Gordon and Elaine H. Gordon, *Centuries of Tutoring: A History of Alternative Education in America and Western Europe* (Lanham, Maryland: University Press of America, 1990), 98–102, 115, 121–124, 130–131, 193–196, 201–216, 262–263, 294–297.

6. Roger Ascham, *The Whole Works of Roger Ascham*, ed. Rev. Dr. Giles. (New York: AMS Press, 1965), 96–104, 120; Gordon, *Tutoring*, 93–98.

7. Cremin, *Colonial Experience*, 124, 173.

8. Houston, *Literacy*, 115, 148.

9. Gerald Lee Gutek, *Education and Schooling in America* (Boston: Allyn and Bacon, 1992), 62–63.

10. Cremin, *Colonial Experience*, 41, 192–193.

11. Margaret Connell Szasz, *Indian Education in the American Colonies 1607–1783* (Albuquerque: University of New Mexico Press, 1988), 27–28.

12. Marcus Wilson Jernegan, *Laboring and Dependent Classes in Colonial America 1607–1783* (Chicago: University of Chicago Press, 1931), 64–65.

13. Szasz, *Indian Education*, 26–27; Cremin, *Colonial Experience*, 237; James Axtell, *The School upon a Hill* (New Haven: Yale University Press, 1974), 21.

14. Edmund S. Morgan, *The Puritan Family: Religion and Domestic Relations in Seventeenth Century New England*, rev. ed. (New York: Harper & Row, 1966), 90–91.

15. Gerald F. Moran and Maris A. Vinovskis, *Religion, Family and the Life Course* (Ann Arbor: University of Michigan Press, 1992), 117, 119.

16. Cremin, *Colonial Experience*, 156.

17. Kenneth A. Lockridge, *Literacy in Colonial New England: An Enquiry into the Social Context of Literacy in the Early Modern West* (New York: Norton, 1974), 38.

18. Morgan, *Puritan Family*, 98–99.

19. Cremin, *Colonial Experience*, 50–52.

20. Szasz, *Indian Education*, 29.

21. *The Dictionary of American Biography*, vol. 2 (New York: C. Scribners, 1928), 577.

22. Robert Francis Seybolt, *The Private Schools of Colonial Boston* (Cambridge: Harvard University Press, 1935), 3–10; Gordon, *Centuries of Tutoring*, 249–250, 3–10.

23. Nathaniel B. Shurtleff, ed., *Records of the Governor and Company of the Massachusetts Bay in New England*, vol. 2 (Boston: William White, 1853–1864), 6–7.

24. Marcus W. Jernegan, *Colonial America*, 67; Alice Felt Tyler, *Freedom's Ferment* (New York: Harper & Row, 1962), 227.

25. Shurtleff, *Records of Massachusetts*, 84–99.

26. Ibid.

27. Jernegan, *Colonial America*, 84–85.

28. Moran, *Religion, Family*, 124.

29. Cremin, *Colonial Experience*, 181.

30. Shurtleff, *Records of Massachusetts*, 203.

31. Ibid.

32. J. Hammond Trumbull, ed., *The Public Records of the Colony of Connecticut*, vol. 2 (Hartford: Brown and Parsons, 1850–1890), 520–521; David Pulsifer, ed., *Records of the Colony of New Plymouth in New England*, vol. 11 (Boston: William White, 1861), 142, 246–247; George Staughton, Thomas McCament, and Benjamin Nead, eds., *Charter to William Penn, and Laws of the Province of Pennsylvania, Passed Between the Years 1682 and 1700* (Harrisburg: Lane S. Hart, 1879), 142.

33. "Watertown Records I," Watertown, Massachusetts, 1894, in *Children and Youth in America: A Documentary History*, ed. Robert H. Bremner, vol. 1, 1600–1865 (Cambridge: Harvard University Press, 1970), 41.

34. Geraldine Joanne Murphy, "Massachusetts Bay Colony: The Role of Government in Education" (Ph.D. diss., Radcliffe College, 1960), Chapter iii.

35. Moran, *Religion, Family*, 124.

36. Maris A. Vinovskis, "Family and Schooling in Colonial and Nineteenth-Century America," *Journal of Family History* 12 (1987): 24; Axtell, *School upon a Hill*, 179; Cremin, *Colonial Experience*, 124.

37. Josiah Cotton, "Extracts from the Diary of Josiah Cotton," *Publications of the Colonial Society of Massachusetts* 26 (1924–26): 278.

38. Gerald Gutek, *Education and Schooling in America*, 63; Cremin, *Colonial Experience*, 134; H. Warren Button and Eugene F. Provenzo, Jr., *History of Education and Culture in America* (Englewood Cliffs: Prentice-Hall, 1983), 14–15; Laura Arksey, Nancy Pries, and Marcia Reed, *American Diaries: An Annotated Bibliography of Published American Diaries and Journals, Vol. 1, Diaries Written from 1492 to 1844* (Detroit, Michigan: Gale Research Co., 1983), 47–48.

39. M. G. Hall, ed., "The Autobiography of Increase Mather," *Proceedings of the American Antiquarian Society* 71 (1961): 278.

40. E. Jennifer Monaghan, "Family Literacy in Early 18th Century Boston: Cotton Mather and His Children," *Reading Research Quarterly* 26 (October–December 1991): 346, 349. This is the same Cotton Mather who helped to preside over the infamous Salem Witch Trials. His participation in this unfortunate hysterical event has for many years minimized acknowledgement of his contribution to early American literacy practices.

41. Ibid., 346–353.

42. Ibid., 354–356, 363–366.

43. Cremin, *Colonial Experience*, 187.

44. Sheldon S. Cohen, *A History of Colonial Education 1607–1776* (New York: Wiley, 1974), 20–21.

45. Cremin, *Colonial Experience*, 505; Alice Morse Earle, *Child Life in Colonial Days* (New York: Macmillan, 1899; reprint Stockbridge, Massachusetts: Berkshire House Publishers, 1993), 134.

46. Cremin, *Colonial Experience*, 505, 192, 237, 493.

47. Harlan Updegraff, *The Origin of the Moving School in Massachusetts* (New York: Teachers College, Columbia University, 1908), 107–116, 171.

48. E. Jennifer Monaghan, "Literacy Instruction and Gender in Colonial New England," *American Quarterly* 40 (March 1988): 23.

49. Cremin, *Colonial Experience*, 128–129.

50. Axtell, *School upon a Hill*, 53, 175–176.

51. David Tyack and Elizabeth Hansot, *Learning Together: A History of Coeducation in American Schools* (New Haven: Yale University Press, 1990), 19; Updegraff, *Moving School*, 138.

52. William Newell, "Memoir of the Rev. Convers Francis," *Proceedings of the Massachusetts Historical Society* (March 1865): 236.

53. "Autobiography of Rev. John Barnard," *Collections of the Massachusetts Historical Society* 3 (1836): 178.

54. Monaghan, "Literacy Instruction," 23, 33; Updegraff, *Moving School*, 152.

55. Walter H. Small, *Early New England Schools* (Boston: Ginn, 1914; reprint, New York: Arno Press, 1969), 163.

56. Ibid.

57. Ibid., 165–167.

58. Ibid., 162; Updegraff, *Moving School*, 152.

59. Ibid., 140; Barbara Beatty, *Preschool Education in America: The Culture of Young Children from the Colonial Era to the Present* (New Haven: Yale University Press, 1995), 23.

60. Small, *Early New England Schools*, 186.

61. Cohen, *Colonial Education*, 90; Updegraff, *Moving Schools*, 128.

62. Updegraff, *Moving Schools*, 144, 148; Small, *Early New England Schools*, 64–65.

63. Nancy F. Cott, *The Bonds of Womanhood: Women's Sphere in New England 1780–1835* (New Haven: Yale University Press, 1977), 30–31.

64. Thomas Woody, *A History of Women's Education in the United States*, vol. 1 (New York: Science Press, 1929), 192; *Boston Gazette*, March 21–22 (S.), 1719/20. "Samuel Granger Late of London" admitted an inhabitant and licensed "to keep School to teach writeing, Logick & Merchants Acco" in this Town," Jan. 27, 1719/20 (B.R., xiii, 65). He opened his school on Mar. 7, 1719/20 (B.G., Feb. 29–Mar. 7, 1719/20). Sir Charles Hobby's house stood on the north corner of Rawson's Lane (now Bromfield Street) and Marlborough (now Washington) Street. "The Diary of Samuel Sewall" (5 *Coll. Mass. Host. Soc.*, vii, 245). entry of Mar. 8, 1719/20: "Col. Fitch express'd himself as much prising Mr.

Granger's Accomplishment to Teach Writing; never such a Person in Boston before. Reslves to send his Son to him; has told him he will do so." See also B.G., Sept 2–9, 8–16, 1723; Aug 31–Sept 7, 1724; Aug 30–Sept 6, 27–Oct 4, 4–11, 18–25, 1725; Jan 3–10, 10–17, 1725/26; Sept 4–11, 11–18, 1727; *Boston Weekly News Letter*, Aug 26–Sept 2, 16–23, 23–30, 1725; May 3–10, 17–24, 1733.

65. *A Report of the Record Commissioners of the City of Boston, Containing the Boston Records from 1660 to 1701* (Boston: Rockwell and Churchill, 1881), 36. Among the best early works on the private entrepreneurial teacher in the colonial era is: Robert Francis Seybolt, *Source Studies in American Colonial Education* (Urbana: University of Illinois Press, 1925).

66. Mrs. Slack, *The American Instructor or Young Man's Best Companion*, 9th ed. (Philadelphia: B. Franklin and D. Hall, 1748).

67. *Dictionary of American Biography*, vol. 1, 60–61.

68. John Adams, *Adams Family Correspondence*, ed. L. H. Butterfield, 4 vols. (Cambridge, Massachusetts: Harvard University, The Belknap Press, 1963). Their four children were Abigail (b. 14 July 1765), John Quincy (b. 11 July 1767), Charles (b. 29 May 1770), and Thomas Boylston Adams (b. 15 September 1772).

69. John Adams to Abigail Adams, 26 September 1775, *AFC*, 1:286; 29 October 1775, *AFC*, 1:317–318; 28 August 1774, *AFC*, 1:145; 7 July 1776, *AFC*, 2:39.

70. John Adams to Thomas Boylston Adams, 20 October 1775, *AFC*, 1:305; John Adams to Abigail Adams, 12 May 1780, *AFC*, 3:342.

71. John Adams to Abigail Adams, 18 February 1783, *Letters of John Adams Addressed to His Wife*, ed. C. F. Adams, vol. 2 (Boston: Freeman and Bolles, 1841), 89–90.

72. Abigail Adams to Mary Warren, 16 July 1773, *AFC*, 1:85; Abigail Adams to Isaac Smith, Jr., 16 March 1763, *AFC*, 1:4.

73. Abigail Adams to Mary Warren, 16 July 1773, *AFC*, 1:85.

74. Mary Warren to Abigail Adams, 25 July 1773, *AFC*, 1:86–87.

75. Abigail Adams to Abigail Adams Smith, *Letters of Mrs. Adams*, vol 2. (Boston: Charles C. Little and James Brown, 1841), 24; Abigail Adams to Abigail Adams Smith, 218–219.

76. Cremin, *Colonial Experience*, 134.

77. Szasz, *Indian Education*, 38.

78. Christopher M. Jedrey, *The World of John Cleaveland: Family and Community in Eighteenth Century New England* (New York: Norton, 1979), 18.

79. Ibid., 98.

80. Ibid., 98–100.

81. Ibid., 101–102 Jedrey's estimates are based on Joseph Perkins' ledger in the Essex Institute, Salem, Massachusetts.

82. Rhode Island was the only New England colony that did not enact schooling legislation. In 1769 Providence finally voted to build three schoolhouses. Cohen, *History of Colonial Education*, 86, 92.

83. Jon Teaford, "The Transformation of Massachusetts Education, 1670–1780," *History of Education Quarterly* 10 (Fall 1970): 301.

84. Cohen, *History of Colonial Education*, 93; Richard B. Morris, ed., *Encyclopedia of American History* (New York: Harper & Row, 1970), 507.

85. Tyack, *Learning Together*, 18.

86. Kathryn Kish Sklar, "The Schooling of Girls and Changing Community Values in Massachusetts Towns, 1750–1820," *History of Education Quarterly* 33 (Winter 1993):

511; Joel Perlmann, Silvana R. Siddali, and Keith Whitescarver, "Literacy, Schooling, and Teaching among New England Women 1730–1820," *History of Education Quarterly* 37 (Summer 1997): 117, 123.

87. Arthur W. Calhoun, *A Social History of the American Family from Colonial Times to the Present*, vol. 1. *Colonial Period* (New York: Barnes & Noble, 1945), 83–84.

88. Gordon, *Centuries of Tutoring*, 172. The term "bluestocking" seems to have its origins in gatherings held around 1750 at the London home of Mrs. Mary Montague (1689–1762). As a child Mary had studied with her brother's tutors, learning Latin, Greek, French, and Italian. At Mrs. Montague's, instead of card playing, the chief recreation at women's evening parties, more intellectual conversation was held on literary subjects. Eminent men of letters often took part. Many attended without "full dress." One of these was Mr. Benjamin Stillingfleet. He habitually wore grey or blue worsted, instead of black silk stockings. In reference to this Admiral Boscawen (1806) derisively dubbed the coterie "the blue stocking society" (as not constituting a dressed assembly). From this time on, learned women who supported educational reform were depreciated by the term "blue stockingers," "blue stocking ladies," later abbreviated to "blues." *Oxford English Dictionary*, vol. 1, c.v. Bluestocking (Oxford: Oxford University Press, 1933).

89. Calhoun, *Social History*, 84.

90. Gerald F. Moran and Maris A. Vinovskis, "The Great Care of Godly Parents: Early Childhood in Puritan New England," in *Religion, Family and the Life Course: Explorations in the Social History of Early America* (Ann Arbor: The University of Michigan Press, 1992), 24–37; Vinovskis, "Family and Schooling," 23.

91. James Russell Trumbull, *History of Northampton, Massachusetts from Its Settlement in 1654* (Northampton, Massachusetts: Gazette Printing Company, 1902), 586.

92. Sklar, "The Schooling of Girls," 516; Cott, *The Bonds of Womanhood*, 30.

93. Linda Auwers, "Reading the Marks of the Past: Exploring Female Literacy in Colonial Windsor, Connecticut," *Historical Methods* 13 (Fall 1980): 204.

94. Ibid., 212.

95. Gordon, *Centuries of Tutoring*, 210–211; Bea Howe, *A Galaxy of Governesses* (London: Derek Verschoyle, 1954), 81–82; Auwers, "Reading the Marks," 213.

96. Lois Barber Arnold, *Four Lives in Science: Women's Education in the Nineteenth Century* (New York: Schocken Books, 1984), 4–5.

97. Katherine Anthony, *First Lady of the Revolution: The Life of Mercy Otis Warren* (New York: Doubleday & Company, 1958), 19–61; J. H. Powell, "The War of the Pamphlets," in *A Literary History of the United States*, rev. ed., eds. Robert E. Spiller et al. (New York: Macmillan, 1953), 133–134; Joan Hoff and Sharon L. Bollinger, "Mercy Otis Warren: Playwright, Poet and Historian of the American Revolution," in *Female Scholars: A Tradition of Learned Women before 1800*, ed. J. R. Brink (Montreal: Eden Press Women's Publications, 1980), 161–163.

98. Geraldine Youcha, *Minding the Children: Child Care in America from Colonial Times to the Present* (New York: Scribner, 1995), 18.

99. Jernegan, *Laboring and Dependent Classes*, 88–89, 101.

100. Ibid., 112–113; Youcha, *Minding the Children*, 23–24.

101. Monaghan, "Literacy Instruction," 27–29.

102. Axtell, *School upon a Hill*, 170–171. Boston, by comparison being a large city, built more functional school buildings.

103. Szasz, *Indian Education*, 36.

104. Earle, *Child Life*, 68–69; Jernegan, *Laboring and Dependent Classes*, 76–77.

105. Small, *Early New England Schools*, 98–99.

106. Earle, *Child Life*, 69.

107. Nila Banton Smith, *American Reading Instruction* (Newark, Delaware: International Reading Association, 1986), 31.

108. Monaghan, "Family Literacy," 348.

109. James L. Axtell, ed., *The Educational Writings of John Locke* (Cambridge: Cambridge University Press, 1968), 270, 321, 325; Earle, *Child Life*, 117; Cremin, *Colonial Experience*, 362. Locke's ideas were further popularized in the colonies by the local publications of detailed educational study plans for children, including James Burgh, *The Dignity of Human Nature* (1754), and Isaac Watts, *Discourse on the Education of Children and Youth* (1753).

110. Smith, *American Reading*, 6; The two-volume *History of the Horn-Book* by Andrew White Tuer (London, 1896) offers an interesting and exhaustive account on this basic literacy device.

111. Ibid., 7.

112. *The New England Primer* (Boston: E. Draper, c. 1785); Paul Leicester Ford, ed., *The New England Primer* (New York: Teachers College Press, 1962), 13–16, 19; Cremin, *Colonial Experience*, 393.

113. Ford, *Primer*, 45–46; Cremin, *Colonial Experience*, 394.

114. E. Jennifer Monaghan, *A Common Heritage: Noah Webster's Blue-Back Speller* (Hamden, Connecticut: Archon Books, 1983), 31–32; Cremin, *Colonial Experience*, 129.

115. Earle, *Child Life*, 179–180.

116. Monaghan, "Literacy Instruction," 21.

117. Cremin, *Colonial Experience*, 40–41; Calhoun, *Social History*, 115.

118. Cremin, *Colonial Experience*, 129, 185.

119. Smith, *American Reading*, 25–28; Monaghan, *A Common Heritage*, 32.

120. Morgan, *Puritan Family*, 101; Cremin, *Colonial Experience*, 174.

Chapter 2

From "Dukes" to "Friends":
Literacy in the Middle Atlantic Colonies

REGIONAL DIFFERENCES

Literacy practices in the Middle Atlantic Colonies often followed New England instructional forms. However, in the Middle Atlantic colonies social conditions frequently were less favorable than in New England for developing an educated populace. The fact that these colonies were settled by immigrants who differed in country of origin, language, and religion constrained governmental action on education. For example, when the rule of New York passed from the Netherlands to England in 1664, the first code of laws (the Duke's Law, 1665) seems to have been designed to accommodate the practices of the Dutch population. The sole provision regarding education was that officials should admonish the inhabitants to instruct children and servants in religion and the laws of the country as well as educate them for employment.[1]

In the Middle Atlantic colonies, as elsewhere, the family remained the principal agent of literacy for children. This was a common social idea. Education usually began with some form of tutoring at home in reading and writing. The colonial household farm or plantation persisted as the basic economic unit in a largely frontier and rural society. Against this background literacy spread through both formal and informal intellectual and technical education. Parents and siblings taught reading in the home from hornbooks, primers, catechisms, and Bibles. Many parents sent their children to a neighbor, "usually a poor widow," who operated a dame school.[2]

By 1776 about 100,000 people lived in the American colonies' principal cities—Boston, New York, Philadelphia, Newport, and Charleston. Even including the secondary towns, only an estimated one of every sixteen colonists lived in an urban environment. Only here was family education eclipsed as the primary agent of literacy by the presence of schools.[3] But even the major cities of the central colonies suffered from one major drawback: a lack of public schools.

The specific schooling arrangements of the middle colonies often were dominated by religious and ethnic groups that in some ways shaped much more pluralistic schools, which were more representative of future American education than the town school system of New England. Since most schools were sectarian or private, many children, especially in the predominantly rural districts, had no access to literacy instruction except in their own home.[4] Besides the lack of public support for funding schools, why did this happen?

Prejudices and laws set by mainstream Protestant groups limited the access of many families to education. For example, most Catholic children were educated at home, by necessity. Maryland had the largest Catholic population in all the colonies, but public Catholic religious services were outlawed. Catholics could not vote or hold office, and Catholic schools were illegal for many years.

As early as 1640 a former Jesuit operated a school for 20 years at Newton, Maryland. This school operated only intermittently until the early 1700s, supported by gifts of land and cattle from wealthy Catholics in the area. Another clandestine school at Bohemic Manor (1745) operated in much the same manner. Since these schools had to exist by stealth, students experienced irregular class sessions.[5]

In early New York, Colonel Thomas Dongan, an Irish Catholic, was appointed the colony's governor (1683–1688). He brought with him an English Jesuit, Thomas Harvey, who with two other English Jesuits, opened a chapel and small school at Fort James. Some of the colony's leading non-Catholic families enrolled their sons along with the children of Catholic families. However, upon the coronation in England of William and Mary, who were Protestant, the school succumbed to the anti-Catholic colonial administrators who came into power.[6] As we will see time and again, private education would become an essential component for early literacy throughout the middle colonies.

NEW YORK

Before New York existed, the Dutch established their own city of New Amsterdam (1626). They provided little opportunity for literacy education. A few children were taught at home by private tutors, and others attended parochial schools.

John Styvesant, Director General of the Dutch colony, New Netherlands, employed (1662) Aegidius Luyak to tutor his children in Latin, Greek, writing, and arithmetic. Luyak later was appointed rector of the New Amsterdam Latin School. In similar circumstances Jacques Cortelyou came to America as the private tutor for the son of a Dutch family. He was the first settler of the village of New Utrecht.[7]

By 1664 New Netherlands had a population of just over 5,000, with a dozen Dutch villages, including New Amsterdam, a few Puritan townships on Long

Island, and scattered, small Finnish and Swedish settlements along the Delaware River.[8]

The schools of New Amsterdam were run in a joint collaboration between church and state. It was universally accepted that the Dutch schoolmaster would teach religion through the catechism in the schoolroom, and on Sundays he was also the "voorlexer," the reader during church services, as well as the sexton. The contract for the teacher at the Dutch settlement of Flatbush, Long Island (1682), detailed these other religious duties in addition to teaching the children. He rang the church bell on Sunday. He read the Bible at service in church, led the singing, and sometimes read the sermon. As sexton he provided the water for baptisms and the bread and wine for communion. He also delivered invitations to funerals and carried other messages. Sometimes he was pressed into service to dig graves and often to visit the sick of his community.

The civil authorities divided the financial responsibilities for these parochial schools. The Lord Directors of the Dutch West India Company paid the salaries of the New Amsterdam schoolmasters out of the company's general funds. Local authorities generally furnished the school quarters, which meant they provided the schoolmaster with a free house to be used as both a schoolroom and a residence. However, each child also paid tuition based on the subjects taken.[9]

Both boys and girls began school at the age of seven. The school was held in the largest room of the schoolmaster's house. School was held six days a week (half days on Wednesday and Saturday), usually between 8:00 A.M. and 4:00 P.M., with a midday two-hour dinner recess. The schoolroom was equipped with the master's desk and with chairs and backless benches for the children, with tables for writing. The boys and girls sat in separate parts of the room, with the girls farthest from the master.

The Dutch of America followed the educational traditions of the fatherland promulgated in 1636 "for schoolmasters going to the East or West Indies": reading and writing for both girls and boys, but with little arithmetic except in the more commercial atmosphere of New Amsterdam and Albany. The Dutch seemed to have been ahead of their New England neighbors regarding girls' education. However, though all of the boys and most of the girls entered the writing class, many girls, because they were needed at home, did not even learn to write their names.[10]

The first book in the Dutch curriculum was an alphabetical reader called the "cock book," named after the crowing cock on its title page. Its contents included: the alphabet in different type sizes, vowels and syllables, the Ten Commandments, the Creed, the Lord's Prayer, the prayer of Solomon, morning and evening prayers, church ceremonies for baptism and communion, and later the Dutch counting table.

Next the child received a reading book consisting of gospels and other selections from the New Testament. Later texts included the Old Testament, history selections, psalm books, and the Heidelberg Catechism, the official doctrine of the Dutch Reformed Church.[11]

The New Amsterdam parochial school persisted through the American Revolution (1776–1783) under the support of the Dutch Reformed Church of the city. However, since only Dutch was taught, with the spread of the English language the practical value of these schools began to decline. The Dutch schools became more and more charity schools, particularly after the Revolution.

The male schoolmaster seemed to dominate this educational system. Although dame schools were common in seventeenth-century Holland, there is surprisingly little recorded of them in New York during the Dutch or English colonial period.[12]

In 1664 the English seized the New Netherlands and renamed the colony and city New York. Certainly, the Dutch influence on education persisted through the parochial schools both in the city and in Albany, Flatbush, Schenectady, and other Dutch enclaves.

New Yorkers throughout the colonial period found this unorganized approach to literacy appealing and well suited for their amalgamated Dutch-English population. Literacy was largely an individual's responsibility. Schools were not the essential institutions of literacy; rather, a combination of the family, apprenticeships, and the churches served this function. The unregulated and diverse parochial schools operated by the Dutch Reformed, the Anglicans, and the Jews dominated education throughout the eighteenth century. Periodic attempts were made to move in the direction of public schools: an Assembly act of 1702, an English school in New York City in 1705, another act passed in 1732 that established a public school to teach 20 pupils (the school closed in 1738). But most children still relied on private tuition-based schools or learned to read and write at home.[13]

Many historians agree that between at least 1695 and 1775 most children in New York City were tutored in these basic literacy skills at home.[14] Families combined religious education and reading instruction. One student, John Pintard, remembered how "My uncle had in his family a copy of Beausobre's French Bible—every page of which contained a picture of the Bible history. Brought up in the strictest manner, he would allow us to read no book but the Bible." Stephen Allen, the son of a carpenter, was born in 1767. When he was seven, his father died, and he was sent to live with his schoolmaster uncle, James Giles. Stephen remembered that his uncle, "would frequently insist on my reading to him. And although I barely knew how to read at that early age, much less comprehend what I read, I nevertheless received some benefit from the operation." Both boys by the age of 10 received classroom instruction in a school.[15]

But most "schools" were short lived, for teaching arrangements were often temporary, schoolmasters moved from city to city, and students sought out different masters for different subjects. The typical teacher held more than one job and advertised his expertise as a teacher educated in England.

Unlike European society at that time, private tutors (professional masters) for individual students were simply impractical in the colonies, except on the isolated plantation, primarily because there were too few qualified tutors. This did not mean that tutors or governesses were entirely absent from the educational scene. Both often used colonial newspapers to advertise for students. In eighteenth-century Boston, New York, Philadelphia, Savannah, and other cities, newspapers provided a good medium for these prospective teachers.[16] Other tutors posted notices at the town hall, post office, or local inn.

These are to give Notice, that there is just arrived here a Certain Person and his Wife fit for any Town, to teach School, both Latin, and to Read and Write English, and his Wife for teaching Needle Work, any Person that wants such may be informed at the Post-Office in Boston (1718).[17]

These teachers often taught both children and adults, acting as schoolmasters for children by day and tutors for adults in the evening. William Elphinston advertised for students in the *New York Mercury* between 1765 and 1767.

William Elphinston

Teaches persons of both sexes, from 12 years of age and upwards, who never wrote before, to write a good legible hand, in 7 weeks one hour per day, at home or abroad.[18]

The typical "school" was held in a rented schoolroom where the master lived. Most students attended these day schools only after first acquiring basic literacy at home, then moved on either to another, more advanced school or an apprenticed trade. Many of these private schoolmasters advertised both "public" and "private" hours. During their "private" hours, students were tutored singly or in small groups. "Private" classes were composed of students who were congenial with each other. Between "private" hours or "between schools," the masters instructed students at their own homes. The fees for private home tutoring was always higher than for classroom instruction.

Adult evening schools in New York, Boston, and Philadelphia were also private ventures. Beginning in the seventeenth century and continuing throughout the colonial period, they were the product of private schoolmasters. Many indentured apprentices attended and studied reading, writing, and arithmetic, thereby fulfilling the literacy obligations of the apprentice's master.

A large part of the rise in literacy in New York City, during the seventeenth century and most certainly the eighteenth, can be traced to these entrepreneurial schoolmasters (see Table 2.1 and Table 2.2). There is strong evidence that these private teachers often offered basic instruction in reading, writing, and math

Table 2.1
New York City Schoolmasters 1638–1783

	1638-1688	1689-1783
Parochial and town schoolmasters	11	27
Private schoolmasters	16	206
Total	27	233

Source: From *American Education: The Colonial Experience 1607–1783* by Lawrence A. Cremin. Copyright © 1970 by Lawrence A. Cremin. Reprinted by permission of HarperCollins Publishers Inc.

Table 2.2
New York City Households and Teachers (Five-Year Averages)

Years	Population	Households	Children	Teachers	Children per Teacher	
1700-1704	4587	829	1241	5.0	248.2	
1705-1709	5060	888	1378	5.6	246.1	
1710-1714	5862	1028	1586	2.8	566.4	
1715-1719	6805	1194	1789	4.2	426.0	
1720-1724	9670	1696	1991	6.4	311.1	Average 357.5
1725-1729	8635	1515	2197	7.2	305.1	
1730-1734	9600	1684	2388	7.2	331.7	
1735-1739	10619	1862	2592	6.2	418.1	
1740-1744	11249	1974	2704	7.4	365.4	
1745-1749	11852	2079	2799	9.8	280.0	
1750-1754	12511	2195	2960	15.8	187.3	
1755-1759	13719	2407	3246	15.6	208.1	Average 253.7
1760-1764	16569	2907	3882	16.6	233.9	
1765-1769	19510	3423	4528	13.6	332.9	
1770-1774	21885	3822	5184	18.5	280.2	

Source: From *American Education: The Colonial Experience 1607–1783* by Lawrence A. Cremin. Copyright © 1970 by Lawrence A. Cremin. Reprinted by permission of HarperCollins Publishers Inc.

even when their advertised specialties lay elsewhere. But the majority of children missed "schooling" altogether and were lucky to receive even meager instruction at home or from a neighbor.[19]

Strange as it may seem to our modern ideals, a genuine prejudice seemed to exist against free public schools. Those "public" schools in New York that did receive a subsidy from the state were considered "charity schools," operated by the Dutch Reformed congregations, the Jewish community, and the Society for the Propagation of the Gospel (SPG). They were looked down upon as schools for poor parishioners and others who could not provide any other education for their children. As "middle-class" parents were usually wary of becoming identified with pauperism, they kept their children away from these charity schools. Additional parental bias against the Church of England kept many children away from the SPG schools, since tracts, sermon, and Anglican books were used in abundance.

Despite these prejudices, during the colonial period a very slow but steady shift occurred in which literacy came to be identified less with the family, a particular person, or a schoolmaster and more with an institution. Finally, by 1805 the free public grammar school emerged in New York.[20]

PENNSYLVANIA

William Penn (1644–1718), the founder of Pennsylvania (1682) and its first proprietor (governor), was a Quaker (a member of the Society of Friends) and as such was doubly committed to literacy education as a fundamental instrument of public order and enlightenment. Education was provided for in the instrument of government that governed the colony, which was drawn up even before Penn left England. It promoted practical education. Penn's second act of government supporting basic literacy in reading, writing, and the scriptures was adopted by the General Assembly in 1683.[21]

Unfortunately, because of the religious and ethnic diversity of the colony, no government financial support for education was enacted. Other obstacles included strong opposition to the Quaker's proprietary rule and the public's general unwillingness to devote as much time as William Penn considered necessary to a child's education. Instead both the Quakers and the large population of German Protestants stressed informal home literacy.[22]

Private financial support for the Quaker schools came from a variety of sources. These included student tuition, legacies and special gifts, bequests, land issues, and housing rentals built on school property. But Quaker schools were established at a slow pace. In October 1683, Enoch Flower from Wiltshire, England, was named the schoolmaster of Philadelphia's first school. The William Penn Charter School (1689) followed. Provincial leaders left the responsibility for establishing and maintaining schools to the Quaker Yearly Meeting of Philadelphia and other similar meetings across Pennsylvania. By 1750 there were only 40 Quaker schools in the entire colony.[23]

Though William Penn regarded education as a public necessity, he employed a private tutor for his own family. Penn had been raised according to the English system of home tutorial education. As a result he personally preferred to "have an ingenious person in the house to teach them (his children) than to send them to schools." Like many other parents, perhaps, he thought that too many evil impressions were received at the private schools of the 1600s and 1700s from too many poorly paid and often inadequately educated schoolmasters.[24]

The frequent use of tutors in Philadelphia was due in part to parents employing them to prepare sons for the Latin Schools founded in that city (see Table 2.3 and Table 2.4). These tutors were sought in England to teach boys Latin, Greek, and arithmetic. The first secondary school in Pennsylvania was established (1758) on land first used by a tutor to teach local children.[25]

Another check to the spread of Quaker schools was their sectarian approach to education. This meant, as in other parochial schools, an indoctrination in the history and beliefs of the Society of Friends. Penn, like other Quakers, felt a contempt for any inordinate pursuit of learning. Unlike the Puritans or the Presbyterians, the Quakers did not organize a college-educated ministry. Therefore, they did not participate in the founding of colleges to train the clergy or the establishment of grammar schools to prepare students for college attendance. Instead, they sought to establish basic literacy by teaching children "useful knowledge such as is consistent with truth and godliness."

Though the Quakers may not have supported at least the outer symbols of intellectualism, they became known for the openness of their schooling. Their

Table 2.3
Philadelphia Schoolmasters 1689–1783

Parochial and town schoolmasters	76	(includes Philadelphia academy)
Private schoolmasters	207	
Total	283	

Source: From *American Education: The Colonial Experience 1607–1783* by Lawrence A. Cremin. Copyright © 1970 by Lawrence A. Cremin. Reprinted by permission of HarperCollins Publishers Inc.

parochial schools did charge tuition to all, but not to the poor. They supported education for all—the wealthy but also the dispossessed, the Indians, African Americans, and women. This stance was truly revolutionary for that time.[26]

More practical applied subjects were studied in Quaker schools than in the grammar schools in New England. Educator Thomas Budd accurately outlined Quaker ideas about their concept of literacy and how it was to be used in *Good Order Established in Pennsylvania and New Jersey in America* (1685). All children were to learn to read, write, and use arithmetic. Boys were to receive instruction in bookkeeping, carpentry, the making of clocks and watches, weaving, or shoemaking. Girls were to learn the spinning of flax and wool, the knitting of gloves and stockings, sewing and all sorts of useful needlework, and straw-working for hats or bas-

Table 2.4
Philadelphia Households and Teachers (Five-Year Averages)

Years	Population	Households	Children	Teachers	Children per Teacher	
1700-1704	2132	374	581	3.0	193.7	
1705-1709	2514	441	684	2.8	244.3	
1710-1714	2896	508	775	2.0	387.5	
1715-1719	3278	576	861	2.2	391.5	
1720-1724	3877	680	1001	2.4	417.1	Average 297.2
1725-1729	4803	843	1218	5.0	243.6	
1730-1734	5728	1005	1425	6.2	229.8	
1735-1739	6948	1219	1696	5.8	292.4	
1740-1744	8529	1496	2029	5.4	375.7	
1745-1749	9991	1753	2359	8.4	280.8	
1750-1754	11298	1982	2675	15.2	176.0	
1755-1759	12410	2130	2868	20.0	143.4	Average 175.3
1760-1764	12710	2230	2979	16.8	177.3	
1765-1769	12913	2262	2997	23.4	128.1	
1770-1774	13115	2301	3106	21.2	146.5	

Source: From *American Education: The Colonial Experience 1607–1783* by Lawrence A. Cremin. Copyright © 1970 by Lawrence A. Cremin. Reprinted by permission of HarperCollins Publishers Inc.

kets. This was a practical education for a self-sufficient frontier society. Most Quaker boys learned a trade from their fathers or became apprentices.[27]

The normal age for beginning education was between ages six and eight. Pupils stayed in school until about age 14. As we have already noted, higher education was completely alien to the early Quakers. While Harvard was founded in 1636, and Yale in 1701, the first Quaker college did not award degrees until 1856. During the colonial period college education was predominantly theological. The Quakers believed that every man had a spark of the divine and that no amount of formal learning in theology or philosophy could strengthen the truth. Universities were disliked because they trained a "hireling ministry" who could preach nothing but "the dead Letter," and not the Gospel. Quakers were also biased against the other educated professions of law and medicine. When they did enter these fields, it was through apprenticeship rather than advanced schooling.[28]

Many other religious denominations also had an impact on literacy by establishing elementary schools throughout the colony of Pennsylvania. The Anglican Society for the Propagation of the Gospel in Foreign Parts (SPG) opened a number of charity schools in the Philadelphia region, including a school for African Americans. The SPG received a royal charter from King William III in 1701. This agency became the vehicle for the largest missionary effort mounted by the Anglican Church up to that time. From the date of its founding until 1783, ministers and teachers supported by the SPG spread out across the American colonies, establishing at least 169 stations. Though the major focus of SPG activities was in Pennsylvania and New York, their preaching and extensive literacy-instruction activities extended from New Hampshire to Georgia. More than 80 schoolmasters offered children basic literacy education through this charity-school system.[29]

SPG schoolmasters taught in log cabins, meetinghouses, private dwellings, and premises of every description. Countless combinations—boys and girls; young men and women; white, Indian, and African American; free, indentured, and slave; High Church and dissenter—participated in classes that spanned the whole gamut of education from basic literacy and the catechism to the classics.

On the Pennsylvania frontier, children occupied with spring planting or the fall harvest attended summer school to achieve rudimentary literacy. Many SPG teachers opened night schools because slaves and indentured servants could not attend day schools. However, other older and younger people such as apprentices also attended these night-school classes. Anglicans and many dissenters' children were sent to the SPG to learn to read.[30]

The SPG schools offered the equivalent of an English school curriculum. However, they drew on a remarkably wide range of instructional materials. Thousands of Bibles, Common Prayer books, church catechisms, and pamphlets of every description were used in their schools. By 1757 no less than 13,000 of these titles had been distributed by the SPG in its efforts to increase fundamental literacy and teach Christianity. This large distribution of printed material on the frontier was very important, since it was so difficult for most people to acquire publications of any kind.

Beginning with the rote instruction of reading, based almost completely on the scriptures, students advanced first to writing and then to ciphering (arithmetic). Many boys completing this program were apprenticed. Girls generally received little education beyond reading, religion, and needlework. Though the SPG had limited success in gaining converts, this agency made a significant contribution to literacy in Pennsylvania and the other American colonies.[31]

Literacy instruction also was offered by other religious denominations that established schools, particularly throughout rural Pennsylvania. Even before William Penn (1681), the Swedes and Dutch had established settlements on the banks of the Delaware River. Their churches' ministers were often itinerant schoolmasters who followed the common educational practices of rural Sweden. In order to cover large sections of the country, they moved from one home to another in a prescribed order, conducting a migratory school. Evert Pietersen from New Castle wrote in 1657 how he had begun such a school with 25 children. "For families living far from churches, ministers and their assistants visited families as far as practical, and in conjunction with parents, taught the young what they could, at least to read and write and recite Bible lessons and the catechism." Certainly this educational adaptation must have been widely practiced by other educators throughout the American colonies. We will later revisit this practice of a "circuit-riding tutor" on the American Western frontier.[32]

Moravian immigrants had by 1755 established 20 schools for their fellow German settlers. However, they maintained an open-admissions policy and taught Scots-Irish and English as well as German children. These schools also tried, with some degree of success, to provide bilingual teachers for their diverse student population.

The German Reformed and Lutheran church schools in Pennsylvania also supported the growth of literacy. The Reformed Church operated five schools in 1741, 18 in 1750, and 35 in 1760 and had grown to 63 schools by 1775. This support for basic literacy was counterbalanced by the fact that 49 congregations in 1760 were without schools and that even by 1775 only half of their 126 churches had made any provision for formal literacy education.

The Lutheran response in rural areas was even weaker. By 1750 only about 20 Lutheran schools were operating, though by 1775 this number had doubled. The dispersed pattern of German frontier settlement (with the typical school radius of five or six miles), made it difficult to find enough students to pay the teacher an acceptable wage. Most parents were unable or unwilling, by paying higher fees, to compensate for the small number of students.

In addition to these denominations, the Scots-Irish Presbyterians also founded many primary schools for their children, particularly in the frontier counties of western Pennsylvania. They brought with them a great interest in education. Wherever they built their homes, they immediately constructed a church and school. In their minds religion and education were closely if not inseparably allied. Judge Chambers tells us about settlers in the Kittochtinny Valley:

Simultaneous with the organization of congregations by these settlers, was the establishment of schoolhouses in every neighborhood. In these schools were taught little more than the rudiments of education, of which a part was generally obtained at home, under parental instruction.[33]

All of these literacy activities by different religious denominations combined educational principles that closely allied the efforts of the home, meetinghouse, and school. Among the outstanding teachers who typified this philosophy was Christopher Dock, who first arrived in Pennsylvania from Germany around 1714. Shortly thereafter Dock opened his first school and continued teaching almost without interruption until his death in 1771.

Though Dock had been well educated in the classics, like William Penn he believed in a much more utilitarian approach to education for children. His first school was held in an old log Mennonite meetinghouse. Dock used a modified monitorial system, in which older students helped in the instruction of younger children. Religious music played a central role in his curriculum.

By 1738 he had opened two other schools; he alternated teaching for three consecutive days in each. Pupils in each school were encouraged to write letters to the pupils in the other schools. Usually these letters asked questions about an incident in the Bible. Dock was the mailman between his schools. Letter writing was a curriculum tool that promoted constructive language exercises by his students.

Dock's school management also successfully dealt with children of varying religious denominations without ignoring Christian doctrine, on the one hand, or raising sectarian controversy, on the other. On the vast eighteenth-century Pennsylvania frontier, with its scattered mixture of peoples, Dock's literacy practices as a pragmatic colonial schoolmaster were probably representative of the heterogeneous reality of each denomination's schools.

Dock's educational success caused some parents to urge him to write a treatise on his methods of organizing and conducting a school. In 1750 Dock wrote *Schulordnung (School Management)*; when finally published in 1764, it was one of the earliest systematic discussions of American common schooling in a pluralistic society. Dock wrote his book as a guide for both teachers and parents on how to conduct a better school.[34]

Outside the main center of Philadelphia, a significant level of literacy was never attained in colonial Pennsylvania. A general plan to provide basic literacy through public schools in colonial Pennsylvania was never followed because of the heterogeneous population to an extent unknown in any other colony. The Quakers, English, Scots-Irish, Germans, Welsh, Swedish, and Dutch colonists split into so many different religious denominations that conflicting social, political, and theological beliefs retarded any united efforts to support literacy education.

Throughout the period families continued to be dispersed over a vast wilderness area. The French and Indian Wars brought long periods of virtual anarchy on the frontier, inhibited travel, and destroyed many families. Incessant wars also meant a heavier tax burden. These basic life-and-death matters lessened the importance of literacy to such a great extent that the literacy revolution occurring in some of the other colonies never really got off the ground in Pennsylvania.

By 1775, not only was the number of scholarly men and women, particularly in rural areas, small, but comparatively few adults could do more than read, write, and do simple arithmetic. Many children and adults throughout the colony remained wholly illiterate.[35]

NEW JERSEY

Like the colonists of Pennsylvania, the settlers of New Jersey were most diverse in nationality and religion. The colony was at first divided between East and West Jersey, with William Penn and the Quakers (1682) purchasing East Jersey. Not until 1702 were these two provinces united under a royal governor. As a result the development of literacy was a very fractured affair for the people of New Jersey.

In 1693 the Quakers of East New Jersey enacted a law that delegated to the inhabitants of each town the responsibility for establishing schools. How well this was followed is unknown. But it seemed necessary to reaffirm the need for basic literacy by passing a new act in 1695 that appointed three schoolmasters in each town.

Beyond the Quakers' efforts general education seemed to reach a low ebb during the period of the royal governors (1702–1776). Though the College of New Jersey (later Princeton) was established in 1746 and Queen's College (later Rutgers) in 1766, there was little public effort to provide basic literacy education. Whatever instruction occurred rested upon the individual initiative of parents and parochial schools. Not until 1816 did New Jersey provide public funding for state education.[36]

Early New Jersey settlers were Dutch, Swedish, English, Scottish, and German Protestant immigrants. The New England Puritans who settled in eastern New Jersey appointed a schoolmaster for Newark in 1676, about 10 years after their arrival. Dame schools were widely used, and private tutors also provided basic literacy education. By comparison, the Swedish settlers, who lived in West Jersey before the English annexed them, waited until 1714 to appoint a regular schoolmaster.[37]

The Quakers were the predominant religious group in central and southern New Jersey. Through their meetinghouse schools they educated youth in ethics, practicality, and piety. As we have seen, the Quakers placed a particular emphasis on apprenticeship education. They relocated many poor and orphan children to homes where they would receive a basic education and often a skilled trade. For over one hundred years (until about 1866) the Quaker schools remained active in New Jersey.[38]

The Anglicans opened their first New Jersey school in 1712 under the sponsorship of the Society for the Propagation of the Gospel (SPG). This schoolhouse and other later classrooms were operated as charity schools.

After 1660 many Scots-Irish Presbyterians settled in New Jersey. Because of their strong belief in religious education, many parochial schools were attached to their local churches. Among the elementary schools they established in the colony was an Indian school (1746) at Crossweeksung. Because of this great religious diversity, literacy education in New Jersey remained heavily dependent upon the private initiative of individual churches throughout the colonial period.[39]

WOMEN'S LITERACY

The literacy education of girls fared no better throughout the middle colonies than in New England. Most Dutch or English girls received very meager schooling. In her *Memoir of an American Lady*, Anne Grant wrote in the first half of the 1700s of the limited educational opportunities available to women in colonial Albany, New York.

It was at that time very difficult to procure the means of instruction in those districts; female education was in consequence conducted on a very limited scale; girls learned needlework (in which they were indeed both skillful and ingenious), from their mothers and aunts; they were taught, too, at that period to read, in Dutch, the Bible, and a few Calvinistic tracts of the devotional kind. But in the infancy of the settlement few girls read English; when they did they were thought accomplished; they generally spoke it, however imperfectly, and a few were taught writing.[40]

As already noted, girls in New York City did attend private tuition-based schools or were educated at home. But the depth of their literacy instruction was usually far less than that provided to males.

The education of women in New Jersey was distinctly domestic. Newspapers of the mid-1700s published letters complaining that too much education for women led them to neglect their butter-making, weaving, spinning, and cooking. The prevailing public sentiment was that a knowledge of books weaned women from their domestic duties. So pervasive was this viewpoint that it retarded women's literacy. Only among the Quakers were women given public positions as approved ministers and a better education.[41]

However, these general anti-education attitudes toward women were not held by everyone in the middle colonies. By the 1750s and 1760s, Philadelphia became a center of educational debate and innovation that also included women. In 1754 Anthony Benezet opened an advanced girls' school that was modeled on the Latin school opened to boys. Foremost among Philadelphia schoolmasters was David James Dove, who was recruited from England in 1751 by Benjamin Franklin as master of English at the new academy opened in the city. Two years later Dove was forced to resign because he had augmented his meager academy salary by conducting a private school for girls in his leisure hours. He immediately opened a new boarding school in Philadelphia for both boys and girls. During the two decades of his career as a schoolmaster Dove continued to be extremely popular and taught hundreds of girls and boys in Philadelphia and its vicinity. He also trained a number of able future teachers who followed his concepts of educating everyone.[42]

Another ardent supporter of female education in local Philadelphian society was Benjamin Rush (1745–1813), American physician, educator, and signer of the Declaration of Independence. In *Thoughts upon Female Education* (1787), he expressed the view that women had to assume the responsibility for the education of the family's children at home. They were the principal guardians of domestic and moral authority. The new American republic required mothers to educate their sons in the principles of liberty and government to prepare them for future public office.[43]

In colonial American society, women were perceived as the ideal educators of their own children. To prepare women for vital roles, Rush and other colonial leaders, such as Washington, Jefferson, and Adams, strongly encouraged education for women at home. Formal schooling was seen as an alternative, but only if private tutoring at home was impractical.[44]

For a woman's tutorial education Rush advocated English, penmanship, arithmetic, bookkeeping, and geography, as well as readings in history and biography. John Adams also included the study of French and Latin grammar. Both Benjamin Franklin and Thomas Jefferson offered an extensive selection from world literature that included Shakespeare, Molière, Racine, Pope, Addison, Dryden, and the *Moral Tales* from the leading English domestic educator, Maria Edgeworth. They also recommended contemporary novels such as *Pamela* (1740), *Clarissa* (1747), and *Sir Charles Grandison* (1753) by Samuel Richardson (1689–1761), a London printer and novelist.[45] This influential eighteenth-century figure used his widely read novels to advance personal theories on the tutorial education of women in England and colonial America. In *Pamela*, Richardson has his central character avidly studying John Locke's *Some Thoughts Concerning Education* (1693), one of the most influential books ever written in England about home tutoring.

Richardson advanced the concept that a mother must begin a child's education at home and carry it to a fairly advanced stage. Girls and boys at first had the same tutorial lessons. Even later, when their curricula diverged, girls were still to learn spelling, good handwriting, French, Italian, and translation of Latin authors. Young women were also to read from the Bible, Milton, and Addison and to learn history and geography. If a woman's childhood education were deficient, her husband was to remedy any lack by providing her with appropriate private tutors.[46]

In 1783 Thomas Jefferson wrote his daughter Martha, who lived in Philadelphia, giving his instruction on the proper education for a genteel young lady. He had hired a Mrs. Thomas Hopkinson as Martha's tutor. Martha's daily education schedule included:

8:00–10:00 a.m.   Music Instruction
10:00–1:00 p.m.   Dancing/drawing lessons on alternate days

1:00–2:00 p.m.	Draw on the day you dance and write a letter the next day.
3:00–4:00 p.m.	French lesson
4:00–5:00 p.m.	Music practice
5:00–Bedtime	Read English literature and practice composition.

Jefferson urged his daughter, "never spell a word wrong," for "it produces great praise to a lady to spell well." The central purpose for Martha's education Jefferson thought was for her to become "good and accomplished" by becoming well read and highly literate. This was the best means to prepare Martha to assume her ultimate role as a genteel married woman.[47]

Franklin and Jefferson also included in their tutoring curriculum *The Ladies Library* (1714), three volumes edited anonymously by an Englishwoman, which collected together a number of writers on women's education including Mary Astell and John Locke, who both supported education at home. The widespread popularity of this work, which was published in many editions, made their views well known throughout colonial America.[48]

We must not be surprised to see a direct correlation between the era of the "learned ladies" in eighteenth-century England and a parallel development through colonial tutorial education. Hannah More, Elizabeth Elstob, Mary Wollstonecraft, Elizabeth Carter, Mary Astell, Maria Edgeworth, and other "bluestockings," had great influence on American educational practices. Many of these women were advocates of tutoring children at home.[49]

In colonial America economic activity and frontier conditions often took men from home and gave women greater social responsibilities. Whether a frontier mother or a city dweller, most women lived a better life in America and were more literate than their European sisters. By eighteenth-century standards, many mothers in the middle colonies were able to provide their daughters with a good literacy education at home.[50]

"PRIVATE" VERSUS "PUBLIC" LITERACY

The great diversity of ethnic groups settling in the Middle Atlantic colonies had the result of limiting literacy education for their population. Unlike New England, the many different religious beliefs and languages raised formidable social barriers to any unified community response. The geography alone was prohibitive to the spread of literacy since the region contained a large, trackless frontier wilderness with widely scattered towns and villages. It was practically impossible to provide this dispersed population with adequate schools or schoolmasters.

Literacy opportunities were further narrowed since these colonies seldom taxed themselves to establish community schools. There were even few public subsidies of private education programs. The public literacy laws were only weakly enforced. There is no accurate way to determine the exact number of children or adults who were taught in a schoolhouse or by private schoolmasters, tutors, or parents. With only a few notable exceptions, there was little public commitment to schooling and literacy in the middle colonies.

NOTES

1. "Lawes Established by the Authority of His Majesties. Letters, Patents, Granted to His Royall Highness James Duke of Yorke and Albany," *Collections of the New York Historical Society*, 1 (1809): 334; Michael Kammen, *Colonial New York: A History* (New York: Charles Scribner's Sons, 1975), 75–83; Lawrence A. Cremin, *American Education: The Colonial Experience 1607–1783* (New York: Harper & Row, 1970), 125.

2. Robert H. Bremner, ed., *Children and Youth in America: A Documentary History*, vol. 1, 1600–1865 (Cambridge: Harvard University Press, 1970), 27, 72–73; Cremin, *Colonial Experience*, 483.

3. Margaret Connell Szasz, *Indian Education in the American Colonies, 1607–1783* (Albuquerque: University of New Mexico Press, 1988), 31–32.

4. Ibid., 41.

5. John Tracy Ellis, *Catholics in Colonial America* (Baltimore: Helicon Press, 1965), 349; Timothy Walch, *Parish School: American Catholic Parochial Education from Colonial Times to the Present* (New York: Crossroad Publishing Co., 1996), 14.

6. Ellis, *Catholics*, 367.

7. William Heard Kilpatrick, *The Dutch Schools of New Netherland and Colonial New York* (United States Bureau of Education, Bulletin 12 (1912); reprint, New York: Arno Press, 1969), 105, 110.

8. Cremin, *Colonial Experience*, 242.

9. Kilpatrick, *New Netherland*, 81, 93–94; Alice Morse Earle, *Child Life in Colonial Days* (New York: Macmillan, 1899; reprint, Stockbridge, Massachusetts: Berkshire House Publishers, 1993), 74–75.

10. Kilpatrick, *New Netherland*, 220–222, 226–227.

11. Ibid., 225–227.

12. Ibid., 110, 140, 159.

13. Carl F. Kaestle, *The Evolution of an Urban School System: New York City, 1750–1850* (Cambridge: Harvard University Press, 1973), 186; Kammen, *Colonial New York*, 248–249.

14. Stanley K. Schultz, *The Culture Factory* (New York: Oxford University Press, 1973), 5; Kaestle, *Urban School*, 2, 25; Kammen, *Colonial New York*, 249.

15. John Pintard, "Reminiscences," Box 3, Pintard Papers, New York Historical Society; Stephen Allen, "Memoirs 1767–1852," typescript, John C. Travis, ed., New York, 1927, at New York Historical Society.

16. Wilson Smith, ed., *Theories of Education in Early America* (New York: Bobbs-Merrill Co., 1973), 61; Governesses of the period advertised for a position in *Pennsylvania Gazette, American Weekly Mercury, New York Gazette, New York Mercury, Weekly Post Boy*: Thomas Woody, *A History of Women's Education in the United States*, vol. 1 (New York: Science Press, 1929), 192; Tutors of the period advertised for a position in *Boston Gazette and County Journal, Gazette of the State of Georgia, New York Mercury*. Huey B. Long, "Adult Basic Education in Colonial America," *Adult Literacy and Basic Education* 7 (1983): 55.

17. Robert Francis Seybolt, ed., *The Private Schools of Colonial Boston* (Cambridge: Harvard University Press, 1935), 14–15.

18. *New York Mercury*, April 1, 1765.

19. Kammen, *Colonial New York*, 249; Kaestle, *Urban School*, 25; Robert Francis Seybolt, "Source Studies in American Colonial History: The Private School," *University of Illinois Bulletin* 23 (1925): 93–94; Seybolt, *The Evening School in Colonial America* (Urbana: University of Illinois Press, 1925; reprint New York: Arno Press, 1971), 9, 10, 11, 13, 14, 21, 59. The best early works on the literacy education provided by private entrepreneurial teachers during the provincial era are Seybolt's *Evening School*; "The Evening Schools of Colonial New York City" in *Fifteenth Annual Report of the [New York State] Education Department* (1919), I, 630–652; "New York Colonial Schoolmasters," ibid., 653–669; "The S.P.G. Myth: A Note on Education in Colonial New York," *Journal of Educational Research* 13 (1926): 129–137; "Schoolmasters of Colonial Philadelphia," *The Pennsylvania Magazine of History and Biography* 52 (1928): 361–371; and Seybolt, *Private Schools of Colonial Boston*. These are admirably complemented by the pertinent material in Carl and Jessica Bridenbaugh, *Rebels and Gentlemen: Philadelphia in the Age of Franklin* (New York: Oxford University Press, 1962), and Carl Bridenbaugh, *Cities in the Wilderness: The First Century of Urban Life in America, 1625–1742* (New York: Alfred A. Knopf, 1955); Cremin, *Colonial Experience*, 537–540.

20. Kammen, *Colonial New York*, 248–250; Leonard J. Trinterud, *The Forming of an American Tradition: A Reexamination of Colonial Presbyterianism* (Freeport, New York: Books for Libraries Press, 1949), 200–201.

21. George Staughton, Thomas McCamant, and Benjamin Nead, eds., *Charter to William Penn, and Laws of the Province of Pennsylvania, Passed Between the Years 1682 and 1700* (Harrisburg, Pennsylvania: Lane S. Hart, 1879), 142.

22. Sheldon S. Cohen, *A History of Colonial Education 1607–1776* (New York: Wiley, 1974), 181–182.

23. Thomas Woody, *Early Quaker Education in Pennsylvania* (New York: Teachers College, Columbia University, 1920; reprinted, New York: Arno Press, 1969), 83; James Pyle Wickersham, *A History of Education in Pennsylvania* (Lancaster, Pennsylvania: Inquirer Publishing Company, 1888), 41; Cremin, *Colonial Experience*, 307.

24. Thomas Woody, *Quaker Education in the Colony and State of New Jersey* (Philadelphia: University of Pennsylvania, 1923; reprint, New York: Arno Press, 1969), 8–10; Woody, *Education in Pennsylvania*, 29–30.

25. Szasz, *American Colonies*, 40; Cremin, *Colonial Experience*, 305.

26. Szasz, *American Colonies*, 41; Cremin, *Colonial Experience*, 537; Cohen, *History of Colonial Education*, 183.

27. Thomas Budd, *Good Order Established in Pennsylvania and New Jersey in America* (Philadelphia: no publisher, 1685), 4; Cohen, a *History of Colonial Education*, 95.

28. Cohen, a *History of Colonial Education*, 121, 127.

29. Trinterud, *American Tradition*, 201; Cremin, *Colonial Experience*, 342.

30. John Hellawell Calam, "Parsons and Pedagogues: The S.P.G. Adventure in American Education" (Ph.D. diss., University of Michigan, 1969), 191, 193, 311–312.

31. Calam, "Parsons," 103, 196–197, 308–309; Szasz, *American Colonies*, 39; Edgar W. Knight, *A Documentary History of Education in the South before 1860*, vol. 1 (Chapel Hill: University of North Carolina Press, 1949), 62–77.

32. Wickersham, *Education in Pennsylvania*, 3, 12, 16.

33. Cohen, *History of Colonial Education*, 184; Alan Tully, "Literacy Levels and Educational Development in Rural Pennsylvania 1729–1775," *Pennsylvania History* 39 (April 1972): 301–312; Wickersham, *Education in Pennsylvania*, 105–106.

34. Martin G. Brumbaugh, *The Life and Works of Christopher Dock* (Philadelphia: J.B. Lippincott, 1908; reprint, New York: Arno Press, 1969), 12–15, 20; Cremin, *Colonial Experience*, 308–309. The monitorial school adapted by Dock was very popular in England by the late eighteenth/early nineteenth century, but in use even earlier. For more information on these schools consult Andrew Bell, *Bell's Mutual Tuition and Moral Discipline*, (London, 1832); Joseph Lancaster, *Improvements in Education as It Respects the Industrious Classes of the Community* (London, 1803). David, Salmon, ed., *The Practical Parts of Lancaster's Improvements and Bell's Experiment* (1805); reprint, Cambridge: University Press, 1932).

35. Tully, "Rural Pennsylvania," 311; Wickersham, *Education in Pennsylvania*, 255.

36. Woody, *Quaker Education in New Jersey*, 1–5.

37. Roscoe West, *Elementary Education in New Jersey: A History* (Princeton: D. Van Nostrand, 1964), 4; Cohen, *History of Colonial Education*, 172–173.

38. Cohen, *History of Colonial Education*, 172; West, *Elementary Education*, 5.

39. West, *Elementary Education*, 9; Cohen, *History of Colonial Education*, 172.

40. Anne MacVicar Grant, *Memoir of an American Lady* (New York: Dodd, Mead, 1901), 62.

41. Arthur W. Calhoun, *A Social History of the American Family*, vol. 1 (New York: Barnes & Noble, 1945), 187–188.

42. Cremin, *Colonial Experience*, 378. J. William Frost, *The Quaker Family in Colonial America* (New York: St. Martin's Press, 1973), 127; Bridenbaugh, *Rebels and Gentlemen*, 36–37.

43. Benjamin Rush, *Thoughts upon Female Education* (Philadelphia: Richard and Hall, 1787), 5–7.

44. George Washington, *The Writings of George Washington*, W. C. Ford, ed., vol. 12 (New York: G. P. Putnam's Sons, 1889–1893), 84–86, 200; Thomas Jefferson, *The Writings of Thomas Jefferson*, H. A. Washington, ed., vol. 7 (Washington D.C.: Taylor and Maury, 1853–1854), 101; John Adams, *Familiar Letters of John Adams and His Wife Abigail Adams During the Revolution*, C. F. Adams, ed. (New York: Hurd and Houghton, 1876), 219–330.

45. Rush, *Thoughts*, 7–13; Benjamin Franklin, *The Works of Benjamin Franklin*, Jared Sparks, ed., vol. 7 (Boston: C. Tappan, 1844–1848), 153, 166–167; Jefferson, *Writings*, vol. 7, 102.

46. Mary Sumner Benson, *Women in Eighteenth Century America* (New York: Columbia University Press, 1935), 45–50.

47. Edwin Morris Betts and James Adam Bear, eds., *The Family Letters of Thomas Jefferson* (Columbia: University of Missouri Press, 1966), 19–20, 30, 52, 71.

48. Benson, *Eighteenth Century America*, 22–23; Richard Steele, *The Ladies Library*, 3 vols. (London: J. Tonson, 1714).

49. Benson, *Eighteenth Century America*, 72. Edward E. Gordon and Elaine, H. Gordon, *Centuries of Tutoring* (Lanham, Maryland: University Press of America, 1990), 168–182.

50. Benson, *Eighteenth Century America*, 314–316.

Chapter 3

"Old Field Schools" and Tidewater Tutors: The Southern Colonies

ISOLATING ENVIRONMENT

Although portions of the middle colonies and New England were rural, neither area encountered the extreme dispersion of population that typified the southern colonies. This physical environment and the region's unique population imposed some severe limitations on literacy opportunities.

The means for providing literacy instruction were quite varied. It was usually out of the question for most families to send their child to any school. But small farmers or planters sometimes opened cooperative elementary schools to provide basic literacy for their families. A remodeled old tobacco shed or a one-room schoolhouse in an infertile field "long abandoned to pine and broom-straw" became the site of the southern "old field schools." There the local neighbors united to hire a schoolmaster, perhaps an indentured servant, to teach basic literacy skills.[1]

Denominational schools were another important source of literacy throughout the region. Many Anglican churches established a local parish school. The Society for the Propagation of the Gospel (SPG) introduced its charity schools in the early 1700s and led in the establishment of schools for African-American children throughout the southern colonies. But the greatest impact of denominational literacy followed the later 1700s religious revival movement by the Scots-Irish and Germans.

Presbyterian schools also proliferated in the Piedmont section of Virginia and the backwoods of the Carolinas. By 1775 southern Quakers had opened several schools in Virginia and North Carolina. In Georgia the Moravians began the colony's earliest school at Irene. They later opened a school in Wachovia, North Carolina.[2]

Charleston and the few other southern towns of any size established grammar schools, but these urban schools served only a few children. Apprenticeship education practices were common in the South as in all the American colonies and represented a significant literacy practice.

The dominant Tidewater planter aristocracy pursued other literacy options for their children's schooling. William Byrd of Westover plantation in Virginia was well educated in Latin, Greek, and Hebrew. He also wrote extensively and amassed a personal library of more than 3,000 books, a private collection matched only by Cotton Mather in Massachusetts. Byrd could not find a good-enough education for his children in the southern colonies, so like many other southern aristocrats, he chose to send all four of his children to England for their education.

A more practical solution was employing a residential tutor. This literacy alternative followed the educational practices of the eighteenth-century English aristocracy. Tutoring became very popular, particularly in Virginia and the Carolinas. As we will now see, the overall southern colonial response to literacy was far different than that of their neighbors to the north.[3]

TO HAVE AN INCLINATION TO LEARN—VIRGINIA

Literacy developed in colonial Virginia around three distinct groups: planters, white servants and craftsmen, and African-American slaves. The planter group itself was subdivided into two categories. The aristocratic planter class owned large tracts of land, buildings, and slaves. The lesser planters and small farmers owned much less land, maybe only a few acres, and held few slaves or, in many instances, none at all. It was the comparatively small aristocratic planter class that largely set up the pattern for literacy development and was mainly responsible for any literacy legislation passed by the colony.[4]

The white servant and craftsman class was formed from the unique economic conditions existing in seventeenth-century England. An indenturement system was created so that men, women, and even children could find the economic means to emigrate to the colonies. The master would advance the passage money, and the servant would labor for a set term of years. At the end of their contract both master and servant were given a grant of about 50 acres of land. Indentured servants became such an important part of the southern colonies that they constituted by 1671 nearly one-sixth of the entire white population. Some indentured persons even became educators in order to earn passage to America.

However, by the early 1700s in Virginia the African-American slave became an even more important part of this labor system. In 1754 slaves constituted about two-fifths of the total population. The uniqueness of this labor system directly affected the progress of literacy in Virginia.[5]

Like those of its northern neighbors, the first Virginia literacy laws in 1619 and 1631 were tied to furthering religious worship. Parents were responsible for teaching their children, servants, and apprentices to read the catechism. However, unlike New England, the attitude of the colony sharply differed when it came to assuming any public financial obligations for the literacy education of the general population. Instead, the colony assumed a literacy obligation only for orphans, the poor, or those children whose parents were not likely to provide instruction at home or elsewhere. The apprenticeship system was used for these children by including an educational clause in their indenturement contract. The basic assumptions made in Virginia was that education was a private affair and that parents were capable, on a voluntary basis, of providing a basic literacy education for their own children.[6]

Though it seems that families had to bear the total responsibility for literacy, they seemed to do so with remarkable effectiveness, as is indicated by Virginia's high literacy rate throughout the colonial period. Families recruited local teachers as private tutors and brought in educators from England or the northern colonies. Local schoolmasters were paid by guardians to take orphans into their classes or instruct them privately.

The household farm or plantation was the basic economic unit throughout the colony. Against this social backdrop, formal and informal instruction took place in the daily life of a child, with the young learning through both experience and explanation. Reading was taught in the home by parents, siblings, or other relatives, from hornbooks, catechisms, primers, and the Bible. Particularly in the tidewater region extended families were common, sometimes representing two or three generations. This network of relatives had a profound effect on the literacy education of children.[7]

These family literacy practices were recorded by Francis T. Brooke (born 1763):

My father was devoted to the education of his children. He sent my two brother, John, and myself very young to school. We went to several English schools, some of them at home. He finally engaged a private tutor—a Scotch gentleman of the name of Alexander Dunhem, by whom we were taught Latin and Greek. We read with him all the higher classics, and some Greek, the Testament and Aesop's Fables.[8]

Another father, a Colonel William Ball, went to even greater lengths to ensure his children's literacy. Upon his death (1693) Ball's will requested that his wife continue teaching each of their youngest children until they reached age 16. At that time the two elder brothers were to become their tutors.[9]

In the earliest days of colonial Virginia, parents of means who wished to educate a child in school often sent them to England. There they would be educated under the supervision of a family relative, friend, or business acquaintance. Throughout the 1700s wealthy families sent young boys and girls across the Atlantic for an English education. Ursula Byrd was shipped off in 1685 at the age of four. Seventy-five years later three more Byrd children were still being schooled in England. To spur this recruitment, English schools even advertised in Virginia's newspapers.[10]

After 1750 and certainly by the time of the American Revolution (1776), parents felt a growing reluctance to send their children to study abroad. The disadvantage of an English education began to outweigh its obvious advantages. The eighteenth century in England was an era of great corruption. Boys and girls educated there frequently returned home with dissipated health, bad manners, and even worse morals. The expenses of such an education always seemed to be more than any parent anticipated. Closer parent-child relationships led many planters to look for educational alternatives nearer to home. The American Revolution brought a general end to English schooling.[11]

Other families sent their children to local boarding schools, such as the grammar school attached to the College of William and Mary in Williamsburg, Virginia. However, tutoring became the most widespread educational method for those families who could afford it. The planter class in Virginia during the early colonial period used English tutors, and later scholars from the northern colleges, for both boys and girls. Occasionally even indentured servants served as tutors.

In many cases the family tutor also taught relatives and neighbors, and the children were frequently boarded on large estates. Special buildings were created on these plantations to house the tutor and his schoolroom, many consisting of two stories. The tutor lived and slept on the second floor with the schoolroom below.[12] The curriculum in many cases resembled the private school or academy of that time: French, Latin, Greek, and arithmetic. However, the method of instruction was one-to-one. Individualized teaching predominated rather than group activities.[13]

Of course it was not easy to find an educated man (or woman) in the Virginia wilderness to fill the position of tutor (or governess). He needed to be a gentleman, with a college education, who was able to give instruction in Latin, the language of scholars in the eighteenth century. This language was a requirement for any boy who someday wished to become a gentleman.

In 1766 Richard Corbin, a Virginia planter, wrote to a London friend in an earnest plea for a qualified tutor.

I am greatly in want of a tutor for my children, it gives me pain to see them misspending the precious moments of their youth. I must earnestly entreat you therefore to procure me an honest man well skilled in the languages, that writes a good hand, and is thoroughly acquainted with arithmetick & accounts. This is so interesting to me that I flatter myself you will exert your endeavors to engage a gentleman qualified in all respects for this business and send him over by the first ship.[14]

Berkeley Plantation, Virginia, provides us with an excellent profile of these literacy practices. Beginning with the 1618 patent, Berkeley's history was the most thoroughly documented of all the tidewater plantations. Benjamin Harrison II bought the land in 1691. His son, Benjamin Harrison III (1673–1710), was the first child to be tutored in reading and Latin at the plantation. By 1700 his young son, Benjamin Harrison IV, was taught at a small building located on the plantation.[15] He and other neighborhood boys were instructed by a transient tutor to prepare them for the College of William and Mary. Benjamin Harrison V (1726–1791) was also educated in the same manner, becoming governor of Virginia and a signer of the Declaration of Independence (1776).[16]

Newspaper advertisements offer important insight into the world of southern colonial tutors. Planters used the newspaper to seek qualified men as tutors. In their desperate search for tutors, many advertised in colonial newspapers (see Figure 3.1). Landon Carter did so in 1772, offering 50 pounds a year to any tutor who could teach his six grandsons arithmetic, grammar, and writing. Failing in this attempt, Carter employed the local parson as a substitute for slightly above half the salary. Finding qualified tutors was never easy in colonial Virginia.[17]

The teachers themselves advertised their availability in the local community newspaper. From 1733 to 1774 more than four hundred advertisements relating to tutors were published in *The South Carolina Gazette* alone. Scores of similar notices appeared in Virginia, North Carolina, and Georgia during the later colonial and early national period (see Figure 3.2).[18]

It is indeed fortunate that the journals of a number of men who lived or worked in eighteenth-century Virginia have been preserved. They give us a window into the educational and child-rearing practices of the time.

One such journal is that of John Harrower, who lived in the village of Lerwick on Scotland's Shetland Island with his wife, two sons, and a daughter. He emigrated to Virginia as an indentured tutor because "This day (January 26, 1774) being reduced to my last shilling I had, I was obligated to engage to go to Virginia for four years as a schoolmaster for Bedd, Board, washing and five pounds during the whole time."[19]

In Virginia Colonel William Daingerfield decided to hire Harrower as a tutor for his three sons. Daingerfield owned the 1,300-acre Belvedira Plantation located near Fredericksburg. Harrower taught the two youngest boys to read, while the oldest son learned syllabification. Edwin, ten, was just beginning two-syllabled words in his spelling book. Bathurst, six, was still on the alphabet, and William, only four, was just beginning to learn. In addition, Harrower taught them writing, arithmetic, and enunciation. Since the Colonel had been well educated in English, he insisted that Harrower teach them proper formal English. This was not an easy task, since Harrower was not well educated (as his spelling shows), and his accent showed the distinctive Scottish "burr."

[May 27] This morning about 8 am the colonel delivered his three sons to my charge to teach them read, write, and figure. His oldest son Edwin ten years of age, intred into two syllables in the spelling book, Bathourest his second son six years of age in the alphabete and William his third son four years of age does not know the letters. He has likewise a daughter. . . . My schoolhouse is from six to eight in the morning, in the forenoon from nine to twelve, and from three to six in afternoon. . . . [June 14] This morning entered to school Wm. Pattie son of John Pattie wright, and Salley Evens daughter to Thos. Evens Planter. . . . [Monday, 20th] This morning entred to school Philip and Dorothea Edge's Children of Mr. Benjamin Edge, Planter. . . . [Tuesday, 21st] This day Mr. Samuel Edge Planter came to me and begged me to take a son of his to school who was both deaf and dum, and I consented to try what I cu'd do with him. . . . Munday, 17th [Apr., 1775] At 8am I rode to Town. . . . On my aravel in town the first thing I got to do was to dictate and write a love letter from Mr. Anderson to one Peggie

Figure 3.1
Colonial Newspaper Tutoring Position Advertisements

WANTED SOON,

A TUTOR for a private family, who, among other things, thoroughly understands the mathematicks. Also a FARMER, who will undertake the management of about 80 slaves, all settled within six miles of each other, to be employed in making of grain. Any such, well recommended, will meet with encouragement by applying to Mr. *John Mercer* in *Stafford*, or to the subscriber in *Williamsburg*, during the sitting of the present General Court.

    October 10.   **JAMES MERCER.**

–*The Virginia Gazette* (Williamsburg, Alex. Purdie and John Dixon), October 15, 1767, p. [2]; also October 22, 1767, p. [2]; November 5, 1767, p. [4].

I WILL give THIRTY POUNDS a year for a good SCHOOL-MASTER capable of teaching ENGLISH AND ARITHMETICK.

                          SAMUEL DU VAL.

–*The Virginia Gazette* (Williamsburg, William Rind), November 15, 1770, p. [2]; also November 29, 1770, p. [4].

A SOBER, diligent Person, of a good Character, that is qualified to teach Children to write and cypher, and read good *English*, and is willing to agree for 3, 5, or 7 Years, by applying to the Subscriber, living in *Prince-George* County, may meet with an Employer, who will give as an Encouragement to such Person 20 **£** *per Annum.*

                          Theophilus Field

–*The Virginia Gazette* (Williamsburg, W. Park), December 12, 1745, p. [4]; also December 19, 1745, p. [4].

Source: A Documentary History of Education in the South Before 1860.

Dewar at the house of Mr. John Mitchel at the Wilderness. ... [Tuesday, April 23d, 1776] Settled with Mr. Porter for teaching his two sons 12 mos. when he very genteely allowed me £6 for them, besides a present of two silk vests and two pair of nankeen breeches last summer and a gallon of rum at Christenmass, both he and mrs. Porter being extreamly well satisfied with what I hade don to them.[20]

Figure 3.2
Colonial Newspaper Teacher Advertisements

Reading, writing and arithmetick to be taught by *Edward Clark* at the House of one Mrs. *Lydia Viart's* near the new intended Market.
—*The South-Carolina Gazette*, December 13 to December 20, 1735.

Reading, Writing, Arithmetick vulgar and decimal, Geometry, Trigonometry plain and spherical, Mensuration of solid and superficial Bodies, Navigation, Surveying, Gaging, and many other useful Branches of the Mathematicks, Euclid's Elements, Italian, bookkeeping, and Grammar, &c: explain'd and taught in the clearest manner by *Archibald Hamilton*, who may be heard of at Mr. *Coon's* Taylor in *Church-street.* N.B. He attends at any time and Place requir'd to teach, or to keep Books; and is willing upon reasonable and speedy Encouragement yo [sic] undertake a School in Town or Country for teaching all or any Part of what is above specified, otherwise to go off the country.
—*The South-Carolina Gazette*, February 12 to February 19, 1737. Also February 19 to 26 and February 26 to March 5, 1737.

The Subscriber begs leave to inform his friends That he intends opening a school, on Monday the 20th of this instant April, at the house of Mr. Christian Camphire, adjoining the Collector William Spencer, Esq., where he . . . designs teaching Latin, Reading, Writing, and Arithmetic.

James Whitefield

N.B. A few Masters and Misses will be also lodged and boarded.
—*The Georgia Gazette* (Savannah), April 8; April 15, 1766.

Source: *A Documentary History of Education in the South Before 1860.*

As on other plantations, the Belvedira "schoolroom" was a separate building, 20 by 12 feet in size, that stood near the main house. Harrower was successful in recruiting 10 additional scholars. The tutors of wealthier planters' children were often engaged in teaching poorer children and also adults. Harrower taught writing and arithmetic at night to Thomas Brooks, a carpenter living at the adjoining Spotswood Plantation, and on Sunday when Brooks did not go to church. Brooks earned 30 pounds a year as a carpenter as well as his room and board. He paid Harrower 40 shillings a year for this instruction. Unfortunately for them both, after six months Brooks moved over 40 miles away and his tutoring with Harrower ended.[21]

By the time Harrower's journal ends (July 1776) he had accumulated 70 pounds. Unfortunately he died a year later, at age 44. Daingerfield sent this sad news to Harrower's wife and family, whom he had planned to bring to Virginia.[22]

Though such men as Harrower did not offer an advanced literacy education, they could often fulfill the main educational goal of most Virginia planters—to prepare the young man with the practical knowledge needed for his future role as a landowner and to develop in him the character of a gentleman. In 1718 Nathaniel Burwell of Carter's Grove Plantation deplored his son's inattention to his studies. His ignorance of arithmetic would hamper him in "the management of his own affairs." If he did not have a broad base of knowledge, he would be "unfit for any gentleman's conversation and therefore a scandalous person and a shame to his relations, not having one single qualification to recommend him." George Washington agreed when he later, in reference to the education of his young ward Jacky Custis (1771), admitted that "a knowledge of books is the basis upon which other knowledge is to be built." But Washington did not think that "becoming a mere scholar is a desirable education for a gentleman."[23]

By the mid-eighteenth century, tutors were also secured from Princeton and other American colleges. George Mason (1725–1792) the "father" of the U.S. Constitution's Bill of Rights, was educated by private tutors and later studied law under John Mercer. In 1770 he asked his friend John Scott in Virginia to write Thomas Gordon at King's College regarding a tutor for his children at Gunston Hall Plantation (near present-day Washington, D.C.). To the west of the main building a small schoolhouse was built. Here John Mason, George's fourth son, was educated until the age of 16 by several different tutors. First was a Mr. McPherson of Maryland. Afterward two teachers came from Scotland to teach John, a Mr. Davidson and then Mr. Constable. John, his brothers, and a few other boys who were permitted to come as "day scholars" were educated by these tutors, who resided with the Mason family until 1782. Mr. Constable then left the family, "during the revolutionary war, and in these times of trouble, it being very difficult to find schools, I was kept at home without a teacher until the Spring of 1783." Mason also employed as a governess for his daughters, a Miss Newman of Virginia, who lived for some time in the family.[24]

Devereux Jarratt like many other tutors was born in the colonies. He only gradually obtained his own education, often while acting as a private schoolmaster. Jarratt was born in 1732 into a carpenter's family in New Kent County, Virginia. His parents "highest ambition was to teach their children to read, write and understand the fundamental rules of arithmetic."[25] When he was only six years of age Jarratt's father died.

At 8 or 9 years old I was sent to an English school in the neighbourhood and I continued to go to one teacher and others, as opportunity served (though not without great interruptions) till I was 12 or 13. In this time I learned to read in the Bible (though but indifferently) and to write a sorry scrawl, and acquired some knowledge of arithmetic. With this small fund, I left school; and my mother dying about this time, no further care was bestowed on my education.[26]

Jarratt then worked for his older brothers. But he continued his own education by borrowing an arithmetic book for self-study during his noon break from plowing. "I made greater progress in real knowledge and use of figures in one month, than I had done in years, while at school."[27] Time and again we will see that this autodidactic (self-learning) learning method was used throughout America in many different eras to improve personal literacy.

With his limited education it is hard to believe that when Jarratt was only 19, he was invited by Jacob Moan to become the schoolmaster in Albemarle County. However, this paid-subscription school yielded very few pupils, an experience that Jarratt repeated several times before he began his career as a private tutor. Jarratt continued to borrow books to read in the evening by firelight. "I soon became what was called a good reader and my relish for books and reading greatly increased."[28]

Jarratt was then hired by a Mr. Cannon to teach his son as a private tutor while residing at the Cannon home. About this time he decided to become a minister, but he was prevented from making this career change because he did not know Latin or Greek.

After teaching school for six more years he went to live with the family of Mr. Thomas Tabb in Cumberland, Virginia. "I boarded in his house, performed the office of a chaplin [sic] in the family, morning and evening, and still kept up the custom of meeting on Sunday either at my school-house or other private houses."[29]

At this time the Davis family in Cumberland had hired Alexander Martin (who later was elected governor of North Carolina and served several terms in the U.S. Congress) to reside with them and tutor their son in Latin. Martin, who was a graduate of the College of New Jersey (later Princeton), also tutored Jarratt in Latin and Greek. This was paid for by Jarratt's old employer Mr. Canon and Martin's uncle. When Martin returned to New Jersey after a year, Jarratt became the tutor of the Davis son for a year and a half. Jarratt next tutored the children of Thompson Swann and other local children. Finally in 1762, he decided to prepare for Holy Orders in the Anglican Church and sailed to England.

Jarratt's life clearly illustrates that tutoring was not confined to Virginia's elite plantation class. This autobiography is also a remarkable account of a person who rose from modest origins to an official in the Anglican Church in Virginia largely because of a persistent course of self-education.[30]

Another tutor's account of literacy education is from the *Journal and Letters of Philip Vickers Fithian*. It is replete with details of his life, curriculum, and teaching methods. Fithian wrote this journal during 1773–1774 while teaching the two sons, five daughters, and nephew of Colonel and Mrs. Robert Carter of Nomini Hall, Virginia.[31] Colonel Carter was a member of the Virginia Governor's Council. Two young men from Princeton also had taught the Carter children at Nomini Hall before Fithian's arrival. Carter had hired these tutors through President Witherspoon of Princeton.[32]

Philip Vickers Fithian was a young theological graduate of Princeton College in 1773. His northern education had prepared him to become a Presbyterian minister. In some ways this ill-suited him to enjoy, to the fullest extent, the social life of plantation Virginia. However, in addition to his extensive teaching duties, Fithian frequently accompanied the Carters as they dined at friends' homes, attended banquets and balls, conversed with neighbors at the parish church, attended local races, and welcomed frequent guests at Nomini Hall. He was no wallflower.[33]

The plantation was in Westmoreland County, with Carter's landholdings located in various parts of the Northern Neck of Virginia and Fairfax County. Rich planters, as members of the southern aristocracy, used tutors to instruct their sons in every branch of knowledge useful to a gentleman. Fithian's *Journal* is highly representative of this period's educational and child-rearing practices even outside the exclusive planter class.[34]

When Fithian began his duties (November 1773), his annual salary as a resident tutor was fixed at 35 pounds, use of a horse, a personal servant, borrowing books from Mr. Carter's library, and his accommodations. These were generous terms for that time.[35]

The curriculum followed for the five girls, while liberal compared with contemporary customs in Colonial America, lacked any significant depth. Their education was limited mainly to instruction in the English language and simple arithmetic. The eldest daughter at the beginning of Fithian's instruction read the *Spectator*, wrote a good hand, and was starting simple arithmetic. The second daughter was reading the "Spelling books and beginning to write"; the third was "reading the Spelling Books"; the fourth was "spelling in the beginning of the Spelling Books"; and the youngest daughter "beginning her letters." The eldest girl, Priscilla, age 15, soon began studying multiplication with Fithian. All of the girls also received instruction in both vocal and instrumental music and dancing, though Fithian never identified a special tutor for these lessons. Fithian also mentioned that he instructed all the younger children, both girls and boys, in their catechism. It was the only instruction shared by both sexes.[36]

The boys of the family were given an education that went beyond basic literacy, including not only the study of English and arithmetic, but also Latin and Greek. The seventeen-year-old eldest son began reading Sallust (*The Cataline Conspiracy*) and Greek grammar at the inception of Fithian's teaching. Both boys were also taught Latin grammar, Virgil, the Greek Testament, English grammar, reading, writing, and arithmetic.[37]

The Carters' schoolhouse was a brick structure 45 feet long and 27 feet wide, with dormer windows. It was located in a square created by the schoolhouse and other buildings, with the plantation's "Great House" in the center. The school building consisted of five rooms. Two bedrooms occupied the upper floor, where

Fithian lived with a clerk and other servants. The schoolroom occupied the lower floor, with two other adjoining spaces. There was a fireplace in every room. This building seems fairly typical of others used on southern plantations for educational purposes.[38]

Fithian's day began at about seven, when he was roused by a boy who came to light the fire. By the time he was dressed, the children were all gathered in the room below to hear "round one lesson." The meal bell was rung at eight o'clock, and the children went out and at eight-thirty were served breakfast. School resumed at nine-thirty and lasted until the twelve o'clock bell, when the children left for their free time. Lunch was served at two-thirty or three o'clock. Lessons resumed at three-thirty and continued until five o'clock. After school the tutor might "continue in the schoolroom," occupy himself in private, or go over to the "Great House" and sit with Mr. and Mrs. Carter. Dinner was served between eight-thirty and nine. Fithian retired by ten or eleven each evening. This instruction routine was kept each day, Monday through Friday, though two daughters left their lessons on Tuesdays and Thursdays to practice their music. Since the eight students ranged in age from five to 17, many of Fithian's instructional methods were individualized for one-to-one tutorials. At other times group instruction obviously occurred, such as the younger children's catechism lessons. The children also may have tutored each other to complete mastery of a lesson.

In this way the experience of the southern plantation tutor foreshadowed the later work of teachers in one-room, mixed-grade frontier schoolhouses. Fithian's comments on his students also showed that the key to his success as a teacher was the recognition of individual differences.[39] His journal entries also revealed his philosophy as an educator.

Fithian gave extensive written advice to his successor John Peck on both practical teaching methods and the daily life of a tutor. Before becoming a tutor, "You had better go into the school and acquaint yourself with the method of teaching."[40] Fithian warned Peck against forming hasty and ill-founded prejudices. To safeguard his reputation at all times he must "abstain totally from women … and acquit [himself] honorably in the character of a tutor … " so as not to jeopardize his example as a teacher for the Carter family. (In 1773 James Marshall, a tutor at Nomini Hall, had been asked to leave by Mr. Carter, because of his overfondness for the opposite sex.)[41] He told Peck that, "I am not urging these things to discourage you; they are hints for your direction, which, if you will attend to … shall make the remainder of your tasks pleasing, and the whole of it useful."[42]

The student's progress in learning and moral conduct "are wholly under your inspection." A tutor must demonstrate his wisdom but practice humility since, "you come here, it is true, with an intention to teach, but you ought likewise to have an inclination to learn." The most important attribute for success in teaching was diligence, for "without diligence no possible abilities or qualifications can bring children on either with speed or profit."

A tutor must "avoid visible partiality," among his students, and resist giving too many holidays, for it is "a false method" to win a student's effort.

Two things which are most essential for your peace and their advantage. . . . Read over carefully, the lessons in Latin and Greek, in your leisure hours, . . . for your memory is treacherous, . . . it would confound you if you should be accosted by a pert School-Boy, in the midst of a blunder. . . . You ought likewise to do this with those who are working Figures . . . you will thereby convince them of the propriety of their subordination to you and obedience to your instructions. . . . The education of children requires constant unremitting attention.[43]

Tutoring each child separately while maintaining classroom discipline required ingenuity and adaptability by Fithian. Each child was guided according to his or her temperament and capacities in the most fruitful directions. Tutors made this a commonplace practice in the eighteenth century. Based on the writings of Locke and Rousseau, what was then termed the "genius" of every child was considered in planning an individual program of study. Fithian took an obvious personal liking to the Carter children and recorded an intriguing portrait of each child. He exercised a powerful influence over these children.[44] At other times, Fithian, like all other teachers, bemoaned his frustration as a tutor.

When I am bedizen'd [sic] with these clamorous children, sometimes I silently exclaim—Once I was told, now I know I feel how irksome the Pedagoging Scheme is—Fanny—I say, Fanny, don't you hear me, Fanny and Betsy, sit down—pray, Sir, must I multiply here by 32—Yes, thick-Scull.[45]

Yet we can surmise from Fithian's *Journal* that he was somewhat reluctant to leave his pleasant life with the Carter family after a 13-month tenure. Southern colonial family tutors like Fithian enjoyed the highest degree of social prestige among the servants. The tutor was generally accepted in the family as a social equal. Fithian as the Carter family's educator admirably demonstrated the educational precepts that the time demanded of an effective tutor.

In December 1774 Fithian was licensed to preach by the Presbyter of Philadelphia. Less than a year later (October 1775) he married Elizabeth Beatty. Early in 1776 Fithian enlisted as a chaplain in the Continental Army. After the battle of White Plains, New York (October 28, 1776), Fithian died in camp from dysentery and exposure. John Peck, Fithian's successor, made such a good impression as a tutor that he ultimately married one of the Carters' own daughters with her father's blessing.[46]

Tutors as literacy educators remained popular in the South throughout the eighteenth century. *Travels of Four Years and a Half in the United States of America* was the personal chronicle of John Davis, who sought employment as a tutor (1798–1802) while traveling from New York to South Carolina and along the southern coast in between. Davis was born at Salisbury, England, in 1776. At age 11 he first went to sea, eventually visiting China, the Dutch Indies (1787), and Bombay (1790). He served on a Royal Navy frigate during the Napoleonic

Wars (1793). Though Davis never attended school he studied Greek, Latin, and French and published a total of 12 books, most on the subject of America. He allegedly was the first author to romanticize the relationship between Captain John Smith of Jamestown and Pocahontas.[47]

Upon his arrival in America, Davis talked over his idea "to get into some family as a private tutor," with Mr. H. Caritat, a New York bookseller, who heartily discouraged this scheme. "Alas! the labour of Sisyphus in hell is not equal to that of a private tutor in America!"[48] Caritat's description of a good American private tutor was a person who wrote with a good hand, understood all the "intricacies of calculation," and would passively submit to the title "Schoolmaster" by children, or "Cool Mossa" by the blacks. A tutor must also

maintain a profound silence in company to denote your inferiority; . . . Rise with the sun, teach till breakfast, swallow your breakfast and teach till dinner, devour your dinner and teach till tea-time, and from tea-time to bedtime sink into insignificance in the parlour.

Caritat warned Davis that tutors did not receive good wages.[49]

With these admonitions in mind, Davis travelled to Charleston, South Carolina, and advertised in *The Gazette* for a tutorial position in a respectable family. Soon after Davis was interviewed by a local planter and his wife. The parents' main interests defined the limits of their educational expectations. Could Davis "drive well"? (keep order in the schoolroom). Did he use a southern spelling book or the odious Noah Webster northern speller? The planter intended his wife to manage their "school" and expected total submission from a lowly hired tutor. Even with a princely salary of 50 pounds per year, Davis rejected their insulting proposal and soon after journeyed to Virginia seeking better terms of employment.[50]

Mr. Ellicott, a Quaker in Occoquan, Virginia, a small settlement near the town of Colchester, hired Davis to tutor his children for three months. The father wanted his children instructed in reading, writing, and arithmetic. "As to Latin or French, he considered the study of either language an abuse of time; and very calmly desired me not to say another word about it." A little brick structure about three hundred yards from the main house contained a schoolroom and tutor's quarters. It looked out upon the Occoquan River.

At the end of his three-month term Davis lamented that "My condition was growing irksome. . . . I was surrounded by a throng of oafs, who read their lessons with the same tone that Punch makes when he squeaks through a comb." Unbelievably, he was now replaced by an old drunken Irishman named Burbridge. When Ellicott hired him, "he was so drunk that he could with difficulty stand on his legs." Ellicott overruled Davis' objection to hiring a sot as follows:

Friend . . . of all the schoolmasters I ever employed, none taught my children to write so good a hand, as a man who was constantly in a state that bordered on intoxication. They learned more of him in one month than of any other in a quarter.[51]

John Davis then traveled to Mr. Ball's nearby Virginia plantation to teach, for a quarter of a year, his daughters and other nearby children.

The following day every farmer came from the neighbourhood to the house, who had any children to send to my Academy, for such they did me the honour to term the log-hut in which I was to teach. Each man brought his son, or his daughter, and rejoiced that the day was arrived when their little ones could light their tapers at the torch of knowledge! I was confounded at the encomiums they heaped upon a man whom they had never seen before, and was at a loss what construction to put upon their speech. No price was too great for the services I was to render their children; and they all expressed an eagerness to exchange perishable coin for lasting knowledge. If I would continue with them seven years! . . . they would erect for me a brick seminary on a hill not far off; but for the present I was to occupy a log-house.

I now opened what some called an *Academy*,[52] and others an Old Field School; and, however it may be thought that content was never felt within the walls of a seminary, I, for my part, experienced an exception from care, and was not such a fool as to measure the happiness of my condition by what others thought of it.

It was pleasurable to behold my pupils enter the school over which I presided; for they were not composed only of truant boys, but some of the fairest damsels in the country. Two sisters generally rode on one horse to the school-door, and I was not so great a pedagogue as to refuse them my assistance to dismount from their steeds. . . . I proceeded to instruct them, with gentle exhortations to diligence of study.[53]

As literacy educators John Harrower, Devereux Jarratt, Phillip Fithian, and John Davis provide us with excellent examples of the great diversity in educational backgrounds and literacy practices of the colonial Virginia era. There were great differences not only in their national/regional origins (Harrower, Scotland; Jarratt, Virginia; Fithian, New Jersey; and Davis, England), but also what they were prepared to teach. Parents also were directly involved in determining what each child was taught. Likewise, among smaller planters and farmers in Virginia, family influence determined literacy attainments. Such parents either used local tutors, instructed their children themselves, or banded together with neighbors to privately fund and hire a teacher for an old field school.[54]

This almost haphazard system of family-dominated literacy should not be underestimated. The majority of America's "founding fathers" seemingly received an excellent education by combining private tutors and local schoolmasters, including George Washington, Thomas Jefferson, and James Madison.[55]

Washington's own mother, Mary Ball, was educated by a young English tutor. At the age of 15 she wrote, "We have now a young minister living with us who was educated at Oxford, took orders and came over as assistant to Reverend Kemp. The parish is too poor to keep both and he teaches school for his board. He teaches Sister Susie and me and Madam Carter's boy and two girls. I am learning pretty fast."[56]

When it came time to educate her son George, Mary had him first tutored by a convict servant whom George's father had brought over from England as an indentured schoolmaster. George then attended an old field school kept by a Reverend Hobby, the local sexton and pedagogue. From Hobby he received most of his education. For another year George rode his horse to another similar old field school that was 10 miles from his home. He then attended Reverend James Marye's school in Fredericksburg for one year. To reach it, George had to row every morning and night across the Rappahannock River. George Washington's formal education ended at age 13, but it gave him a passionate desire for more self-learning, which would well prepare him to lead the colonies into nationhood.[57]

When it came time to educate his own stepson, John Parke Custis, George Washington hired Reverend Jonathan Boucher as his tutor. Boucher told Washington that he intended to ensure that Custis became "a good Man, if not a learned one." He denounced the literacy practices of the local schools that taught boys "Words rather than things," giving them "a parcel of Lumber by Rote." Instead for several years Boucher educated the young Custis to become a gentleman rather than just a scholar.

In August 1770 Boucher proposed to accompany his pupil on "the grand tour"[58] of Europe to complete his education, "which every gentleman should know, and yet no school nor college can teach him." Although Washington turned down his proposal, he did follow Boucher's advice to send John to King's College (later Columbia) in New York City. Custis remained at school until his marriage at age 20.[59]

Thomas Jefferson's literacy education began when at age five he joined other children at Tuckahoe, Virginia, in a small house in the family's plantation courtyard. There a tutor taught him in what was called "the English school."[60]

James Madison was taught to read and write, as well as the beginnings of arithmetic, at home, by his mother and grandmother. He boarded for a few years (1762–1767) with a Scottish schoolmaster, Donald Robertson, a well-known tutor. The curriculum included Latin, Greek, arithmetic, geography, algebra, geometry, and literature, including Locke. In 1767 a Reverend Thomas Martin, the new pastor at the Madison family parish church, was hired as the family tutor for James, his three brothers, and his sister. During 1767–1768, Madison was tutored at home by Martin to prepare him for admission to the College of New Jersey (Princeton). His college education was cut short in 1772, when he returned home to tutor, "my brothers and sisters in some of the first rudiments of literature." Madison pursued this task until the start of the American Revolution (1775).[61]

DOMESTIC LITERACY IN THE CAROLINAS

Throughout the eighteenth century in both North and South Carolina, the home literacy instruction of children was a common accepted educational custom, both in families of modest means or through tutors and governesses by planters who could afford it. This does not mean, however, that the vast majority of children were either well educated or even partially literate.[62]

Before the American Revolution (1776–1783) many South Carolina planters sent their sons to Oxford or Cambridge to complete their education. Old field schools and private tutors were as commonly used as in Virginia to give Carolina's children their basic literacy skills.[63]

As in Virginia many parents in the Carolinas, out of either personal preference or economic necessity, did undertake at least the basic literacy education (and sometimes much more) of their children upon themselves. The *Memoirs of Martha Laurens Ramsay* offer us a fairly detailed record of how an eighteenth-century mother conducted the day-to-day education of her children at home.[64]

Martha Laurens Ramsay was born in Charleston on November 3, 1759. In 1775 she journeyed with her father Herry Laurens to England. In 1780 he was charged with treason by the British government and imprisoned in the Tower of London. Upon the end of the American Revolution (1783), her father was released and sent to Paris as a minister by the new American government with full power to assist in the peace negotiations. Martha joined him in Paris. They returned to Charleston in 1785. Two years later (January 23, 1787) Martha married David Ramsay, M.D. Over the next 16 years, while living in Charleston, she bore 11 children of whom eight survived.[65]

Soon after she became a mother she carefully studied the writings of the leading domestic educators of that day published in both French and English. "She gave a decided preference to the writings of Mr. Locke and Dr. Witherspoon on that subject (education). The object she proposed to herself was to obtain for her children, health and a well regulated mind."[66]

Martha's earliest curriculum was typical for that day; she taught her children to read their Bibles. As a teaching aid to increase reading comprehension, she employed the prints on scripture history produced by a popular English education writer, Mrs. Trimmer. As they grew older, Martha used other similar contemporary books to connect the Bible to secular history and the Old and New Testaments.[67]

Martha also considered using the educational theories of Rousseau and other modern reformers. However, she considered them all inferior to the prudent use of the rod.[68]

It is quite obvious that as her children's teacher Mrs. Ramsay possessed much more than ordinary intellectual resources and took far more than ordinary pains in her domestic education program. For her oldest children she compiled her own English grammar text, being dissatisfied with the available schoolbooks. Martha taught her children to read from a wide variety of literature. However, she always endeavored to take the time to teach them to read for meaning and substance, rather than just for words. Martha obviously preferred to educate her children to understand ideas rather than to load their memories with the long memorized verses that were popular with educators at that time.

To liven up this learning process, Martha would often prepare questions on the most interesting events of ancient and modern, Asiatic, Roman, English, and biblical history. These she expected her children to answer from their general knowledge on the subject, rather than committing an answer to memory. Martha's memoirs contained three packets of such historical questions used to help her children recall information they had read and combine facts to produce a logical answer.[69]

Mrs. Ramsay thought that no pains were too great, no sacrifice too hard, provided her children were advanced educationally by them. As her sons and daughters grew up, she prepared her sons through a course of home education to enter college. (Her son David was attending Princeton College by 1810.) She taught her daughters with the assistance of a governess and friend, Miss Futerell, and also sent them to local boarding schools.[70]

Martha Ramsay's advanced home education program could not be duplicated by many other parents in South Carolina or any of the other American colonies. But it does show how parents did have access to popular educational literature. Uncounted families throughout the South and in the other regions of colonial America devoted their own steady attention to their children's education. They took a lively personal interest in their children's daily concerns and for childhood literacy forged more personal pathways that many parents in our modern era may now envy.

THE LITERACY OF CHANGE—LOUISIANA

As part of colonial New France, New Orleans added an important dimension to the development of literacy in Louisiana. To secure the continuance of the colony of Louisiana, French colonial administrators, as part of their social and cultural policies, actively supported some types of literacy education.

The Mississippi Valley's first recorded teacher was Francoise de Boisrenaud, who arrived in New Orleans on the ship Pelican (1704). Mademoiselle Boisrenaud provided basic literacy instruction to the colony's young girls in her home and also religious instruction to Indian slave girls. In 1718 she left New Orleans because of poor health.[71]

The city's first lasting agency of literacy education was the Ursuline school and convent. Rather uniquely for this time period, females and minorities were the primary focus of literacy efforts in New Orleans. In order to transform the "savages" of Louisiana into subjects, some semblance of French society was needed in the wilderness. The absence of Frenchwomen was keenly felt, particularly for their role in establishing families that would support the colonizing spirit. It was this urgent desire for the colonial reconstruction of French life that made the literacy activities of the Ursuline nuns so important to local officials. Convent girl graduates were ardently sought after as desirable wives throughout the French colonial period. On the other hand, there was a notable lack of support for the Capuchin (a Catholic order of priests) school for boys. The realities of Louisiana frontier life reemphasized for boys the necessity of more practical apprenticeship education. This was an interesting reversal of the literacy practices found in the English colonies.[72]

As a result, on September 13, 1726, a contract was entered into between the trading company of the Indies that controlled New Orleans for the French Crown and the Ursuline nuns of France. Their order had been the first teaching nuns to bring instruction for girls to Quebec, Canada, in northern New France. Less than a year later the first group of teaching sisters arrived in New Orleans (August 6, 1727). The Ursulines began their work as literacy educators immediately upon their arrival in the city. The first boarding school students were accepted on November 17, 1727, at a small house near their residence, with classes for day students begun soon after. The Ursulines also started afternoon literacy classes for Afro-American and Indian girls.[73]

The curriculum offered the practical and basic literacy subjects needed in a frontier society: reading, writing, arithmetic, sewing, the making of fabric, and the care of silkworms. Of course, all the girls received instruction in religion. Reading was taught from handwritten books and conducted by rote recitation. The morning classes were taught in French, and the afternoon classes in English. Spelling was taught to eight to 10 girls at a time. The nuns chose the brightest girls as peer tutors, known as dixaineres, to drill other students in class lessons. One of their responsibilities was to distribute and collect each day books used for class instruction, since students were never allowed to take any books home.[74]

After 1731 the Ursulines greatly expanded their social services to New Orleans. They began sheltering abused women and caring for large numbers of female orphans. In 1803, just one week after Louisiana had become part of the United States, Governor William C. C. Claiborne visited the convent school. In his letter to Secretary of State James Madison, Claiborne wrote of the deep impression that the Ursulines' literacy education efforts had made on him.

There is an Abbess and eleven Nuns, the sole *object* of whose temporal care is the Education of Female youth;—they at present accommodate *seventy three boarders* and a hundred day Scholars, each of whom contribute to the Support of the House, in proportion to the means and conditions of their respective parents, and many receive their tuition gratis.[75]

The Ursuline convent and school for girls has operated in New Orleans without interruption to this day since its inception in the colony in 1727.[76]

WOMEN'S LIMITED LITERACY OPPORTUNITIES

There were few girls' schools in the colonial South. A more typical source of literacy for women was a domestic education conducted by a mother, an aunt, the brother's tutor, or a governess.[77] In fact, most southern men agreed with their northern brothers that any woman who sought the same level of literacy education as a man was somehow defective, defying her "natural" feminine nature.

In a family that had an interest in literacy, the father tried to provide some schooling for all his children, but usually saw to it that a boy would receive a longer education than his sister. John Foster, who when he died in 1764, left a will stipulating that his sons at age 12 be enrolled in school for two years and then apprenticed in an occupation. He requested that his daughters attend school for only a year.[78]

Educational programs for women were more fully developed, as we have already seen, among prominent and wealthy families. While some fathers like that of Martha Laurens Ramsey provided an advanced education for their daughters, this was not the general rule for that time period. The childhood education of the granddaughter of Martha Washington, Eliza Custis, seems more typical.

Growing up in 1780s Virginia, Eliza was first given her basic literacy education in reading and spelling by her mother and a cousin. Upon her mother's remarriage, Eliza's new stepfather provided her a tutor, and she began reading more sophisticated materials. However, her stepfather drew a line at how well she was to be educated. He told her tutor that Eliza "was an extraordinary child and would if a boy, make a brilliant figure." Eliza's education came to an abrupt halt when she insisted on learning Greek and Latin. Both her tutor and parent refused, since "women ought not to know those things."[79]

During the 50 years prior to the American Revolution women as well as men were sought as tutors. Women were given the title of governess. They taught not only basic literacy but in some instances foreign languages, particularly French. Fithian's *Journal* recorded that two women from England were employed as tutors near Nomini Hall: Miss Garrott was the governess of the daughters of Colonel Tayloe. Sally Panton taught French, writing, and English to Miss Turburville, the daughter of Richard Henry Lee.

Local Southern newspapers offered an extensive record of advertisements seeking women tutors (governesses).

WANTED, AN ELDERLY WOMAN capable of educating and bringing up children. Such a one, well recommended, will hear of good encouragement by applying to the Printer hereof.—The Virginia Gazette, March 8, 1770.

A WELL bred Woman of Character, capable of teaching young Ladies the Degrees of NEEDLEWORK, together with READING and WRITING, etc. etc. will meet with great Encouragement by applying to the ladies in the Borough of NORFOLK.—The Virginia Gazette ([Williamsburg], alex. Puride and John Dixon), November 26, 1772, p. [2].

Conversely, women also advertized as tutors for girls. Some historians believe that these private southern teachers, of either sex, were the forerunners of the first recognized educational institutions of the South. Before 1750, "these schools supplemented in an important way the work of tutors in the household . . . but were found chiefly in the cities."[80]

But even in the largest city in the colonial South, Charleston, the city's *Gospel Messenger* (an Episcopal journal) told parents that only under unusual circumstances should a girl be sent to a day school rather than receive her basic literacy education at home. Only the most dire necessity should separate a girl from her family by exiling her in a boarding school.[81]

Even Thomas Jefferson, who as we have seen was very committed to producing a well-educated daughter, still believed that her prime responsibility was as a domestic manager. Despite the more advanced education he urged her to pursue, Jefferson stressed that she would only become the mistress of her family mainly through learning a variety of "feminine" subjects such as music, drawing, and dancing. Above all, she needed to learn "the needle and domestic economy," for she must be able to sew if she expected to direct the servants' work.[82]

THE PATHWAYS TO LITERACY

From our review we have seen numerous alternatives for gaining access to literacy throughout the American colonies. These personal pathways were often dependent on geographic location, ethnic, cultural, or religious background, and the sex of the child or adult. In some regions, such as New England, an earnest attempt was often made to provide literacy more democratically. Also, this region had the significant advantage that common religious beliefs were enlisted in the pursuit of personal literacy. In reality, however, only a minority of children and adults throughout all the colonies were ever provided access to any meaningful level of learning beyond the most basic literacy (such as signing one's name).

What is more significant is the fact that a child or adult did not have to sit in a schoolhouse to achieve literacy, which more often than not was mastered in a home schoolroom. It is also evident that the home was the center of a child's domestic education in civility, piety, a sense of community responsibility, and often basic career skills. As was recorded again and again, literacy instruction, even in a schoolhouse, was generally done on an individual basis rather than through teaching a group.

Literacy in colonial America relied heavily on two basic institutions, the family and the church. They provided the basic foundation of literacy and the eventual support for the establishment of formal schooling. The reality of life in rural and small-town America, where most farmers and pioneers lived, meant that these same two institutions would continue to dominate the development of literacy throughout America until the dawn of the twentieth century.

Though literacy throughout the American colonies reached only a minority of the population, it had taken root and would grow. During the years of the early American republic until the time of the Civil War, literacy would become an ever more important social force with each passing decade.

NOTES

1. Margaret Connell Szasz, *Indian Education in the American Colonies, 1607–1783* (Albuquerque: University of New Mexico Press, 1988), 41–43; Edmund S. Morgan, *Vir-*

ginians at Home: Family Life in the Eighteenth Century (Williamsburg, Virginia: Colonial Williamsburg, Inc., 1952), 22; Alice Morse, *Child Life in Colonial Days* (Stockbridge, Massachusetts: Berkshire House Publishers, 1993), 65.

2. Sheldon S. Cohen, *A History of Colonial Education 1607–1776* (New York: Wiley, 1974), 129–130; Szasz, *American Colonies*, 41–44.

3. Edgar W. Knight, ed., *A Documentary History of Education in the South Before 1860*, vol. 1 (Chapel Hill: University of North Carolina Press, 1949), 321, 571–573; Szasz, *American Colonies*, 43–44.

4. Marcus Wilson Jernegan, *Laboring and Dependent Classes in Colonial America 1607–1783* (Chicago: University of Chicago Press, 1931), 134.

5. Ibid., 135.

6. Lawrence A. Cremin, *American Education: The Colonial Experience 1607–1786* (New York: Harper & Row, 1970), 125, 155; Jernegan, *Colonial America*, 153–154.

7. Cremin, *Colonial Experience*, 240, 483–484, 531–532.

8. Louise du Bellet Pecquet, *Some Prominent Virginia Families*, vol. 2 (Baltimore: Genealogical Publishing Co., 1972), 344–345.

9. Cremin, *Colonial Experience*, 483.

10. Morgan, *Virginians*, 9–10.

11. Daniel Blake Smith, *Inside the Great House: Planter Life in Eighteenth Century Chesapeake Society* (Ithaca, New York: Cornell University Press, 1980), 107; Morgan, *Virginians*, 10–11.

12. A structure of this type is still standing and can be visited at the Shirley Plantation on the James River near Richmond, Virginia. The famous Confederate general Robert E. Lee was educated at the Shirley Plantation. George Mason also built at Gunston Hall (in Virginia near Mount Vernon) a special structure for the tutor's lessons, though only of one story. This plantation also has been preserved and is open for public view.

13. Morgan, *Virginians*, 11–12; Knight, *Documentary History*, 571–573; William Arthur Maddox, *The Free School Idea in Virginia Before the Civil War* (New York: Columbia University, 1918), 6; Edgar W. Knight, *Public School Education in North Carolina* (Boston: Houghton Mifflin, 1916; reprint, New York: Negro University Press, 1969), 12; Thomas Wood, *A History of Women's Education in the United States*, vol. 1 (New York: Science Press, 1929), 244, 268, 273; Paul Monroe, *Founding of the American Public School System* (New York: Macmillan Co., 1940), 61–62.

14. Morgan, *Virginians*, 13–14.

15. Berkeley Plantation, located on the James River near Richmond, Virginia, has been restored and is open to public view.

16. Clifford Dowdey, *The Great Plantation* (Charles City, Virginia: Berkeley Plantation, 1957), 29, 106, 125–126, 142–143, 197, 236–237.

17. Wood, *Women's Education*, vol. 1, 276; Knight, *Documentary History*, 649–657.

18. Knight, *Documentary History*, 649–660.

19. John Harrower, *The Journal of John Harrower* (Williamsburg, Virginia: Colonial Williamsburg, 1963), xvi, 17.

20. Harrower, *Journal*, xxi, 38–148.

21. H. Warren Button and Eugene F. Provenzo, Jr., *History of Education and Culture in America* (Englewood Cliffs, New Jersey: Prentice-Hall, 1983), 35; Robert E. Brown and B. Katherine Brown, *Virginia 1705–1786: Democracy or Aristocracy?* (East Lansing: Michigan State University Press, 1964), 273; Harrower, *Journal*, 59–122.

22. Harrower, *Journal*, xix, 160, 164.

23. Phillip Vickers Fithian, *Journal and Letters of Phillip Vickers Fithian 1773–1774: A Plantation Tutor of the Old Dominion*, ed. Hunter Dickinson Farish (Williamsburg, Virginia: Colonial Williamsburg, Inc., 1957), xvii; Button, *Education and Culture*, 35–36.

24. Fithian, *Journal*, xix. "The Recollections of John Mason," transcriber Terry Dunn, unabridged edition (Mason Neck, Virginia: Board of Regents of Gunston Hall, 1989), photocopied typescript.

25. Devereux Jarratt, *The Life of Reverend Devereux Jarratt, Rector of Bath Parish, Dinwiddie County, Virginia* (Baltimore: Warner & Hanna, 1806), 14–15.

26. Ibid., 19–20.

27. Ibid., 25.

28. Ibid., 25, 29, 30, 32, 41.

29. Ibid., 45, 52.

30. Ibid., 52–55.

31. The Carter children included Benjamin, 17; Robert, 14; Priscilla, 13; Anne, 11; Frances, 9; Betty, 8; Harriet, 5; and John, 1. Louis Morton, *Robert Carter of Nomini Hall* (Williamsburg, Virginia: Colonial Williamsburg, 1941), 220–222.

32. Morgan, *Virginians at Home*, 13, 14.

33. Fithian, *Journal*, xxxi. Button, *Education and Culture*, 35–36.

34. Morgan, *Virginians at Home*, 12–13. Button, *Education and Culture*, 35–36. Morton, *Robert Carter*, 64–66.

35. Fithian, *Journal*, 6–7. Fithian described Mr. Carter's library as an "over-grown library of law books," Latin and Greek classics, books on divinity and famous writers, Locke, Addison, Young, Pope, Swift and Dryden. Fithian, *Journal*, 26.

36. Ibid., 21–22, 26, 127–128. Morgan, *Virginians at Home*, 15. Woody, *Women's Education*, 277–278.

37. Fithian, *Journal*, 25–26, 62, 74, 77, 127–128, 190. Woody, *Women's Education*, 278.

38. Fithian, *Journal*, 80–81.

39. Ibid., 31–32.

40. Ibid., 143.

41. Morton, *Robert Carter*, 221.

42. Fithian, *Journal*, 162.

43. Ibid., 164–165.

44. Morgan, *Virginians at Home*, 16–17. Woody, *Women's Education*, 278. Fithian, *Journal*, 48–49, 127–128. Fithian, *Journal*, 78.

45. Fithian, *Journal*, 133.

46. Morgan, *Virginians at Home*, 54–55: Fithian, *Journal*, XXXII; Morton, *Robert Carter*, 221.

47. John Davis, *Travels of Four Years and a Half in the U.S.A.*, (New York: Holt, 1909), iii–x.

48. Ibid., 17–18.

49. Ibid., 18–19.

50. Ibid., 52–57.

51. Ibid., 252–255, 336–337.

52. "It is worth while to describe the *Academy* I occupied on Mr. Ball's plantation. It had one room and a half. It stood on blocks about two feet and a half above the ground, where there was free access to the hogs, the dogs, and the poultry. It had no ceiling, nor was the roof lathed or plastered; but covered with shingles. Hence, when it rained, like

the nephew of old *Elwes*, I moved my bed (for I slept in my Academy) to the most comfortable corner. It had one window, but no glass, nor shutter. In the night to remedy this, the mulatto wench who waited on me, contrived very ingeniously to place a square board against the window with one hand, and fix the rail of a broken down fence against it with the other. In the morning when I returned from breakfasting in the "great big-house" (my scholars being collected), I gave the rail a forcible kick with my foot, and down tumbled the board with an awful roar. 'Is not my window,' said I to *Virginia*, 'of a very curious construction?' 'Indeed, indeed, Sir,' replied my fair disciple, 'I think it is a mighty noisy one.'" Ibid., 396–397.

53. Ibid., 395–397.

54. Smith, *Great House*, 293–294.

55. James J. Walsh, *Education of the Founding Fathers of the Republic* (New York: Fordham University Press, 1935), 33–63.

56. Alice Morse Earle, *Child Life in Colonial Days* (New York: Macmillan, 1899; reprint, Stockbridge, Massachusetts: Berkshire House Publishers, 1993), 95.

57. Douglas Southall Freeman, *George Washington*, vol. 1 (New York: Scribner, 1948), 64; Earle, *Child Life*, 65–66.

58. "The Grand Tour" as an educational "vacation" had started in England after 1660 and flourished as an upper-class mobile "finishing" school until the beginning of rail travel, around 1825. The boy student was accompanied by his tutor to continue his education in the local history, culture, arts, etc. of the countries they visited. A common route included London, Dover, Calais, Switzerland, Florence, Venice, Rome, Germany, and Paris. For more details, read Christopher Hibbert, *The Grand Tour* (New York: G. P. Putnam, 1969).

59. Stanislaus Murray Hamilton, *Letters to Washington and Accompanying Papers*, 5 vols. (Boston: Houghton Mifflin, 1898–1902): Vol. 3, 318, 324–325; Vol. 4, 20–22, 74, 84–85, 175–176, 232–233.

60. Jefferson did not like being tutored. One day he played hooky and hid behind an outhouse. He recited the Lord's Prayer that school end. Jefferson remembered how disillusioned he was by the impotence of his own prayers and, as a warning not to expect too much out of heaven, told this story to his grandchildren; Fawn M. Brodie, *Thomas Jefferson: An Intimate History* (New York: Norton and Company, 1974), 49.

61. Irving Brant, *James Madison* (New York: Bobbs-Merrill, 1941), 56–67, 122–123.

62. Knight, *North Carolina*, 12; Arthur W. Calhoun, *A Social History of the American Family from Colonial Times to the Present*, Vol. 1, *Colonial Period*. (New York: Barnes & Noble, 1945), 291.

63. Knight, *Documentary History*, 571–573.

64. David Ramsay, *Memoirs of the Life of Martha Laurens Ramsay*, 2nd ed. (Charlestown, Massachusetts: Samuel Etheridge, 1812).

65. Ramsay, *Memoirs*, 15–27.

66. Ibid., 25–26.

67. Ibid., 27.

68. Ibid., 28.

69. Ibid., 33.

70. Ibid., 45, 28.

71. Clark Robenstine, "French Colonial Policy and the Education of Women and Minorities: Louisiana in the Early Eighteenth Century," *History of Education Quarterly* 32

(Summer 1992): 193; Marcel Girand, *Histoire de la Louisiane Française* (Paris: Presses Universitaires de France, 1953–1966), Vol. 1, 143, 166; Vol. 2, 22; Vol. 3, 342; Robenstine, *Louisiana*, 204, 206–207.

72. Ibid., 197; Sister Joan Marie Aycock, "The Ursuline School in New Orleans," Copy supplied by the author.

73. Robenstine, *Louisiana*, 199.

74. Aycock, "New Orleans," 11, 12, 13; Robenstine, *Louisiana*, 209.

75. Sister Jane Frances Heaney, *A Century of Pioneering: A History of the Ursuline Nuns in New Orleans (1727–1827)* (New Orleans: Ursuline Sisters of New Orleans, Louisiana, 1993), 230.

76. The original building of the Ursuline Convent School (built 1734) is now open to view as a historic site. Robenstine, *Louisiana*, 210.

77. Benson, *Women in Eighteenth Century America*, 309–310.

78. Will of John Foster, Albemarle County Wills, Virginia, 1764, Vol. 2, 163–164.

79. "Eliza Custis, Self-Portrait," *Virginia Magazine of History and Biography* 61 (1953), 93–94.

80. Fithian, *Journal*, 142, 146, 225; Advertisement, *South Carolina Gazette*, April 28, 1757; Advertisement, *Virginia Gazette*, March 8, 1770; Advertisement, *Maryland Gazette*, June 14, 1764; Advertisement, *Maryland Gazette*, December 24, 1772; Woody, *Women's Education*, 280–281.

81. Jane H. Pease and William H. Pease, *Ladies, Women and Wenches: Choice and Constraint in Antebellum Charleston and Boston* (Chapel Hill: The University of North Carolina Press, 1990), 78.

82. Letters, Thomas Jefferson to Martha Jefferson, March 28, 1787, and April 11, 1790, in Sarah N. Randolph, ed., *The Domestic Life of Thomas Jefferson* (New York: Doubleday, 1939), 115, 116, 181.

Part II

Literacy in the Young Republic (1790–1860)

Chapter 4

Literacy in Transition: The Northeast

THE GREAT LITERACY EXPERIMENT

In the northeastern United States, from the time of the American Revolution to the 1830s, the pathways of literacy remained fluid and diverse. The literacy dividing lines between the school and church were blurred, as were those between the family and school. Though schools were part of the terrain of childhood, they remained only a small part. Homes, churches, asylums, orphanages, and factories were sites of significant literacy instruction. Formal literacy education remained for most children only an occasional unsystematic activity. Most rural children learned to read and write at home during evenings or during the slack agricultural seasons of winter and summer.[1]

Significant numbers of Americans pursued basic literacy instruction entirely within their families and churches or through informal methods. The choice of using the schoolhouse or the family schoolroom was usually imposed by physical or social circumstances. As the 1800s progressed, more people had at least some schooling, as state after state passed compulsory attendance laws (yet with little means to enforce them). The formal legal movement that would provide literacy through a system of public schooling was often very experimental, offering considerable variation within a state from community to community, even from school to school. Communities frequently patched together various combinations of private and public financial support and control to meet their schooling needs.

During the 1840s, Lowell, Massachusetts, incorporated Roman Catholic parochial schools, attended by Irish-Catholic students and taught by Irish-Catholic nuns, into the local public school system. Pennsylvania, Ohio, and Wisconsin provided the same kind of support for German-speaking Lutheran students attending Lutheran parochial schools scattered across those states.[2]

Yet in many places schools were maintained only with great difficulty, if at all. In 1803 William Hall settled in Dover, Delaware, and he wrote that

There was then no provision by law in the state for schools. Neighbors or small circles united and hired a teacher for their children. ... The teachers frequently were intemperate whose qualifications seemed to be inability to earn anything in any other way. ... Even in the best neighborhoods teachers of the young frequently were immoral and incapable.[3]

From 1809 until 1833 Pennsylvania provided public education only for those children whose parents were willing to take a pauper's oath. In 1834 Pennsylvania enacted its first public school law. By 1837 only about 42 percent of all children were enrolled in free public schools. Delaware, New Jersey, and Maryland followed a similar pauper school practice, with the added feature that public school teachers were often drawn from the ranks of indentured servants. Of course, these conditions placed a stigma on public school enrollment.[4]

The diversity of schooling during the colonial period persisted into America's early national era with three basic types of schools. The "English" school stressed basic reading, writing, spelling, arithmetic, and often geography and history. In America's predominantly rural society, this basic literacy education was almost always housed in the stereotypical one-room schoolhouse, with pupils of multiple ages and grades. In a small number of urban areas, the English school might be divided between primary and intermediate programs.

In the cities of the northeast, the Latin grammar school for boys continued to focus on a curriculum of Latin and Greek, while also offering more advanced studies including geometry, algebra, and trigonometry.

The academy became the other popular educational alternative of the nineteenth century. Often it was a boarding school that also accepted some day students. As we shall see, these schools offered a mixed bag of subjects from the English or Latin grammar-school curriculum, often whatever was desired by the schoolmaster or his tuition-paying parents.[5]

In these early days of the American Republic, influential political leaders such as Thomas Jefferson conceived the idea of "public education" going far beyond the schooling process. Daniel Webster, in defining the verb "to educate," did not even mention school attendance in the first edition of his famous dictionary (1828). Instead Webster defined education to mean "to instill into the mind principles of the arts, sciences, morals, religion, and behavior. To educate a child well is one of the most important duties of parents and guardians."[6] Influential political economists, such as the Scotsman Adam Smith, viewed domestic education as a far more important foundation of literacy than the schools of that time. In his famous *Wealth of Nations*, Smith did acknowledge the financial utility of schools. But he strongly preferred family domestic education or even tutors and governesses, where the motivation for effort and hence for effectiveness was both clear and direct.[7]

The "book revolution" that occurred in late eighteenth- and early nineteenth-century America rapidly increased the number of titles and books available to the average family. During the 30 years between 1830 and 1850, book publication increased five times over that of the period from 1770 to 1830. "The speed of communications increased dramatically, and literacy penetrated into the countryside." This also helped strengthen a growing domestic education movement and family literacy practices.[8]

Such was the experience of Almira Hart Lincoln (1793–1876) of Berlin, Connecticut, who was the youngest member of her family of 17 children from two marriages. The oldest children always tutored the youngest, turning the home into a school. Almira was 11 before attending her first formal school. Her father Samuel Hart, who was largely self-educated, taught her much more than the fundamentals of reading, writing, and math. Hart taught Almira the philosophies of Locke and Berkeley. They read plays from Shakespeare, Rollin's *Ancient History*, Plutarch's *Lives*, Gibbon's *Rome*, and the poetry of Milton. Almira also read contemporary works on teaching methods such as Hannah More's *Strictures on Female Education*. As an adult, Almira Hart Lincoln became a teacher and authored science textbooks.[9]

THE FAMILY AND READING

Opinion leaders of the time stressed the importance of the family in literacy instruction. This "institution of institutions" supported a vast educational literature of "domestic education" or "fireside education," how-to books providing parents with materials and teaching methods for instructing their children at home.[10] Like the home-schooling movement of today, the "family school" education movement of the nineteenth century was characterized by parent teachers rebelling against "tasked lessons" in a schoolroom. Instead, they saw the function of the educator as being to "draw out," not to "fill up." The origin of the term "domestic education" can be ascribed to a book of that title by the American Herman Humphrey in 1840. The parallel term, "Fireside Education," was the title of an 1841 work by the Englishman S. G. Goodrich. The latter book had far greater impact. It gave the family school movement both a concrete educational philosophy and its instructional methods. Hundreds of additional philosophical works on domestic education for parents were written by educators, clergymen, doctors, and social reformers throughout the remainder of that century and into the beginning of the next. This paralleled a similar movement in England and on the European continent. Many of the most popular titles on this subject were reprinted from European editions or adapted for an American audience. Domestic education was to remain a powerful educational force until it was supplanted by twentieth-century tax-based schooling.[11]

The mother's role as primary tutor was of supreme importance. Though the literature of the period spoke of both parents acting as teachers, most books were written for women. Fathers had increasingly little time to instruct their children because of work commitments. The proponents of that era's "liberal mental culture" viewed learning as a continuous process. The mother was the logical educator since she was the person most closely and constantly associated with the child.

Many of these educational reformers were against educating children beyond their years. This led to the adoption of the Pestalozzian system of object teaching, rather than the "overeducating" of young children (such as teaching four-year-olds Latin, Greek, and philosophy as had been common in the fifteenth through seventeenth centuries). Instead of formal teaching, one mother of a seven-year-old son "contrived to give an air of recreation to his hours of study." Rejecting the classical approach to learning, the "family school" embraced new principles by studying individual differences. The simple, everyday observation of children provided a common meeting ground between the researcher and the practitioner in the raising of children. The legacies of Rousseau, Locke, and Edgeworth were blended, with pleasurable learning as the final goal.

Parental "domestic education" guides offered a unique blend of formal instruction: reading, spelling, the definition of words, penmanship, arithmetic, and the expression of thought, along with character formation in which intellectual, social, moral, and religious elements might be interwoven. Education was more naturally presented at home since these philosophers contended that intellectual cultivation did not thrive in the crowded schoolroom, where children's bodies are cramped and their minds stimulated only artificially. One hour well spent in the "family school" might do more good than a day spent in any schoolroom.[12]

Lydia Sigourney in her book *Letters to Mothers* (1838) told them that this period of home tutoring should be extended into childhood as far as possible.

Why expose it [a child] to the influence of evil example? ... Why yield it to the excitement of promiscuous association, when it has a parent's house, where its innocence may be shielded, and its intellect aided to expand? Does not a mother's tutoring for two to three hours a day give a child more time than a teacher at school?[13]

Similar themes are voiced by the contemporary home-schooling movement.

Goodrich in *Fireside Education* (1841) also saw the parent as "the teacher ... developing and perfecting the various physical, moral and intellectual faculties of their children." The home was a "Fireside Seminary," "the chief engine by which character is formed." The common school was only an auxiliary to the fireside, not a replacement, since the family had the first and primary educational role.[14]

Home Education (1838) told parents that if properly conducted, home schooling was in most cases preferable to regular schooling. Isaac Taylor believed this "especially so for girls." He recommended combining children from different families as a method of improving instruction.[15]

One of the few works published for fathers was John Hall's *On the Education of Children While under the Care of Parents or Guardians* (1835). He too argued in favor of a home education. If a parent was forced by circumstances to send a child to school, Hall counseled him to select one where the mind is "most effectually cultivated and where the moral, manner, general habits and health should be best promoted." He complained that too often the parent's inquiry is limited to "where does schooling come the cheapest? ... The value received makes no part of the estimate. A school is a school." Hall did not view cheapness as a successful determinant of a quality education.[16]

Maria Edgeworth (1768–1849) was a noteworthy early contributor to the domestic education movement. She helped introduce a new, distinctive "children's literature" and also improved educational prospects for women.

Maria was born in Ireland. Her father, Richard (1744–1817), had been educated at Trinity College, Dublin, and Oxford. Her mother, Ann Maria Elders, died when Maria was age six. Richard's second wife died in 1780. In the meantime, Maria attended school at Mrs. Latuffiere's Derby (1775) to learn penmanship, French, Italian, and embroidery. In 1781 she was sent to school at Mrs. Devis's on Upper Wimpole Street in London. Maria remained there only a year. At age 14 she arrived at the family's Irish estate (1782) to be educated by her father. By this time, her father had married a third time. There were 12 children now at home who were to be educated by Edgeworth with Maria's help.[17]

For the next two years Maria was tutored rigorously by her father. She later offered her thanks to the "father who educated me, under providence, I owe all of good or happiness I have enjoyed in life."[18] Richard read aloud to his family from Shakespeare, Milton, and Homer. He encouraged them to read on subjects they could understand, including biography, travel, literature, and science.

Richard was in close touch with progressive movements both in England and on the continent. He was particularly influenced by the "Lunar Society," whose members, though focusing on science, were concerned also with education. They criticized the uselessness of public education that remained too remote from the business of life and morally worthless. In their educational writing Richard and Maria Edgeworth amplified these views, attacking the rote-learning methods found in the contemporary grammar and public schools. They denounced the narrow classical curriculum and the failure of schools to account for individual differences.[19]

Maria later claimed that her father was the first to practice the experimental method in education, as Richard used the Edgeworth family as a laboratory for educational experiments. Edgeworth and his second wife, Honora, collected data for a study of children based on their actual experiences. Their goal was to develop a system to teach reading that stressed reasoning capacity and accounted for individual differences. They conducted experiments with their own children, with Honora noting Edgeworth's questions, the answers of the children, and his explanations.[20]

In *Practical Education* (1798), Richard and Maria combined these personal observations with prevailing education theories. Nothing like *Practical Education* had appeared in England since Locke's *Thoughts on Education* (1693). It was an immediate sensation, attracting a wide audience. This controversial book was widely praised by some intellectuals and strongly denounced by the education establishment. *Practical Education* went into numerous editions, the last in 1822. Maria wrote over half of the material, but most of the specialized curriculum chapters came from her father.

As an educational treatise, *Practical Education* combined the best of Locke and Rousseau with scientific inquiry. It remains a key to progressive eighteenth-century educational thought. Some twentieth-century scholars view it as the most significant work on pedagogy between Locke's *Thoughts* in 1693 and Herbert Spencer's *Essay on Education* in 1861. Edgeworth accepted Locke's associationism as the explanation of how a child's mind can be formed through experientially controlled education. Of equal if not greater importance was Rousseau's influence on Edgeworth regarding the importance of childhood. This is a principle that revolutionized continental education. Edgeworth retained or modified many of Rousseau's theories. He stressed the importance of parents in ordering a child's environment, hence his clear preference for early private domestic rather than public education. He agreed that effective education must be child centered. Rousseau's stress on infancy, childhood, and adolescence as different stages in growth and development encouraged the Edgeworths to begin writing fiction addressed to different age groups.

The Edgeworths believed that learning and happiness were to go hand in hand in a child's education. Happiness in mind was both a condition and goal of a good education. This theory was based on Locke's psychology. Like him, Edgeworth appreciated the educational nature of play (Froebel later called this "insight"). Edgeworth also believed in practical education. The Edgeworths' writings also anticipated those works of Johann Pestalozzi (1746–1827) and Friedrich Froebel (1782–1852), setting the stage for a positive reception of these later theorists.[21]

Practical Education was the first basic handbook written solely for parents on how to teach according to the way children learn. It was to be followed by hundreds of similar works supporting "domestic education." *Practical Education* is crowded with simple illustrations from family experience. The book's 25 essays cover a wide field of learning. A child's "mental faculties" were discussed in: "On Attention," "Memory and Invention," "Taste and Imagination," and "Wit and Judgment."[22]

An earlier work, *The Parent's Assistant* (1796), established Maria Edgeworth as the leading writer for children in England. Until this time very few books had been written especially for the young. Their entertainment was limited to literature designed for their elders.[23] *Moral Tales* (1801) and *Popular Tales* (1804) featured short stories and novelettes for adolescents. "The Good Aunt" and "The Good French Governess," featuring model teachers, provided variations on pupil-teacher relationships and Maria's theory and practice of learning.[24]

Well into the nineteenth century, Maria continued her support of education at home by parents or a governess. Her father's influence was always present, for Maria maintained that all her educational theories came solely from him.

She never credited herself as a significant contributor to educational theory. In 1847 Maria wrote,

How can I return to speak of myself and my works? In truth I have nothing to say of them but what my dear father has said for me in his prefaces to each of them as they came out. These sufficiently explain the moral design, they require no additional explanations, and I have nothing personal to add.[25]

Her *Essays on Professional Education* (1809) offered practical advice on preparation for many professions. As late as 1825, she wrote materials designed for education at home with *Harry and Lucy Concluded; Being The Last Part of Early Lessons*. This book offered science lessons for older children. Her later works taught parents how education can neutralize individual differences, enabling children to enter many professions.[26]

To what extent did families follow the advice of these domestic educators? Among the American readers of Maria Edgeworth was Rachel Van Dyke. Her diary (1810–1815) offers a good example of how family literacy was practiced and gives a realistic picture of the American family in the early nineteenth century.

Rachel (b. 1793) was the daughter of Frederick Van Dyke (b. 1751), a New Brunswick, New Jersey, gentleman. Their household included several brothers and sisters and her cousin Betsy Magoffin, who was tutored almost daily by Rachel. Rachel's diary includes a frank account of her experiences as Betsy's tutor. Her cousin had come to live in their home after her father's death and her virtual abandonment by her mother. "Poor girl," Rachel wrote, "she has been taken about from one place to another from her infancy and no attention has been paid to her education—I will begin tomorrow and try what I can do." Rachel shared her bedroom with Betsy and acted as an important role model for her younger cousin.[27]

Even before Betsy's arrival, Rachel had formed an opinion of her cousin's educational accomplishments from a letter written to her sister. "The meaning of her (Betsy) sentences are good enough—but by the manner in which she expresses her meaning—I judge that she has not been much accustomed to letter writing." Betsy had attended school previously, but

She knows nothing about grammar or geography—I can see she has learnt her lefsons [lessons] as I did mine ... Like a parrot without understanding what I recited. She is a smart girl and tho' rather lazy (like myself) yet by proper instruction she might be made a sensible learned woman. I wish I was capable of teaching her as she ought to be taught.

Rachel constantly lamented her own poor education, which had combined instruction at home with limited school attendance. However, she had already studied chemistry, history, and Latin. Much of Rachel's time was spent alone in her room studying Virgil. This proved very frustrating. She called Latin a "provoking language" and threatened to give up its study more than once.

Each morning Rachel attended to her own self-studies and then gave Betsy her lessons in grammar, spelling, and history. "This I will try to persuade her to do every morning." It was not an easy task. Her sister Lydia laughed at Rachel's attempt at teaching Betsy. But this did not deter her: "Let her laugh I don't care— I will go on and help her but still I will instruct Betsy as long as she will attend to her studies."

The seventeen-year-old Rachel occasionally lamented that her task required too much time, trouble, and patience. Though she found Betsy an intelligent girl, Rachel understood her own limitations and hoped a better educational program could be found at a later date for her cousin.

Betsy began to respond to Rachel's daily attentions. After several months of tutoring, Rachel recorded that, "She (Betsy) is more industrious, more obliging, studies her lessons better and is as good natured as a girl need be." Rachel's tutoring method included teaching Betsy to "parse" (to explain the grammatical usage of a word), a task that proved very difficult. Through daily perseverance they seemed to achieve some success.[28] Rachel also used Betsy's facility to hear and then relate stories. This helped her teach Betsy to use better grammar and improved her vocabulary.[29]

Rachel's tutoring of her cousin was not a social anomaly. The fact that a young woman, without outside direction or support, shouldered the literacy education of a distant relative appears unusual only from a modern perspective. The extended family of early nineteenth-century America remained a highly self-reliant social unit, including within its sphere literacy education both practical and moral. Only over the next century did "schooling" assume such a specialized place in society that most parents came to believe the home could not compete with the schoolhouse.

SUNDAY SCHOOLS AND RELIGIOUS EDUCATION

Religious bodies in America continued to be closely intertwined with the rise of literacy. In addition to operating church day schools and charity schools, many religious groups established Sunday schools to provide basic literacy instruction.

The Sunday school movement was first begun in 1781 in Gloucester, England, by Robert Raikes and imported over the next 20 years to Virginia, New York, Philadelphia, and Boston in the United States. Raikes began his Sunday school for boys who worked in the local factories and thus could not attend day classes during the work week. It offered basic literacy instruction wrapped around a religious curriculum. From its humble Gloucester origins, the Sunday school movement developed into a major international institution.[30]

In 1785 a Sunday school was founded in Virginia. By 1790 the "First Day or Sunday School Society" was created in Philadelphia. There were no public schools in the city at that time. By 1800 more than 2,000 students had been admitted. Many received most if not all of their education in these schools. These

Sunday schools offered the rudiments of reading and writing to children who worked during the week and kept them off the streets on the Sabbath. Until 1815, Sunday schools were relatively few in number in America and enrolled lower-class children. Yet by 1830 they were widely available to large numbers of children from many backgrounds.[31]

Interestingly, Sunday schools operated over the protests of many churchmen who objected to the work of learning to read as a profane act on the Sabbath. But for most religious leaders the acts of saving the unconverted and teaching basic literacy were in perfect harmony. Between 1815 and 1826 interdenominational efforts among Episcopalians, Presbyterians, Methodists, Congregationalists, and Baptists founded literacy/evangelical groups that worked outside their regular church organizations. These included the American Education Society, American Home Missionary Society, American Bible Society, American Tract Society and American Sunday School Union.[32]

As was common in early American schools, these Sunday schools were divided into four grades: infant, elementary, scripture, and senior. The alphabet and words of one syllable were taught in the lowest grade. In the elementary grade students learned to spell out words of two or more syllables. The third grade was for scholars who could read, though often imperfectly. The senior grade was reserved for those who could readily read in the New Testament. An interesting report of the Sunday and Adult School Union (1818–1822) recorded the results of students from ages 17 to 78. "One person, seventy-eight years old, who did not know the alphabet on entering the school, was taught to read with facility and to write a decent hand."[33]

Sunday school groups developed their own educational materials. For beginners there were the alphabet on cards and a simple spelling book that included reading lessons, all of which were taken from the Bible. The publications of the American Tract Society and the American Sunday School Union included a system of readers that became progressively more difficult linguistically and more sophisticated in content. Like the later famous McGuffey Readers, they provided a comprehensive system of reading instruction. In addition, all these publications taught the "fear of God." It was impossible for the evangelical mind to distinguish the instruction of basic literacy and Christian character formation.[34]

Many other children and adults attended Sunday schools because no other formal schooling opportunities were available to them. Sunday schools sprang up in the new factory towns of the northeast. For example, at the Brandywine Manufacturers' Sunday School in Delaware, children of DuPont Company employees and local farmers acquired basic literacy skills and finished their education with Bible readings and lessons in the catechism of their choice. For almost the entire first half of the nineteenth century, this Sunday school each year taught about 150 students reading, writing, spelling, and religion and received a share of the Delaware State School Fund to help pay expenses. This same story was repeated again and again in other factory towns and in newly settled frontier areas.[35]

In 1791 Philadelphia's first Sunday school was created by the First Day Society, an ecumenical group of Episcopalians, Quakers, and Catholics. The group sought to counteract the disintegration of the local apprenticeship system, provide basic literacy, and remove rowdy youth from the streets of Philadelphia on Sunday. By 1800 the popularity of free charity schools reduced the society's student enrollment. The added competition of the Evangelical Sunday Schools finally forced the closing of the First Day Society's school in 1817.[36]

The Male Adult Association was formed in 1815 by an interdenominational Philadelphia group of evangelical laypeople, "to teach Adult Males to read [in order] to excite them to the study of the holy Scriptures." School was taught in rotation on Tuesday and Friday evenings to adults who were primarily "mechanics." Classes were formed based on the students' reading abilities. Adult scholars first learned basic reading from the Bible, then moved on to study the New Testament, writing, and arithmetic. In 1817 the association merged with the Philadelphia Sunday and Adult School Union, and the focus shifted to offering Sunday schools for children and adults who wished to attend.[37]

By 1824 the formation of the American Sunday School Union began the practice of separating literacy and religion, although often imperfectly. Sunday schools still taught basic literacy where no common school existed and provided religious instruction that ranged from a "common denominator" Protestantism to full-scale denominational instruction. The common schools provided basic literacy and moral education (particularly Protestant based) or character training stressing obedience, self-discipline and honesty. They often followed Sunday schools, and in many new communities common schools were organized to complement their predecessors.

The rise of the American public school has usually been portrayed as a product of the struggle by secular forces to free education from the influence of religion, to separate church from state. This modern American education truism is largely a myth. Before twentieth-century, tax-supported compulsory education, America's civil and religious leaders saw republicanism and Christianity as mutually supporting literacy through a community's schools. Ignorance was an enemy of the Republic, not sectarian morality.[38] For this reason, Protestant-based moral education was often subtly and not so subtly woven throughout the common-school curriculum. The Catholic minority had many problems with this arrangement. Catholic communities often assumed the financial burden of building and operating parochial schools.

As early as 1783 St. Mary's parish established a Catholic school in Philadelphia. Finding and keeping schoolmasters was a major problem, since no teaching sisters were in the United States at that time. German Catholics broke away from St. Mary's in 1788 and established Holy Trinity Church and school. Special emphasis was placed on the preservation of the German language and culture. By the 1850s Philadelphia established a Catholic parochial school system.[39]

New York City's first parish school was established by St. Peter's Church in 1800. Over 200 pupils were enrolled by 1806, 500 by 1810. This was followed by St. Patrick's parish school (1815), and two additional schools were founded by the Sisters of Charity during the next few years. By 1842 the State of New York was providing public funding for both Catholic, private and secular schools.[40]

Other religious orders of women also responded to the literacy needs of Catholic children. Between 1809 and 1830, the American branch of the Daughters of Charity founded by Elizabeth Bayley Seton organized 15 schools in 11 cities.

By 1818 in Boston the Ursuline sisters began a convent school that enrolled Protestant as well as Catholic children. They also staffed the first Boston parochial parish school in 1820. Because of the intense poverty of the Irish immigrant population, only three parochial schools operated throughout the 1830s and 1840s. However, Catholic Sunday schools flourished until about 1860.[41]

The publication of Catholic educational materials in the United States is almost as old as the nation itself. The implicit themes of these texts were very similar to those in public common-school texts (but with anti-Catholic invective removed). Beginning in 1785, a Philadelphia priest published *A Spelling Primer for Children with a Catholic Catechism Annexed*. But it was not until the late 1840s, when the publishing industry spread to New York City and Baltimore, that the use of Catholic primers became common in their schools.

The first Catholic literacy primers were commonly modified European texts for American audiences. There was a close parallel between common-school and Catholic primers. Both often emphasized such themes as the educational value of nature; a conservative code of behavior; diligent, honest work habits; and devotion to parents; both included stories about America's "founding fathers," encouraging the emulation of historical figures such as George Washington and Benjamin Franklin.[42]

Seen in a larger context, early Catholic education complemented the literacy programs of other American denominations. Catholics agreed with the literacy and political values implicit in common schooling, but objected to the generic Protestant anti-Catholic teachings that were carried into the common-school movement from its colonial antecedents. As a result, in major cities of the Northeast, many Catholics established a separate educational pathway to provide literacy for their children.[43]

THE AGENTS OF LITERACY

New England in the early eighteenth century remained the bedrock of American literacy. The rapid demographic and economic growth of so many towns ensured the establishment of more schools. Massachusetts had an extensive though decentralized system of public and private district schools.[44]

Warren Burton in *The District School As It Was* (1832) tells us how he acquired his basic literacy in the community school at Wilton, New Hampshire (1804–1818). At the young age of 3½, he began summer school equipped only with an "old Perry's spelling book." He was part of the sixth class with two other boys and one girl.

> He (the teacher) had nothing particularly remarkable about him to my little mind. He had his hands too full of the great things of the great scholars to take much notice of me, excepting to hear me read my Abs four times a day. This exercise he went through like a great machine, and I like a little one.

Burton's "severest duty" was "sitting still." Since, "My lesson in the Abs conveyed no ideas, excited no interest, and of course, occupied but very little of my time." After his first few weeks at "winter school," severe storms kept him at home. The little girl in his class had attended only the first three or four days of that winter term.[45]

Following the learning of lists of syllables and words, Perry's *Speller* progressed to lessons with sentences on abstract moral themes. Although the children could not understand how the lessons applied to them without help, giving such assistance scarcely ever entered the schoolmaster's head or heart. "Indeed we had no other idea of all these easy lessons, tales and fables, than that they were to be syllabled from the tongue in the task of reading."[46] It is no wonder that the writers of domestic education books could argue that the lockstep, dull recitation method used in most schools of the day could hardly motivate many children to learn anything very well.

The art of recitation and elocution practiced in the district school was considered so important to learning that teachers called upon each class to read aloud twice in the morning and twice in the afternoon. This lasted from a quarter to half an hour depending on the size of the class.[47]

Both the district school and the family worked together as the agents of literacy in rural New England. These rural areas were being incorporated into a burgeoning market economy in the early days of the Republic, and the supplementing of home schooling by the establishment of district schools paralleled the spread of that activity. There were four primary ways to attain a basic literacy education in the Upper Connecticut Valley, Vermont, and New Hampshire: through domestic education at home during childhood, through the district school system during later youth, through attending a Sunday school, or through apprenticeship education.[48]

Through 1830 the average literacy level obtained through some combination of these venues was higher than we might expect. Most children learned enough to write a simple letter. Through home, school, or apprenticeship instruction most inhabitants of these areas acquired a fairly good ability to read and understand the grammar in the annual almanac, rural newspapers, basic books like the Bible, hymns, devotional tracts, schoolbooks, and some light fiction and popular nonfiction works. The expansion of personal family libraries and newspaper readership increased this so-called print culture so that by 1810–1815 nearly three-quarters of all these families included some active readers.[49]

These regional New England literacy practices were recorded in the diaries of Elizabeth Buffum Chace and her sister Lucy Buffum Lovell (1806–1899), who lived in Smithfield, Rhode Island.

When I was two years old I began to be taken to the Quaker meeting as well as to school. ... When I was three years old I could read very well.

I remember well standing, when I was just three and a half, between the knees of a young man who was cousin of my father's and reading to a large company of Friends from the Book of Discipline of our Society, much to their amusement, no doubt, if not to their edification. Their praises of my reading rang in my ears for a long time, and I dare say made me a vain, self-conceited little thing.

At the first school in addition to being taught to read we were taught to sew. At meeting we were taught to sit still, which in moderation is no mean accomplishment.

After passing through the school for little ones, (an Infant School), we children— the children in my set in the old village—began receiving our instruction at the Academy. The public school system had not been established in Rhode Island. But our parents were a reading and thinking people, and they intended their children should be well educated.[50]

Their local school was open 52 weeks a year, with no vacations. Elizabeth and Lucy were made to recite from *Murray's Grammar* (a popular text) over and over again before making any practical application of it by analogy or "parsing" a sentence (analyzing its grammar). Suddenly, when Elizabeth was age 12, the schoolmaster handed her a book and told her to study a passage for a parsing lesson. Of course Elizabeth had no idea how to apply any rules of grammar. Luckily for her knuckles, at recess one of the older students gave her a quick peer tutoring lesson on grammar applications.

Still for that time it was a good school, for we had to work out our own salvation by hard study. The master carried all the time in his hand, a ruler with a leather strap nailed over each end. If he caught an eye wandering from the book or if he saw signs of restlessness, or heard a whisper, he gave the offender a smart blow.

Our curriculum was narrow but we made good readers and spellers, and those of us who had the gift, good writers, and we were well grounded in grammar.[51]

Elizabeth and Lucy also went to an evening writing school that was operated by two young brothers who lived in their village. About 1825 a new schoolmaster, George D. Prentice, a Brown University graduate, began teaching in their day school. (Prentice would later become the editor of the *Louisville Courier Journal*.) Until then the sisters had read books obtained only from their own family library and the small village library. This now changed for the better. Every other week their new teacher walked to Providence and obtained books from the Brown University Library and distributed them to his students. Thus Elizabeth and Lucy were given their first opportunity to read the Waverly novels, the works of James Fenimore Cooper, and the poetry of Byron and Scott. This exposure to new kinds of knowledge led these sisters and other children of her generation to accept the new ideas and material changes of the early Industrial Revolution more rapidly and to participate with a growing fascination in important issues of their contemporary world. As an adult Elizabeth became part of the anti-slavery movement.[52]

The evidence is clear that many children in early nineteenth-century New England attended some sort of school well before the area became heavily urbanized or industrialized and even before the existence of school systems. In Massachusetts many towns provided some form of public or private schooling. However, the state's law of 1789 insisted that a child be able to read and write before enrolling in a grammar school. This presumed that the parents would provide these basic literacy skills through domestic education or some type of primary school. A heated political debate occurred in Boston, where the town financed the grammar schools but not the primary schools. Opponents of public primary schools argued that parents should continue to provide the rudiments of literacy at home.[53]

Lucy Larcom (1824–1893) grew up in Charleston, near Boston. She started attending "school" at age two, "as other children about us did," kept by a neighbor everyone called "Aunt Hannah." Her primary school was conducted in her kitchen or sitting room "as best suited her convenience." Lucy learned her "letters" standing at Aunt Hannah's knee while she pointed them out in the spelling book with a pin. She also taught Lucy to read a few passages from the Bible; "whenever I read them now (it does) not fail to bring before me a vision of Aunt Hannah's somewhat sternly smiling lips, with her spectacles just above them, far down on her nose, encouraging me to pronounce the hard words. I think she tried to choose for me the least difficult verses."[54]

As a Boston upper-class child, Elizabeth Rogers Mason Cabot kept a diary (beginning in 1844) that recorded a combination of education at home and through private schools. Elizabeth began her education with a teacher who visited her at home. She then attended a small class at her friend Mary Quincey's home taught by a Miss Watson, who was technically unqualified but forced to teach by the need to earn money in widowhood.[55]

The education of Charles Eliot Norton (1827–1908), whose family was an inheritor of Boston's Puritan heritage, provides another example of the common blending of domestic education and schooling. His mother Catherine took charge of Charlie's education as well as that of his older sisters, Louise and Jane. Since Charlie could not write books like his father Andrew, a Harvard professor, his sisters helped him paste little pictures on blank pages and sew them together. He was reading and probably writing before the age of four. Charlie read Maria Edgeworth's *Harry and Lucy* and *The Little Merchants*. The latter was a good book for a Boston boy whose family had been so closely tied to world trade.[56]

Norton's first writing lessons were preparing letters to his mother, who gently amended his lapses. Catherine taught all her children to admire the written word.[57] At the age of four Norton was sent to a "woman's school" (probably a dame school). Then by age six Charlie began attending a series of grammar schools to learn Latin, Greek, math, and a little geography and history. His father also tutored him in Greek and Latin. However, many other classes also took place at home.

Charlie's sisters, who were totally excluded from his classical grammar schools, received all their education at home. Their father taught them Latin; a friend, Italian; and a governess, French. Charlie also learned French, Italian, and German while sitting in with his sisters' governess as she taught a little class of nine neighborhood children. His sister Jane also studied Dante and other classical literature with Henry Longfellow. To complete their education, all the children were given liberal access to the literary classics and children's literature in their father's extensive home library. By age 18 Norton was admitted to Harvard.[58]

However, critics of that time charged that the many poor children never received an adequate education because their parents could not afford private tuition, lacked basic literacy skills themselves, or were just negligent in their supposed role as domestic educators. The literacy debate in early nineteenth-century Boston was really over who should finance these schools, rather than over the educational needs of young children. Finally, in 1818 the city of Boston assumed the financial responsibility for providing basic literacy through primary schools for children aged four to six.[59]

When a new form of education, the infant school, arrived in early nineteenth-century New England, it focused much attention on the importance of early literacy practices. The infant school movement began in the British Isles and was initially intended to help poor children aged between two and four with their literacy education, an early version of "Head Start." Infant schools became popular among the middle class as well. Robert Owen opened the first infant school at New Lanark, Scotland, in 1816. The schools rapidly spread throughout England, Scotland, and Ireland and first came to America in 1827, at Hartford, Connecticut. They spread quickly throughout the Northeast.[60] Some estimates are that by the 1830s and 1840s as many as 40 percent of three-year-olds in Massachusetts may have been enrolled in these infant literacy schools.[61]

Opinion was divided on teaching the very young to read. Robert Owen at first thought that books should be entirely excluded from the infant schools. However, other educational leaders, such as Samuel Wilderspin, and pressure from parents forced Owen to compromise his position.

The rapid rise of the infant-school literacy phenomenon bordered on becoming a fad. Popular publications such as the *Ladies Magazine* and many local newspapers endorsed the movement. It seemed that anyone could acquire a published infant-school manual and set up his or her own home school with no questions asked. Again and again we will see how easy it was throughout the nineteenth century to declare oneself a "teacher" or "tutor" or "governess" and establish a "school" or an "academy," either in one's home or in a nearby rented building. Since private education was unregulated and the need for childhood literacy was so great, it was easy to acquire students.

In this time period, as in early colonial times, it was quite normal for many young children to receive early literacy instruction at home. Opposition to infant-school literacy arose over a number of social and educational issues. Such leading domestic education experts as Lydia Sigourney and Herman Humphrey denounced the infant schools for not supporting childhood education at home and argued that early intellectual training was unsafe. Such prominent nineteenth-century educational thinkers as Johann Pestalozzi and Johann Friedrich Herbart argued against trying to speed up a child's intellectual development and favored the home for forming a child's educational foundation. They argued that a child's intellect should not be overstimulated before the full physical development of the mind and body.[62]

Other educators took up these warnings partly as a reaction to the growing popularity of the infant-school phenomenon. In 1833 Amariah Brigham, a physician, warned parents "that efforts to develop the minds of young children are frequently injurious; and from instances of disease in children I have witnessed, I am forced to believe that the danger is indeed great." Brigham warned that "early mental excitement" before age six or seven could lead to insanity for the child.[63]

Beginning in the 1830s until 1920, the term "precocity" was applied to using accelerated learning programs with younger children. The effort to persuade parents to abandon infant "precocity" was felt only gradually by the infant schools. However, by the 1860s the transition was completed. Almost no younger children attended these schools; rather, the new kindergarten movement now directed slightly older children into learning-readiness activities and did not attempt to teach them how to read.[64]

Elizabeth Palmer Peabody (1804–1894), founder of the first English-language kindergarten, was influenced by the domestic education practices of her parents. Both mother and father undertook her education at home and later in her mother's school. Elizabeth's father taught her Latin, Greek, French, Italian, and German. Later she published translations in most of these languages and went on to study Polish, Icelandic, and Sanskrit.[65]

Mrs. Peabody "was the ardent practitioner and theorist of the family." She enjoyed teaching and devised a curriculum with her husband that molded her children into well-educated adults. The basis of her educational scheme was "predominately [sic] moral—to fill my mind with images of kind, heroic and thoroughly high-principled people." Elizabeth's mother published two books on the "moral posture" of a good teacher. She trained her daughter to regard a good teacher as "the highest and proper activity of every American woman who loved her country—moral education became to my mind the essence of all education." The Peabodys' philosophy showed the deep influence of the "fireside education" movement, which put moral education at center stage and academic training second.[66]

Elizabeth's curriculum was rigorous and broad. Her parents, in addition to foreign-language instruction, taught her from Murray's English *Grammar*, Blair's *Rhetoric*, and Harme's *Elements of Criticism*. She read Herbert Spencer, Oliver Goldsmith's histories of England, Greece, and Rome, the *Iliad*, the

Odyssey, Fasso's *Jerusalem*, the writings of Maria Edgeworth on domestic education, and many works in the sciences, including those of Charles Darwin.[67]

Before the age of 16, Elizabeth was teaching in her mother's school. Afterward she became the governess of a Maine family. By 1825 Elizabeth became a member of the "transcendental movement" in education, becoming the friend or acquaintance of many great nineteenth-century New England figures, including Ralph Waldo Emerson and Horace Mann.

Emerson, though an ardent supporter of education, was biting in his criticism of contemporary educational institutions. Instead, he supported the "natural" education of the family. "The whole theory of the school is on the nurse's or mother's knee. The child is as hot to learn as the mother is to impart. There is mutual delight." Emerson condemned across the board any effort to replace the "natural" family school with mass school systems to train people cheaply and with military efficiency. "Our modes of education aim to expedite, to save labor; to do for the masses what cannot be done reverently, one by one: say rather, the whole world is needed for the tuition of each pupil." His only remedy for these "quack" practices was "to import into education the wisdom of life. Leave this military hurry and adopt the pace of nature. Her secret is patience." Emerson's journals are an eloquent nineteenth-century testimony to the continuing vitality of the Puritan and Benjamin Franklin traditions of self-education that influenced Elizabeth Peabody and can still be felt throughout America today.[68]

In 1834 Peabody began teaching Latin, mathematics, and geography at the Temple School in Boston. Bronson Alcott, a friend of Emerson, opened this innovative school with about 30 pupils. At that time Alcott was a leading educator in the domestic education movement rooted in Pestalozzi's methods. His support of the domestic education was highlighted in the 1829 article "Maternal Instruction" in the *American Journal of Education*. As Alcott's co-worker, Elizabeth Peabody was deeply influenced by his philosophy in her later educational activities. In 1860 Elizabeth and her sister opened the first American kindergarten based on the concepts of Friedrich Froebel. Until her death in 1894, the educational philosophy of the domestic-education movement appeared in her books, articles, and lectures. Her theories and teaching methods became a permanent part of modern educational practice.[69]

The Temple School founded by Bronson Alcott was but one example of the *academy*, a quintessential American institution that overlapped both the primary schools, at one end of the educational ladder, and the college, at the other. Until eclipsed by the rise of the public high school in the 1880s, the academy as an important literacy-education experiment came in many different shapes, sizes, and forms.[70] Alcott was one of its leading proponents.

Bronson Alcott (1799–1888), the son of a mechanic-farmer, was born in western Connecticut. His mother taught him to read by tracing letters with a stick on their kitchen floor. Though Alcott went to a one-room school that he despised, he was largely self-educated. With his cousin William, he collected a library composed of classics such as *Pilgrim's Progress, Paradise Lost,* and *Robinson Cru-*

soe. Following his mother's example, Bronson started a daily journal. By the end of his life Bronson Alcott had written 61 volumes.[71]

Bronson tried a number of different professions. For five years he was a peddler in Virginia and the Carolinas; then, during the winter of 1823–24, he embarked on a career as an education entrepreneur by becoming a schoolmaster in Cheshire, Connecticut. Bronson called his fee-based school "The Cheshire Pestalozzian School." Combining his knowledge of the Swiss educator with other educational theories and the transcendental philosophy, Bronson Alcott became a truly original educational thinker.

In his one-room school he introduced a startling variety of curricular innovations. At his own expense he purchased a student library of over one hundred books. Children no longer sat on a long bench but at individual desks. He decorated the schoolroom with flowers and pine boughs. He taught children geography by making a map of the yard outside the school. Reading was no longer taught by the rote memorization of phonics, but by relating pictures to words; arithmetic by assembling beans and blocks of wood. The outward experimental nature of the school attracted educators who came to see it. One even proclaimed it "the best common school in the state—probably in the United States."

But problems were brewing, since Bronson also taught his students the transcendental belief in individual communion between man and the divine as the only true religious experience. True religion must be an experience unique to each individual. Parents began raising objections to the strange new school's teaching methods and then to his subversive doctrines, which shunned connections with organized religious groups.

Soon parental discontent was very open, and Alcott's pupils were sent to other competing community schools. Over the next few years Alcott moved from school to school in Boston and Philadelphia, repeating this same failing educational formula again and again.[72]

However, Bronson's most interesting educational experiment was conducted on his two daughters, Anna and Louisa. For four years he kept a daily journal that eventually totaled 2,500 pages on their home-schooling development. Louisa and her sister received an excellent tutorial education from their parents and friends. Sophia Hawthorne taught Louisa her alphabet. Henry David Thoreau tutored her in botany. The girls read Shakespeare, Plato, and Thucydides as well as popular authors such as Dickens and Scott. Emerson gave Louisa access to his library, and she made good use of it. All of this was an excellent preparation for Louisa May Alcott's later career as a successful writer.[73]

With Elizabeth Peabody as his assistant, Alcott's most famous academy, the Temple School, started on September 22, 1834. From 20 to 30 children came that first day. They were all under 10 years of age except for a few older girls. Alcott put into practice all of his educational theories in attractive and artistic surroundings. The number of students soon increased to 40.

Discipline was very strict, but reading and spelling were taught with much active learning. The children were taught to write a daily journal to document spiritual happiness. Peabody explained that Alcott considered "early education as a leading of the young mind to self-education. He leads them, in the first place, to the contemplation of spirit as it unveils itself within themselves."[74]

By the fall of 1836 even Elizabeth Peabody was becoming disillusioned with Bronson's constant insistence on the inherent "saintliness of children." But the major cause of the failure of Temple School was the publication of Bronson's *Conversations with Children on the Gospels* (1837). The Boston newspapers attacked both the sexual aspects of *Conversations* and its blasphemy of daring to treat Jesus as a human being. The following year, the withdrawal of financial support forced the school into Bronson's home. When in June 1839 he admitted Susan Robinson, a black child, all except one parent withdrew their children, finally closing the academy and ending Alcott's work as a schoolmaster.[75]

But as agents of literacy, the private academies run by Bronson Alcott and legions of other educational entrepreneurs were abundantly spread across the educational landscape of the Northeast. Harriot K. Hunt offers us in her *Glances and Glimpses* (1856) the fascinating story of how these academies functioned in Boston.

Harriot (born 1805) was first taught at home by her mother. "We went (Harriot and a younger sister), while yet quite young, to a school kept by Misses Hannah and Elizabeth Brown. ... Next went to Mrs. Carter (1810). ... [It] was a private school: we never attended the public schools; they were not then the carefully modelled institutions they now are."[76]

As a young adult Hunt set up her own first school in April, 1827. "The felt necessities of my soul urged me to open for myself some path of usefulness. As our house was large for so small a family, my parents gave me a pleasant chamber overlooking the broad blue ocean, and there I opened a school and became a teacher."[77]

Her father's ill health and problems with the family business motivated Harriot to establish her own academy. "The pleasant room was soon alive with happy childhood, and I tried to profit by the wise tact that had led me along, in leading others. The ninth of April, 1827, found me in my schoolroom with eight pupils, and when the following October came, I had twenty-three."[78]

The academy's success caused Harriot to compare her career as an educator to the more typical life of her contemporaries.

Many of my former schoolmates at this time, had no other employment than muslin work (i.e., sewing at home). Of course, we were still on visiting terms, though I had lost some caste by becoming useful. I was struck at an early period, by the selfish, contemptible indolence they indulged in, as by the lamentable ennui it occasioned. ... A chasm had yawned between our friendships,—for I was at work—they were at play. Our lives had nothing in common. My school was a grand use to me, for it not only called out gratitude to my parents, for the advantage they had given me, but also for the delight, and enthusiasm with which I pursued the occupation. I was an enigma to those who had once been school girls with me. They knew not the magic of usefulness.[79]

After the death of her father, Harriot built a schoolhouse in the garden so that the family might be able to rent their home. In 1833 she engaged a friend and neighbor to take over her school for six months. Shortly thereafter, Harriot left her schoolmistress days behind, and changed careers to become a doctor.[80] Harriot's academy was most typical for this time period, born out of financial necessity and lasting only a short period of time.

Elizabeth Peabody, whose career we previously traced, was not the only member of her family who contributed to the development of education. Her sister Mary, after a long secret courtship, married Horace Mann. Mary supported her husband's quest for public education, but educated their children—Horace, Jr., George, and Benjamin—at home. Mary's methods of tutoring were innovative but not always successful. In the hope of helping Benjamin become bilingual, she and her husband tried speaking only in French to him. The boy's speech became such a muddle that she abandoned the attempt.[81]

Mary also demonstrated her scholarly concern for improved early childhood education in the translation of "Princes in France: Their Education and Teachers" (1880). This article discussed the strengths and weaknesses of the seventeenth-century tutorial education of the princes of France. Mary Mann's commitment to the common school movement did not prevent her personal practice and study of domestic education.[82]

Horace Mann (1796–1859), through his development of the common-school model, inaugurated a new era in American education and the history of literacy. A native of Franklin, Massachusetts, up to age 17 Mann was educated primarily at home and in church, as well as through intermittent schooling, occasional tutoring, and his own systematic self-study in the town library. Upon his graduation as valedictorian from Brown University (1819), Mann served as a legal apprentice and then returned to Brown for several years as a tutor in Latin and Greek. Upon his admission to the bar (1823), he developed a successful law practice before winning a seat in the state legislature. He served in the house from 1827 to 1833, then was elected to the senate in 1834. As president of that body, he helped push through a bill to establish a state board of education (1837). He then agreed to be appointed its secretary, the one paid office established by the legislature. For the next 12 years (1837–48) Horace Mann conducted a local and national campaign to gain popular support for nonsectarian education. He articulated a particularly American theory of education—that the bedrock of the republic was its literate masses.[83]

Education then, beyond all other devices of human origin, is a great equalizer of the conditions of men—the balance wheel of the social machinery. ... The greatest of all the arts in political economy is to change a consumer into a producer ... and this to be directly obtained by increasing his intelligence. For mere delving an ignorant man is but little better than a swine, whom he so much resembles in his appetites, and surpasses in his powerful mischief.[84]

As secretary of the board he conducted an intensive study of education and even travelled to Europe (1843) to conduct a five-month survey of European educational conditions. The components of his educational revolution in Massachusetts included establishing in 1839 the first American teachers' college, then termed a "normal school"; making six months the minimum duration of the school year; enforcing the state's high-school law so that the number of high schools for boys and girls rose from 18 in 1840 to over 100 in 1860; and contributing to the enactment of a state truancy law (1852) that had teeth.

Yet it is important to understand that Mann never recommended mandatory compulsory school attendance for all children. His goal was to require children to attend either regularly or not at all. Mann wished to popularize school attendance among parents, but not to compel all to attend. It would be almost another 70 years until mandatory, compulsory public-school attendance would gain enough public support to be enacted in every state. The path to literacy for many Americans would still remain a long road filled with many detours.[85]

Between 1800 and 1860 literacy instruction for most children in the northeastern states was left to the private initiative of parents or benevolent institutions. These conditions denied significant literacy educational opportunities to many children even though most of the northern states had, at least on paper, some sort of public primary school system.[86]

Sarah Ann Remington lived in the Genesee Valley in rural western New York. After she married Benjamin (1803–1888), Sarah raised three children—Jeremiah, Edwin, and Margaret. Like many other women in rural New York, she taught all three of her children the fundamentals of literacy. Later, in the 1850s, her eldest son Jeremiah attended Union College in Schenectady, New York.[87] For that time the seemingly big leap from the family schoolroom to the college classroom was not all that uncommon.

James Fenimore Cooper (1789–1851) had a similar, though more advanced, domestic educational experience. In 1800, after attending the village school, Cooper was sent to live with a private tutor in Albany, New York. For two years he was tutored in the rector's household of St. Peter's Church. Shortly thereafter, at age 14, Cooper entered Yale University.[88]

The career of Abiah Warren Hiller (1817–1863) illustrates the transition of literacy from a private to a more institutionalized process. Abiah was born in Jeffrey, New Hampshire. After attending her village school, she went to Chesterfield Academy, one of only 12 private academies in that state. In her late teens, Abiah began teaching in the local common schools, sometimes living at home but also, while teaching in other districts, frequently boarding in her students' homes. During the winter of 1838–39 she had a large class that included several older students. One was William Hiller, age 20, a laborer who was also learning to become a carpenter.[89]

After teaching in New York City in the late winter of 1840, Hiller moved to McDonough, a village with a population of around 1,500 in upstate New York, to which her parents had moved. With her father's help, she converted a sitting room in her parents' home into a classroom and opened her own academy. Abiah was a successful educational entrepreneur. Her school was so popular that, in a role reversal, her students awarded their teacher a certificate of merit.

We the undersigned tender our unfeigned thanks to you, for the uniform kindness, and attention with which you have treated us, and would also say that we are well satisfied with your school, and believe you have spared no exertions on your part for the promotion of our education.

Nine students signed this certificate, among them her carpenter student William Hiller. He had returned to his home town of McDonough and promptly enrolled in Abiah's school.[90]

In 1842, after the death of her father, she married her 23-year-old student William. Abiah was then age 25. She soon gave birth to two daughters, Phebe Anna (1843) and Josephine (1845).

Abiah, in 1848, prepared to move to Richmond, Virginia. She rented out her home and classroom rather than selling them. The local superintendent of common schools wrote a glowing letter saying her teaching had "ever been popular and satisfactory to her patrons" and commending her as a model teacher, noting that "most of our female and some of our male teachers have fitted themselves for teaching under her tuition." Rare praise for an agent of literacy.[91]

But by 1849 Abiah had returned to McDonough without her husband. (He was traveling to San Francisco via Cape Horn as a "49er" participating with many others in the California gold rush.) Abiah reopened her school. By the fall of 1850 she had enrolled 20 children and noted that "more are coming, so I have business enough for the present."

Then on March 26, 1851, tragedy struck, as Abiah's home and school burned down. Successful entrepreneur that she was, Abiah immediately rebuilt a bigger classroom. The house was 28 feet square with 18-foot rafters. Her schoolroom was 16 feet by 20 feet, with an eight-foot ceiling. The blackboard in the classroom bore her motto on its border, the byword of Abiah's students for decades to come: "What Man has done, Man may do."[92]

Abiah distributed broadsides for her new "Select School" throughout McDonough (see Figure 4.1). It advertised her new house and the school it housed as offering "Extra Studies" ... "taught on reasonable terms." She also encouraged boarding students to room with her as a supplement to the student's tuition. Abiah soon had 10 students attending her classes. Later both of her daughters became public school teachers. Abiah continued to operate a school throughout the 1850s; she died of diphtheria in 1863, at age 58.[93]

In the urban area of New York City around 1820, nearly half of all children were illiterate, because their parents were too poor to pay school fees for private education, too proud to accept charity through church-affiliated charity schools, or too indifferent. Private tutors and independent teachers who ran "pay schools" were the most pervasive forms of literacy education. Some of these teachers reduced their fees for poor students.[94]

Literacy actually began to shrink in the early 1800s as New York became more heterogeneous, immigration swelled, and poverty grew because of a labor surplus. The rate of church-going among many slum dwellers was low. The ap-

Figure 4.1
Broadside for Abiah Hiller's School

SELECT SCHOOL!

Mrs. A. S. Hiller

Respectfully informs the citizens of McDonough, that she will commence School in her new house, near McDonough Village, on Monday, Sept.   185 , where she will teach the branches usually taught in similar schools.

Terms : From $1,50 to $3,00 per quarter, (of 12 weeks each.)

EXTRA STUDIES.

Drawing and Painting with water colors, Theorem Painting, Map Drawing, Card Drawing, Wax work, &c., &c., taught on reasonable terms.

Board can be obtained in the family of the teacher on reasonable terms ; also, those wishing to board themselves can be accommodated, for a small compensation per week.

Thankful for past favors, the teacher humbly solicits a continuance of public patronage.

June 21, 1851.

Source: Northwest Museum of Arts & Culture/Eastern Washington State Historical Society, Spokane, Washington Dunning Collection.

prenticeship system declined with the growth of mass production stemming from the early Industrial Revolution. In response to this crisis Thomas Eddy, a Quaker, in 1805 spearheaded the founding of the Free School Society to provide basic literacy education for the churchless poor. This was almost immediately expanded to include all poor children since the denominational charity schools were swamped by applicants. The first Free Society school opened in 1806. Later with the aid of both city and state funds, a large school designed to use a monitorial instruction program was finished in 1809 and another opened in 1811.[95]

The steady demand for increased literacy in early nineteenth-century New York City coincided with the introduction of the British monitorial system, in which a few adult teachers supervised student "monitors" (peer-tutors) in teaching large numbers of other children. Here was a cheap teaching method to meet the demands of mass urban literacy.

The monitorial school had its origins in the work of Andrew Bell and Joseph Lancaster.[96] An English schoolteacher, Andrew Bell (1753–1832), while superintendent of a school in Madras, India, designed a system of tutoring with an older boy teaching an entire class using the aid of younger assistants (monitors).[97]

Almost simultaneously the schoolmaster Joseph Lancaster (1778–1838) opened a small grammar school in England (January 1, 1798). He was such an excellent teacher that his success nearly overwhelmed him. By June of 1801 he was teaching 350 boys in an enlarged school. Lancaster found himself with too many pupils and little money to hire assistants. The idea of student monitors came to him. Lancaster thought he had made one of the most "useful discoveries" in the history of civilization.[98]

Lancaster soon published *Improvements in Education As It Respects the Industrious Classes of the Community* (1803), which gave a detailed description of how to operate a monitorial school using student tutors. Both Bell and Lancaster later became very contentious over the origin of "their" idea. Since Lancaster was the first to outline his program with *Improvements in Education*, he became the far better known advocate of the monitorial method.[99]

The concept of the monitorial school movement came into existence because of continued widespread opposition to publicly funded education for the poor. To cope with the burgeoning population of nineteenth-century England, the charity schools sought a cheap and efficient educational system that could enroll large numbers of children.[100]

Lancaster's system of monitors had 1,000 students taught by one adult teacher. It featured an elaborate set of rules, routines, and methods for tutoring. Students sat in neat symmetrical rows in a huge classroom. Teaching was done mechanically and with precision. The teacher drilled older children; the older children taught groups of younger children; they in turn taught still younger ones. This ripple effect greatly enhanced the effort of the master (teacher). Lancaster developed for the tutors manuals of prescribed teaching procedures that clearly outlined and systematized every aspect of the instructional process.

Lancaster's system featured economy of expense and efficiency of instruction. It disciplined by routine, motivated through competition. "I have ever found, the surest way to cure a mischievous boy was to make him a monitor. I never knew anything succeed much better, if as well."[101]

Unlike a graded system, students were promoted to a new group whenever they had demonstrated their competence. Students of 10 to 12 worked around a monitor. When one failed, the next child was given a chance to answer and move to a higher position. At the heart of this curriculum was moral discipline that inculcated values of obedience, subordination, promptness, and regularity. Individualized instruction made the system function. Instead of traditional schoolroom recitations and birch-enforced authority, Lancaster's student tutors aimed at internalized discipline through proper motivation.[102]

The Lancastrian system has been called "the most widespread and successful educational reform in the Western world during the first thirty years of the nineteenth century."[103] It was a basic tutorial method applied to classroom instruction. Its success was based upon increased motivation and competition, which replaced cruel corporal punishment. "A child could proceed at his or her own rate in each subject."[104] Monitorial education relied on many concepts developed by earlier tutor-philosophers.

Children felt comfortable as "monitors." Many had already acted as peer tutors at home for their brothers and sisters. The "monitorial school movement" became an outgrowth of the "domestic education movement" as a form of mass education in basic skills using peer tutors of small groups, rather than teacher-conducted classrooms.

Because a large number of students were needed to make a Lancasterian school "cost effective," the system was confined largely to cities.[105] "The speed and breadth of its adoption in American cities was remarkable."[106] Starting with the Free School Society of New York City, other cities followed: Philadelphia, through the Association of Friends for the Instruction of the Poor, 1808; Albany, New York, 1810; by 1817 the North Carolina legislature had recommended the system statewide. Monitorial schools were formed throughout New York State, Connecticut, Pennsylvania, Maryland, Virginia, Ohio, and Kentucky. Joseph Lancaster rode the crest of his success. In 1818 he came to America and lectured across the country.[107]

One of the most unexpected legacies of these tutor-driven schools was that many provided the basis for later urban public school systems. The monitorial schools were one of the origins of the free public school. The New York City Board of Education (est. 1842) absorbed monitorial schools of the Free School Society in 1853. A similar process occurred in Philadelphia, Baltimore, and Schenectady.[108] As we shall see later, the use of student tutors would prove useful on the American frontier. A reliance on children teaching children in one-room schoolhouses as a supplement to direct teacher instruction persisted into the twentieth century.[109]

LITERACY TOOLS AND METHODS

By the early 1800s the teaching of reading had evolved from using the horn-book and primer of colonial days to using a rising tide of publications called spellers and readers. It is important to understand that these new "spelling" books' primary purpose was to teach children how to read. Teaching spelling was only a secondary consideration. The so-called spelling books were given that title, because spelling had long been used as the chief method to teach reading. Children were taught to spell words out and then to pronounce them. This was then called the "pronouncing form" or "alphabet method." Only after 1820 were both the "whole word" method and the "phonetic" method suggested as alternative teaching remedies for the failings of the alphabet method.[110]

Noah Webster's *The American Spelling Book* (1783) became a rip-roaring best-seller reaching a total distribution of 24 million copies. The royalties from this book alone (only a cent a book) provided Noah with enough support to write his famous dictionary (1828).[111]

In 1778 Noah Webster graduated from Yale College intending to become a lawyer. Because of the depressed economy following the Revolutionary War, he turned to teaching in two Connecticut grammar schools. His success as a teacher led Webster to open his own private academy in Sharon by placing the following newspaper advertisement:

The subscriber, desirous of promoting Education, so essential to the interest of a free people, proposes immediately to open a school at Sharon, in which young Gentlemen and Ladies may be instructed in Reading, Writing, Mathematicks, the English Language, and if desired, the Latin and Greek Languages—in Geography, Vocal Music, &c. at the moderate price of Six Dollars and two thirds per quarter per Scholar. The strictest attention will be paid to the studies, the manners and the morals of youth, by the public's very humble servant,
    NOAH WEBSTER, Jun
Sharon, June 1, 1781

His academy opened the following month with students from some of the town's leading families.[112]

Webster closed this academy after only eight days. He then traveled to Goshen, New York, where he opened a "classical school." While thus engaged, Webster began to compile his speller, which he sought to make a "tool in America's struggle for cultural independence from Great Britain." As a young teacher, Webster became aware that all the educational primers in use were still British. His speller was written by an American, in the new American Republic freed from tyranny and dependence upon Europe. Webster's speller was to promote what he later called a "federal language," to counter that period's significant variations in English among the regions of the United States.[113]

Webster actually published three books: a speller, a grammar, and a reader. Only his *American Spelling Book*, which became popularly known as the "blueback speller," was to become a success—the most widely sold book in nineteenth-century America. The speller was not a breakthrough book, but largely an improvement on Thomas Dilworth's *A New Guide to the English Tongue* (1747), the most popular spelling book in the colonies, with over 40 editions by 1785. Webster's key improvements were a system of points to indicate correct pronunciation and as complete a list of polysyllabic words as could be found.[114]

As already mentioned, Webster and his imitators taught children to read by an extremely conservative technique: the "pronouncing-form method." Sometimes all the children in a one-room school would go through an oral exercise of sing-song drills, such as spelling a group of words, listing state capitals, or reciting the multiplication tables. Sometimes small groups would recite together, or one student would engage in a question-and-answer drill with the teacher. In between these teacher-led instructional processes was a good deal of peer or cross-age tutoring. In most parts of the young United States, rural one-room schools, with two- to three-month winter and summer terms, typically included 40 to 60 boys and girls from 5 to 18 years of age.[115]

Webster's old "blue-back speller," a book of 158 pages, achieved such fame that when he published his first dictionary (1828), it became an instant success, since most of those who now admired the dictionary had learned to read from the speller. Webster became a most beloved patriot author and a leading figure in American education as he wrote a series of other textbooks.[116]

WOMEN'S LITERACY VERSUS THE "CULT OF DOMESTICITY"

By the 1840s basic literacy was virtually universal among New England men and women. This is in sharp contrast to 60 years earlier, when only about half of all New England women could sign their names. A significant evolution in women's literacy began to increase opportunities for women both to learn and to use their literacy skills in teaching careers.[117]

In the half-century after the American Revolution, the best-educated women were either self-taught or, as we have seen, tutored at home by teachers or relatives. Although institutions offering secondary education for girls were established, many were temporary, underfinanced, haphazard ventures that catered more to society's demands for an "ornamental education" than to a more useful basic literacy. A study of one hundred New England middle- to upper-middle-class women's diaries, memoirs, and letters tells us how the dominant educational philosophy of that day, the "cult of domesticity," argued that women should be trained to know their "stations" as daughter, sister, wife, or mother. A strong prejudice persisted against "learned women."[118]

As a result, absurd arguments persisted that denied many women even a basic literacy education. When women were first taught writing, opposition arose in many communities on the grounds that a woman would forge her father's or husband's name if she learned to read and write. Learning geography was also opposed, since it would make a woman dissatisfied with her home and desirous of travel! The clergy prophesied "the dissolution of all family bonds" when in 1829 New York first publicly examined a girl in geometry.[119]

Even as late as 1848, when the first woman dared to present herself for admission to the Harvard medical course, she was rejected. One college president wrote in 1855 after the Regents of the State of New York chartered the first woman's college (Troy Female Seminary), "the idea of giving women a man's education is too ridiculous to appear credible." A professor at a well-known eastern college also added, "to my mind this borders on the vulgar."[120]

Luckily, there were notable exceptions to this trend. When Boston established public primary schools after 1818, they were open from their inception to both girls and boys. Built into this system were single-gender schools, with six grammar schools solely for boys and five exclusively for girls. However, it is estimated that Boston's public schools educated only about 55 percent of the city's school-age population (1845).[121]

Across New England, in Connecticut, New Hampshire, Maine, and Massachusetts, female academies provided girls' secondary education, but academies for boys also admitted girls. These schools usually segregated girls' instruction by teaching them in a separate classroom, in another part of a shared classroom, during different school hours, or during a summer-school program. Unfortunately we have seen how ephemeral these learning establishments were, often lasting only as long as a teacher's need for money and/or his or her ability to attract local students.[122]

American popular opinion regarding the utility of women's literacy shifted gradually, so that by mid-century a consensus in its favor seems to have emerged. As summer schools opened for more girls with a curriculum that included both reading and writing, basic literacy came within the grasp of more women, but only if they persisted in seeking it.

A good example of the fractured literacy opportunities that society offered girls was recorded in the 1828 diary of Lavinia Bailey Kelly, who was born in 1818 at Northwood, New Hampshire.

The first school that I attended was kept by Miss Mary Frost of Andover, Mass. . . . in the summer of 1822. In the summer of the following years I attended school kept by Miss Frost, 1823, Miss Matilda Prentice 1824, Miss Martha Mead, 1825, Miss Prentice 1826, Miss Harriet Nealy 1827. In the winters I never attended school. In the spring of this year (1828) I was at Warner, and attended a school kept by Miss Sally Lyman about a fortnight.

Lavinia studied geography, writing, learning to work lace, and other female "accomplishments" at these schools.[123]

Almost all female schools punctuated their education for women with these so-called accomplishments, which were designed to enable girls to attract men, gain husbands, maintain homes, and manage families. An innovative nineteenth-century educator, Emma Willard, strongly objected to the existing conditions of women's education. She established the Troy Female Seminary (1821) in Troy,

New York, as the first U.S. college-level institution for women. Willard protested that existing schools were often unequipped, poorly staffed, and transitory, with an unstandardized curriculum. She further objected that the school's directors usually devised their curricula on the basis of what would enlarge tuition receipts, which frequently meant concentrating on "accomplishments." Willard sent to Governor De Witt Clinton of New York *A Plan for Improving Female Education* (1819), which ultimately led to the historic chartering of her college. Willard was a staunch advocate of providing women instruction in subjects such as mathematics, the sciences, and philosophy, from which they traditionally had been excluded.[124]

The schools and academies begun in the first half of the nineteenth century to educate girls exclusively were almost always conducted by women. Schoolteaching was one of the few careers outside the home that was considered socially acceptable for gentlewomen. Teaching was often an essential means of support for unmarried women in America and England. Young women could find four different types of teaching jobs: summer-school teacher, a position at a private academy, a governess for an individual family, or an instructress in an early town elementary school.[125]

A study of female employment in Massachusetts education from 1834 to 1860 shows that approximately one out of five white women in the state were employed as schoolteachers at some time. Most women teachers at best had received a common-school education or had a domestic education experience. Perhaps, by 1860, about one new teacher in six had been prepared through a normal school or teachers' college.

For this reason women were usually only allowed to teach small children, who were more easily disciplined and less disruptive than older ones. Young women teachers' pay was very low, with a customary portion taken for food and lodging received by "boarding around" in the homes of their pupils. The same was true for a governess. Faced with these living conditions, many women chose marriage after a short tenure as a teacher. However, for women who sought independence, teaching provided a measure of freedom through gainful employment. For many women, a teaching career created a limbo-like transitional state between a parent's home and a future marriage, though even here women were usually under the watchful eye of a male school board or private employer. As we will see, this trend toward female-dominated primary education would accelerate across America as the nineteenth century progressed and continue to the present era.[126]

LITERACY'S DRUMBEAT

During the first 60 years of the nineteenth century, children raised in the northeastern states who received any literacy education did so mainly through private instruction at home or through sectarian institutions. Surprisingly, the states' support of literacy came in a distant third. Societal conditions withheld literacy from the majority of children, though by the Civil War (1860) a gradual cultural shift had occurred favoring broader literacy opportunities for both boys and girls. This continued increase of literacy among the population of the early northeastern United States can be traced to three primary sources: the popularity of the domestic education/fireside education literacy movement; the significant role played by Sunday schools, private academies, and sectarian education; and the beginnings of a meaningful system of state-funded common schools backed by compulsory attendance laws.

In the early day of the American Republic, a unique coalition of religious bodies and state governments supported literacy education. But the numerous entrepreneurial private academies, faddish monitorial/infant schools, and ever more numerous one-room subscription or pay schools were also important agents of literacy. A wide variety of educational choices thus persisted through the early years of the American Republic.

Though literacy was still assumed to be largely a personal or family responsibility, such notables as Horace Mann and Noah Webster began to transform literacy from a privilege for some into a popular American grassroots social movement. In Massachusetts, Mann successfully lobbied to establish schooling laws that required a child to attend school either regularly or not at all. Webster, through his "old blue-back speller" became the publicly accepted "patriot author" of a widely accepted basic literacy curriculum that swept across all sections of the United States. This was an exciting pivotal period for literacy in America. One hundred years later, in the early twentieth century, from this foundation in the northeastern states came tax-supported, compulsory public schools that would offer at least a basic literacy education to all.

NOTES

1. David Tyack and Elizabeth Hansot, *Learning Together: A History of Coeducation in American Schools* (New Haven: Yale University Press, 1990), 3, 59; Barbara Finkelstein and Kathy Vandell, "The Schooling of American Childhood: The Emergence of Learning Communities," in *A Century of Childhood*, ed. Mary Lynn Stevens Heininger (Rochester, New York: The Margaret Woodbury Strong Museum, 1984), 65, 67.

2. Lawrence A. Cremin, *American Education: The National Experience 1783–1876* (New York: Harper & Row, 1980), 164, 172.

3. Arthur W. Calhoun, *A Social History of the American Family, Vol II: From Independence Through the Civil War* (New York: Barnes & Noble, 1945), 59.

4. Ibid.; James Pyle Wickersham, *A History of Education in Pennsylvania* (Lancaster, Pennsylvania: Inquirer Publishing Company, 1886), 273; Samuel Elliot Morison, *The History of the American People* (New York: Oxford University Press, 1965), 531.

5. Roscoe L. West, *Elementary Education in New Jersey: A History* (Princeton, New Jersey: Van Nostrand, 1964), 17; Cremin, *National Experience*, 388–389.

6. Noah Webster, *A Collection of Papers on Political Literacy and Moral Subjects* (New York: Webster & Clark, 1843), 246.

7. Adam Smith, *An Inquiry into the Nature and Causes of the Wealth of Nations* (New York: Random House, 1937), 681.

8. Carl F. Kaestle et al., *Literacy in the United States: Readers and Reading since 1880* (New Haven: Yale University Press, 1991), 52–54.

9. Lois Barber Arnold, *Four Lives in Science: Women's Education in the Nineteenth Century* (New York: Schocken Books, 1984), 38–39.

10. Lee Soltow and Edward Stevens, *The Rise of Literacy and the Common School in the United States: A Socioeconomic Analysis to 1870* (Chicago: University of Chicago Press, 1981), 65.

11. Herman Humphrey, *Domestic Education* (Amherst, Massachusetts: J.S.C. Adams, 1840); S. G. Goodrich, *Fireside Education* (London: William Smith, 1841); Anne L. Kuhn, *The Mother's Role in Childhood Education: New England Concepts* (New Haven: Yale University Press, 1947), 108.

12. Kuhn, *Childhood Education*, 72, 79, 101, 106, 107, 108, 119, 175, 178–203. Other representative works on "domestic education" include John Abbott, *The Mother at Home* (Boston: Crocker and Brewster, 1833); Theodore Dwight, *The Father's Book* (Springfield, Massachusetts: G&C Merriam, 1834); Warren Burton, *Helps to Education in the Homes of Our Country* (Boston: Crosby and Nichols, 1863); Annie Allen, *Home, School and Vacation* (Boston: Houghton Mifflin, 1907); Ellen Celia Lombard, *Home Education* (Washington, D.C.: Government Printing Office, 1919); Ellen C. Lombard was the secretary of the Home Education Division, U.S. Bureau of Education.

13. Lydia Sigourney, *Letters of Mothers* (Hartford, Connecticut: Hudson and Skinner, 1838), 107.

14. Goodrich, *Fireside Education*, iv–v, 15–20.

15. Isaac Taylor, *Home Education* (New York: D. Appleton and Company, 1838), 10–11.

16. John Hall, *On the Education of Children While under the Care of Parents or Guardians* (New York: John P. Haven, 1835), 11, 33–34, 153–154.

17. Elizabeth Harden, *Maria Edgeworth* (Boston: Twayne Publishers, 1984), 7–9; James Newcomer, *Maria Edgeworth* (Lewisburg: Bucknell University Press, 1973), 15, 17.

18. Harden, *Maria Edgeworth*, 10.

19. Ibid., 11, 5, 6.

20. Ibid., 6, 25.

21. Richard Lovell Edgeworth and Maria Edgeworth, *Practical Education*, 2 vols. (London: J. Johnson, 1798); John Locke, *Some Thoughts Concerning Education*, Peter Gay, ed. (New York: Columbia University Press, 1964); Herbert Spencer, *Essay on Education and Kindred Subjects* (London: J.M. Dent, 1914); John William Adamson, *English Education* (Cambridge: Cambridge University Press, 1930), 105–106; Newcomer, *Maria Edgeworth*, 31–38.

22. Elizabeth Inglis-Jones, *The Great Maria* (Westport, Connecticut: Greenwood Press, 1959), 51; Harden, *Maria Edgeworth*, 24–27; Edgeworth, *Practical Education*.

23. Maria Edgeworth, *The Parent's Assistant or Stories for Children*, 4 vols. (London: Printed for J. Johnson by G. Woodfall, 1800); Maria Edgeworth, *Early Lessons*, 5 vols. (London: Printed by J. Johnson, 1801–1803); Newcomer, *Maria Edgeworth*, 28–29; Harden, *Maria Edgeworth*, 6, 120.

24. Maria Edgeworth, *Moral Tales*, 3 vols. (London: Printed for J. Johnson, 1802); Maria Edgeworth, *Popular Tales* (London: Printed for J. Johnson by C. Mercier, 1804); Harden, *Maria Edgeworth*, 33–34; Bea Howe, *A Galaxy of Governesses* (London: Dereck Verschoyle, 1954), 58–59.

25. Maria Edgeworth, *Maria Edgeworth: Chosen Letters*, ed. F. V. Barry (New York: Houghton Mifflin, 1931), 447–449.

26. Maria Edgeworth, *Essays on Professional Education*, 2 vols. (London: Printed for J. Johnson, 1811); Maria Edgeworth, *Harry and Lucy Concluded, Being The Last Part of Early Lessons*, 3 vols. (Boston: Munroe and Francis, 1825); Newcomer, *Maria Edgeworth*, 18–19, 42; Harden, *Maria Edgeworth*, 75–76.

27. Rachel Van Dyke, Diary, 6 October 1810–16 May 1811, 27 November 1810, 12 December 1810, Rutgers University Library, New Brunswick, New Jersey.

28. Ibid., 16 October 1810, 28 February 1811, 27 October 1810, 21 January 1811, 4 December 1810, 3 November 1810, 22 January 1811, 29 January 1811, 31 January 1811, 9 February 1811, 14 February 1811.

29. Ibid., 28 November 1810, 25 February 1811; Kuhn, *Childhood Education*, 12, 37, 41, 159.

30. Lloyd P. Jorgenson, *The State and the Non-Public School 1825–1925* (Columbia: University of Missouri Press, 1987), 11; Cremin, *National Experience*, 66.

31. Jorgenson, *Non-Public School*, 12; Cremin, *National Experience*, 66.

32. Soltow, *Rise of Literacy*, 15.

33. Edwin W. Rice, *The Sunday-School Movement, 1780–1917, and the American Sunday School Union, 1817–1917* (Philadelphia: American Sunday School Union, 1917; reprint, New York: Arno Press, 1971), 74–75; Soltow, *Rise of Literacy*, 17.

34. Rice, *Sunday-School*, 74; Cremin, *National Experience*, 70.

35. Anne M. Boylan, *Sunday School: The Formation of an American Institution 1790–1880* (New Haven: Yale University Press, 1988), 23.

36. Ibid., 7–9.

37. Ibid., 15.

38. Soltow, *Rise of Literacy*, 17; Jorgenson, *Non-Public School*, 13; Boylan, *Sunday School*, 53; Cremin, *National Experience*, 66.

39. Timothy Walch, *Parish School: American Catholic Parochial Education from Colonial Times to the Present* (New York: Crossroad Publishing, Co., 1996), 17.

40. Ibid., 18–19.

41. Ibid, 1, 20, 24, 38–39.

42. Timothy Walch, "Catholic Schoolbooks and American Values," in *Enlightening the Next Generation: Catholics and Their Schools, 1830–1980*, ed. F. Michael Perko (New York: Garland, 1988), 270–274.

43. Walch, *Parish School*, 27.

44. John Demos and Sarane Spence Boocock, *Turning Points: Historical and Sociological Essays on the Family* (Chicago: University of Chicago Press, 1978), 48.

45. Warren Burton, *The District School As It Was* (New York: T.Y. Crowell Company, 1928; reprint, New York: Arno Press, 1969), 16, 18–19.

46. Ibid., 52.

47. Ibid., 53–54.

48. Maris A. Vinovskis, *Education, Society and Economic Opportunity: A Historical Perspective on Persistent Issues* (New Haven: Yale University Press, 1995), 121, 22, 128.

49. Ibid., 125–127.

50. Elizabeth Buffum Chace and Lucy Buffum Lovell, *Two Quaker Sisters: From the Original Diaries of Elizabeth Buffum Chace and Lucy Buffum Lovell* (New York: Liveright Publishing Corporation, 1937), 18–19.

51. Ibid., 23–24.

52. Ibid., 28–29.

53. Demos, *Turning Points*, 48–50.

54. Lucy Larcom, *A New England Girlhood* (Boston: Northeastern University Press, 1986), 38–48.

55. Elizabeth Rogers Mason Cabot, *More than Common Powers of Perception: The Diary of Elizabeth Rogers Mason Cabot* (Boston: Beacon, 1991), 14–15.

56. James Turner, *The Liberal Education of Charles Eliot Norton* (Baltimore: The Johns Hopkins University Press, 1999), 32. Norton became a famous Harvard University professor in art history and a champion in the study of the humanities. He was a contemporary of Longfellow, Emerson, and other nineteenth-century New England intellectuals.

57. Ibid., 33. His mother was particularly successful with her son, who authored over a dozen books, wrote or edited several hundred articles, and was the editor of the *North American Review* and a founder of *The Nation*, both important nineteenth-century journals.

58. Ibid., 33, 37–38, 40.

59. Demos, *Turning Points*, 48–50.

60. Vinovskis, *Education*, 17–18.

61. Gerald F. Moran and Maris A. Vinovskis, *Religion, Family and the Life Course* (Ann Arbor: University of Michigan Press, 1992), 121; Maris A. Vinovskis, "Trends in Massachusetts Education, 1826–1860," *History of Education Quarterly* 12 (Winter 1972): 52.

62. Johann Henrich Pestalozzi, *Leonard and Gertrude*, Eva Channing, trans. (Boston: D.C. Heath, 1885); Johann Friedrich Herbart, *The Science of Education* (Boston: D.C. Heath, 1893), 6, 10; Johann Friedrich Herbart, *Outlines of Educational Doctrine* (New York: Macmillan, 1911), 318–320; Edward E. Gordon and Elaine H. Gordon, *Centuries of Tutoring* (Lanham, Maryland: University Press of America, 1990), 162–166, 218; Demos, *Turning Points*, 56–57.

63. Amariah Brigham, *Remarks on the Influence of Mental Cultivation and Mental Excitement upon Health* (Boston: Marsh, Capen & Lyon, 1833).

64. Moran, *Family*, 122; Vinovskis, *Education*, 36–37; Demos, *Turning Points*, 71–73.

65. Hersha Sue Fisher, "The Education of Elizabeth Peabody" (Ed.D. dissertation, Harvard University, 1980), 23, 29, 42–43; Megan Marshall, "The Sisters Who Showed the Way," *American Heritage* 38 (September-October 1987): 58–66.

66. Fisher, "The Education of Elizabeth Peabody," 30, 31, 35.

67. Ibid., 36, 37, 43.

68. Ralph Waldo Emerson, *The Journals of Ralph Waldo Emerson, 1820–1872*, 10 vols., ed. Edward Waldo Emerson and Waldo Emerson Forbes (Cambridge: Riverside Press, 1909–1914), vol. 10, 135, 143, 144, 126, 148, 149, 153–154, 155.

69. Fisher, "The Education of Elizabeth Peabody," i, ii, iii, 23; Kuhn, *Childhood Education*, 59–61.

70. Cremin, *National Experience*, 165.

71. Madelon Bedell, *The Alcotts* (New York: Clarkson N. Potter, 1980), 10–12.

72. Ibid., 17–18.

73. Ibid., 57; Louisa May Alcott, *Work, A Story of Experience* (New York: Schocken Books, 1977), xi–xii.

74. Alcott, *Life*, 243–244, 245, 247.

75. Bedell, *The Alcotts*, 120, 132, 145, 149; George E. Haefner, *A Critical Estimate of the Educational Theories and Practices of A. Bronson Alcott* (New York: Columbia University Press, 1937; reprint, Westport, Connecticut: Greenwood Press, 1970), 32–34.

76. Harriot Hunt, *Glances and Glimpses* (Boston: J.P. Jewett & Co., 1856), 15–16.

77. Ibid., 54.

78. Ibid., 55.

79. Ibid., 57.

80. Ibid., 75.

81. Marshall, "The Sisters," 60, 62.

82. Mrs. Horace Mann, trans., "Princes in France: Their Education and Teachers, from *Compayre Histoires Critique de l'Education*," *The American Journal of Education* 30 (1880): 465–490.

83. Cremin, *National Experience*, 134–136.

84. Horace Mann, "Twelfth Annual Report of Horace Mann as Secretary of Massachusetts State Board of Education" (1848), in *Documents of American History*, vol. 2, ed. Henry Steele Commager (New York: Appleton Century Crofts, 1963), 317–319.

85. Richard B. Morris, ed., *Encyclopedia of American History* (New York: Harper & Row, 1970), 247, 750; Samuel Eliot Morison, *The Oxford History of the American People* (New York: Oxford University Press, 1965), 530; Morris, *American History*, 247; Cremin, *National Experience*, 156.

86. Morison, *American People*, 530.

87. Gerald W. McFarland, *A Scattered People: An American Family Moves West* (New York: Pantheon Books, 1985), 91–103.

88. Dumas Malone, ed., *Dictionary of American Biography*, vol. 4 (New York: Charles Scribner's Sons, 1933), 400.

89. Linda Peavy and Ursula Smith, *Women in Waiting in the Westward Movement: Life on the Home Frontier* (Norman: University of Oklahoma Press, 1994), 44–46.

90. Ibid., 48–49; Dunning Collection, Northwest Museum of Arts & Culture/Eastern Washington State Historical Society, Spokane, Washington.

91. Peavy, *Women in Waiting*, 52–54.

92. Ibid., 63, 67, 71, 302.

93. Ibid., 85–86.

94. Morison, *American People*, 530; Carl F. Kaestle, *The Evolution of an Urban School System: New York City, 1750–1850* (Cambridge: Harvard University Press, 1973), 28, 49.

95. Ibid., 83–84, 160.

96. Andrew Bell, *Bell's Mutual Tuition and Moral Discipline* (London: C.J.G. & F. Livingston, 1832), 75. A Monitorial School "text" was published in India in 1797 and 1815 as an early attempt at an English language textbook; John Miller, *The Tutor* (Serampore, 1797; Calcutta, 1815; reprint, Menston: Scholar Press, 1971).

97. Vernon L. Allen, ed., *Children As Teachers* (New York: Academic Press, 1976), 13; Val D. Rust, *Alternatives in Education* (London: Sage Publications, 1977), 113.

98. David Salmon, ed., *The Practical Parts of Lancaster's Improvements and Bell's Experiment* (Cambridge: Cambridge University Press, 1932), viii–ix.

99. Joseph Lancaster, *Improvements in Education As It Respects the Industrious Classes of the Community* (London: Darton and Harvey, 1803), 31–32; Lilya Wagner, *Peer Teaching: Historical Perspective* (Westport, Connecticut: Greenwood Press, 1982), 61–84.

100. Harold Silver, *The Concept of Popular Education: A Study of Ideas and Social Movements in the Early Nineteenth Century* (London: MacGibbon and Kee, 1965), 17–67; R. K. Webb, *Modern England* (New York: Dodd, Mead and Company, 1971), 154.

101. Lancaster, *Improvements*, 31–32.

102. Carl F. Kaestle, ed., *Joseph Lancaster and the Monitorial School Movement* (New York: Teachers College Press, 1973), 4, 6–8; Carl F. Kaestle, *Pillars of the Republic* (New York: Hill and Wang, 1983), 67; Allen, *Children As Teachers*, 13–16.

103. Kaestle, *Pillars*, 41.

104. Ibid.

105. Ibid., 18, 41–43.

106. Ibid., 42–43.

107. Lancaster had moved from city to city, constantly complaining, planning great things and never doing them. In 1838 he was living in New York working on yet another unfinished book. While crossing a city street, he was trampled and killed by a runaway horse. Ibid., 41–43.

108. John Franklin Reigart, *The Lancasterian System of Instruction in the Schools of New York City* (New York: Teachers College, Columbia University, 1916; reprint, New York: Arno Press, 1969), 1–6; William Oland Bourne, *History of the Public School Society of the City of New York* (New York: W. Wood and Company, 1870), 28–47; Kaestle, *Pillars*, 56–57.

109. "Little Schools on the Prairie Still Teach a Big Lesson," *Smithsonian* 16 (October 1985): 118–128; Lilya Wagner, *Peer Teaching*, 134–202.

110. Cremin, *National Experience*, 391; E. Jennifer Monaghan, *A Common Heritage: Noah Webster's Blue-Back Speller* (Hamden, Connecticut: Archon Books, 1983), 31–33.

111. Noah Webster, *A Grammatical Institute of the English Language. Comprising an Easy, Concise, and Systematic Method of Education, Designed for the Use of English Schools in America*, Part I (Hartford: Hudson & Goodwin, 1783); Monaghan, *Common Heritage*, 31; Nila Banton Smith, *American Reading Instruction* (Newark, Delaware: International Reading Association, 1986), 45.

112. Smith, *American Reading*, 44; *Connecticut Courant and Weekly Intelligence*, Hartford, June 5, 1781; Monaghan, *Common Heritage*, 24.

113. Monaghan, *Common Heritage*, 26, 197; Alice Felt Tyler, *Freedom's Ferment* (New York: Harper & Row, 1962), 231–232.

114. Monaghan, *Common Heritage*, 30, 32, 201, 204.

115. William J. Gilmore, *Reading Becomes a Necessity of Life: Material and Cultural Life in Rural New England 1780–1835* (Knoxville: University of Tennessee Press, 1989), 37; West, *Elementary Education*, 25; H. Alan Robinson, Vincent Faraone, Daniel R. Hittleman, and Elizabeth Unruh, *Reading Comprehension Instruction, 1783–1987: A Review of Research and Trends* (Newark, Delaware: International Reading Association, 1990), 59–60; Cremin, *National Experience*, 395.

116. Smith, *American Reading*, 45; Monaghan, *Common Heritage*, 201.

117. Nancy Cott, *The Bonds of Womanhood: Women's Sphere in New England 1780–1835* (New Haven: Yale University Press, 1977), 101; Kenneth A. Lockridge, *Literacy in Colonial New England* (New York: Norton, 1974), 38–42, 57–58.

118. Cott, *Womanhood*, 110, 122; Tyack and Hansot, *Learning Together*, 39.

119. Calhoun, *American Family*, 89.

120. Ibid., 90.

121. Jane H. Pease, and William H. Pease. *Ladies, Women and Wenches: Choice and Constraint in Antebellum Charleston and Boston* (Chapel Hill: University of North Carolina Press, 1990), 63, 65, 69, 70.

122. Cott, *Womanhood*, 113.

123. Diary of Lavinia Bailey Kelly (Cilly), undated entry of 1828, New Hampshire Historical Society.

124. Emma Willard, *A Plan for Improving Female Education* (Middlebury, Vermont: Middlebury College, 1918); Cott, *Womanhood*, 32–35, 115–116; Morris, *American History*, 803.

125. Cott, *Womanhood*, 32–35, 114–115; Gordon, *Centuries of Tutoring*, 210–211.

126. Richard M. Bernard and Maris A. Vinovskis, "The Female School Teacher in Ante-Bellum Massachusetts," *Journal of Social History* 10 (March 1977): 332–345.

Chapter 5

"Lay the Cornerstone More Firmly": The Antebellum South

A FRACTURED ODYSSEY

Literacy education in the antebellum South (1800–1860) was at best uneven and fluctuating, since society in most states showed little support for a formal common-school system. In fact, prior to the 1850s, free compulsory schools were a rarity in the entire South.

In many states, laws were passed or elaborate permissive educational systems were designed, only to be ignored. Although legislation providing for some form of publicly supported schooling was passed in South Carolina (1811), Virginia (1820), Maryland (1825), North Carolina (1839), New Orleans (1841), and Louisiana (1845), this did not result in the availability of literacy education for most southern children. North Carolina and Alabama actually began moving in that direction only to be interrupted by the Civil War (1861–1865). North Carolina was the only southern state that did develop a functioning state primary-school system of any comprehensiveness and vigor. Charleston, South Carolina, also seems to have made an effort at establishing free, charity schools before 1815. As we will see, even within these systems there was considerable variation of literacy practices from community to community, even from school to school. One thing seems to be certain, an infinite mixing of private, public, and domestic education programs resulted in an interweaving of these alternatives in the lives of many children. It should come as no surprise that, with this fractured approach to literacy, by one measure (1860) illiteracy among native-born southern whites stood at about 20 percent, compared to .042 percent among native-born New Englanders.

Fear that African-American literacy would undermine slavery as a viable economic institution led to numerous laws attempting to prohibit schools for blacks.

There could be no public support for mass literacy across the South until this issue was resolved by the Civil War. We will consider the African-American quest for literacy in Chapter 9.[1]

The popularity of "domestic education" was not confined to New England during America's early national period. As during the colonial period, throughout the South parents provided tutors for many children's basic literacy education, except now parents also acted as teachers. Most planters lived in isolated rural areas where children would have to leave home to attend any school above the primary level. Literacy education very often began at home, with the mother as the domestic educator, as in North Carolina, where Hannah Gaston established a precise home-class schedule. Each day her six-year-old son recited "six or seven lessons."[2] Other families employed private tutors or governesses, continuing to build the typical earlier colonial plantation style schoolrooms and dwellings for their teachers.[3] Many of these instructors proved to be poor teachers or highly transitory. Sudden resignations were all too common.[4] A plantation parent, Anne W. Johnson, described this predicament (1848) and probably an equally common solution: "I am now teaching the young children, our Teacher left us about three weeks since. I think she will not return."[5]

Parents often believed their children needed more advanced schooling by the age of 14. However, many parents of girls did not view a faraway school as clearly superior to a plantation education. Young women gathered together in seminaries might become "corrupted by other students."[6] Many used these schools as a last resort because, as one planter argued, "I have many objections to boarding schools generally but it is almost impossible to educate our Daughters entirely at home."[7]

As qualified teachers were difficult to find in many areas of the rural South, southern families looked to the North for literacy educators.[8] Margaret Clark Griffis (1838–1913) was the daughter of a prosperous Philadelphia business family. After the financial panic of 1857, her father's business failed, and Margaret was forced to begin her career as a governess (1857–1866).[9] She was hired as a live-in governess by a succession of mainly southern families. Her educational curriculum was similar for all her students: English, French, and music. Margaret struggled to establish a good interpersonal relationship with each family to combat the great loneliness she experienced when separated from her own kin.

Clark's first experience as a southern literacy educator began at Meriwether Plantation near Tiptoville, Tennessee. For over one year she taught the five children of the Isler family. Margaret was so successful that her employer William B. Isler offered to double her salary if she would stay for another year. Clark tells us, "He thought the children improved under my care more than with any other teacher they have ever had." She was also popular with her students so that they "seem to think that I belong to them and must not go away."[10]

Perhaps anticipating the outbreak of the Civil War, Margaret left the Meriwether Plantation; over the next seven years her work as a literacy educator took her gradually northward. She taught children near Centreville, Virginia

(1859–1860), and Washington, D.C. (1861), and in two Philadelphia families (1864–1866).[11]

During this time as a literacy educator Margaret never stopped her own self-education, reading the poetry of Shelley and the books of James Fenimore Cooper and studying both French and German.[12] Though Griffis was often bitter over being separated from her mother, she never seemed to consider her career as a governess an unusual or burdensome occupation. This might be explained in part by the fact that Margaret's personal odyssey as a literacy educator, who worked for so many different families spread across a large geographic area, was undoubtedly being repeated by thousands of other women and men at that time throughout the South and in other parts of the world. In fact, Margaret later traveled (1871–1872) to Japan and taught in a Tokyo high school. She finished her career teaching at a Philadelphia girls' school (1875–1898).[13]

To better understand the fractured odyssey of antebellum southern literacy, let us now review the experiences of students in different states.

"STIRRING THEM UP A LITTLE"—VIRGINIA

William C. Preston was raised at Aspenvale in Washington County. Beginning in 1780, Peter Byrnes, an Irish weaver by trade, begun teaching successive Preston family children. He taught William (1800–1812) his letters, to read the New Testament, and to cipher as far as the rule of three. William remembered that "I learned with facility and was I suppose of good behavior. . . . We never failed to love and cherish him." Byrnes died at age 82 and was buried in the family plot.[14]

The next step in my education was to be placed under the tuition of a Mr. Hercules Whaley, a private tutor brought into the family, a man of rare and curious accomplishments. My father picked him up in the remote valleys of Lee County . . . [and] prevailed upon him to enter our family as a tutor. He continued with us for many years but there was always a mystery hanging about him . . . we gradually learned that he was a native of New York, that he had been bred for the ministry, that he had become an actor and at length had joined Gen. Wayne's army as a dragoon. . . . He was found to be a capital Latin scholar, familiar with the classics continued in that language, not ignorant of Greek, and speaking French pretty well . . . and read and recited poetry with exquisite power . . . he would be seized with such enthusiasm as to rise from his seat, assume a theatrical attitude in the floor and acclaim it with dramatic intonations swept away with excitement.

. . . He took charge of my entire training . . . we rose and walked and sat together and slept in the same room, so that my process of education was continually going on.

. . . Whaley and I read together most of the Latin classics and many of the English, for my father had a very good library. But my parents thought . . . that their boy ought to be sent to a public school, and so at 14 I was sent to what was called the Washington College at Lexington (now Washington and Lee University), a college superintended by lazy and ignorant Presbyterian preachers, and filled with dirty boys of low manners and morals. In six months at this place I unlearned as much as it was possible for a boy of sprightly parts to unlearn in six months.[15]

Then being "affected with some slight hemorrhage of the lungs," Preston was sent farther south to a warmer climate. His father had always planned for him to go to a southern college as "I was to be a well educated man and then to study law as my life time profession." Preston, while traveling to Florida, detoured to Columbia, South Carolina, and enrolled there as a college sophomore in December 1809. "I graduated with distinction in 1812, having gone through pretty much such acquaintances [subjects] as I had made under Whaley [his tutor]."[16] Thus through what must now seem to our modern perspective a highly unorthodox education, William Preston became a highly literate adult. This unsystematic educational program seems to have been repeated for many other southern children of that time by families who had the economic means to orchestrate it.

Eleanor Agnes Lee (1841–1873) was the fifth child of Robert E. Lee and Mary Anne Randolph Custis, whose father was the adopted son of George Washington (whom General Lee idolized.) Agnes was raised on the Custis Plantation in Arlington, overlooking Washington, D.C.[17] In 1852 her mother, Mary Anne Randolph Custis Lee, hired a governess, Susan Poor, to teach Agnes and her sister Anne in the hope of "stirring them up a little."[18]

Susan Poor established a specific "schoolroom" for her pupils at Arlington. Among the few things we know was that her curriculum included an emphasis on writing skills. "Miss Sue says I must keep a journal it will improve my 'style.' At any rate it will be amusing in after years to know what I did and felt when I was young!"[19]

Even though her governess left in July 1853, Agnes continued her journal until 1858, which offers us an account of her girlhood in antebellum America. Unfortunately, she stopped writing before the outbreak of the Civil War (1861–1865). The proximity of the Custis plantation to Washington, D.C., and her father's defection to the Confederacy made their home one of the first pieces of Southern real estate occupied by Union forces in the earliest days of the war. Agnes' personal insights on her famous father during these tumultuous war years might have given us some valuable sidelights on this famous American.[20]

A completely different perspective on literacy education in antebellum Virginia is contained in the diary of Jane Gibbs. She chronicled her life as a teacher in Nelson County, Virginia, at the Green Pond School. On March 27, 1857, Colonel Fitzpatrick, a local planter, hired Jane to teach the local children writing, French (and possibly Latin) for a salary of 50 dollars a year and her room and board. This was typical of the arrangements local rural communities made with itinerant schoolmasters. From that date until November, 1859, Jane recorded her daily activities with her "scholars." Fifteen children began attending daily school at Green Pond. In the summer months (July 1857) this number fell to one or two students. In the autumn Jane taught about six pupils individually, each on a different day of the week. Children occasionally stayed with their teacher overnight. While teaching, Jane continued her own self-study of Latin and professional reading.

The fact that she remained at one post for at least three years was very unusual. Most similar schoolmasters were very itinerant. One possible reason was that the families around Green Pond School liked Jane's teaching. They invited her frequently to their homes for parties and religious gatherings.

A religious woman, Jane Gibbs introduced her diary with a concise personal philosophy that gave an insight to her effectiveness as a teacher.

Marks!

Good disciple—good order is [sic] the life of a school. Make your pupils respect [you] and they will have you—teach them politeness and charity for one another.[21]

The urban areas of Virginia present a far different picture of literacy education, offering a mixture of charity schools, subscription schools, and even adult night schools.

Night School to Be Opened in Martinsburg, Virginia

Night School.—James Maxwell respectfully informs the Citizens of Martinsburg, that he will commence a Night School on Monday evening the 12th inst. in which will be taught Spelling, Reading, Writing and Arithmetic, including Vulgar and Decimal Fractions, the extraction of the Square, Cube and Biquadrate Roots, &c. Attendance from early candle-light to half past nine.—*Martinsburg Gazette and Public Advertiser*, October 15, 1829.[22]

Mechanics in two other Virginia cities also formed short-lived night schools. However, these adult literacy programs were unusual for Virginia and not typical for other urban areas throughout the antebellum South.[23]

Petersburg, Virginia, offers us a good contrasting example of the state of antebellum southern literacy in an urban area. By 1830 Petersburg had a vibrant, burgeoning economy due to a diverse manufacturing base. A population of 3,440 whites, 2,032 free blacks, and 2,850 slaves made it Virginia's fourth largest city, and one of the larger urban areas of the South.[24]

The region around Petersburg in 1825 contained more than a dozen private academies. They were all tuition-based and expensive. They opened and closed with great regularity, as was the common pattern for such nineteenth-century schools. The academies usually offered a classical education based on studying Latin and Greek. However, the Anderson Seminary did offer Petersburg's students a free basic education and between 1821 and 1830 enrolled about 400 students. But since it was the "poor school" or "charity school," many families shunned it for their children.

These schools hardly met the literacy needs of the region. As late as 1840 fewer than 35 percent of the 411 children aged 5–20 attended any of these schools at any time. Only 6 percent of the student population (117) attended the Anderson free school. A tax-supported common school did not open in Petersburg until after the Civil War.[25]

The Petersburg Benevolent Mechanics' Association (PBMA) was founded in 1825 as an education agency for mechanics, journeyman, and especially apprentices. It attempted to promote these ends by sponsoring a Sunday school, a library, public lectures, and a night school.

In 1825 the PBMA opened their evening literacy school for their members' apprentices and children. Seventy-six young men and children initially registered to attend two evenings a week for basic literacy instruction in reading, writing, and arithmetic. Unfortunately attendance soon fell because of the school's poor location and the nature and hours of the apprentices' work. They could not attend at an early hour, and the evening hours were too short for a meaningful instruction period.[26]

Though some of these adolescent apprentices may already have acquired a basic education, the lack of common schools must have left the majority of Petersburg residents with less than adequate literacy skills. Even so it appears that many parents and apprentices thought that an apprenticeship was "an education in and of itself" and that literacy was just not that important. This is substantiated by the School Committee's annual report for 1841, which noted that of 45 enrolled night-school students, 14 could not read (an illiteracy rate of 31 percent).[27]

Between 1844 and 1846, PBMA night-school attendance averaged around 13 students, a depressingly low enrollment. By 1850 the board of the PBMA admitted its failure and closed the school. The educational aversion shown by both masters and their apprentices reflected a wider societal belief in the antebellum South that basic literacy was not a necessary prerequisite for improving one's life. One can only speculate on the cost of such ambivalence.[28] Certainly this literacy deficiency of so many Virginians must have applied a great cultural and economic brake to the development of the state and the entire region.

THE ACADEMIES OF KENTUCKY AND TENNESSEE

During the antebellum period in Kentucky and Tennessee, plantation owners and the landed gentry of small farmers supported small private academies or employed private tutors and governesses for their children's education. But in the mountain communities of those states a lack of educational opportunities doomed most children to illiteracy.[29]

The Autobiography of Amos Kendall (1872) shows how a tutor for a private family might have far more to cope with than strictly educational matters. In May 1814, Amos Kendall, a Dartmouth College graduate, met a Mrs. Henry Clay (the wife of U.S. Congressman Henry Clay "the great compromiser"), who had recently returned to Kentucky from Washington, D.C. She successfully recruited him to become the tutor for five of her seven children. Previously her two eldest boys, Theodore, about age 13, and Thomas, age 12, had attended a very "ill-regulated" private academy in Jessamine County, Kentucky. Three girls were also to be tutored by Kendall. Mrs. Clay agreed to pay him $300 a year, his board, and the use of Mr. Clay's library to teach her family. Kendall accepted under the condition that he would be at liberty after six months to leave the position upon furnishing a well-qualified substitute.[30]

He arrived at Ashland Plantation (located today in Lexington, Kentucky) on May 10, 1814, and began teaching three days later.

My two boys, I perceive, have not been very well taught, and know almost nothing either of Latin or English grammar. They have begun *Caesar's Commentaries*, and after having recited, I make them write out a translation of the whole, which I intend they shall copy in a book. This is with the design, not only of impressing it more strongly upon the memory, but improving them in writing and English grammar.[31]

Kendall's educational program with the three daughters was very different, centering on literacy skills.

The oldest girl reads and writes, and bids fair to make an excellent scholar. The second knows little of reading, and seems to be idle, although a fine little girl. The third is yet in her Abs. The whole of them are passionate, and have never been governed at all. But they are by no means unmanageable.[32]

Kendall's problems then began to multiply.

May 14
    Thomas refused this afternoon to go to his lesson; but on being carried into the room, he yielded.
    May 20
    I find the children, especially the boys under my care, have been indulged till they are almost ungovernable. The oldest, Theodore, has the most amicable disposition, but Thomas is the smartest boy. They have been accustomed to fight each other, so that, they could not be boarded at the same place. Their father is almost always absent, and their mother has been so for nearly two years past, and they have been left to their own management.[33]
    May 29
    While Mrs. Clay was absent, Thomas became so enraged with some slaves and threatening them, "exerted all his little power to kill them." (Kendall held him inside a plantation office until he cooled off.)[34]
    June 9
    This evening Thomas got into a rage after the departure of the company, and at Mrs. Clay's request I dragged him, not very tenderly, into the office. He fought me like a tiger and cussed me with all his might. "You dammed Yankee rascal," cried he, "you have been trying to make yourself of great consequence among the ladies this evening."

Kendall cuffed him once or twice but did not feel charged to whip him. Mrs. Clay ordered him off to bed. The next day Thomas remained in bed until Kendall had gone to breakfast. Afterwards alone with his mother, he burst into tears. "He wished to ask pardon of me, but feared the other children would laugh at him." Later he came with his mother, who asked Kendall's pardon for him.[35]

August 23

Mrs. Clay being gone, the care of the boys devolved in a great measure on me. Hearing a great noise in the kitchen, I went in, and found Theodore swearing in a great rage, with a knife drawn in an attitude to stab one of the big negroes. I did not want to inquire the cause, but seized him by the collar, took the knife away, and very expeditiously had him in the house. If he were my boy I would break him of such tricks if it cost blood.[36]

On October 17, Kendall received notice that his application to study law had been granted.[37]

April 29, 1815

Resigned my sceptre to Mr. Kilpatrick. Though the behavior of Mr. Clay's children out of school has not been very agreeable, yet their attention to study and their good hearts, and uniformly respectful conduct towards me, have attached me considerably to them, and I cannot leave them without regret. Yet, I cannot but feel a glow of joy that my pedagogical labors are closed, and ardently hope I shall never be under the necessity of resuming them.[38]

Amos Kendall left Ashland Plantation and went to Georgetown to read the law of Kentucky. It is obvious that being an agent of literacy could in those times be neither an easy or a safe occupation. Henry Clay as a national political leader of great importance once said, "I'd rather be right than be President!" He certainly seemed to have much to learn about being an effective parent and role model for his own sons, rather than expecting a tutor to somehow make up the difference.[39]

By comparison the life of Julia A. Tevis, as a literacy educator, was far more peaceful, but certainly very arduous and eventful. Julia was born in 1799 and started her first schooling at age four in a rustic one-room school in Clarke County, Kentucky. When she was seven her family moved to Paris, Virginia, where Julia attended a village school; they then moved again, to Winchester, Virginia. There she was enrolled in a female academy operated by a Presbyterian and Dutch Reformed minister.[40]

For three consecutive years, in the morning was two columns in *Walker's Dictionary* [a popular reader/spelling book], giving the definitions and parts of speech. We spelled in large classes, and regularly turned each other down—the one who retained her place at the head of the class for the whole week, bearing off the prize-ticket on Friday afternoon.[41]

In 1813, Julia's family moved to Washington, D.C. Her education under a Mr. and Mrs. Simpson was primarily devoted to music, drawing, French, and various kinds of embroidery (the so-called female accomplishments).[42]

A boarding school on Pennsylvania Avenue run by Mrs. Stone, an English-woman, became the next home for Julia and her three younger sisters. The same "feminine" curriculum continued, complicated by a French "governess" who did not understand enough English to correct their translations, a task delegated out of necessity to the drawing teacher.[43]

Her father's bankruptcy then caused Julia to turn to education as a career. She moved to Wytheville, Virginia, where she boarded with family friends, the Smyths, and opened her first academy.

I rented a large upper room in a house contiguous to General Smyth's. The kindness of my parents relieved me from all trouble and expense as regarded desks, benches, etc. My schoolroom was neatly fitted up for the accommodation of 30 or 40 pupils. All the little misses in the village attended—some grown girls—and a few little boys. A few of the girls were larger and considerably taller than the teacher.[44]

Julia also gave private lessons in drawing, French, and music. As she soon found herself overwhelmed with students, Julia sent for a sister to help teach in her academy. With her own limited educational preparation, what were Julia's basic literacy instructional methods?

I used the monitorial system to some extent, which gave me an hour in the morning and evening to attend to my French and Drawing; but in the same room where the whole school was seated; thus I had the opportunity of overlooking the appointed monitors (students), who heard the recitations of the younger children, and taught the a, b, abs, as successfully as I could have done it myself.[45]

The death of Julia's father left her family destitute. Her mother and sister moved to Wytheville into a house big enough to accommodate six to eight pay-ing outside student boarders. Julia's academy continued to prosper, with girls from North Carolina and neighboring counties in Virginia filling her mother's boardinghouse.[46]

In the next phase of her career as an educator, Captain Frank Smith, of Abing-ton, Virginia, invited Julia to become the family governess for his only child, "offering a salary equal to the present income of the school." As an added ben-efit a comfortable residence, one-half mile from Smith's home, was made avail-able for her entire family. This residence was promptly turned into a day-school for young girls.[47]

Julia became the governess to nine-year-old Mary Smith and three cousins near her age. The girls also took dancing lessons, "from a queer little man by the name of Fry." Julia described her philosophy of individualized tutorial instruc-tion in the following way.

We had daily exercise in music, French, and drawing but experience had taught me that the elementary branches of spelling, reading, and arithmetic should be learned at an early age, for these are the *arts* by which the sciences are to be acquired. ... Our language deserves the highest degree of attention; and to expect children to become acquainted with the principles of learning simply by hearing others talk, is ridiculous and absurd. A child may learn to spell correctly before its powers of thought are well developed. In spelling, children should be made to enunciate and pronounce each sylla-ble distinctly; and spelling books and dictionaries will not complete the course. Words, sentences, and even whole pages should be dictated to them; the words spelled incor-rectly underlined by the teacher and the pupil made to correct them.[48]

A major change now occurred in Julia's life when on March 9, 1824, she mar-ried John Tevis, a Methodist minister. John rode a preaching circuit of 900 square miles. In the late summer of 1824 Julia joined her husband back in Kentucky, where on December 28, 1824, she gave birth to a son, Benjamin Pendleton. Soon after, in March 1825, the Tevis family settled in Shelbyville, Kentucky, which at that time had an academy for boys and girls and a coeducational dame school.[49]

Julia immediately opened a new academy in her home with "18 or 20" girls, four as boarders with at least two girls in their teens.

Few of my pupils had been subjected to the wholesome discipline of a well-regulated school, thus they required to be taught the simplest rudiments of knowledge. Some had been properly instructed, but so irregularly and by so many different teachers, that I found it necessary to tear down a portion of the superstructure and lay the cor-nerstone more firmly—preparatory to the cultivation of thorough intellectual habits.[50]

Julia's small school was called the Science Hill Female Academy. After a few weeks her academy increased to approximately 40 students from 10 to 15 years of age. The number of boarders grew to the capacity of her house.[51]

Her lifetime success as an educator could be measured by the unusual longevity of her school. During the 50th anniversary celebration of Science Hill Female Academy, on March 25, 1875, Julia opened her house to welcome back her old pupils. Out of 3,000 previous students, some 300 girls returned, repre-senting every class since 1825. This was an outstanding personal tribute to her educational accomplishments in antebellum Kentucky.[52]

A CAROLINA CORRESPONDENCE

In the Carolinas free charity schools supported by the city of Charleston, pri-vate academies, and domestic education all made their contributions to literacy education. In Charleston between 1820 and 1840, the city's free schools each year taught from 250 to 550 pupils whose parents complied with the means test to prove their poverty. One-third to two-fifths of these students were girls. These coeducational institutions provided basic literacy instruction in reading, spelling, arithmetic, grammar and geography. In 1841 a grammar school was set aside for male education. These free schools provided a literacy education for at most 20 percent of Charleston's white children, or less than 10 percent of all children be-tween the ages of five and fifteen. Girls received fewer basic literacy opportuni-ties and were excluded from the city's high school and college.[53]

Other children relied on the numerous private academies subsidized by benev-olent societies or organized by private educational entrepreneurs whose only income came from student fees. The Fellowship Society used income from its $50,000 endowment to operate a coeducational primary school. The South Car-olina Society sponsored secondary-level academies in the 1820s open to both boys and girls.[54]

Most of Charleston's private academies were owned by individuals acting as independent educators. As we have seen, these academies were often situated in rented rooms or a private home. A man might be the schoolmaster, but more commonly a woman, a family group, a married couple, a widow and her daugh-ters, or even sisters provided the school's staff. These academies had the barest minimum of financial backing. They constantly opened and abruptly closed. Anyone could proclaim himself or herself a teacher or open an academy, adver-tising for both students and teachers in the Carolina's myriad newspapers, as shown in the following advertisement.[55]

Lumberton Academy, North Carolina, Desires Teachers, 1848

To Teachers

The Proprietors of the Lumberton Academy wish to engage the services of a teacher, capable of preparing Scholars for any of the classes at the University. It is believed that the Institution will yield—if a good teacher can be procured, who will take charge of it permanently—$750 to $1000 per annum.

Application either by letter or in person, to either of the subscribers at Lumberton, N.C. will be promptly attended to.

R.S. French
R.E. Troy
Fayetteville Observer, May 8, 1848[56]

In the years of the antebellum period, the town of Warrenton, North Car-olina, acquired a reputation as a literacy center, as it became the home of the Warrenton Male Academy (1786), the Falkener School for Girls (1802), and the Warrenton Female Academy (1809). The last-named institution was founded by Jacob Mordecai, patriarch of a Jewish family in the area.[57]

Mordecai was a largely self-taught businessman born in Philadelphia in 1762. He moved to Warrenton in 1792 and opened a store that failed in 1807. Before these business reverses, Mordecai had become a prominent citizen in this small town; the trustees of the Male Academy offered to help him support his wife and 10 children by inviting him to take charge of it. Two years later Mordecai was approached by another group of citizens to open an academy for young ladies, even though Warrenton already had a girls' school. Probably because of financial inducements, in 1809 the Warrenton Female Academy opened with Mordecai as the chief instructor, assisted by Rachel, his daughter, who had just turned 20 years of age.

Soon her sisters, Ellen and Caroline, and brother, Solomon, joined the enter-prise. The whole family ultimately became involved in the academy either as teachers or in caring for the physical and moral well-being of the young ladies. A Mr. Miller also was hired to teach music. The school was so successful that the enrollment rose from an initial 50 students to over 100. By the end of July, 1810, there were also over 50 boarders at the academy. After a fire burned the school down in 1811, Mordecai bought a permanent school building. Additional teachers were hired for French and drawing.[58]

In preparing herself for her duties, Rachel turned to the books on education written by England's Maria Edgeworth and her father Richard. As we have seen the Edgeworths' first book *Practical Education* (1798) was widely read by parents and teachers on both sides of the Atlantic. Rachel began a correspondence with Maria Edgeworth that was taken up by succeeding generations, continuing almost 100 years, until 1942. Edgeworth's educational ideals regarding the nature and practice of literacy made a profound impression on Rachel and on many other American educators.[59]

Their correspondence provides a visible link between a receptive audience in North Carolina and European progressive education ideas such as the following: The education of women should be taken seriously. A child's potential for learning should be developed for personal and social gain. To make this happen, discrimination based on personal prejudices must be set aside. The teacher should be a guide and facilitator, rather than an authoritarian figure using fear to induce learning. The teacher needs to create a positive learning environment that will reduce fear and encourage the child to risk learning something new. These were very heady ideas for the nineteenth-century antebellum South, and it is significant that they were being practiced by the Mordecai family in their rural women's academy until it closed, in 1834.[60]

Many North Carolina planters kept their children close to home, mixing attendance at a local academy with domestic education by the mother. In larger families with mothers burdened by a multiplicity of plantation chores, this led to a more haphazard instruction. Isaac and Harriet Avery's third son, learned his alphabet at home by the age of three. However, his mother complained that she never seemed to have enough time to tutor him.[61]

Other parents sent their children to the local small subscription academies of the type we have described, but often with mixed results. As Joseph B. Skinner found for his five-year-old daughter, "I have the last two days sent Penelope to school for two hours, but she has not yet been prevailed upon to say a single letter—I am in hope to succeed today, although it hurts me very much to see her depressed or mortified."[62] For other children school attendance was not very rigorous. Mary S. Henderson complained that her five-year-old son had learned very little, "because his teacher took no pains to instruct him.[63]

Some planters sponsored their own plantation schools or employed a tutor or governess. The temporary nature of the commitment made by plantation tutors is illustrated by Charles William Holbrook, a tutor on a North Carolina plantation. Holbrook graduated from Williams College in Massachusetts and soon after took up his tutorial position in Rockingham County, North Carolina. Seven other classmates out of 35 also became teachers, but all later switched to other occupations. The South offered abundant opportunities for the entrepreneurial educator to organize a school. Charles was hired to tutor the children of two brothers, Thomas and Rawley Gallaway. He had four students, three boys and one girl. After one year as a plantation tutor he moved to Greensboro, where for the next five years he was the "professor" of his own school. From a practical standpoint it must have proven very difficult for even most affluent planter families to enroll their children consistently in any educational programs whether with a tutor/governess or at local academies that functioned so irregularly.[64]

THE DEEP SOUTH: GEORGIA, MISSISSIPPI, AND LOUISIANA

Wilkes County, Georgia

This Indenture made this 3rd of January 1820 witnefseth [sic] that John H.D. Bond doth covenant with the several subscribers whose names are under written, to teach a school and instruct the Pupils that may be committed to his care in Reading, Writing, and Arithmetic, five days in each week (Muster days excepted) [local militia musters] with all the care, afsiduity [sic], and attention, in his power, for the term of nine months from his commencement in consideration of which service in of Tuition we the under written subscribers do promise to pay; or cause to be paid, unto the said, H.D. Bond, or cover the sum of eight dollars per scholar. As given under our hands the day and date above written.[65]

The preceding subscription school covenant was typical for this antebellum period in Georgia and indeed throughout most of the nineteenth-century South. Seventeen parents in northeastern Wilkes County signed this "covenant" and placed the exact number of students each pledged to get the school started, a total of 22 scholars. For a base pay of $176, H. D. Bond pledged to teach their community's children for at least nine months before he could move on (which most schoolmasters seemed to do with astonishing regularity).

The children who received some form of basic literacy education were fortunate. For those at the bottom rung of the economic spectrum, the "common folks," including small farmers or families who lived in remote mountain areas, domestic education was their children's only chance at literacy. Before the Civil War at least two generations grew up in northern Georgia with a limited education. Many were totally illiterate.[66]

Georgia's plantation owners, like their counterparts in other southern states, imported tutors from the North and even England. In 1793 Eli Whitney, a recent Yale College graduate, journeyed to the South and became a tutor on a Georgia plantation. Although he failed to make any notable contributions to the history of literacy while at that plantation, he did invent the cotton gin, making cotton raised by slave labor an important cash crop. Thus he helped guarantee

the Civil War (1861–1865). A further irony was Whitney's ineffective government patent on his innovation. The cotton gin was so simple almost any mechanic could copy it, and many did.[67]

One tutor's perspective helps complete our picture of home education in antebellum Georgia. Amelia Akehurst Lines (1827–1886) arrived in America from
England in 1829. During 1857–1858 her letters described the difficult life of a
Georgia plantation tutor-governess. She led both a lonely and a professionally
precarious existence.

February 7, 1858
    To Mr. Lines,
    Very rarely does any thing occur to relieve the monotony of my life at present; and
yet time does not hang heavily, or pass wearily away as I imagined it would: every day
cares and duties have given it wings. Through the day I am constantly with my pupils,
either in the school room, in the nursery, at the piano or on the play ground. Never
feel free from care until they are locked in the arms of slumber; then I "draw a long
breath" and sit down to read or write.
    Receive this as a token of regard,
    From Jennie [Amelia's nickname]

February 16, 1858
    My Dear Sister,
    Mrs. Shelman has a lady [interested] as governess [to replace Amelia]. She is in
Philadelphia and has been South three years and liked so well that she is anxious to
return. She has written two letters to Mrs. Shelman, and I should judge it very desirous to secure this situation. Mrs. Shelman is very much pleased,—says she shall
send for her. I am of course feeling very anxious. In many respects this is not a desirable place but it is decidedly comfortable and easy; and sure. I had made up my mind to
remain until I secured a pleasanter home or saved enough to take me home.
    Your sister,
    Jennie

Like many other nineteenth-century tutor-governesses, Jennie dreamed of
escape from her profession. After exchanging many woeful letters with "Mr.
Lines" (a Connecticut printer), she succeeded in marrying him in August 1859.[68]

Samuel Worthington and his two brothers owned cotton plantations close to
each other in Washington County, located near the Mississippi River north of
Vicksburg. Amanda, Samuel's daughter, kept a journal that recorded her educational experiences. The three brothers hired a private teacher, who organized a
school called the "Point Worthington Academy." It moved from one plantation
to another. Classes were held from six to seven months a year. Each brother took
the responsibility of maintaining the school on his own property for about two
months a year. This arrangement was in operation for a number of years during the mid-1850s; however, it is not known how long the school existed.[69]

This academy, which bore the name of Samuel Worthington's plantation, also
admitted a few other students from neighboring families. All the students were
grouped into various classes according to age. However, there was only one

teacher for this entire "academy." Amanda first started attending this school when she was 12 years old. Her earlier education probably took place at another local academy.[70]

Later Amanda was sent to a French music school in New Orleans, but she returned home at the outbreak of the Civil War. There she was enrolled at a small school called the "Butterbean Academy" with eight other boys and girls, three of whom were the plantation overseer's children. Miss Georgia Richardson, age 20, was her teacher.[71]

Amanda attended classes six hours a day Monday through Friday, from January to July 1862. However, her attendance was irregular because of sickness, probably malaria. School hours were kept flexible to accommodate severely rainy weather conditions. Sometimes classes were canceled or limited to a single session, from 8:00 A.M. to 2:00 P.M.[72]

The Butterbean Academy's curriculum included poetry, science, history, theology, drawing, and music. Amanda also studied rhetoric, with an original composition due each Monday. Miss Richardson also gave Amanda private music lessons at her home on Monday and Thursday afternoons.[73]

In the fall of 1862, Miss Richardson had to quit teaching because "she was threatened with consumption." Her resignation and the increased war activity along the Mississippi River led to the closing of the Butterbean Academy. Samuel Worthington made an effort to continue his children's education at home by hiring an itinerant preacher as their tutor. But this effort proved futile since the tutor was away most of the time preaching. As far as we know, Amanda never did finish her education, because of the tumultuous events that rocked the state of Mississippi during the Civil War.[74]

In an earlier, quieter era, a Selma Plantation diarist, a governess whose name was probably Margaret Wilson recorded her work as a literacy educator between 1835 and 1837. The plantation was located about a mile north of Washington, Mississippi, which had been the former territorial capital (1802–1830). Margaret Lindsay Smith, the widow of Captain Smith, lived on Selma Plantation with her only daughter, Mary, and Maria Chambers, a single woman related by marriage.[75]

Washington, Mississippi, was the first stop on the Natchez Trace, as it heads northeast from the river toward Nashville. For a time the town prospered, before Natchez stole its commerce and the capital was moved to Jackson. In the 1830s Jefferson College still flourished as the oldest institution of higher education in the "Old Southwest." Elizabeth Academy for Girls, created in 1819, was also in operation.[76]

Even with these local education resources, Margaret Smith decided that her daughter Mary needed a governess and logically turned to the city of Pittsburgh as an educational resource. For more than a generation an active trade route flourished along the Ohio and Mississippi Rivers from western Pennsylvania to Natchez. Countless people had migrated downriver, so why not also import a northern governess?

It appears that our governess Margaret Wilson had fled southwest after being rejected by a man she names only as "the Shadow." We do not know if Margaret intended for this to be only a brief sojourn or the new beginning of a lifetime's work. She did seem to miss Pittsburgh, referring to herself as "a poor desolate Exile."[77]

Margaret's own education to become a governess seems to have been largely limited to the traditional female "accomplishments." She played the piano and the guitar. Margaret read the latest popular literature and wrote poetry and songs. She also claimed to know French and to have French ancestors.[78]

In June 1835, Margaret changed from tutoring only Mary by taking in another pupil. "Mrs. Smith has the kindness to encourage me to increase my school." Later that same month a third pupil was "added to my formidable number. . . . I have now the prospect of three scholars for next summer, they would all be very good and profitable.[79]

However, by the end of 1836 Margaret was ready to turn over her duties to her successor, another woman with the name of Margaret. The new governess does not appear very enthusiastic about the assignment, for it seems that she had already taught Mary Smith at an earlier date. "What business had I to come back, a little more money, and perhaps I shall be disappointed in that, it looks very much like it thus far."[80]

On April 7, 1837, Miss Wilson writes,

I would not let Margaret [the new governess] come into the school on Friday for good luck sake, but I have been writing for her a system of regulation for the different studies and exercises of every day. I hope it may be of some service to her.

[Wednesday April 12]

Margaret stays in school with me all day, I wonder if she is not both frightened and disgusted at the task before her—I think she is in bad spirits about it.

Margaret Wilson left Selma Plantation in early May 1837. For many women in the antebellum South, it would seem that being a private literacy educator was a lonely and dispiriting occupation.[81]

A more positive personal experience was the domestic literacy education given by Ann Lewis Hardeman (1803–1868) to the children of her extended family. Born in Tennessee, one of seven children, by 1849 she was living at her brother William's plantation, a few miles south of Jackson, Mississippi. Though William's wife Mary was childless, living also with them were the six children of Ann's deceased sister Sarah, as well as her sister Caroline and their mother.[82]

Ann's diary begins in June 1850, while she is struggling to become the family's domestic literacy educator and to meet and understand the responsibilities of motherhood, without either having the formal title or being able to exercise the prerogatives of a mother. Her sister's children ranged in age from James, at twelve, though Oscar, nine, Adelaide, seven, Annie, five, Edward, three, and Sarah, only one.[83]

The educational program that Ann supervised alternated sporadically between school attendance and domestic education. Academies seemed to open or close in the typical haphazard manner of that time, with Ann destined to fill in the literacy gaps for each child.

Wednesday, July 24
James and Oscar's school closed yesterday in the afternoon—their teachers gave them a treat of ice cream and distributed the rewards. James got McAuley's *History of England*. This morning he has commenced teaching the little ones in due form—Oscar—Adelaide and Betty (a cousin)—Edward occasionally. [cross-age tutoring][84]

Tuesday, August 20
Have commenced teaching the children since yesterday morning, succeeded quite well.

Friday, August 23
Have succeeded tolerably well with the children during the past week. They are much happier than when they do not say lessons. Adelaide commenced Geography this morning.

August 27
The children said lessons very well for about 10 days.

October 15
... the boys started to school to Dr. Barbee 30th September on Monday—doing tolerably well. Adelaide still recites her lessons to me.

1851
Thursday, January 16
Children all well except colds, learning tolerably well. Bettie is learning to read and Adelaide to write.

Saturday, January 25
Dr. Barbee gave up his school on Tuesday 20th. Mr. Holman their former teacher will take school again.

Tuesday, February 4
James and Oscar commenced school today under Mr. Holman's tuition—8 scholars present.

Thursday, March 6
Adelaide commenced "Parley's first Book of History" this morning, did very well

Sunday, March 9
The children doing very well. Adelaide said her lessons without giving me any trouble during the past weeks—think she will succeed very well with her History.

1852
Monday, February 9, Noon
The 3 younger children, Adelaide, Bettie and Edward have recommenced their lessons at home during an interval of 2½ months they have recited no lessons. ... Edward has not said regularly his lesson is now on the 23rd page of "Webster's Elementary" Speller beginning with the 22 lesson—

Monday, March 1 One O'clock
Have commenced with the children on Rev. Mr. Lewins plan—have heard their lessons for to-day.[85]

In 1853 James is again hired to tutor his brothers and sisters during the summer vacation.

Monday, August 1

He will have Oscar, Adelaide, Bettie, Edward, Willie and Josey Bowman [a cousin]—Oscar and Adelaide at the rate of $1.50 per month the balance at $1, he has been teaching about 10 days and has succeeded so far very well.

1855

Thursday, October 5

James went to College this morning—I have engaged Oscar's services as teacher at 50 ct per week.

1857

Monday, April 20

Adelaide and Bettie went to school. [evidently the Jackson High School for Young Ladies run by Mrs. Ozanne]

1859

Sunday, July 10

Our dear James arrived with his uncle William from Oxford [a local school] where he had spent the last 4 years to complete his term at College [today the University of Mississippi]. I do not hesitate to say that he has in every respect fulfilled the expectations of his entire family.[86]

Also in 1859 Oscar, Betty, and Adelaide were sent north to a school in Burlington, New Jersey. "I need not record the pain it gave me to give them up," Ann writes, after being for nine years their surrogate mother and primary literacy educator.[87]

The Civil War (1861–1865) now intervened and nullified much of Ann's careful nurturing of these children. While serving with his cousin, the famous Confederate calvary leader J.E.B. Stuart, James was killed at the Second Battle of Manassas, Virginia, in September 1862. Less than six months later William died (March 1863) after a short, sharp illness. Six weeks later Oscar was killed in battle. Only Edward was left to soldier on, surviving the war to become a carpenter. Ann lived long enough to see two of her students become educators. Adelaide made a living as a schoolteacher, and Bettie became a governess.[88]

The patterns of literacy development for antebellum Louisiana were similar in many ways to other areas of the South. Charity schools, "old-field schools," so-called academies, and private family tutors were the mainstays of literacy. Most of these antebellum tutors were self-made entrepreneurs, many from the North, who came south to seek personal career opportunities by attaching themselves to the so-called southern plantation aristocracy. One such member of that class in the Lower South was John Hampden Randolph.

In 1841 he purchased Nottoway Plantation in Iberville Parish, Louisiana. There Randolph planted sugar on several thousand acres with a labor force of 195 slaves. He employed a resident physician to care for their health, white Arkansans to process the sugar, and Irish immigrants to dig drainage ditches. For Randolph's children's education he hired a northern college graduate as their primary literacy educator and separate itinerant music and dancing teachers. Later, as young men, Randolph's sons attended either the University of Virginia or Rensselaer Polytechnic. His daughters were sent to a fashionable girls' finishing school in Baltimore to finish their education.[89]

AN EDUCATIONAL MOSAIC

Literacy education throughout the antebellum South can be characterized as a rich mosaic of individual or small-group initiatives led by dedicated and often well-educated literacy schoolmasters supplemented by domestic educators. They existed in sharp relief to a general societal ambivalence about literacy that pervaded the largely agricultural, rural antebellum South. Across this landscape many people seemed to believe that a basic literacy education was not a necessary prerequisite for improving one's life. This "literacy disenfranchisement" extended to most of the working classes and the African Americans and certainly supported this era's politically correct view about the minimal mental cultivation appropriate for women. These social attitudes help explain the lack of any comparable common-school movement developing across the South until after the Civil War.

With that said, the programs of evening schools, academies, charity schools, subscription schools, and plantation schools, though sometimes ephemeral and unsystematic, certainly demonstrate that many southern parents and educators did care a great deal about literacy. We have seen how Margaret Clark Griffis, Hercules Whaley, Julia Tevis, Rachel Mordecai, Amelia Akehurst Lines, and Ann Lewis Hardeman productively labored in such places as the Science Hill Female Academy, the Butterbean Academy, and the PBMA Evening School. They overcame general indifference to satisfy the personal desire of a growing number of parents that their children should receive at least a basic literacy education. Their lives provide us a striking example of what southern literacy educators could achieve for that time.

NOTES

1. Lawrence Cremin, *American Education: The National Experience 1783–1876* (New York: Harper & Row, 1980), 71–172; Samuel Eliot Morison, *The Oxford History of the American People* (New York: Oxford University Press, 1965), 511; Arthur W. Calhoun, *A Social History of the American Family* (New York: Barnes & Noble, 1945), 340; Barbara L. Bellows, *Benevolence Among Slaveholders: Assisting the Poor in Charleston 1670–1860* (Baton Rouge: Louisiana State University Press, 1993); Janet Duitsman Cornelius, *"When I Can Read My Title Clear": Literacy, Slavery, and Religion in the Antebellum South* (Columbia: University of South Carolina Press, 1991), 33.

2. Alexander Gaston to William Gaston, 9 July 1813, Gaston Papers, Southern Historical Collection, Library of the University of North Carolina, Chapel Hill, North Carolina.

3. John D. Hawkins to ABC, 31 August 1828, Hawkins Family Papers, Southern Historical Collection, Library of the University of North Carolina, Chapel Hill, North Carolina.

4. William P. Little to William Polk, 11 November 1822, Polk and Yeatmann Family Papers, Southern Historical Collection, Library of the University of North Carolina, Chapel Hill, North Carolina.

5. Anne W. Johnson to Charles E. Johnson, Jr., May, n.d. (ca. 1848), Johnson Papers, Duke University Library, Durham, North Carolina.

6. John Hope Franklin, *A Southern Odyssey: Travelers in the Antebellum North* (Baton Rouge: Louisiana State University Press, 1976), 73.

7. Joseph Pearson to William Gaston, 3 July 1823, Gaston Papers, Southern Historical Collection, Library of the University of North Carolina, Chapel Hill, North Carolina.

8. Morison, *Oxford History*, 502.

9. Margaret Clark Griffis, Diary, 1 January 1858; 27 September 1866, Rutgers University Library, New Brunswick, New Jersey.

10. Ibid., 2 January 1858, 2 June 1858, 29 June 1858, 22 September 1858.

11. Ibid., 18 November 1859, 10 February 1860, 1 February 1861, 20 November 1864, 17 November 1865.

12. Ibid., 2 January 1858 to 4 June 1858, 5 November 1859, 17 February 1861, 13 March 1861.

13. Ibid., 11 February 1860; general entries.

14. Minnie Clare Yarborough, ed., *The Reminiscences of William C. Preston* (Chapel Hill: University of North Carolina Press, 1933), 2.

15. Ibid., 3–5.

16. Ibid., 5–6.

17. The Custis-Lee Mansion still exists and is open to the public.

18. Agnes Lee, *Growing Up in the 1850's: The Journal of Agnes Lee*, ed. Mary Custis Lee de Butts (Chapel Hill: University of North Carolina Press, 1984), xi, xvii, 3.

19. Ibid., 4, 10.

20. Ibid., 4, 16.

21. Jane Gibbs, Diary, 27 March 1857 to 30 November 1859, Library of Virginia, Richmond, Virginia.

22. Edgar Knight, ed., *A Documentary History of Education in the South before 1860*, vol. 4 (Chapel Hill: University of North Carolina Press, 1949), 36.

23. James D. Watkinson, "Reluctant Scholars: Apprentices and the Petersburg (Virginia) Benevolent Mechanic's Association School," *History of Education Quarterly* 36 (Winter 1996): 433.

24. Ibid., 429.

25. John W. Boitnott, "Secondary Education in Virginia 1845–1870." (Ph.D. diss., University of Virginia, 1935), 317–318; James G. Scott and Edward A. Wyatt IV, *Petersburg's Story: A History of Petersburg, Va.* (Petersburg, Virginia: 1960), 118.

26. Watkinson, "Reluctant Scholars," 434.

27. Ibid., 435–436, 443.

28. Ibid., 444–448.

29. Calhoun, *American Family*, 59.

30. Amos Kendall, *The Autobiography of Amos Kendall* (Boston: Lee & Shepard, 1872), 115.

31. Ashland is today open to view in the city of Lexington, Kentucky. Ibid., 116.

32. Ibid.

33. Ibid.

34. Ibid., 117.

35. Ibid., 117–118.

36. Ibid., 124.

37. Ibid., 131.

38. Ibid., 142.

39. Ibid.

40. Julia A. Tevis, *Sixty Years in a School Room* (Cincinnati: Western Methodist Book Concern, 1878), 54–56.

41. Ibid., 67–68.

42. Ibid., 84.

43. Ibid., 118.

44. Ibid., 164.

45. Ibid., 175.

46. Ibid., 190–191.

47. Ibid., 192, 195.

48. Ibid., 197, 208–210.

49. Ibid., 259–263, 315–316.

50. Ibid., 321, 322.

51. Ibid., 324.

52. Ibid., 484.

53. Jane H. Pease and William H. Pease, *Ladies, Women and Wenches: Choice and Constraint in Antebellum Charleston and Boston* (Chapel Hill: University of North Carolina Press, 1990), 77.

54. Ibid., 77–78.

55. Ibid., 79.

56. Knight, *Documentary History*, 48.

57. Brian W. Taylor, "The Edgeworths' Influence on the Warrenton Female Academy," *Vitae Scholasticae* 14 (Spring 1995): 61.

58. Ibid., 61–62.

59. Ibid., 62–63.

60. Other schools were even named after them, such as the Edgeworth Seminary in Greensboro, North Carolina. See Mary Kelley "Reading Women/Women Reading: The Making of Learned Woman in Antebellum America," *Journal of American History* 83 (September 1996): 401, 417; Taylor, "Warrenton Female Academy," 64, 70–71.

61. Isaac T. Avery to W. B. Lenoir, January 11, 1824, in Lenoir Family Papers, Southern Historical Collection, Library of the University of North Carolina, Chapel Hill, North Carolina.

62. Joseph B. Skinner to Joshua Skinner, June 17, 1823, in Skinner Family Papers, Southern Historical Collection Library of the University of North Carolina, Chapel Hill, North Carolina.

63. Mary S. Henderson, Diary, June 30, 1855, in Henderson Papers, Southern Historical Collection, Library of the University of North Carolina, Chapel Hill, North Carolina.

64. D. D. Hall, "A Yankee Tutor in the Old South," *The New England Quarterly* 33 (1960): 82–91.

65. Subscription School Covenant, Wilkes County, Georgia, January 3, 1820, Panhandle Plains Historic Museum Research Center, Canyon, Texas.

66. Calhoun, *American Family*, 348.

67. Shirley Abbott, *The National Museum of American History* (New York: Abrams, 1981), 131.

68. Amelia Akehurst Lines, *To Raise Myself a Little: The Diaries and Letters of Jennie, a Georgia Teacher 1851–1886*, ed. Thomas Dyer (Athens, Georgia: University of Georgia Press, 1982), xiii, 74, 77–78, 78–79.

69. Journal of Amanda Worthington, two vols., and Worthington Family Papers, Southern Historical Collection, University of North Carolina, Chapel Hill, North Carolina;

Samuel Worthington, Papers of Washington County Historical Society, Jackson, Mississippi; Clifford C. Norse, "School Life of Amanda Worthington of Washington County 1857–1862," *Journal of Mississippi History* 34 (1972): 109.

70. Ibid., 9.

71. Ibid., 110–111.

72. Ibid., 111–112.

73. Ibid., 113–114.

74. Ibid., 115–116.

75. Michael O'Brien, ed., *An Evening When Alone: Four Journals of Single Women in the South 1827–67* (Charlottesville: University of Virginia Press, 1993), 15–16.

76. Ibid., 17.

77. Ibid., 17–18.

78. Ibid., 20.

79. Ibid., 109, 112, 145.

80. Ibid., 132.

81. Ibid., 150.

82. Ann L. Hardeman, Diary, 3 vols., Oscar J. E. Stuart Papers, Mississippi Department of Archives and History, Jackson, Mississippi; O'Brien, *Journals of Single Women*, 32, 33, 46, 48.

83. O'Brien, *Journals of Single Women*, 227.

84. Ibid., 222.

85. Ibid., 223, 225, 229–230, 231, 240.

86. Ibid., 245, 256, 269, 283.

87. Ibid., 286.

88. Ibid., 43–44.

89. Morison, *Oxford History*, 502.

Part III

Literacy and the Frontier Experience (1790–1900)

Chapter 6

"Jack of All Trades, Master of Some": Pioneer Educators of the Midwest

MIDWESTERN ROOTS

After the American Revolution ended (1783), pioneers leaving the eastern seaboard states moved westward looking for new farmland. They migrated to the territories of the Middle West without degenerating into a colonial people, confident of retaining their full civil, political, and educational liberties. This important legal framework was the crowning accomplishment of the Northwest Ordinance, which permanently defined the political and educational development of the future Midwestern states.

Adopted by Congress on July 13, 1787, the Northwest Ordinance was both visionary and practical. Of uncertain authorship, its origins lie with both the earlier plans of Thomas Jefferson and the later work by James Monroe. Individual territorial status was given after the population reached 5,000 free males, with statehood conferred at 60,000. Most importantly the new states were "on an equal footing with the original states in all respects whatsoever." These new, sparsely populated states had the same potential power in Congress as older, much larger states, including the right to provide public financial support for education.[1]

Ohio, Indiana, Illinois, Michigan, and Wisconsin were all carved out of the Northwest Territory. However, the ordinance established an important legal precedent, and all subsequent new territories down to present-day Alaska and Hawaii were organized according to its legal framework.[2]

While reviewing how literacy developed in the Midwest and other regions of the United States, it is useful to recall that these historical events did not occur in a vacuum. The wider social, economic, and political contexts provide vital perspective on the overall cultural evolution of literacy, which is lacking in the study of educational development as a series of isolated events.

PRAIRIE LITERACY: ILLINOIS

For contemporary readers it may seem strange that Trappist monks were responsible for the earliest recorded literacy activities in Illinois. Here is how it happened. The new territorial Governor Ninian Edwards and Nicholas Jarrot, a respected French resident, persuaded a Kentucky community of Trappist monks, led by a Father Urbain Guillet, to settle in 1809 at Cahokia, Illinois. These vegetarian monks laid out gardens, cared for the sick, and opened a free school. Unfortunately, meager harvests and disease so thinned their ranks that the surviving monks returned east in 1813. Their one lasting legacy, "Monks' Mound," the huge Indian mound on which they lived, was named after them.[3]

On April 18, 1818, President Monroe signed legislation creating the State of Illinois. This enabling act earmarked 3 percent of the proceeds from Illinois' federal land sales to support education.[4] However, these meager financial resources and public indifference severely limited literacy in the early years after Illinois statehood. Public education was virtually nonexistent. Literacy education practices were at best sporadic, uneven, and private.[5]

In 1824 State Senator Joseph Duncan, who later would become a governor of Illinois, introduced a "Free School Law" similar to a plan drafted by Thomas Jefferson when he was governor of Virginia. The act authorized the raising of local taxes for education, local contracts, and popularly elected school officers. The bill passed both houses of the legislature and was signed by Governor Edward Coles on January 15, 1825. This free common-school law opened literacy to all white citizens to the age of 21. Unfortunately, within two years the law's taxation feature hardened opposition, so that in 1827 another bill gutted the Free School Law, declaring that no person could "be taxed without his consent." This meant that local school districts could authorize taxation only after every taxpayer in the district agreed in writing to be taxed! This resuscitated the popular private academies and subscription schools supported with quarterly fees paid by parents. Only in 1855 did the state finally begin to create a structure for giving every child a free literacy education.[6]

There was little doubt that there existed a need for literacy on what was then the western frontier. Theron Baldwin, a future trustee of Illinois College at Jacksonville wrote about the extensive illiteracy on the Illinois prairie. A typical 1820s village of 52 families contained 27 households in which no member could read, write, or cipher. As late as 1840 another survey estimated that of the 472,000 free adults living in Illinois, only about 27,000 persons over 21 years of age could either read or write.[7]

Numerous individuals operating with various motives and at many levels of ability endeavored to make a living by teaching. They opened subscription schools here and there throughout the state; some lasted for a few weeks or months, while others enjoyed greater longevity. The schoolmasters running these academies advertised for students, stating the terms of the school, and charged each student a fixed tuition that ranged from $3.50 to $7 per quarter, per pupil. Typically these teachers also accepted room and board at the pupils' homes as a form of payment, generally moving from family to family every few weeks.

At the age of 20, Stephen A. Douglas, the future U.S. Senator from Illinois, arrived in the fall of 1833 at the town of Winchester. After searching for students, he set up a school with 40 scholars. Each parent paid him $3 per quarter. As was common at the time, Douglas regarded his teaching as just a stopgap measure to put food on his table while preparing for another career. He read the law while he taught, and by March 1834 Douglas was admitted to the bar and closed his school to later enter politics.[8]

Susan Short May was born in 1836 in Kendall County. She describes a subscription school she attended near her village of Bristol.

The first school which I can remember attending was a tuition school, taught by a dear, lovable woman, probably not over twenty-five years of age, who we were permitted to call "Aunt Polly." The school room was one room in her brother's house. The little children sat on a low bench without a back, which ran through the middle of the room. The older children had desks.

She taught both patriotism and history in rhyme. And we also sang, or rather intoned, the kings and queens of England.[9]

Most frontier schools were of the crudest type. Many were one-room log cabins with oiled paper for windows. Desks and benches were rough-hewn puncheons (split logs round side down, with logs driven into auger holes). In winter the only heat came from an open fireplace that warmed only those fortunate enough to be close to the fire. In warm weather swarms of flies and mosquitoes abounded, making learning difficult. Discipline was maintained by the vigorous and frequent application of the rod of authority to the seat of understanding. Parents often lacked the knowledge or experience to hire good teachers. A report on schoolmasters in Illinois and Missouri during the 1830s stated that one-third were public nuisances due to incompetence or immorality, one-third did as much harm as good, and only about one-third were of some use in teaching basic literacy.[10]

Some Illinois towns did make an effort to provide a decent literacy education. Consider, for example, Naples, Illinois, which by 1836 had three hundred settlers drawn from nearly every state and a few families from England. Like many other towns in the Prairie State, Naples's diverse population and small size made interdenominational cooperation in educational matters a necessity. An important common bond stemmed from the mutual concern for the education of the community's children. In other towns like Kaskaskia, the Reverend Desmoulin taught Latin and French. A New England schoolmistress ran a school at Salu. In 1829 Aratus Kent operated a Latin and Greek grammar school in Galena. Alton, Illinois, used the endowment from one hundred lots to provide a free public education. By 1830 girls' schools began to open, such as the Monticello Seminary (1838) just north of Alton. This school educated generations of women before closing in 1971.[11]

Many churches in Illinois, as the agents of Eastern missionary societies, also maintained vigorous and varied literacy programs. Circuit-riding ministers functioned simultaneously as preachers and as itinerant literacy teachers.

An early example comes from the personal reminiscences of Mary Otwell. Her husband, Seth Otwell, was a Methodist circuit rider when Mary first arrived in Carlinville, Macoupin County, in 1831. Schooling at that time was being offered in every type of public and private building imaginable. This also included their log home, which served as the community's first official schoolhouse. "Wide planks were thrown down," Mary relates, "loose for flooring, they half way covering the sleepers upon which they rested. As the building was set upon logs laid under the corners, I used to be afraid lest the wolves that we heard howling around the house should crawl under and come up between the sleepers, and try to make our acquaintance."[12]

It was about the year '34 that the school building known as the "Old Seminary" was built. The first teachers were Mr. and Mrs. Cooley and Miss Almira Packard, afterwards Mrs. Whipple. They were pretty good teachers. . . .

About the same time Braxton Eastham came from Kentucky and settled in Carlinville. . . . They removed to a cabin near where they now live. This cabin was in later days used for a school house called "Good Intent." Later it was used as chicken house. . . .

Uncle Jarrott assisted in organizing the first Sunday School in the place, and afterwards to carry it on—filling, I believe the office of superintendent. His sons Joseph, Wesley and Ferguson, were old enough to form a little school, at least there was a beginning around which to gather in the other children of the town.

From these humble beginnings Mary's recollections give us a picture of buildings serving many functions and of people playing many different educational roles.[13]

Another view of the literacy educational activities among the residents of Macoupin County can be found in the educational pursuits of Edmund Multanowski. He was hired in 1856 by eighteen Carlinville German Lutheran families. Multanowski supported himself entirely through periodic subscriptions for holding religious services. However, his duties were as much academic as religious. As a circuit-riding tutor-educator, Multanowski ran a school two days a week in Carlinville and on two other days rode through the surrounding countryside teaching as he went. He instructed children who were not members of the Lutheran church for a fee of 25 cents per day. These parents also provided Multanowski with transportation out to the hinterland and back. By the 1860s his successor, in addition to running a day school, had begun to conduct evening adult Bible school. The day school grew to the point that by 1865, another teacher was hired permanently.[14]

What all these literacy activities ultimately accomplished was recorded in the U.S. Census of 1850. In Macoupin County the census recorded 72 common schools with 73 teachers and 1,958 students. However, when all of the other private academies, schools, Sunday schools, and home schools of every variety were added, the same census reported that 3,356 students attended school. If these figures are accurate, they translate into about 90 percent of the total county school-age population of 3,715 (ages 5–14) spending some time in some type of school. This was no small literacy achievement for an Illinois frontier area. Unfortunately, not all the other Illinois counties followed Macoupin's educational example,[15] though many other educators seemed to try.

The Massachusetts Education Missionary Society was organized to support pastors and other reliable persons who wished to go to western states and become elementary school teachers. In return these teachers agreed to conduct nonsectarian common schools and to promote general literacy in every possible way. The Baptists also supported a seminary in Illinois that was located first at Rock Springs and later in Upper Alton. The seminary enrolled prospective schoolteachers at reduced tuition, if they agreed to teach for a period in Illinois. Sectarian Baptist teaching, however, was confined to conducting Sunday schools on the Lord's Day.[16]

In the pioneer prairie states like Illinois, the struggle for literacy required the alliance of people of many different religious persuasions.[17] The Congregational ministers of the American Home Missionary Society sent to Illinois after 1827 reported high levels of illiteracy among the Kentucky and Tennessee frontier people they encountered in Southern Illinois. For example, Theron Baldwin enrolled 105 pupils in his Vandalia Sunday school in the spring of 1830. He was amazed to find that only 37 could read. In visits to nearly settlements, of 52 families less than half contained even one literate child or adult. Though Baldwin organized a Sunday school there, "to gather in if possible young and old, and learn them to read," he urged his superiors in New York to send more schoolteachers West.[18]

While Baldwin continued to petition his New York superiors for teachers, Mrs. Theron Baldwin and another home missionary's wife, Mrs. John F. Brooks, formed on October 4, 1833, the Ladies Education Society of Jacksonville, Illinois, allegedly the oldest women's organization in the United States. This organization helped needy and worthy women to obtain an education and paid all or part of their tuition. Based on their successful fund-raising in the East, the society awarded tuition grants, some as little as $5, to pupils in many parts of Illinois, Michigan, Wisconsin, and Nebraska. In most cases the girls receiving these grants provided their own board by working in the homes of families that were near the tutor who gave them instruction. In addition to tuition, the society sometimes purchased the students' books.[19]

The Ladies Education Society's goal was not only to educate these girls but also to train them for a teaching career. Therefore, most of the girls receiving aid were at least 12 years old. The society's members believed it would be easier to educate young women already in the Midwest who knew how to endure hardship than to recruit female teachers from the East. However, no pledges ever were required from these students, who could attend the school of their own choice.[20]

The interest of these ministers' wives in literacy brought an incalculable benefit to the Midwest. By 1848 about 500 students were receiving literacy instruction from the society's teachers. Pastor Baldwin further advanced this effort by establishing the Monticello Female Seminary, which trained scores of girls as literacy instructors.[21]

One of these women was Emma Morse Loomis, who had been born in Maine, in 1848, before moving to Illinois.

After leaving school, [the Female Academy in Jacksonville], I was governess to three little girls in their county home. Their mother preferred it that way, did not like to send them to the county school. . . . I was recommended to the mother of these little girls—8, 10, 12—by my professor. I taught there two years.[22]

In 1839 Jacksonville opened the Illinois School for the Deaf and later (1849) the Illinois School for the Blind. All of these educational activities provided a critical mass for literacy backed by local sentiment in favor of education.

About the same time (1846), Lucy Larcum began her life as an itinerant district-school teacher. She spent a few months teaching in one school in the district before moving on to the next one-room schoolhouse. Illiteracy was rampant. Whole families could not read or write. Sometimes parents did not understand that their children could learn to do so. Lucy received a salary of $14 a month as she taught in Waterloo, Lebanon, Sugar Creek, and Woodburn, Illinois.

Teaching conditions remained very primitive, as can be imagined from Lucy's description of a typical schoolroom.

Tis built of unhewn logs, laid "criss-cross," as we used to say in the lane; the chunks filled up with mud, except those which are not filled up "at all, at all," and the chimney is stuck on behind the house.

They never had a school in this district before. . . . I asked one new scholar how old she was. "Don't know," she said, "never was inside of a schoolhouse before."[23]

Most rural Illinois communities failed to provide any public education. Abraham Lincoln (1809–1865) received a basic literacy education mainly at home. He attended school very briefly. As a young man in Illinois he was tutored to become a surveyor (1833) by Mentor Graham, a former schoolmaster. Graham's daughter related how many nights at midnight she woke up to see Lincoln and her father figuring and explaining by the fireside using Robert Gibson's *The Theory and Practice of Surveying*. These lessons and self-education enabled Lincoln to become a surveyor. Several years later Lincoln rode into Springfield to read the law under the tutelage of lawyers Henry E. Dunner and J. T. Stuart. By 1837, Lincoln began a very successful law practice with Stuart.[24] As president, drawing on his own educational upbringing, Lincoln had his youngest son, Willie, tutored at the White House. Alexander Williamson, a genteel Scotsman, taught Willie (1861–1862) until the child's premature death.[25]

Another prominent figure in Illinois history, Frances E. Willard, whose childhood years were divided between Illinois and Wisconsin, was taught at home first by her mother and then by a young neighbor. Her mother maintained an evening school for her three children and the hired hands.

When Frances was 12, her family hired Miss Burdick, an 18-year-old woman, to teach Willard, her sister, and two girls from a nearby family. The girls ranged from age eight to fourteen. "For two summers Miss Burdick carried on her institution of four pupils, the second summer a few more coming in, and gave an elaborate exhibition at the close."[26]

Willard's father and a neighbor built a district school about a mile from her home. She began attending this school at age 14, taught by a Professor Hodge, a Yale graduate of English birth. "Accustomed to teach men, he bent himself gently to the task of pointing out ABC's to the youngest. . . . he was a fine reader and his greatest pleasure seemed to be when his older pupils rendered to his satisfaction some gem from the English poets, in which he trained us carefully." Willard studied with him only for about four months and then received instruction from a rapid succession of other teachers during her four subsequent years in this school.

In 1857 Willard and her younger sister were sent to the Milwaukee Female College. But a year later they transferred to the North Western Female College in Evanston, Illinois. During six weeks of the summer of 1858, Willard taught in her old Wisconsin district school.[27]

In her journal Willard recorded with growing unease the coming of the Civil War during the fall of 1860. Willard's primary concern was for her friend Mary Bannister's safety as a governess teaching in Tennessee. Luckily, by early December, Bannister had terminated her tutoring contract and returned to Evanston, thus avoiding being a Yankee in the South after the outbreak of the Civil War (April 1861).[28] Willard was then confronted with the unpleasant dilemma that weighed heavily on all young unmarried women of her time: "Not to be at all, or else to be a teacher." She decided to enter the schoolroom. "Between 1858 when I began, and 1874 when I forever ceased to be a pedagogue, I had 13 separate seasons of teaching in 11 separate institutions and six separate towns." What may now appear to have been a rather haphazard career seems to have been typical for most nineteenth-century male and female teachers.[29]

During the summer of 1860 Willard taught in a district school in Harlem, Illinois, an area west of Chicago. But her "school life" was almost unendurable.

6 June 1860

Here I have twenty-seven scholars. Five "ABC darians," the rest all under twelve years old except two girls and one boy. The school house leaks, is small, dirty and meanly constructed as a whole. The children are more than half Germans, the rest Irish and uncultivated (Oh how emphatically so!) Americans. I have class in Botany, U.S. History, Algebra, Arithmetic, & Grammar. . . .

I don't want to punish them but,—here's the philosophy of it: I have tried to appeal to their consciences,—I can not find that they have any; to their "honors," they have none;—to their pride, it is latent; to their ambition, it is wanting; to their good nature;— it is underdeveloped. Nothing remains, but appealing to their *nerves*;—they understand that! When I *strike* and the tingling, painful sensation creeps over their brown little palms, they wake up, and never otherwise. ... Those who have been trained at home require little discipline—they are studious, quiet and obedient, and I have pleasure in them.

[They] ... are my "civilized pupils"—. ... But what are these among the many? Seven, out of an average of thirty-seven.[30]

In the future, Willard would abandon education and become nationally famous as the leader of the Women's Christian Temperance Union, headquartered to this day in Evanston, Illinois.

Illinois State lawmakers in 1855 finally assumed overall responsibility for education by levying a property tax. These funds were further buttressed by sales of the sixteenth section of each township, the "school section." Meanwhile many church-affiliated institutions of higher learning had burgeoned on the prairies: St. Xavier College (1846), Rosary College (1848), Illinois Wesleyan University (1850), Northwestern University (1851), Eureka College (1855), Lake Forest College (1857), Wheaton College (1860), and many others. Though many failed within a few years, some did attract out-of-state students and survive to this day.[31]

However, even these encouraging educational steps did not mean that universal literacy was growing throughout the state. For example, in western Schuyler County, by 1861 about 63 percent of students under the age of 21 attended school. By 1871 this figure had tumbled to just 56 percent and by 1881 had slipped to under 55 percent. Though the new Illinois constitution of 1870 charged the General Assembly to establish an "efficient system of free schools," not until 1915 would Illinois adopt the necessary legislation requiring tax-supported, mandatory, compulsory education for all children between the ages of seven and sixteen.[32]

How does this overview of early Illinois literacy compare to educational practices in nearby states? While there was much common ground, we also will find some remarkable variations in the way literacy was attained in the other states of the Midwest.

LITERACY'S LIMITS: MISSOURI

When Chicago was only a village, St. Louis was a major Midwestern city, because of its key location on the Mississippi River, which made it the hub for the fur trade of the Far West. St. Louis was founded in 1764 by Pierre Laclede Liguest as the northernmost trading post of French Louisiana. To keep this city from being handed over to the British after France's defeat in the French and Indian War, St. Louis was given to Spain through a secret treaty. For the next 37 years, St. Louis remained an important commercial trading center, attracting many French refugees from the former lands of New France. It remained under Spanish political rule until the Louisiana purchase by the United States in 1803.[33]

Among the early St. Louis literacy educators was the Society of the Sacred Heart, a French order of nuns. They came to the city in 1827 and founded an educational institution that endures to this day. Like the Ursuline nuns in New Orleans, the Sacred Heart sisters began a variety of education programs for women, including an academy, a free school, and a Sunday school for African Americans. In addition, 20 orphans were continually under the sisters' care.[34]

For girls from families who could afford to pay for schooling, the Sacred Heart Academy was started in 1827 with an enrollment of about 20 girls. Both boarding and day-school divisions offered a five-year educational program. From 1840 to 1860 between 70 and 80 pupils were enrolled in the academy. The literacy impact of the academy was probably most striking in its earliest days. However, even as St. Louis grew, its contribution to literacy remained significant.[35]

For an entire decade the free school of the Sacred Heart was the only institution offering a literacy education to poor girls on a large scale. Its enrollment of 30 students in 1827 rose to 93 pupils in May 1832. Both English- and French-speaking girls attended, with the former taught by an Irish and the latter a French nun. The Sunday school for African-American girls appears to have remained operating until 1847, when Missouri enacted a law prohibiting all African-American education.

The students in the free school were divided into three classes. They received basic literacy instruction in reading, writing, spelling, arithmetic, and religion. In the 1830s, for a small fee, these girls could also enroll in a more advanced department to be taught grammar, geography, and sewing.

Though the prejudices of that time required that this "free school" and the academy meet in separate buildings, free-school pupils took part in the general graduation exercises, distribution of academic prizes, and membership in the honorary "confraternity of the Sacred Heart."[36]

In 1830, when the city's population reached about 5,000, St. Louis possessed two coeducational schools and two female seminaries. There were also a few other short-lived subscription schools. Many families with means sent their children to school out of state.[37]

The first St. Louis public schools were not opened until 1838. They charged fees until 1847, when these schools became entirely free.[38] Literacy practices recorded by the U.S. Census of 1840 revealed that only one student in five (266 out of 1,200 children receiving any education) attended the St. Louis public schools. The majority of children were either educated at home or attended private schools.[39]

A study of literacy in St. Louis between 1840 and 1870 also found that many middle- and upper-class children were privately educated at home. Many of these students had tutors from Europe. To finish their education, these students frequently attended eastern U.S. colleges or journeyed to Europe.[40]

Thus the school programs conducted by the Society of the Sacred Heart were a very significant contribution to literacy education in St. Louis in terms of both number and diversity. In the summer of 1829 the "five schools" that included middle/upper-class, African-American, orphaned, and poor females enrolled over one hundred girls and young women. By 1839 their combined enrollment well exceeded 200.[41]

The separation of literacy instruction into these various schools and groups of girls may seem objectionable by today's diversity standards. By the societal conventions of the early nineteenth century, the Academy of the Sacred Heart in St. Louis pushed to the limits the concept of providing universal literacy instruction by defying many local prejudices and reaching out to girls from every segment of that community.[42]

Outside St. Louis, parents on the prairies of Missouri looked to subscription schools to educate their sons and daughters. These early schools were often in people's homes, churches, log cabins, or sparse frame buildings built for the purpose. An example in 1825 was a coeducational Troy, Missouri, subscription school that charged tuition of $1.25 per student for a four-month term, held either during the summer months, between planting and harvest, or during the winter season. Girls frequently obtained more education than the boys, since the girls were able to remain in the schoolroom while the boys had to work in the farm fields.[43]

This, however, was not true for all Missouri settlers. A group of Germans from Russia came to Perry County, Missouri, to found a colony in which they could maintain their religious beliefs. They held the general opinion that a girl's education should be limited to the most basic literacy abilities such as learning the catechism and hymns. In general, rural Germans did not value education until it became difficult to give land to each son. School attendance reflected these attitudes, with fewer rural girls than boys attending school even as late as the 1920s.[44] Advanced education for girls had been unknown in Russia and was unusual in America, the exception being among the more progressive elements of the Mennonites. Many Germans from Russia therefore objected to female schoolteachers and did not want their daughters to become schoolmistresses.[45]

ISLANDS OF HIGH HOPE: IOWA/NEBRASKA/KANSAS

Many narratives of teachers and pupils in the frontier Midwest provide stark testimony about the harsh conditions, primitive circumstances, and isolation that accompanied their journey to literacy. Many early Iowa subscription-school teachers simply organized classrooms in their own homes.[46] Schoolhouses often were islands unto themselves so that the teacher had both to manage the school building and many other aspects of nurturing children. Anna Johnson's description of her job as a rural Iowa teacher as "many-faceted" was certainly not an understatement.

I not only taught, but was also an administrator, mother, doctor, nurse, judge, and jury, artist, cook, librarian, custodian or janitor, carpenter or fixer, advisor, psychologist, disciplinarian, and humanitarian. I might say that I was "Jack of all trades and master of some." In this rural community I was very close to the children and all the parents and many others in the area. Their problems often became my problems, which sometimes made my task even harder.[47]

Epidemics were one of these problems. Many schools were devastated by typhoid, diphtheria, and scarlet fever. A Nebraska teacher, Sarah Jane Price, recorded in her diary how she and her students coped with these deaths while still carrying on with literacy learning.

Thursday, Feb. 6th, 1879
    I had fifteen scholars today. Those who have essays to write were busy as tomorrow is the day to read them. . . . Susie is not better, indeed she is somewhat worse. I fear she will never be any better. . . .
    Friday, Feb. 7th, 1879
    This has been a very nice day. I had a full school. This afternoon was the time for essays. Addie had one on old bachelors which was responded to by Will Arnold on old maids, very humorous. Sherman had one on natural history which was very funny. David Tyler had one about our old brown hen which was so funny he could hardly read it himself.
    Tuesday, Feb. 11th, 1879
    I have not written any in my journal since last Friday because I have had no time, so I will snatch a few moments tonight, although I must sleep a little less. Susie died on last Saturday. Lon came home about three and said they thought she was dying and wanted me to come and so I got ready without delay and went, but got there just as she died. She knew everything until the last and talked very good to them. Al said she died so happy and hoped they would all die as she was dying. Her funeral was preached by Bro. Smith, a very good sermon and I hope much good was done. I helped to dress her and washed her myself. She had a sweet smile on her face.[48]

Extremely cold weather on the prairie was another often overwhelming issue faced by Jane. Low temperatures made school attendance very difficult, particularly for younger children. Jane ended the winter term in January 1880 with very mixed feelings toward her success as a teacher.

I believe it is about as near a failure as I ever made in teaching, not from any fault of my own, but because there were so few scholars in the district and they [are] so small that they could not attend regularly in cold weather. But I am through and glad of it and hope I have done some good.[49]

The professional motivation of literacy educators like Jane often transcended monetary rewards or even concerns about education and the physical well-being of their pupils. Many of these teachers were alone and unmarried, and the healthy affection that developed between them and their children was similar to the relationships in an extended family.[50] Near Sterling, Kansas, Catherine Wiggins portrayed this relationship while teaching in the Goodwill School as "more like a large, well-ordered and congenial family of some 24 members."[51] Other teachers who recognized this kinship, such as Sarah Huftalen and Mary

Jones, felt that their Iowa schoolhouses were their "school-homes."[52] Or the Nebraska teacher who saw that the best way to introduce literacy to young beginning readers was to emphasize the close linkage between the child's home and the concept of the school family. "Really our school is a family."[53]

Literacy agents usually were members of the local community. Commonly a one-room school was taught by a young woman who had just graduated from that local school or one nearby. Such was the case in the educational career of Nancy Higgins. Nancy was first educated (1875) at District School No. 1, built on her father's land near Douglas Grove, Iowa. This was a subscription school taught by a Mrs. E. D. Eubank, who had recently settled in the area. A prairie fire had destroyed the logs to be used for the school, so a sod schoolhouse was built on the Higgins farm, where Nancy and her sisters and brothers attended class.

Less than ten years later, in the spring of 1882, Nancy had earned her teaching certificate at the coeducational Gibbon Academy, a Baptist boarding school, in Gibbon, Nebraska. She then signed a contract to become a teacher at another sod schoolhouse, District No. 4, in Custer County, Iowa. Nancy started with an enrollment of 45 children with an age span of four to seventeen.

However, Nancy quit District No. 4 after only one school term. She instead returned to live at home and teach that fall at District No. 1. Now faced with only 16 scholars she encountered a new challenge. Among her pupils were her two sisters and five nieces and nephews. Family members were a common enough feature at these prairie academies, since so many teachers lived at home. This certainly must have presented an added trial for many of these inexperienced teachers, since their siblings and other relatives were in a unique position to test their teacher's patience and sense of discipline. In this instance Nancy recorded in her attendance book how a brother and nephew would reach into the sod wall near their seats to pull out clods of sod and then flip them at other children when she wasn't looking. Nancy continued to teach until April, 1883, when she married William C. Gaddis, a homesteader from Iowa, who built a sod house just three miles from the Higgins farm.[54]

Though many young schoolteachers ended their teaching careers by marrying, the individual autonomy and community recognition given to these women made this career choice very attractive. As the prairie's chief agent's of literacy, the high hopes of many settler families were vested in these country schoolmarms.

Another perspective on the community's involvement in literacy was provided by Herbert Quick, who was born in 1861 and was little more than four years old when he started attending the Pine Creek schoolhouse in Grundy County, Iowa. His older brother Charles tried to teach Herbert the alphabet before entering school, "but I remember having a fit of stubbornness and refusing to look at the mysterious things."

The teacher was Maggie Livingstone, who was known as a good teacher, but strict. . . .
    I have just looked at a copy of a twenty-year-old edition of the *McGuffey's First Reader*. It has not a single lesson that was in the one I took in my trembling hand when Maggie Livingstone called me to her to begin learning my letters. . . .

I became immediately the fair-haired marvel of the little school.... The alphabet lasted me less than a week, and I romped through the "a-b, abs" which followed it. I had the old-fashioned instruction which began with the a, b, c's and proceeded regularly to words of one, two and three syllables, without much reference to what the words meant.[55]

Quick explains in his autobiography *One Man's Life* (1925) how existence in those rather primitive times (1860–1870s) on the prairie was similar to living in a desert—with few oases. Though there was little "stark illiteracy," there was a general "coldness towards books." "My father never read anything. My mother was passionately fond of reading; but we had no books." Quick describes himself as "a bookish boy in a bookless home in a bookless society." Then how did Quick acquire an education that "has led to a career devoted in a large part to literacy creation"?

The answer to this literacy riddle can be given in one word: "self-education." Quick wrote, "uncultured people like that of the Middle West in America grappled with the task of educating itself ... though we were quite unaware of it, our whole systems (of schools) in Iowa was a sort of Lancastrian system.... The children taught one another." In fact, his entire society instructed one another. Teachers "often literally studied at night the lessons they taught the next day ... keeping one lesson ahead of their pupils." (Has anything really changed for many teachers today?)

I have in years not long past had letters from elderly men and women who held certificates as teachers in the schools when I was young. They were the letters of persons just above the plane of illiteracy. Yet, they did a most important work in education.... Those illiterate teachers were the rudimentary organs, formed by the society out of its own flesh and blood, which have developed into colleges and universities.... Poor and inefficient as they were, I speak of them with reverence.[56]

Quick was a very bright student and "learned by heart the lessons of the classes in advance of me by listening." He advanced so rapidly that "in this little domain of learning, I was the wonder of the school, and grew to be the possessor of something like celebrity." By the time he was almost 16, Quick passed the certificate examination and began his own career as a teacher.[57]

Quick's observations well illustrate that the concept of literacy at a particular time and place is shaped by societal standards. For this reason, literacy has remained difficult to measure in absolute terms, since America's literacy standards have evolved so radically over the past two hundred years.

The importance of one-room schools in the development of literacy in the Midwest seems very clear. The typical prairie one-room school was ungraded, with pupils ranging in age from four through twenty and sometimes even older. Individual attendance was erratic, being determined by seasonal farming needs. However, children were accepted into a school at any time during a term. This often meant that enrollment could decline to as few as two students or rise to forty or more with only one teacher.[58]

Basic literacy instruction in reading, language arts, grammar, spelling, and writing occupied about half of the class time. The most widely used reading textbooks were Webster's blue-backed spellers early in the century and the *McGuffey's Readers*, especially the 1879 edition that sold more than 60 million copies. These texts offered readers morality stories generally defined by nonsectarian Christian tenets, national unity and pride, and self-betterment.[59]

Students were grouped either approximately at the same grade level or by the textbooks they could read and comprehend, but not by chronological age. The brightest pupils went at their own pace and were seldom held back by teachers because of the artificial boundaries of grade levels. This meant that as a student completed one textbook in a subject, he or she moved up to the next more difficult book. Teachers commonly had pupils of different ages learning from the same grade-level textbooks. Literacy instruction was given by grouping the pupils through individualized, self-paced instruction, with an emphasis on independent study and extensive use of peer or cross-age tutoring. The younger children often learned materials by listening to the recitations of those more advanced. If the school had a small enrollment, less than 15, the teacher gave individualized tutorial instruction throughout most of the day. These diverse and inventive teaching methods crept into the teachers' repertoire, since by the late nineteenth century they were required to attend yearly institutes. Critics of these teachers might have considered them progressive if they had not been in one-room schools. Through these diverse educational practices these one-room schools became one of nineteenth-century America's most effective literacy-instruction models.[60]

Certainly settler support for literacy instruction in these public coeducational, one-room schoolhouses was almost universal across the prairie states. The total number of children enrolled in these schools rose at a spectacular rate between 1860 to 1895. In Iowa, for example, the number of children in schools rose from about 36,600 in 1858 to almost 534,000 in 1895. In 1858 only about 16 percent of Iowa's school-age children were enrolled in schools; by 1895 this figure soared to nearly 75 percent of this state's school-age population. It is important to note that by the early 1900s the majority of all the schoolchildren in the United States still attended over 200,000 one-room county schools.[61]

A DYNASTY OF LEARNING: INDIANA/OHIO

With nineteenth-century literacy education in the state of Indiana we can glimpse the evolution from the frontier to more settled communities. Private subscription schools predominated, supplementing literacy education begun at home. It was not until 1848 that the Hoosier State passed its first free public school act.[62] The three-generation story of the Kennedy family offers us an insightful portrayal of their day-to-day struggle to provide Indiana children and adults basic literacy.

The Kennedys were "a dynasty of schoolteachers" whose sway extended from 1820 to 1919. Grandfather Thomas Kennedy faced his first years as a literacy educator (1820) in a small Bourbon County, Kentucky, log schoolhouse. Between 1830 and 1840 the county's population declined by 4,000. Six of those who left (1836) were Thomas, his wife Martha, and their four children. They settled near Bainbridge, Indiana, in a two-room log cabin at Big Walnut Creek.[63]

Thomas had limited preparation to become an agent of literacy. He had never attended a college or even an academy. Tom's only formal education had come through attending a rustic school for "a snatch or two." But a certain family tradition toward education, begun earlier in Virginia, made him the very man that the elders of these rural communities agreed should instruct their youth.

"Thomas had a leaning toward knowledge." His family had taught him to read and write at home so well that he devoured what few books and newspapers were in reach. Thomas knew grammar well enough that his neighbors thought he spoke in public with "real book English." He could cipher, wrote a good, round hand, and knew about history and geography. Most important, he continued to read and learn anew throughout his life. What more could people desire of a teacher?[64]

Thomas shopped around Putnam County, Indiana, from year to year for the best teaching job he could find. This often meant a walk or ride of several miles mornings and evenings. Hospitality was still free in the rural Middle West. Occasionally Thomas boarded around, particularly on a stormy night. He found that teacher earnings varied widely according to a neighborhood's opinion of the value of learning and its relative poverty. Teacher's fees for a three-month school term ranged from 50 cents to $1.75 per pupil including room and board with the patrons.[65]

A peculiar Indiana State law in 1833 set $60 as the maximum teacher pay for this three-month school year. "These educational monopolists must be curbed somehow!" Since certain charlatans had collected their fee in advance and then skipped town, the law also required that teachers were to be paid only at the end of each term. At that time, they never expected to be paid in cash. Around 95 percent of a teacher's salary came usually in commodities or labor. At the end of each term, Thomas took a wagon to school in order to haul away his pay: potatoes, homespun yarn, oats, corn, cured and fresh meat, home-woven rag carpets, or even some trapped furs. A blacksmith's family would pay its school fee in horseshoeing, another in hauling; some pupils worked on Thomas's farm clearing, hoeing, or plowing.[66]

Running a farm and teaching school in-between was not an easy way of life, so there was always a shortage of competent teachers. Also, Indiana did not issue its first teaching license until 1850. However, an 1837 law did authorize a circuit court to appoint examiners to review the qualifications of applicants and certify their fitness to teach. Unfortunately, this often failed to eliminate the unqualified because the teachers often knew more than the examiners! As a result an odd assortment of characters, good, bad, and indifferent, became teachers. It was not a surprise that in 1833 Indiana's Governor Noble bitterly complained that "the profession is not in that repute that it should be."[67]

Judge David D. Banta of Franklin recalled the odd assortment of Hoosier schoolmasters he knew: "the one-eyed teacher, the one-legged teacher, the single-handed teacher, the teacher who had fits, the teacher who got drunk on Saturday and whipped the whole school on Monday." Putting aside that time's lack of sensitivity to the disabled, while some teachers were incompetent misfits, most were praised by their pupils for their scholarship, devotion, and good fellowship.[68]

In the autumn of 1849, Thomas's son Benjamin landed his first job as a teacher, "at the young age of seventeen." He taught in his home district in "the very school where he had been a pupil only yesterday." There actually were a few pupils in Ben's school who were older than he. Some were even bigger.

Teaching equipment and methods were also as primitive as in his father's day. The school had only a few more books, and Ben still had to whittle the student's pens. Older students continued to be sent out into the forest once or twice a week to cut firewood. His school building fit the description by the state superintendent: "dilapidated log buildings situated in some out-of-the way place in the woods ... [near] the largest and deepest mudhole of the county."

Ben's school did have one new "gadget." A paddle was hung beside the door with "In" cut on one side of it and "Out" on the other. If a student left the schoolroom, he turned the paddle to read "Out." When he came back, he turned it to "In." "This was considered an enormously clever device."[69]

Ben's sister Caroline also began teaching in a neighboring district. It took a longer time for her to become a teacher (early 1850s) since there remained a strong prejudice against women teachers in that region of Indiana. Since Ben, Caroline, and their father were all teaching in the same sparsely settled county, other would-be teachers began to grumble that too many Kennedy teachers were forming a family monopoly. In March 1856, to relieve this criticism of his family, Ben moved to Franklin, near Indianapolis, about 50 miles from home. There he was immediately hired in a chance encounter with John Doty, a township trustee.

I believe you're just the man we're looking for out in our district.... We had a feller that tried to teach our school, beginnin' last fall, but the big boys made it so lively for him, he finally give up, and the rest of the winter we haven't had any school. They mighty nigh tore the house down and throwed it out the winder.[70]

By the following Monday, they had drawn up a contract for Ben to teach at the Doty School on a subscription basis for 10 weeks at so much per pupil, since the regular term had passed for the free school according to existing Indiana law. Within two or three days, 35 students had been registered. But there was one hitch.

"Have you got an examination ce'tif'cate?" asked Mr. Doty. "No," said Ben. "I've never been examined. Up in Putnam County they didn't seem to think it was necessary." "Well, they're kinder strict down here," Doty explained.[71]

On Saturday they drove Doty's wagon to Franklin and found the official examiner's office. The oral examination consisted of the following questions:

1. "When and by whom was America discovered?"
2. "If sugar is six and a quarter cents a pound, how many pounds could be purchased with 50 cents?"
3. "Correct this sentence: 'Me and Mary is playing.'"

Ben answered all the test questions correctly, which occupied all of three minutes.

"There is one thing more," said the examiner, as he handed his pen to Ben. "Write this sentence, 'The Good alone are great.'" Ben did so, and the official scanned his penmanship carefully.

Very neat writing. Plain, legible. You appear to be a competent instructor, Mr. Kennedy. I'll give a trial license, and next year, according to law, you'll have to pass another examination for a permanent license.[72]

With this simple test Ben began the remaining half century as a basic literacy educator in Johnson County. The following autumn he was given the Doty school again, but for the regular term. Two years after his first teacher examination, Ben passed his second. David Banta, a young Franklin attorney, examined him as they walked to the county courthouse picking their way through the mud as they crossed the street.

Now, give me the genders of the following nouns: Boys, Girls, Children, Books. [Ben answered correctly.]
You'll do, Mr. Kennedy. Come into the county trustee's office and I'll have your permanent license issued right away.

That was the last certificate examination that Benjamin Kennedy ever underwent![73]

Benjamin's son Millard began teaching at the age of 19. He retired in 1919. Thomas, Benjamin, Caroline, and Millard's dynasty as literacy educators, although their incumbencies overlapped, amounted to about 140 teaching years. Their three lifetimes witnessed an evolution from the primitive log, one-room school to the modern city school with students riding to it in a bus. They had a profound impact on the development of their communities during their 99 years (1820–1919) as the agents of literacy in rural Indiana. Millard Kennedy humbly characterized what they accomplished when he wrote

We Kennedys may not have set the world afire in our century of progress, but we all toiled hard and honestly, I think, at the job of community leadership which was ours ex officio, and our friends, patrons and superior officers seemed to think we did pretty well with it.[74]

This legacy of literacy was repeated by countless other educators across nineteenth-century America. They helped to ensure that widespread basic literacy became one of the major socioeconomic foundation stones that would help make the next 100 years truly "the American century."

Another unique literacy variation in Indiana was the presence of the planned community at New Harmony. Throughout America's history, both religious and nonreligious groups have organized utopian communities where they sought to create a perfect society and practice their beliefs without interference. These include the Shakers at Pleasant Hill, Kentucky; the Mormons at Salt Lake City, Utah; the Inspirationists at Amana, Iowa; or the Owenites at New Harmony, Indiana.[75]

Robert Owen (1771–1858), a British social reformer, was famous for his reform at the mill town of New Lanark in Scotland, where he experimented with ways to improve the living and working conditions of the common laborer, including opening an infant school. In 1824 Owen sold his New Lanark holdings and through a partnership with the American philanthropist William Maclure purchased New Harmony. This was heralded as a major event in its day. At a joint session of the U.S. Congress attended by the president and his cabinet, Owen unveiled his plan to create a model community at New Harmony where all property would be held in common.

Maclure organized the educational component of this experiment, bringing with him a noted group of educators. This included Joseph Neef, who sought to advance literacy by using the educational methods of Johann Heinrich Pestalozzi (1746–1826), a Swiss reformer. Pestalozzi had espoused the use of education as a tool for social regeneration.[76]

Neef organized three schools during his tenure at New Harmony. These included an infant school, a boarding school enrolling students ages 5 to 12, and an adult school. Neef, who had been teaching assistant of Pestalozzi, organized his New Harmony literacy activities based on four basic Pestalozzian principles:

1. Child freedom based upon natural development.
2. Direct experience with the world and its activities.
3. The use of the senses in training pupils in observation and judgment.
4. Cooperation between the school and home, and between parents and teachers.[77]

At the infant school instruction was shared by Neef's wife and Marie Fretageot, also a native of France brought to American by Maclure. She had opened a Pestalozzian school in Philadelphia before being invited to teach at New Harmony. At its peak the infant school enrolled more than one hundred children aged two to five.

Joseph Neef was the superintendent of the higher school enrolling about two hundred students five through twelve years old. Since it was a community boarding school, both New Harmony children and a number of nonresidents were enrolled in a program centered on industrial education. Children were instructed in useful trades and occupations. Pupils chose an occupation for themselves or were assigned a trade if unable to make a decision.[78]

Surprisingly, Owen's New Lanark schools gave no literacy instruction! This is hard to understand since Neef had written his own distinctive methods book for reading and writing instruction (1813). The basic philosophical differences between Maclure, Owen, and Neef helped to permanently undermine the community. Owen supported Lancastrian monitorial education, rather than Pesstalozzian concepts. Neef used Pestalozzian methods in his higher school, though Maclure's industrial education approach was also imprinted throughout the curriculum. Neef left after only two years as these conflicting efforts frustrated New Harmony's literacy education efforts and certainly contributed to the final disintegration of the community.[79] A utopian model certainly offered no guarantee that literacy education would be more effective than that in the rest of Indiana. In fact, New Harmony seems to have offered its residents less literacy rather than more.

Probably due to its geographic proximity to the eastern states, Ohio state agencies began dealing with education earlier in the nineteenth century. In 1830 Ohio passed its first free public elementary school act. Six years later Calvin E. Stowe recommended dividing the state's educational institutions into elementary, grammar, and high school grades based on his *Report on Elementary Institutions in Europe* (1836). Yet by the next year the state's first superintendent of public schools freely conceded in his first annual report, "It is certain that many of those reported as public are, in fact, private schools."[80]

One such private school was the Hamilton and Rossville Academy described by its operator Chauncy Giles in December 1841 as "a very pleasant, orderly school of sixteen scholars." By March 1845, this school had grown to 45 students. His sister-in-law, Rowena Lakey, gave this summary of his teaching methods: "His object seemed to be to cultivate a love of knowledge, to form a habit of acquiring it; and at the same time he tried to make it practical in every possible way."[81]

To illustrate,

In teaching a class of beginners in arithmetic, he kept them practising notation and numeration until they each and all could write and read numbers with the greatest ease and correctness. Meanwhile, to keep up their interest, the exercises were varied by some examples in addition or by learning the tables, etc. . . . By this time the multiplication tables and the other tables were as familiar to the children as A,B,C. They take pride in buying and furnishing houses, making dry-goods bills and settling them, all of which they find interesting and rather amusing exercises; and incidentally the idea enters their minds that this study might be of some use to them in the future.[82]

Giles also varied his literacy instruction methods to accommodate the younger students' learning styles.

Mr. Giles did not insist upon the little ones sitting up straight and still by the hour, neither did he expect them to give their attention to any particular subject more than a few minutes at a time. Their lessons were very short and rehearsals frequent, and their slates and pencils were always at hand ready for use, and they did use them a great deal.... They had learned a variety of pretty little songs for children which they delighted in singing, and singing and marching were much relied upon to relieve the little ones of long sitting.[83]

With this variety of instructional methods it is easy to understand why some private academy schoolmasters were popular with many parents. One of his pupils' mothers remarked that she sometimes felt it was extravagant to send all her children to Mr. Giles, "but when she saw the little ones so happy she felt she could well afford the extra expense." The educational methods that the more progressive private schools offered ensured their survival, as rote-learning was still prevalent in most public common schools.[84]

In southern Ohio, east of Cincinnati, Sina Sharon Chaney began teaching the rural Appalachian poor in her state. These local schoolchildren were of mixed English, Irish, Scots, and Flemish stock. From 1871 to 1883 Chaney taught in a school in which the teacher's salary was paid by a tax levied by the state of Ohio, but no other form of government support was received.

Sina taught up to 40 students ranging in age from five to twenty for a five-month term with only two holidays. Her curriculum consisted for the most part of the traditional literacy subjects: the ABCs, reading, penmanship, composition, grammar, spelling, public speaking, arithmetic, mental arithmetic (without paper), algebra, and geography. Although this was an ungraded school, Sina set up five levels of reading and math instruction. She taught by combining subjects. Written composition was important and was practiced by every student; recitation drills were frequent. Student peer tutoring was used daily.

Moral precepts were stressed, and the rules and regulations emphasized respect for authority. Sina motivated her pupils through a positive reward system of "head marks" or personal achievement points. At the end of each term, the "annual party" gave the pupils the opportunity to participate in a public performance in which each child demonstrated what had been learned on the road to literacy.[85]

TO CULTIVATE A LOVE OF KNOWLEDGE

The people who settled the Midwest adapted many of the literacy practices of the eastern United States to an expansive prairie environment. Later European immigrants, church/missionary groups and even utopian societies added to this educational mix.

Limited public schooling until the later nineteenth century meant that the prairie variety of literacy education leaned heavily upon subscription schools of all types. The one-room school, whether built of logs, sod, or clapboard, remained a fixture on the prairies until the 1950s. Private academies, convent schools, and ever-present domestic education began to address some of the literacy needs of girls and African Americans. These settlers' real thirst for knowledge elevated the notion of personal self-education to an important American core cultural concept. This was part of that urge "to get ahead," to be in charge of one's own destiny, what was to be later called "Yankee ingenuity." On those vast treeless expanses many Midwest families began to understand that cultivating a love of knowledge was essential to mastering what at times could be an inhospitable physical environment. Self-education at home or in one-room schools might help explain some of the remarkable growth of colleges in nineteenth-century Illinois and elsewhere.

The ordinary Midwestern farming family began to recognize that literacy was essential. These farmers knew that without cash they could never rise above the hardships of pioneering or living in a sod house or log cabin. Literacy helped them bring about the shift from self-sufficient to commercial farming that swept through the Midwest during 1800–1850. Farm boys (and girls) were now taught to strive for achievement with literacy as their essential tool.[86]

But for many of these families the Midwest was only a stopover for perhaps a single generation. The lure of gold, cattle, free public lands, and the wide open spaces of the Far West would stretch the literacy needs of Americans to the Pacific shore.

NOTES

1. "The Northwest Ordinance," in *Documents of American History*, Vol. 1, Henry Steele Commager, ed. (New York: Appleton-Century-Crofts, 1963), 128–132; Richard B. Morris, ed., *Encyclopedia of American History* (New York: Harper & Row, 1974), 117; James E. Davis, *Frontier Illinois* (Bloomington, Indiana: Indiana University Press, 1998), 94–96.

2. Samuel Eliot Morison, *The Oxford History of the American People* (New York: Oxford University Press, 1965), 300–301.

3. Davis, *Frontier Illinois*, 126.

4. Ibid., 163.

5. Ibid., 171, 241.

6. Ibid., 172, 241; John Clayton, *The Illinois Fact Book and Historical Almanac* (Carbondale: Southern Illinois University Press, 1970), 164.

7. Clayton, *Illinois Fact Book*, 165; Davis, *Frontier Illinois*, 241–242.

8. Davis, *Frontier Illinois*, 172–173.

9. Susan Short May, "The Story of Her Ancestry and of Her Early Life in Illinois," *Journal of the Illinois State Historical Society* 6 (April 1913): 123–125.

10. Clayton, *Illinois Fact Book*, 165.

11. Timothy Smith, "Protestant Schooling and American Nationality 1800–1850," *Journal of American History* 53 (March 1967): 688; Davis, *Frontier Illinois*, 172, 242.

12. Mrs. Mary Byram Wright (Mary Otwell), "Personal Recollection of the Early Settlement of Carlinville, Illinois," *Journal of the Illinois State Historical Society* 18 (1925–26): 671.

13. Ibid., 676–677, 681–683.

14. Lawrence A. Cremin, *American Education: The National Experience 1783–1876* (New York: Harper & Row, 1980), 437–438.

15. By 1870 Macoupin County school attendance was 8,201 out of a total school-age population of 10,954, with most children attending the public schools; U.S. Bureau of the Census, *The Seventh Census of the United States 1850*, 738–746, 696–699, 722, 725; U.S. Bureau of the Census, *Statistics of the United States Compiled from the Original Returns and Being the Final Exhibit of the Eighth Census 1860*, 374–375; *Statistics of Population, Ninth Census* (1870), 408, 626; Cremin, *National Experience*, 434–435.

16. Smith, "Protestant Schooling," 689–690.

17. David Tyack, "The Kingdom of God and the Common School: Protestant Ministers and the Educational Awakening in the West," *Harvard Educational Review* 36 (Fall, 1966): 447–469.

18. Letter, Theron Baldwin to Absalon Peters, May 21, 1830, American Home Missionary Society Correspondence, Chicago Theological Seminary, Chicago, Illinois.

19. "Protestant Schooling," 690–691; Helen Hinde, "The Early Days of the Ladies Education Society of Jacksonville, Illinois," *Illinois Heritage* 2 (Fall-Winter 1999): 23.

20. Hinde, "Ladies Education Society," 24–25.

21. Ibid., 25; Smith, "Protestant Schooling," 692.

22. Mark E. Nackman and Darryl K. Paton, "Recollections of an Illinois Woman," *Western Illinois Regional Studies* 1 (Spring 1978): 33.

23. Lucy Larcum, *Lucy Larcum: Life, Letters and Diary* (Boston: Houghton Mifflin, 1894; reprint, New York: Gale Research, 1970), 28, 33, 34.

24. Carl Sandburg, *Abraham Lincoln: The Prairie Years*, vol. 1 (New York: Harcourt, Brace, 1926), 169, 203–204, 217.

25. Justin G. Turner and Linda Levitt Turner, *Mary Todd Lincoln* (New York: Alfred A. Knopf, 1972): 247–248.

26. Frances E. Willard, *Glimpses of Fifty Years* (Chicago: H. J. Smith & Co., 1889), 73, 77, 81.

27. Ibid., 81–82.

28. Frances E. Willard, *Writing Out My Heart*, Carolyn Gifford, ed. (Urbana: University of Illinois Press, 1995), 29–34.

29. Willard, *Glimpses of Fifty Years*, 133.

30. Willard, *Writing Out My Heart*, 70, 78.

31. Davis, *Frontier Illinois*, 414–415; Clayton, *Illinois Fact Book*, 165.

32. Davis *Frontier Illinois*, 407.

33. William H. Goetzmann, *Exploration and Empire* (New York: W.W. Norton, 1966), 14.

34. Nikola Baumgarten, "Education and Democracy in Frontier St. Louis: The Society of the Sacred Heart," *History of Education Quarterly* 34 (Summer 1994): 173.

35. Ibid.

36. Ibid., 175–176.

37. Ibid., 173.

38. Ibid., 172; *The Sixth Census 1840* (Washington, D.C.: U.S. Census Office, 1840), 203–211.

39. Selwyn Troen, *The Public and the Schools: Shaping the St. Louis System 1838–1920* (Columbia, Missouri: University of Missouri Press, 1975), 10–11.

40. *Sixth Census*, 203–211.

41. Baumgarten, "Frontier St. Louis," 191–192.

42. Glenda Riley, *The Female Frontier: A Comparative View of Women on the Prairie and the Plains* (Lawrence, Kansas: University of Kansas, 1988), 53–54.

43. Linda Schelbitzki Pickle, *Contented Among Strangers: Rural German-Speaking Women and Their Families in the Nineteenth Century Midwest* (Urbana: University of Illinois Press, 1996), 140.

44. Ibid., 140, 152.

45. George Carroll, *Pioneer Life in and Around Cedar Rapids Iowa from 1839 to 1849* (Cedar Rapids, Iowa: Iowa Printing & Binding House, 1895), 195.

46. Anna Johnson, "Recollections of a Country School Teacher," *Annals of Iowa* 42 (Winter 1975): 500.

47. Sarah Jane Price, Diaries 1878–1895 and miscellaneous papers. Nebraska State Historical Society, Lincoln Nebraska.

48. Ibid.

49. Mary Hurlbut Cordier, *Schoolwomen of the Prairies and Plains* (Albuquerque: University of New Mexico Press, 1992), 131.

50. Kenneth Wiggins Porter, ed., "Country Schoolteachers, 1898–1902, Rice County, Kansas," *Kansas Magazine* (1961): 44.

51. Cordier, *Schoolwomen*, 131.

52. Ibid., 132.

53. Ibid., 160–161.

54. Herbert Quick, *One Man's Life* (Indianapolis: The Bobs-Merrill Company, 1925), 99, 100, 157.

55. Ibid., 153–156.

56. Ibid., 100, 248.

57. Cordier, *Schoolwomen*, 116.

58. Carl F. Kaestle, "Literacy and Diversity: Themes from a Social History of the American Reading Public," *History of Education Quarterly* 28 (Winter, 1988): 523–549.

59. Anna Marie Murphy and Cullen Murphy, "Onward, Upward with McGuffey and Those Readers," *Smithsonian* 15 (November 1984): 184, John H. Westerhoff, *McGuffey and His Readers: Piety, Morality, and Education in Nineteenth Century America* (Nashville: Abington Press, 1978), 23.

60. J. Galen Saylor, *Who Planned the Curriculum? A Curriculum Plans Reservoir Model with Historical Examples* (West Lafayette, Indiana: Kappa Delta Pi, 1982), 171; Andrew Gulliford, *America's Country Schools* (Washington, D.C.: The Preservation Press, 1984), 34; Johnson, "Country School Teacher," 500; Cordier, *Schoolwomen*, 116–117; Wayne E. Fuller, "The Teacher in the Country School," in Donald Warren, ed., *American Teachers: Histories of a Profession at Work* (New York: Macmillan Publishing Company, 1989), 106.

61. Cordier, *Schoolwomen*, 23; *The Statistical History of the United States from Colonial Times to the Present* (Stamford: Fairfield Publishers, 1965), 208.

62. Morison, *History of the American People*, 531.

63. Millard Fillmore Kennedy, *Schoolmaster of Yesterday* (New York: McGraw-Hill, 1940), 3, 12, 33, 36.

64. Ibid., 10–11.

65. Ibid., 38, 40.

66. Ibid., 39.

67. Ibid., 72, 75.

68. Ibid., 72.

69. Ibid., 94, 95, 99, 101.

70. Ibid., 94, 116–118.

71. Ibid., 119–120.

72. Ibid., 121–122.

73. Ibid., 122–123.

74. Ibid., 3–5.

75. Gerald and Patricia Gutek, *Experiencing America's Past: A Travel Guide to Museum Villages* (New York: John Wiley & Sons, Inc., 1986), 2. Many restored and recreated villages are opened to the public across the United States. Pleasant Hill, New Harmony, Amana, Williamsburg, and other sites are carefully described in this book, as is their educational significance.

76. Ibid., 223; Gerald Lee Gutek, *Joseph Neef: The Americanization of Pestalozzianism* (Montgomery, Alabama: University of Alabama Press, 1978), 34–35; Gerald Lee Gutek, *Education and Schooling in America* (Boston: Allyn and Bacon, 1992), 240–243.

77. Gutek, *Neef*, 9, 41, 42; Gerald Lee Gutek, *Pestalozzi and Education* (New York: Random House, 1968), 165.

78. Gutek, *Neef*, 41, 45–47.

79. Ibid., 46, 56–57, 62; Joseph Neef, *The Method of Instructing Children Rationally in the Arts of Reading and Writing* (Printed by the author, 1813).

80. Lloyd P. Jorgenson, *The State and the Non-Public School 1825–1925* (Columbia: University of Missouri Press, 1987), 6; Morison, *History of the American People*, 531; Ohio Superintendent of Common Schools, *First Annual Report of the Superintendent of Common Schools*, made to the thirty-sixth general counsel of the State of Ohio, January 1838, by Samuel Lewis (Columbus, Ohio: S. Medary, 1838), 46.

81. Chauncy Giles, *The Life of Chauncy Giles as Told in His Diary and Correspondence*, compiled and edited by Carrie Giles Carter (Boston: New-Church Union, 1920), 61, 80.

82. Ibid., 80–81.

83. Ibid., 82.

84. Ibid., 82.

85. Russell S. Fling, "The Diary of Sina Sharon Chaney" (paper delivered at the One-Room School Conference, DeKalb, Illinois, June 21, 2000).

86. Richard Hofstadter, *The Age of Reform* (New York: Vintage Books, 1955), 123–159.

Chapter 7

"An Eternity Job": Riding the Literacy Circuit on the Western Frontier

THE WIDE OPEN SPACES

In the United States by 1800, approximately 700,000 whites lived west of the Appalachian Mountains. In less than four decades after the purchase of the Louisiana Territory from France (1803), more than 4.5 million settlers had moved into the Mississippi River Valley and its tributaries. The American West began to fill with a flood of people fleeing from the disruptions of the Industrial Revolution in the eastern United States or the revolutions and wars of Europe. By 1815 one million acres of federal land had been sold to these pioneers; 1.5 million acres were sold in 1816, 2 million acres in 1817, and 2.5 million acres in 1818. Squatters accounted for countless more acres. Often starting from St. Joseph, Missouri, this exodus west traveled on wagon trains that might consist of 11 wagons, 20 men, and eight families, who brought children with them or soon produced offspring. They traveled westward about 12 miles on a good day. Road conditions, hostile Indians, weather (rain and snow), and how many miles to the next water were among their main concerns.

They had little time for education, though Emma Hill remembers that on the way west, her parents let her read romantic novels and *Pilgrim's Progress*. Surely other children did the same. How were children to become literate in this remote "great American desert"?[1]

Western conditions such as vast distances, social attitude, and cost continuously worked against parental efforts to establish a system of schooling.[2] Contemporary historians can cite little evidence about the existence or extent of literacy before 1850. In the main they have examined only people's ability to sign marriage registers, wills, army rolls, and other legal documents.[3] In the earliest stages of western settlements, married women often educated their own children at home or set up simple home schools to offer basic literacy to local children.[4]

Any school attendance was often difficult since on ranches and farms all the family's hands were often needed to work the land from early spring until winter. Harsh weather conditions conspired to keep children at home. Long daily trips made the domestic literacy option much more attractive for many parents and children. School attendance lagged in the thinly populated farming and ranching areas of the Dakotas and Wyoming. At a heavy personal cost of time and effort, parents taught their children the fundamentals of literacy. One literacy study (1989) even claims that parents did such a good job that the literacy rate in the Far West (1900) among children over 10 was only slightly below that of schoolchildren in the Ohio Valley and slightly higher than in New England.[5]

Home instruction was the earliest form of literacy education for most children on the western frontier. For some it would be their best. To teach their children, parents relied on available books and publications. Families taught each other reading, history, and household skills. Reading was taught somewhat later than in colonial times. Many immigrant households taught one culture and language at home while the children learned English at school. Most of these western children were taught in one-room schools, which still numbered over 200,000 as late as 1916.[6]

A critical element that contributed to the success of instruction at home was the "book revolution" that occurred in late eighteenth- and early nineteenth-century America. This was highlighted by the beginning of mass market fiction through the production of cheap books, reprints, and dime novels. This rapidly increased the number of titles available to the average family. The speed of communications increased dramatically, and literacy penetrated into remote geographical areas.[7] By 1870 results of this literacy phenomenon caused a western traveler to observe, "It was a perpetual surprise to me to hear girls whose whole life had been spent on the Plains or in the backwoods talk of Longfellow, and Bryant, Dickens and Thackeray, Scott and Cooper when they came in from milking.... Nobody could talk more understandingly, criticize more justly or appreciate more fully everything in their authors that related to natural feeling."[8]

The Sunday school movement also made its contributions to western literacy. A lack of public schools gave these a greater importance for a longer time in many communities. American Sunday School Union missionaries were often the only available educators. The Methodists had a significant impact through their mass circulation of low-priced books, pamphlets, and religious tracts. They introduced books into regions almost devoid of reading materials, thereby helping many westerners develop the reading habit.[9]

More affluent families also had the time to use these periodicals and books to teach their children. Elizabeth Fisk, a Montana railroad manager's wife, wrote her mother.

You should see what a literary family we are this morning. While I am writing, Eleanor is studying and printing her lesson and Katie is trying to follow her example and has established herself with a book at her little table and is muttering away at herself, seemingly entirely absorbed in her task.[10]

Elizabeth began tutoring her daughter Eleanor at age five, and her sister Katie at age two. On a typical day she directed her children at light housekeeping, tutored them for an hour, heard their recitations, and then supervised their written exercises. The girls then had at least an hour to play before dinner.[11]

In fact it seems that most western parents and their children showed a surprising interest in getting an education. However, they usually had to compromise between literacy and the frontier's demands and opportunities. This meant that school attendance was choppier and less consistent than east of the Mississippi. In the Dakotas and Wyoming, where farming and ranching reigned supreme and the population was thinly spread, school attendance dropped. In 1867–68 only 27 percent of Montana's school-age children attended class. However, a majority of westerners of all ages had at least some exposure to literacy.

This pattern—as one student put it, "education by broken doses"—was the rule for boys and young men. As in Midwestern one-room schools, girls often outnumbered boys among students under 12, since sons were often kept at home to help at heavy labor. At a greater age (16 or 17), daughters began assuming domestic duties, while older males used their increased independence to attend school. Older students were almost all young men. So boys alternated between school and work from the age of six to their twenties or even later, while girls, if they went to school, did so at a younger age. However, as we will see, many young women became teachers in these western schools.

This stuttering literacy system accounts for the astounding range of ages often present in frontier one-room schools. A 21-student class list from Montezuma, Colorado, shows the youngest as age six and the oldest 19. Susie Crocket's Oklahoma classroom was full of beards. Six-year-old Charley O'Kieffe's desk-mate was 34. The Madison County, Montana, school board saw this trend as a great financial opportunity. They ordered every adult student over the age of 20 to pay a dollar a week in tuition.[12]

This early form of schooling on the plains worked very well for some adults like Gabriel Lundy. In his autobiography, *Pursuit of Knowledge*, he tells the story of how he was born in Parker, South Dakota (1886), and educated as an adult. His parents who were from Norway returned there, leaving him in the United States. Gabriel worked for a Norwegian tenant farmer who did not see any benefit in sending him to public school.

As a teenager Gabriel did carpentry work and took a correspondence course in building construction. This only increased his intense desire to read and study in school. For two winters he attended the public school in Petersburg, North Dakota, while supporting himself doing janitorial work. His fourth-grade teacher, Grace Wheeler, encouraged her 17-year-old pupil and advanced Gabriel to the sixth grade. That year he could attend only 47 days of school.

By 1906, at the age of 20, Gabriel enrolled in the sub-preparatory class at the Fargo Agricultural College, again supporting himself as a janitor. After three years he was able to transfer to the university in Grand Forks, where he studied German and Norwegian and took extra courses at the Model High School.

Graduating in 1914, Gabriel taught at South Dakota Normal School in Spearfish. He then studied agricultural economics, graduating from the University of Wisconsin with a Master's of Science degree in 1917. Gabriel began teaching agricultural economics (1926) at South Dakota State College in Brookings and ended his career as its department head. His own passion for learning in turn would help countless other students on the western plains.[13]

The American West was in many regions so sparsely settled that it often was impractical to establish a local school. Charles Gallagher, born in 1884, was one of nine children. His parent's ranch in far eastern Nevada was separated by six miles from the nearest neighbor. The closest town was 20 miles south of the ranch. The "local" doctor was in a town 13 miles in the opposite direction. In an emergency it took so long to get the doctor, Gallagher remembered, that "the patient was either better or dead."

Charles attended a one-room school built by his family and the nearest neighbor. There he learned to read but also studied algebra, geometry, physics, shorthand, and bookkeeping. At the age of 16, Charles earned his primary certificate and began teaching in the Gallagher home. After breakfast and milking the cows, he taught from seven in the morning until four in the afternoon. Then he did his evening chores. Charles's class of three students consisted of his sister, a cousin, and a neighbor boy named Albert, who thought that Charles was a "fine teacher."[14] Many other western children had similar domestic education literacy experiences.

Lucinda Dalton was only three when her father began tutoring her each evening after working all day in the California diggings, so that she would "not be ignorant as well as poor."[15] Bennett Seymour also gave candle-lit home-tutoring sessions in California Gulch, Colorado, for his own children and neighborhood youngsters. Often single men traveling the frontier helped mothers tutor their children. Even if this meant extra work and expense, western frontier women entertained and fed these itinerant teachers in the hope that their children might listen to and learn from another adult who helped break the isolation.

Scattered evidence seems to back up the effectiveness of these domestic education programs. Charles Draper from Montana entered and graduated early from his state's normal school (teacher training). He had attended school for only 23 months of his 16 years, but he had been extensively tutored at home by family members.

In 1879 Alma Kirkpatrick came to teach school in Montana's Beaverhead Valley. She was amazed to discover that most valley children had read extensively on their own at home and had attained a broader knowledge base than most comparable Midwestern schooled youngsters. It appears on balance that for many children on the western frontier a home-literacy education was better than adequate.[16]

These "wandering schoolmasters" of the West held classes in many a cabin of mud-daubed logs, where boards served as desks and shingles with bits of coal as slates and blackboards. They charged what they could get and boarded around. They taught from Noah Webster's blue-backed speller, Jedidiah Morse's geography, and Nicholas Pike's arithmetic. This was no sedentary calling. One wandering schoolmaster in Colorado recalled beginning one day's teaching by strangling with his bare hands a wildcat that had gotten into the schoolroom.[17]

Many of these pioneer teachers were also the daughters of the first generally literate western women. They increased their life choices by preparing to become teachers. Flora Davis Winslow, one such teacher, tells us that "I teach school because I wish to be independent and not beholden to my friends for my livelihood."[18]

In other instances the frontier population was so dispersed that teachers failed to find enough students to organize one-room schoolhouses. Such was the case of Callie Wright (1830–1870), a "circuit-riding teacher" on the southeastern Texas frontier.

TEXAS

Caledonia (Callie) Wright was the daughter of Dr. and Mrs. W. J. Wright. The family had come to Texas from Mississippi about 1850 and bought a farm on the Colorado River near Columbus. Callie was part of a large family and undoubtedly had much practice at domestic education before she ever became a frontier teacher. As an adult she became a schoolteacher. However, because of the remote nature of the Texas frontier, she did not find a position even as an itinerant schoolmaster in a one-room schoolhouse. Instead, between 1863 and 1867, Callie became a "circuit-riding tutor" for children on remote ranches isolated from alternative forms of rural education.[19]

Callie's letters to her family revealed the arduous nature of education that was typical of the American frontier. Some students studied at home under the guidance of their parents. Her own sister Jodie was a domestic scholar, partially for economic reasons.

Jodie you wrote to me that you had commenced studying at home. I am glad to hear of it most especially from you for I know it is time and you will try to learn for you know that you have to pay your own schooling and you ought to try and learn all you can at home.

The long distances children traveled to school had a direct relationship on school attendance and scholarship. In another letter she tells her sister that

Silas is going to town to school, I don't expect he will do much good at it this winter, for it will be too cold to ride so far.... Silas has started to school, John Hilley, John Finchback and him started to Bartsop day before yesterday. They will get there today if nothing happens to them, they went in a little two horse wagon.[20]

In some instances, frontier children who traveled a great distance to school did not live at home, but boarded in town. Callie told her sister that "Silas is going to school in Columbus, he eats at Jack Naves and rooms with the teacher." Callie mentioned these room-and-board arrangements throughout her letters.

But other children were either too young for such arrangements, too poor to pay school tuition and boarding fees, or in ill health. Also, many children were needed to work the family farm and could not easily attend a regular school. Callie taught these children, riding from home to home and sometimes spending a few days at each location before riding on. At each home her basic literacy curriculum consisted of reading, writing, arithmetic, history, and geography. Her detailed record of these activities as a "circuit-riding tutor" were for the years 1865 and 1866.

I commenced teaching Dan and Laura today, which I expect will be very tedious for neither one is scholarly enough to be interesting. I get eight dollars per month, but don't consider it a compensation for the sacrifice I make but I do it for accommodations for there wasn't a school convenient and neither one is well enough to board.

Another child boarded at a nearby ranch and was seen by Callie each week for instruction.[21] Callie visited other nearby ranches, weather permitting (as part of her circuit), but always returned "home" to teach Dan and Laura Alley. This was at the height of the Civil War. Her letters are a mixture of personal comments on these daily literacy education activities punctuated with comments damning the Yankees for the varmints everyone knew them to be. These arrangements continued until the end of 1865.

With the start of a new year, Callie began looking for "ten or twelve scholars" and had already been promised three students. After the end of the Civil War economic conditions became very depressed throughout the South. Callie told her sister, "There are more people in the South that don't know what to do than ever seen before." She would be grateful to find a handful of children to teach, since "that would be better than doing nothing."

However, Callie's days as a "circuit-riding tutor" ended in 1867, with her marriage to C. D. Clapp. Sadly, only three years later she died from unknown causes and was buried on the family farm near Columbus, Texas.[22]

From Callie's and other first-person accounts, a general pattern of four stages of development emerges in reviewing later nineteenth-century literacy practices in Texas and throughout the American West. In the first stage of literacy, since ranches or farms were separated by great distances, the family tutored their own children or supplemented this instruction by hiring a teacher. Thus "circuit-riding educators" like Callie Wright were a variation on the subscription-school system. In the second stage of development after travel had improved because of better roads and any potential Indian danger had ceased, children from several families gathered at one schoolroom on a ranch. Stage three witnessed the collaboration of small towns in building a one-room schoolhouse and hiring a subscription schoolteacher who boarded around with local families. Sometime between 1890 and 1920, public schools took over the administration of all these local schools, though hundreds of thousands of students in the western states would remain in one-room, multi-grade schools taught by one teacher until the 1950s. Although the Texas legislature in 1856 offered its first financial support for "free public schools," it was not until September 1871 that the first totally free public school opened in Texas. Mandatory attendance came much later.[23]

Speaking about her education in the Texas Panhandle, Mary Ann Goodnight (born 1839) recalled,

I don't know what it is about me that makes people ask me where I went to college. Why, I never went to college at all or to any other school. There were no colleges in Texas nor public schools either when I was a girl. My only teachers were my father and mother, both of whom were well-educated for their times. Then too, I learned a lot from Nature.

Mary Ann later taught at several subscription schools around her home near Weatherford.[24]

Even as late as 1890 Frances Somerville remembers the first school she attended in the town of Wellington. "Miss Dona Russell conducted one upstairs in our house for some twelve or fifteen of the neighbor's children. My three brothers and my sister went so I too would slip upstairs and listen."[25]

James Nunn, a Texas native (born 1858), brought a herd of cattle to Scurry County in 1879 to establish his ranch. His brothers had done the same two years earlier. Nunn had been taught in a rural one-room school, and later attended Georgetown University.

Women were very scarce in this part of the country. During the first years I was here, 1879, I saw only three women.... It was thirty miles to the nearest doctor, and there were no schools, no churches or "no nothing." I taught J. I. Green's children to read and write on Sundays.[26]

Mrs. L. A. Knight lived at Hale Center (near today's Amarillo) in 1887 when the country was a vast treeless expanse of open range undivided by fences.

As the county was not yet organized and no public schools were to be had, the first thought of the parents was the education of their children. It is often thought that pioneer people were uneducated, but each of these eight parents (the first families living at Hale Center) were graduates of colleges, therefore they realized the need of an education.

The school was held in a shed room of the Graves' home. The salary of the tutors was paid by these four families, however any child who wished to was allowed to attend the school. This was the first school in Hale County; built in 1887–1888.... They also had in this school a circulating library. The teachers would send to the Boston libraries and get the best books and magazines to be had.... These pioneers subscribed to magazines and newspapers too.[27]

About ten years later (1896–97) Judge C. T. Kerr taught in a Panhandle three-county school with about 35 pupils in eight grades. Six months of "public school" were funded by the state, and two months of "private school" were paid for by local parents.[28]

Conditions in these one-room school districts remained primitive. In Pampa, Texas, on particularly bad weather days, Mr. Thomas had all the children stay indoors. They played games on one side of the schoolroom to help keep the lightweight building from blowing over during a Panhandle windstorm.[29]

The Swenson and Allen Ranch consisted of over 500,000 acres of open range in four West Texas Panhandle counties. It was so big that it had its own school. Ethel Schnaufer taught from 15 to 26 students during her four-year tenure (1910–1914) in the ranch's one-room school. A ranch with its own public school can still be found in the Panhandle of twenty-first-century Texas.[30]

More typical were small community schools like the one-room school near Weatherford. Jefferson Davis Hunter (born 1870) remembers attending the Dean Schoolhouse, which was about 20 feet square. The building had a dirt floor and was also used for church and social gatherings. The local circuit-riding preacher came through the county and stopped once a month at the Dean Schoolhouse. "He would come in and stack his gun in the corner with those of the other church goers. They all carried guns as protection from the Comanches."[31] The threat of an "Indian scare" was a constant part of daily West Texas life in the 1870s.

These local schools were usually begun through the efforts of a community activist like William Horace Hickox, a stock raiser and farmer. In 1890 he circulated a petition for the creation of a school. These families suffered many hardships, inconveniences, deprivations, droughts, and blizzards common to pioneer life. At times their only fuel was dried cow-chips and their only vegetables were "pig-weeds." During the terrible high-plains winters they were unable to get to town for six weeks at a time. Yet all the 22 families who lived in Carson County signed Hickox's petition because they all recognized the importance of not depriving their children what they deemed a life essential—a basic literacy education.

As money could not be had from the county or state with which to build the schoolhouse, donations were made. Land was donated and Q. Moore of Claude donated most of the lumber. Soon they had a 20 × 30 foot building which served a community center. It was named "Lone Star," Mrs. Masters says, for it certainly was a star in their sky in those pioneer days. The state then furnished the teacher, a Miss Potts, who taught three summer sessions, which began in March and closed in November. This arrangement was made necessary on account of distance that some pupils had to travel to get to school, and winter weather was bad.[32]

Live Oak School in Parker County was attended by the then seven-year-old Elizabeth Montgomery Neelley. She remembered the building on "the edge of a glade, with great live oak trees standing guard round about." It was a "beautiful location" on the treeless Texas plains.

The pupils, each and all, brought the books which their parents had carried to school. What an assortment! Only one book was universal, Webster's Blue-Back Speller. I carried a dog-eared copy of that. My Appleton's Third Arithmetic was the only one of its kind in school. I remember that some of the grown boys had geographies. Sometimes they let us young ones look at the pictures. But with all this motley array of textbooks our teacher was able to assemble us in classes. And study and achievement went smoothly as well-oiled machinery.

A blackboard was across the entire end of the house and the privilege of using the beautiful white sticks of chalk was a glorious adventure. Here we learned our "figures" and the beginnings of arithmetic. Soon the teacher asked us if we had slates that we could bring to school (another relic of our parents' school equipment). When he asked me, I replied, "I have a piece of one," and when he laughed I couldn't understand why.

That very afternoon father rode horseback to the store at Agnes and when he returned with various necessities crammed in a lovely whole slate and also a brand-new Blue-Back speller. How proud I was to carry them to school next day and to have teacher take notice of them. Mother sewed a cloth cover over my new book and folded some "thumbpapers" to place where my thumb (perhaps sometimes grimy) would rest on the page as I held the book in my hand. My slate was equipped thus; Father bored a hole in the frame with a gimlet and in this were tied two long strong cords. On the end of one cord was fastened a slate pencil. I still never forget that a tiny representation of the United States flag was pasted around the upper end of the pencil. On the end of the other cord was fastened a sponge.

When we got out slates full of "sums" and the teacher had inspected them we were supposed to go to the water bucket and pour a few drops on to wash the slate clean again. I must confess though that we were so eager on the track of knowledge (for want of a more elegant explanation) that we often spat on our slates and then applied the sponge vigorously. We had not advanced in modern sanitary knowledge and equipment at that time. We all drank from the same dipper. Our minds were clear and receptive, however; and I think they were freer from moral pollution than the minds of many such groups in our present day.

In all this crudeness we were unspeakably blest with one innovation. An agent, offering modern school supplies, had called on the trustees and showed them his wares. The trustees in turn consulted with Uncle Fuller and a rather complete outfit was purchased. This called forth some protest among the patrons. They had never had such "trimmings" to their education program. There was a fine globe which stood on the teacher's desk, and many charts to place in position on a tripod when being used. These pertained to numbers and various arithmetic knowledge and to beautiful handwriting. Also there was a numeral frame, with its varicolored balls strung on wires that helped beginners to add, subtract, multiply, and divide. There were realistic red apples cut in sections from halves to sixteenth in order that we might comprehend fractions. Best of all to me were the "dissected maps." No game on earth has to me been so fascinating, and the foundation of geography was laid almost overnight.

Included in the purchase was a large wall clock in highly polished wood octagon-shaped cabinet. Our teacher used this as lesson material, for many did not know how to tell time by the clock. When that school was over there had been a great step taken in the march of progress among the young of that community. The rudiments of essential knowledge had been indelibly stamped on young minds.

I think that was the smoothest running school I ever attended, and this the happiest bunch of youngsters with which I was ever associated.[33]

NEW MEXICO/ARIZONA

General literacy education in New Mexico and Arizona was delayed because of a controversy that arose over the very nature of public schooling. Because of the states' history as former Spanish/Mexican colonies, there were many Catholic leaders who wanted tax income to go directly to parochial schools and to allow clergy to teach in public classrooms. By 1875 Arizona had a centralized tax-based, nonsectarian public school system operating parallel to parochial schools. However, it was not until 1891 that New Mexico followed with a similar schooling program.[34]

Early literacy education in Arizona often took place in very primitive settings. For instance, the diary of Angeline M. Brown, who began teaching at the Lowes Tonto Academy on the banks of Tonto Creek in 1880, amply illustrates the hardships of frontier conditions. The schoolhouse itself was only 10 by 12 feet in size with "a dirt floor, brush sides like our house and no door. And only seats for 12."

Angeline lived only about half a mile from the Tonto Academy in equally ramshackle housing. "Our 'house' is primitive in the extreme and our furniture more so ... presently I get used to these ridiculous huts of mud and poles or poles and weeds and mud—as the case may be!" One incredulous neighbor asked Angeline, "You teach down there? Its like putting a humming bird into a mud lark's nest."

Much of the other local housing appeared to be equally rustic. Angeline's neighbor John Vingard's one-room house was 16 by 16 feet in area, a "dirt-floor pole house, thatched flat roof, no windows but open spaces in the side. It has a rough fireplace."

Her journal records how difficult life could be for a teacher in the Arizona territory.

September 28, 1880
    "School began with just four scholars this morn."
    October 11, 1880
    "Alice too ill to go to school and 'Six Bits' (their horse) has run away so Johnnie being lame couldn't come to school, but Clara, Willie, Abbie and the Armer's (four children) were there.
    A few days earlier, While I was holding her (Six Bits) and saddling her—she bit us. Maybe she should be renamed six bites."
    October 15, 1880
    "School is progressing nicely, a quieter, more obedient set I never saw."
    October 18, 1880
    Fifteen Apache warriors attacked Angeline's home but were beaten off and fled back to the mountains.
    October 20, 1880
    After the Indian attack Angeline resumed teaching to only four students.
    October 26, 1880
    In the middle of the night 100 stampeding cattle wrecked her house and almost killed Angeline. Only her quick-witted action saved her from serious injuries.

November 8, 1880

Twenty-three pupils attending schools with seats for only twelve.

November 11, 1880

"Twenty five scholars today. Awful cold and winds and so crowded."

November 12, 1880

During a geography class, a large Gila monster attached itself to the hem of Angeline's dress, much to the amusement of her pupils. "Just leave it be," they counseled her. "It will fall off on its own!"

December 2, 1880

The Gila monster comes out every morning by the schoolhouse to sun himself. "I've taken to picking him up gingerly by the tail and putting him back on my desk ... where he suns himself and snaps at an unaware fly and seems to greatly enjoy himself."

December 15, 1880

Nineteen students crammed into her tiny schoolroom. "I've an idea now about how much room Noah had left in the ark."

January 4, 1881

Angeline's teaching career abruptly ends when she is elected to the Arizona Legislature as the "Enrolling and Engrossing Clerk of the House." This meant that she registered a proposed bill and also registered a new law passed by the legislature.[35]

Thus concluded Angeline Brown's career as a literacy educator and her battle with the hazards of the Arizona frontier. Those hoping to survive in the Arizona of the 1880s certainly had to know how to defend themselves from an often hostile natural environment.

On September 9, 1850, New Mexico became a new territory of the United States. From that time until 1891, New Mexico became a battleground between Anglo-American Protestants and native New Mexican Catholics who fought over the issue of public support for literacy education.[36]

Anglo-Americans, who comprised at best one-tenth of the population, imposed upon the new territory their secular attitudes toward citizenship. In particular was a belief that the American common school was a primary agent to support democracy.

Before becoming part of the United States, New Mexico had been settled almost entirely by Spanish-speaking Catholic immigrants from Mexico. While it was part of the empire of Spain (Mexico declared its independence in 1810), civil law was largely subordinate to the canon law of the Catholic Church. Large tracts of land in New Mexico, Arizona, California, and Texas had originally been settled as church missions by Franciscan friars. They attempted to colonize the Spanish Southwest by converting the native Indians to Catholicism and teaching them to become farmers or undertake a manual trade. This mission system reached its height in California before the Mexican Revolution which resulted in secularization of mission property by Mexican authorities. Though this colonization scheme failed, it had significant long-term consequences for the rise and nature of educational institutions throughout the southwestern United States. (We will explore the impact of the missions on Indian literacy in Chapter 8.)[37]

Prior to 1846 New Mexico mission schools seemed to be exclusively for boys with the local clergy as teachers. This changed in 1850, when John B. Lamy arrived as the first bishop of the Diocese of Santa Fe. Lamy invited the Sisters of Charity, the Sisters of Loretto, the Christian Brothers, and the Society of Jesus (Jesuits) to staff the parochial schools. With these literacy efforts, the church maintained significant control of education in New Mexico until the early 1870s.[38] By that time 44 primary schools had been opened throughout the territory, but only five of these were "public schools" following the American common-school model. William Ritch, the New Mexico Territorial Commissioner of Education, estimated that perhaps 17 percent of all school-age children (5,114 out of 29,312) attended any type of school. However, many parents taught their own children. One example was Donaciano Vigil, who was appointed the first governor of the territory. "The son learned from his father the elementary studies which he followed up with close application and ... receiving such books as the limited supply of his town permitted."[39] We can only speculate how many other children received a domestic literacy education; undoubtedly, there were many.

The appointment of William Gillette Ritch as territorial secretary and his subsequent "Report on Education" (1874) renewed the public school debate. A staunch Episcopalian motivated by his personal hatred of Catholicism, Ritch was determined to establish an "American" educational system for New Mexico. He denounced the condition of education as backward and in article after article called for a tax-supported public school system.[40]

These reports did not immediately change the public's attitudes toward establishing broader literacy education opportunities. Only in February of 1891 did the legislature finally adopt "An Act Establishing Common Schools in the Territory of New Mexico." Even then Catholic priests and nuns remained teaching in public schools until 1951. This clash of two different cultures left a legacy of bitterness that seriously impeded the advance of literacy education in New Mexico.[41]

KANSAS

On the mid-nineteenth-century Kansas plains there were few schools. Literate mothers took on the personal responsibility of tutoring their children in the privacy of the family cabin. They taught basic skills first to their own children, then to any neighboring youngsters. Often the family Bible was the first text, from which were taught the alphabet and beginning reading. In this "family schoolroom" the hard dirt cabin floor served as a blackboard with long pointed sticks as chalk to scratch out letters and numbers. Children memorized grammar rules and recited history dates. Spelling contests between siblings were common literacy practices.[42]

During the 1870s one such parent, Anne Bingham, remembered how she used her paltry supply of books to teach her daughter, while performing the daily chores. "Many times I went about with a book in one hand and a broom in the other."[43]

Norwegian women settlers often promoted literacy practices for their children and themselves. Non-English-speaking women used newspapers and books to educate themselves in reading English. One woman recalled that although her grandmother had little formal education, she "availed herself of every opportunity and learned to speak and write the English language as well, mostly by studying and reading by night. These women also commonly formed book discussion clubs or literary circles to further literacy self-improvement. Many mothers, in turn, taught their sons and daughters how to read, write and speak in both English and Norwegian."[44]

It was not until the 1870s that rural schools gained a real foothold in Kansas. However, since there were few schoolhouses, some were established in a larger home's upstairs rooms. The transformation from domestic education to a formal school system remained a slow, haphazard process throughout Kansas and most of the West.[45]

Anna Webber was one of these early Kansas public school teachers. She kept a diary of her first teaching assignment during a twelve-week school term during May–July 1881 in Mitchell County.

May 9
The school house ... is a small frame house. ... It has 3 windows and a door. There is [sic] no benches, seats, black board or writing desks. I am now sitting on the floor with my paper on "the teacher's chair" which is as high as my chin, (almost). For seats we have 2 boards placed on rocks.

May 13
If a person wants to write, they have to sit down on the floor and lay their paper on one of the old board seats, or place the paper on a book and hold it on your lap—of which either one is very uncomfortable writing position.

May 24
I have had so much trouble with Charles A. It seems impossible for him to learn the alphabet. He is such a careless, lazy little rascal. He seems to take no interest whatever in trying to learn. I don't know what to do with him.

May 30
School day has arrived again. And I have six new scholars. But the best is, they have brought a table for us to use. They did not get the seats.

June 4
I am teaching today. I have only eight scholars. The wind is blowing real hard, and it is quite warm.

June 7
It has been so warm that the scholars could hardly study.

July 5
The seats finally came but no blackboard. It is all over and done with. And I am just a little glad and considerable tired.

By the end of her term Anna almost got her classroom equipped. After this rather inauspicious start, it seems somewhat amazing that she continued teaching. In 1890 she joined the staff of the Kansas Industrial School for Girls at Be-loit.[46]

Many other Kansas teachers also faced limited resources in their schoolrooms. A confusing conglomeration of textbooks were supplied by the students. Black-boards were found in most classrooms, but maps and globes were usually miss-ing. Teachers frequently were even called upon to furnish the children with ink and quill pens.[47]

Teaching in Kansas and much of the plains offered these young teachers low pay, poor working conditions, only seasonal employment, and the sole respon-sibility for the physical maintenance of the schoolroom. One 16-year-old Kansas teacher in 1890 was paid only $20 per month to instruct 10 students. From her meager pay she deducted 25 cents per day to rent a pony for her 20-mile round-trip ride to school. Her 14-square-foot schoolhouse was a sod hut with half win-dows, a dirt floor, no plaster on its walls, and no books. To compensate, students brought to school whatever materials they found at home.[48]

One Kansas student of this time gave this informal recollection of her one-room school.

"I remember the first school I attended," explained Roxanna Rice, "a room crowded full of big boys and girls, noise and confusion with now and then a howl from some boy that was being whipped.... The boy with us wore a paddle fastened around his neck. On this paddle were pasted several letters of the alphabet and these were changed every day. How I envied that boy because his folks were making so much pains with him. The attention given him I coveted.... I do not know how I learned to read. We had the En-glish reader and the spelling book—Webster's great spelling book that saved the lan-guage of the country from being put into little local dialects. My brother, older than myself, complained one day that his lesson was hard. Someone took the reader and read it to him. I thought it was very fine. To my surprise I could read it without a hitch."[49]

For many of these frontier literacy educators, life in a crude one-room school-house was an unhappy time to be endured for only a few years before marriage. Yet many dedicated women found fulfillment in such settings. One grateful schoolmarm wrote, "I'm thankful God gave me friends and opened the way for me to get into work for which I was fitted and took delight in. I consider teach-ing an eternity job. Who can tell how far-reaching may be the ideals implanted in the heart and mind of a little child?"[50]

NEBRASKA

A daunting array of negative environmental conditions also encouraged do-mestic literacy in Nebraska. They included vast distances between families, the threat of Indian attack, and a transient, uncertain population base. In certain in-stances, population surges further complicated schooling efforts. During the late 1870s Nebraska experienced a series of wet years. A tidal wave of hopeful farmers sent the school-age population soaring by almost 13 percent in one year, from 92,000 to over 104,000. Even though on paper two hundred new schools were organized, construction was completed on only 19 buildings. Of equal significance, the teaching force grew by only six to instruct almost 12,000 new potential students. In light of these statistics it is not surprising that many parents considered literacy education at home not just an option, but a necessity.[51]

George White's family lived near Haiglier, Nebraska. The two nearest schools were four to five miles distant, which meant there was no school for his two children during the winter. His wife Mary remembered how "often I held a school book in one hand and wielded a white-wash brush with the other. At other times I propped a book in front of the wash-tub. . . . Sometimes I was to sit down comfortably in a chair and teach my rebellious child who seemed determined not to learn. I was just as equally determined she would, so after awhile she in cheerful spirit, continued her lessons day by day."[52]

The Whites had added two more daughters to their family when a new schoolhouse was built. Unfortunately it was on the other side of the river. The children were forced to get across, "as best they could." "Sometimes they waded, sometimes in winter they had to jump from cake to cake of ice. Sometimes they mired down in quicksand."[53]

For these reasons, though the Whites' children received some public schooling, their parents educated them mainly at home. This seems to be typical for many other Nebraska children of that time. The Whites did very well with their home schooling. They reared eight children; of these, six were daughters, all of whom later enjoyed careers as schoolteachers.[54]

In January 1870 Isabelle Simmons Stewart (age 16) began teaching 16–18 pupils in a two-room log house called the Bertwell School District. The Chatman family lived in the other room. Her salary was $10 per month, and the district paid her board of $1.50 per week. Of the locale Isabelle tells us, "as far as the eye could see there was nothing but the vast-rolling prairie."[55]

Much of Nebraska in the 1870s was only then being opened up for settlement. W. H. Hotze first attended school in 1877, in the town of Indianola, Red Willow Creek County. Built only the year before, the school was staffed by Katie Dunning, age 19, who had attended school and been further coached by her mother, a former schoolteacher. Hotze recalled, "so everything went fine although some pupils were older than she. . . . Mother had taught me some at home, letters, numbers, and simple words, a hour each morning. . . . Father led me into the school room one morning carrying my dinner pail and introduced me to the teacher. . . . There were no free lunches or free textbooks either then. . . . At Christmas time the black diphtheria plague struck killing four in our school including a fellow 6 years old. School was closed for 2 months."[56]

Simon Van Doran's five children were educated in a private subscription school in his residence. Other settlers to the east and south of his homestead wished to collaborate in an opportunity to educate their children. In 1879 they built a sod schoolhouse behind a bluff that skirted the river, since this location was thought to be safer from Indian war parties that customarily skirted the banks of the river.[57] He tells us that "It was not until 1880 that School District No. 81, Webster County, received its proper designation from the authorities at Red Cloud. The number of the district and the right to organize were all that it did receive."[58]

The ceiling of the school was a layer of willows upon which earth and sod had been thrown. In the winter, snakes seeking heat would come out of it. Boys armed themselves with sticks and the teacher with a pitchfork to get rid of them. Once a rattlesnake appeared.

For a time all lost track of him, which made the situation all the more tense....Perhaps it was half an hour, perhaps two hours that we all sat motionless with mingled uncertainty and terror....As the fury of the reptile reached a climax his body gradually assumed a spiral form, from which the head was raised for a strike. But in the uncanny motion of his coil he lost completely his unstable equilibrium on the log, so that his "strike" was transformed into a sinuous, writhing plunge that came to an awful termination upon the stove, the top of which had become since early morning a dull crimson....[His] body curled into a sizzling mass like a bacon frying in a spider of hot grease....The teacher Dean Smith, a fine young man, cautioned us again and again: "It's the hidden enemy that's dangerous."[59]

We don't know if perhaps that day the class did get a "free lunch."

Not all early Nebraska schools were housed in such an exciting environment. In Sutton by 1884 the old courthouse became a school. The first floor was turned into a one-room school for all grades below high school. The second floor was used as an armory. "Grown men of Russian and German descent were sent to school to learn to speak English as well as read and write it, and recited sociably with small girls five or six years of age."[60]

Anna Bemis Cutler started at Sutton School in 1884.

My kindergarten course was short—in fact, completed in one day, for it consisted of being given a little pack of colored pieces of wood and told to separate them according to their colors. This took all of five minutes and then I was promoted to the first grade, c class.

   Here I stood with my toes neatly placed against a crack in the floor, (wide cracks between boards, filled with dust), and taking a pointer in hand, was told to put it on the kitty on the chart. This I did successfully; but when being asked to read the word beside the picture, I naturally said, "kitty," it was a surprise to have the next reader say, "cat" and pass above in the line. However, this experience told me to pay attention to the letters and work on the chart. I had long since learned my letters, sitting on the floor and copying from the newspaper in my father's hands above me, "The Chicago Tribune," "The Des Moines Register," or some big headline.[61]

In 1884 Isabel Fodge Cornish began teaching school in Ortello Valley. By December this 15-year-old teacher in short skirts and long braids entered the new schoolhouse, which was equipped with a rickety table and a feeble chair salvaged from her grandmother's unoccupied sod cabin. A square woodburning stove was lent by Rev. William Elliott. Six wooden benches had been made for her six students, but also for the local adults who would also use the building to attend church services or community meetings. At teacher training school, Isabel had been shown how to make a crude blackboard: apply a compound of soot or "lampblack" to a kind of building paper. With six feet of this so-called blackboard in place and the purchase of a box of chalk, the new schoolhouse was ready for its occupants.

Because the schoolroom floor was only dirt, Isabel's feet were frosted during the cold winter of 1884. To insulate the floor, a quantity of straw was put down. This did make the schoolroom warmer. Unfortunately it also proved to be a breeding ground for fleas. Isabel commented, "This was not conducive to quiet study but did afford the children some bodily activity."[62]

A few years later Isabel married another teacher, A. B. Cornish. He was forced to use some ingenuity when his class of eight beginners came to school with six different kinds of readers.

On the first day one small boy came without a book. In response to questions he said, "Maw can't find it anywhere." The resourceful teacher took a book from his pocket, a small account book, contributed by some patent medicine firm, and printed in it the lessons to be learned. Each day the child came bookless and each day the lesson was printed. But at last one day in he walked with a reader. When asked how he had acquired it, he replied, "Why, maw swept under the bed yesterday and found it."[63]

In view of the privations of early Nebraska parents, teachers and children, it is amazing that literacy education advanced at all. But these settlers endured adversity and hardship on almost every front. The frontier culture of tenacity and fortitude served them well in the struggle to attain literacy. Parents and teacher saw literacy education for their children (and sometimes themselves) as another important part of the process to open up and settle the American West.

OREGON

Rev. Robert Baird, a Presbyterian scholar, once explained to a European audience that America's predilection for separating church and state actually had encouraged rather than discouraged religious involvement in education. "Primary instruction in the United States owes almost everything to religion," Baird asserted.[64]

Protestant evangelical clergymen spread the gospel of the common school movement in the West as a civilizing mission against ignorance, barbarism, and the Roman Catholic Church. Though many of these itinerant preachers were themselves poorly educated, a substantial number of the clergy who went west were well-educated graduates of Yale, Princeton, or the Andover Theological Seminary.[65]

In 1848, when George Atkinson arrived in Oregon as the first member of the American Home Mission Society (AHMS), there were only a few private schools run by freelance teacher-entrepreneurs. Aaron J. Hyde traded two dogs for a Portland town lot and there opened the first school in town. A frustrated farmer, B. F. Dowell, opened a subscription school in July 1851. Twenty-six students paid eight dollars each for a three-month school term. Dowell's literacy efforts prospered, for his enrollment rose to 39 scholars by early August, and he continued as a successful educational entrepreneur until the April 1852 Rogue's River gold strike. His comfortable teacher income of $60 per month had been his prime incentive, since nothing in his diary suggests any real attraction to education. Many opportunists migrated west looking for easy money. A few months after leaving the classroom, Dowell was selling whiskey and cigars to miners rather than digging for gold.[66]

By the time Atkinson died (1889), the literacy education landscape had changed dramatically. Public education was flourishing throughout Oregon. In fact, Atkinson had become known as "the father of the common school in the state."[67] The AHMS had made it a major part of his mission to create "churches, schools, whatever would benefit humanity"[68]

The AHMS, as well as other Protestant groups, were also motivated by the fears of the proselytizing efforts of the Roman Catholics, who were also rushing to build their own schools and churches. By 1838 Oregon had three bishops, 27 priests, 13 sisters, and two schools. This included a girls' school right next to Atkinson's house, reinforcing in his mind the idea that "by ... education ... the Catholics will get their influence." Particularly galling was the fact that some Protestants were enrolling their daughters in this academy.[69] Actually all of this religiously motivated educational competition was a good thing for Oregon's early settlers. We must remember that these private schools offered parents a range of literacy choices; in many cases, because of the absence of public education, they were the only game in town.

As we have seen in other geographic regions of America, Protestant ministers supplemented their meager religious salaries by teaching school or even by becoming school superintendents. They saw no clear division between private and public education, except for Roman Catholic schools. In fact, Oregon ministers were enthusiastically recruited by both religious and public schools—some even became prominent in public teacher associations.[70]

The political explanation was that Protestantism served as a cultural common denominator. Its elements included discreet praying, Bible reading without comment as part of the curriculum, and ministers as teachers or as public school officials. These educational practices seemed part of being an "American" and inseparable from the mores of that time. Today's lack of a common denominator, generic Protestantism, prevents this merging of public education and moral authority.[71]

LITERACY IN THE "NEW ZION"

In April 1830 Joseph Smith established the Church of Jesus Christ of Latter-day Saints (Mormonism) as a true American religion. The church espoused many radical religious concepts. Because the concept of plural marriage (polygamy) was viewed with such hostility by contemporary American society, the Mormons were largely forced into deliberate economic and social isolation. In 1847 their pilgrimage was completed when the Mormons arrived in the Great Salt Lake Valley of Utah. Beginning in the 1890s, Mormonism began changing in ways that made it possible for its adherents to participate in the American political and social arena. Today Utah is much more heterogeneous, with large numbers of non-Mormons living in the state.[72]

James M. Monroe joined the Mormon Church on September 4, 1841. Later that same year he was ordained to a lesser priesthood. Monroe kept a journal while living in Utica (1841–42) and Nauvoo, Illinois (1845). It was in Nauvoo that he became the private tutor of both the children of Joseph Smith (who was murdered by an Illinois mob in 1844) and those of Brigham Young (who took over Mormon leadership) and Brother Taylor. He taught one group of children in the morning and the other children in the afternoons. These classes Monroe called his "two schools" though they were held in private homes.[73] "I think I never felt my inability and incapacity of instructing children ... ," he wrote.

I was reading a book for the benefit of teachers.... I almost despaired of ever being able to come up to the standard.... [I want to] impress upon his mind [a student named Frederick], the fact that I am his friend and desire his improvement. I feel very much interested in these children and am determined to do my best to study their characters and dispositions and thereby be enabled to pursue the best course to give them a good education.[74]

Monroe developed a rather unique approach to discipline. Instead of publicly scolding his pupils, he wrote letters to the children who misbehaved. He taught them addition, subtraction, multiplication, and composition. Monroe told them tales that stressed the importance of "punctuality," the "consequences of idleness" and "the advantages of industry." He was in school up to eight hours each day.[75]

Self-improvement also occupied a great deal of Monroe's day. His studies included photography, phrenology, botany, algebra, and elocution.[76]

April 25, 1845
My interest in my pupils seems rather to increase than to diminish and I take a great deal of pleasure in instructing them.[77]
May 1, 1845
My scholars seems to take hold well in general. Several individuals wish to get their children in my school but I don't care about taking them.[78]

Monroe's classes did gradually increase, until he had about a dozen students in each of his "schools."[79] However, all these literacy arrangements seemed very tentative, since, "Brigham wished every one to be prepared for danger which he said was the best way to keep it away."[80] In 1847 Brigham Young was installed as the Mormons' second prophet. Under his leadership Young led 147 weary

Saints out of danger by making a 1,300-mile pilgrimage to Utah. There they could build a new Zion under Mormon self-government. By the end of 1848, some 5,000 Mormons had arrived in the region, which Brigham Young called Deseret.[81]

When the Mormons first arrived in Utah, it was common for literacy education to be offered in private homes. Ungraded subscription schools offered the first "public education." Mary Jane Dilworth held the first class (1847) in an old military tent three months after the group arrived. Though the territorial legislature by 1851 had mandated a local tax supporting public schools, the results were uneven. The availability of literacy education in a specific Mormon settlement was governed both by the local community's ability to pay a school-fund tax and their cultural support of "book learning."[82]

Susa Young Gates (1856–1933) was among the first-born generation in this new Mormon "City of God." Her father, Brigham Young, counted her one of his 46 children by an estimated 55 plural wives. Susa was the first child to be born in the "Lion House." Brigham Young had his home architecturally designed to accommodate the communal living of 12 wives, 19 daughters and eight sons. During the 14 years that Susa lived in the Lion House, she was privately tutored at home or at a nearby primarily family school.[83]

Brigham Young had a major influence on the content of Susa's education. He once told his children's private tutor "not to teach the multiplication tables without the spirit of the Lord." Education should develop practical skills and serve basic literacy needs. Both boys and girls should be given equal educational opportunities. Mothers had a special role in the education of their children. Discipline should be maintained by using object lessons rather than physical punishment. But above all, education was to be used to promote the Mormon faith.[84]

Susa was first educated in the basement of the Lion House by Harriet Campbell Cook, one of Brigham Young's wives. This home school held class from nine to ten, recess until eleven, dinner at twelve, school from one-thirty to two-thirty, a half-hour recess, then school from three to four. A stepsister and a tutor hired by her father also gave Susa music lessons. Many of Young's other children also developed musical talent.[85]

At age nine Susa began attending a private school that had been built across the street from the Lion House. It was primarily composed of her numerous siblings, with a few neighborhood children. Karl Maeser, a German born Dresden-trained educator, became her teacher. The education philosophies of Froebel, Herbart, and Pestalozzi were a major component of Maeser's teaching methods. He was later often referred to as the "Pestalozzi of the Rockies" because of his advocacy of child-centered education, the central role of the family, and changing behavior through moral object lessons. These educational philosophies had a major influence on Susa and her domestic education.[86]

Only in 1870, at the age of 14, did she begin her formal education, when she enrolled at the University Deseret (later to become the University of Utah). She took classes in stenography, telegraphy, and baking and edited the school's paper.

Perhaps because of a sheltered childhood, she eloped after only one year in school. However, in 1878, after her father died and she endured a painful divorce, Susa enrolled at the Brigham Young Academy in Provo. She was soon asked to establish a music department. With the advice of Karl Maeser, her childhood tutor, Susa made a great success of this venture, which continued until her second marriage, in 1880.[87]

As she grew older, Susa traveled extensively and became a considerable force in the campaign for women's suffrage. Susa met Susan B. Anthony, Clara Barton, and Charlotte Perkins Gilman and became known as Brigham Young's most famous daughter. She briefly attended Harvard University in 1892. As a skilled writer, editor, and talented public speaker, Susa became a vigorous advocate for women enrolling in high school and college. She served actively on the Board of Trustees at both Brigham Young Academy (now Brigham Young University), and the Utah State Agricultural College (now Utah State University).[88]

The frontier experience of Mormon women like Susa in some ways exemplifies the greater educational opportunities given females throughout the American West. Whether out of religious convictions or environmental necessity, women achieved a greater degree of independence at a younger age and became teachers in greater numbers. These trends paralleled other social developments for women in the American West. In 1869, the Wyoming Territory gave women the right to vote in local elections. This was long before the U.S. Constitution extended the voting franchise to women with the ratification of the Nineteenth Amendment (1920). Other western states followed Wyoming's lead. Without doubt the central role played by women in the spread of literacy expedited many fundamental social changes throughout the West.[89]

"IDEALS IMPLANTED IN THE HEART AND MIND"

For most Americans the settling of the Far West conjures up images of Indians, mountain men, wagon trains, cattle, and cowboys. Certainly the gunfighter has been oversold in American popular culture as being far more significant in day-to-day Western life than literacy. This is not the first time that popular images have distorted the realities of daily life. Yet even in the movie classic *High Noon*, the local schoolmarm had an important role.

There is a major geographic difference between America west of the Mississippi and the eastern United States. In those nineteenth-century wide-open spaces of the West, there was "no nothing." Yet one of the first thoughts of the settlers who were so lightly sprinkled across the landscape was the education of their children. As a group they believed that literacy was "a life essential." For many western families their remoteness made domestic education a necessity, not an option. If children could, they attended sod, clapboard, or even straw one-room schools for "broken doses" of "stuttering literacy." The Lone Star School in Kansas, the Live Oak School in Nebraska, or the Tonto Academy in Arizona are representative of tens of thousands of rudimentary frontier schools in which most children and teachers experienced "an important time of learning."

We are amazed at how these schools overcame the harsh, even dangerous, physical conditions and their meager equipment. Yet these children often wrote in glowing terms how their little schools functioned, "like well oiled machinery" and that they were "the happiest bunch of kids." Perhaps one explanation was that their circuit-riding teachers who relished their independence often "considered teaching an eternity job." Or shared the motivation of one schoolmarm who was "thankful God opened the way to get into work I took delight in."

We also must not minimize the efforts of the American Home Mission Society, the Mormons, the Catholic mission schools, and numerous other church groups who supported literacy education throughout the West. Each in turn made their own vital contributions that have often continued to this present day.

But what impresses us most about the West is the often-expressed "passion for learning," whether through self-education, family schooling, or the establishment of subscription schools. Was this phenomenon largely due to the determination of large numbers of immigrants who were resolved that their first-generation American children "not be ignorant as well as poor"? Or did the same pioneer stamina that helped tame a harsh wilderness increase their resolve in pursuing family literacy? Certainly their literacy experiences opens a new insightful human chapter on how the West was really won.

For all the progress made toward a more literate nineteenth-century America, there were also parts of that society that had limited opportunities: American Indians and African Americans. We will examine their personal struggles for knowledge from the early colonial era to the later nineteenth century in Part IV.

NOTES

1. Mark Derr, *The Frontiersman* (New York: William Morrow and Company, 1993), 59, 64; Harriet Bunyard, Diary, Henry E. Huntington Library, San Marino, California; Elliott West, *Growing Up with the Country: Childhood on the Western Frontier* (Albuquerque: University of New Mexico Press, 1989), 181. This is the most significant published general history of western frontier education. Well researched with an excellent bibliography.

2. West, *Growing Up*, 179.

3. Carl F. Kaestle et al., *Literacy in the United States: Readers and Reading Since 1880* (New Haven: Yale University Press, 1991), 11.

4. Julie Roy Jeffrey, *Frontier Women: The Trans-Mississippi West 1840–1880* (New York: Hill and Wang, 1979), 70, 88, 90.

5. West, *Growing Up*, 179, 189, 190; U.S. Bureau of the Census, *Twelfth Census of the United States*, 1900 Population, vol. 2, ci–cii, cxv–cxvi.

6. West, *Growing Up*, 180, 181; Lawrence A. Cremin, *American Education: The National Experience 1783–1876* (New York: Harper & Row, 1980), 374–377, *The Statistical History of the United States* (Stamford, Connecticut: Fairfield Publishers, 1965), 208.

7. Kaestle, *Literacy*, 52–54.

8. Fitz Hugh Ludlow, *The Heart of the Continent: A Record of Travel Across the Plains and in Oregon* (New York: Hurd and Houghton, 1870), 29–30.

9. Lloyd P. Jorgenson, *The State and the Non-Public School 1825–1925* (Columbia: University of Missouri Press, 1987), 13; Lee Soltow and Edward Stevens, *The Rise of Literacy and the Common School in the United States: A Socioeconomic Analysis to 1870* (Chicago: University of Chicago Press, 1981), 15.

10. Elizabeth Fisk, Fisk Family Papers, March 22, 1875, box 6, folder 10, Collection #31, Montana Historical Society, Helena, Montana.

11. West, *Growing Up*, 183.

12. Ibid., 189–190, 196–197.

13. Gabriel Lundy, "Pursuit of Knowledge," unpublished biography, University of North Dakota Libraries, Grand Forks, North Dakota; Elizabeth Hampsten, *Settler's Children: Growing Up on the Great Plains* (Norman: University of Oklahoma Press, 1991), 42–43.

14. West, *Growing Up*, 145–146.

15. Ibid., 183.

16. Ibid., 183–184.

17. Dixon Wecter, "Literary Culture on the Frontier," in *A Literary History of the United States*, rev. ed., ed. Robert F. Spiller et al. (New York: Macmillan, 1953), 653–654.

18. Polly Welts Kaufman, *Women Teachers on the Frontier* (New Haven: Yale University Press, 1984), xxi–xxii.

19. Josepha Wright, Papers, 1863–1867, The University of Texas Library, Austin, Texas. Callie wrote these letters on her frontier teaching experiences to her youngest sister, Josepha (Jodie) Wright.

20. Callie Wright to Jodie Wright, 11 November 1864; Callie Wright to Jodie Wright, 30 March 1863; Callie Wright to Jodie Wright, 11 November 1864; Callie Wright to Jodie Wright, 26 January 1865, Josepha Wright Papers.

21. Callie Wright to Jodie Wright, 16 June 1865, Josepha Wright Papers.

22. Callie Wright to Jodie Wright, 8 October 1865; Callie Wright to Jodie Wright, 9 January 1866, Josepha Wright Papers.

23. Frederick Eby, *Education in Texas: Source Materials* (University of Texas Bulletin, no. 1824, 1918), 291; P. B. Grissom, "A History of Education in Texas," unpublished paper, Panhandle Plains Museum Library, Canyon, Texas; West, *Growing Up*, 186.

24. Mary Ann Goodnight, Memoir, Panhandle Plains Museum Library, Canyon, Texas.

25. M. C. Somerville, Memoir, July 19, 1940. Panhandle Plains Museum Library, Canyon, Texas.

26. Letter to Omah Ryan, July 25–26, 1937, Panhandle Plains Museum Library, Canyon, Texas.

27. Memoirs of Mrs. L. A. Knight, Oral History by Kermit Mitchell, Summer 1936, in Panhandle Plains Museum Library, Canyon, Texas.

28. Interview of Judge C. T. Kerr by Robert M. Buckfield, November 12, 1947, Amarillo, Texas, in Panhandle Plains Museum Library, Canyon, Texas.

29. Kay Crouch, "The History of Education in Pampa, Texas from 1903–1917," unpublished paper, West Texas State University, 1968, in Panhandle Plains Museum Library, Canyon, Texas.

30. Interview of Ethel Schnaufer April, 1974, Campo, Colorado, by Leslie Schnaufer in Panhandle Plains Museum Library, Canyon, Texas.

31. Memoirs of Jefferson Davis Hunter, oral history written by Cornelia Hunter, August 4, 1936, in Panhandle Plains Museum Library, Canyon, Texas.

32. Inez Blankenship, Sketch of the Life of W. H. Hickox, August 20, 1935, in Panhandle Plains Museum Library, Canyon, Texas.

33. Mrs. Elizabeth Montgomery Neelley, "Pioneer-Life of Early Settlers," written especially for the *Semi-Weekly Farm News* in Panhandle Plains Museum Library, Canyon, Texas.

34. Dianna Everett, "The Public School Debate in New Mexico (1850–1891)," *Arizona and the West* 26 (Summer 1984): 107–134.

35. Angeline M. Brown, Diary, Entries September 25–December 2, 1880, Henry E. Huntington Library, San Marino, California.

36. Everett, "The Public School Debate," 107.

37. William G. Ritch, *Education in New Mexico 1875*, Third Annual Report to the National Bureau of Education, 1876, Ritch Papers, Huntington Library, San Marino, California; Bernardo P. Gallegos, *Literacy, Education and Society in New Mexico 1693–1821* (Albuquerque: University of New Mexico Press, 1992), 10–18; At an earlier date the Spanish had established the same mission school model in parts of South America in order to colonize their empire.

38. Everett, "Public School Debate," 108–109.

39. William Ritch, *Report of the Commissioner of Education 1873–74* (Washington, D.C., 1874), 330; Everett, "Public School Debate," 110; Ritch, *New Mexico 1875*, 15–16.

40. Everett, "Public School Debate," 112–114.

41. Everett, "Public School Debate," 133–134; *Zeller vs. Huff* (1950) 55, State Supreme Court of New Mexico, 501–532.

42. Joanna L. Stratton, *Pioneer Women: Voices from the Kansas Frontier* (New York: Simon and Schuster, 1981), 157–160.

43. Anne E. Bingham, "Sixteen Years on a Kansas Farm 1870–1886," Kansas State Historical Society Collections 15 (1919/20): 520.

44. Glenda Riley, *The Female Frontier: A Comparative View of Women on the Prairie and the Plains* (Lawrence: University of Kansas, 1988), 36, 174–175.

45. Stratton, *Pioneer Women*, 168.

46. Lila Gravatt Schrimsher, ed., "The Diary of Anna Webber: Early Day Teacher of Mitchell County," *Kansas Historical Quarterly* 38 (Autumn 1970): 320–337.

47. Riley, *Female Frontier*, 105, 122–124.

48. Ibid., 122–124.

49. Stratton, *Pioneer Women*, 159–160.

50. Ibid., 170.

51. West, *Growing Up*, 188.

52. Sod House Memories, unpublished paper, Nebraska State Historical Society, Lincoln, Nebraska, 68–69.

53. Ibid., 69.

54. Ibid., 69–70.

55. Isabelle Simmons Stewart, Reminiscence, May 8, 1925, Nebraska State Historical Society, Lincoln, Nebraska

56. W. H. Hotze, "Pioneer School Days in Southwest Nebraska: A Reminiscence," *Nebraska History* 33 (March, 1952): 43–45.

57. Loulie Ayer Beall, "A Webster County School," *Nebraska History* 23 (July–Sept. 1942): 195.

58. Ibid., 196.

59. Ibid., 197–199.

60. Anna Bemis Cutler, "The First School at Sutton," *Nebraska History* 23 (July–Sept 1942): 210–211.

61. Ibid., 211–213.

62. Isabel Fodge Cornish, "A Pioneer Teacher's Reminiscences," in *Pioneer Stories, Custer County Nebraska* (Broken Bow, Nebraska: The Custer County Co., 1943), 37–38.

63. Ibid., 38.

64. David Tyack, "The Kingdom of God and the Common School," *Harvard Educational Review* 36 (Fall 1966): 447–448.

65. Ibid., 450.

66. West, *Growing Up*, 187–188.

67. Tyack, "Common School," 456.

68. Nancy Atkinson, ed., *Biography of Rev. G. H. Atkinson* (Portland, Oregon: F. W. Bates and Co. 1893), 280, 184.

69. Tyack, "Common School," 460.

70. Ibid., 461–463.

71. Ibid., 466–469.

72. Patricia A. Lynott, "The Education of the Thirteenth Apostle: Susa Young Gates, 1856–1933," *Vitae Scholasticae* 16 (Fall, 1997): 72–73, 89; Leonard J. Arrington and Davis Bitton, *The Mormon Experience: A History of the Latter-Day Saints*, 2nd ed. (Urbana: University of Illinois Press, 1992); Brigham H. Roberts, *A Comprehensive History of the Church of Jesus Christ of Latter Day Saints: Century I*, 6 vols. (Salt Lake City, Utah: Deseret News Press, 1930). This is the standard Mormon history of their settlement in Utah.

73. James M. Monroe, Journal, Mormon File, Henry E. Huntington Library, San Marino, California.

74. Ibid., April 22, 1845.

75. Ibid., April 22, 23, 29; May 1, 1845.

76. Ibid., April 23, 25; May 2, 3, 7, 1845.

77. Ibid., April 25, 1845.

78. Ibid., May 1, 1845.

79. Ibid., May 5, 1845.

80. Ibid., May 4, 1845.

81. Lynott, "Thirteenth Apostle," 73; Samuel Eliot Morison, *The Oxford History of the American People* (New York: Oxford University Press, 1965), 548.

82. Lynott, "Thirteenth Apostle," 75, 90.

83. Ibid., 76–77.

84. Ibid., 81.

85. Ibid., 78, 83.

86. Ibid., 82–83.

87. Ibid., 83–84.

88. Ibid., 72, 87.

89. Ibid., 88.

Part IV

Literacy Outside the Mainstream (1620–1900)

Chapter 8

Literacy as a Mission: Native Americans

DEAD MEN TELL NO TALES: THE FATAL EFFECT OF INDIAN LITERACY

As late as 1910 the U.S. Department of Interior's Bureau of Indian Affairs still operated 27 industrial schools for the Native American Indians. These boarding schools or industrial facilities were the government's final effort to acculturate American Indians in a process that had begun as early as 1649 with colonial New England religious mission and day schools.[1]

Educational efforts to offer America's Indians literacy must be seen in the overall context of the violent and aggressive history of white-Indian relations. With the dawn of the Industrial Age, American Indian culture was threatened not just by change but by total destruction as the world became a virtually unrecognizable place to the American Indian. Before the twentieth century, the religious fervor of missionaries to secure literacy, civilization, and justice for the American Indian was often a one-sided affair. Indians always desired justice, but white civilization and literacy never attracted any great numbers.[2]

With few exceptions the literacy missionaries showed little regard for Indian cultures, which they believed were "savage." Literacy was their best tool for initiating the American Indian to the ways of "civilization" before introducing them to Christianity. Literacy became the chief means of acculturation. Indians were expected to repudiate their identities and learn to talk, act, dress, and live like white men and women. These Indian literacy efforts occurred while most whites generally assumed that such a leap was impossible or even undesirable.[3]

Generally all whites agreed that Indian culture, power, and autonomy had to make way for white civilization (i.e., land for settlement). Literacy as a part of that Indian conversion played only a relatively small role in the full dimensions of the white-Indian conflict between the sixteenth and twentieth centuries. However, for the relatively small numbers of Indians who chose to participate, intimate contact with white civilization often proved fatal. Smallpox and other diseases ravaged this population, in union with alcoholism and continuous sniping by land-hungry white settlers.

There were ethically responsible white men and women who made a sincere effort to reach out and help the American Indian through literacy education. Indians also developed their own written native languages in an effort to preserve their tribal cultures through becoming literate.

NEW ENGLAND INDIAN "UTOPIAS"

The Wampanoag Indians gave a warm welcome to the Pilgrim fathers when they first arrived at Massachusetts Bay (1620). The colony's original 1628 charter considered Indian conversion an integral part of the Puritan goal to establish a holy utopia in the New World, "to win the natives of the country to the knowledge and obedience of the only true God and Savior of mankind." There were actually few Indians to convert since repeated epidemics before and after white settlement culminated in a catastrophic 1633 smallpox outbreak. Many Indians in Massachusetts Bay were hastily converted on their deathbeds. These Indians often left their orphaned children to the care of English families. Indian children underwent Anglicization through the twin process of acquiring literacy and Christianity. One young teenage Indian, John Sassamon, may well have been among them. By entering the ranks of a very small group of bilingual New Englanders, the vast majority of whom were Indian, he would play a major role in Indian literacy and regional history.[4]

As early as March 1644 five sachems (chiefs) of the Massachusetts tribe submitted their people and their lands to the colony. They also agreed "from time to time" to participate in religious instruction. John Eliot (1604–1690), a Cambridge College graduate, preached his first successful sermon to an Indian audience on October 28, 1646.[5] Shortly afterward (1649) Parliament established a corporation to aid New England missionary efforts, soon to become known as the New England Company. It served as the major source of funds and administration for Indian literacy in seventeenth-century New England.[6]

But more than Indian converts, the English wanted Indian land. It took about 20 times as much land to support an Indian hunter as to feed a Puritan. The Algonquin tribes of New England wanted tools such as iron hoes and firearms that the English had to offer, but close proximity to the whites left only a few alive due to plague and pox. The Massachusetts Indians shrank from a total population of about 9,000–12,000 to a mere 900–1,200 people. Other tribes suffered equivalent losses. In southern New England by the time of King Philip's War (1675), out of a population of about 10,000 Indians, perhaps 2,500 to 3,500 Indians had converted to Christianity. Only a small percentage of this total received any literacy instruction.[7] But even this was an astonishing success in light of the negative Puritan attitudes about native culture. A large part of these results came from the literacy work of John Eliot, one of the most remarkable leaders of seventeenth-century New England. He organized 14 "Praying Indian Towns" in western Massachusetts and Connecticut on a utopian vision of a "Christian Commonwealth" governed according to the Bible. Each village supported a school taught by an Indian schoolmaster. Eliot also developed and published an Indian Bible and other books in the Algonquian language, undoubtedly assisted by two Indian assistants Cockenoe and Sassamon.[8]

Eliot arrived in New England in 1631 and struggled as a minister for a dozen years in the rude settlement of Roxbury. In the early 1640s he took Cockenoe, an Indian boy made prisoner in the Pequot War of 1637, into his house. Cockenoe had been a servant to a Dorchester planter and could speak and even read English. He became Eliot's interpreter. Remarkably, by 1646 this hard-working missionary was able to preach his first sermon in the Massachusetts language. The Indian language was very difficult. Cotton Mather had once remarked that Indian words were so long he thought they must have been growing since the confusion at the Tower of Babel.[9]

Cockenoe returned to his native Long Island in 1649, to act as an interpreter between the local Montauk Indians and the English. John Sassamon, whom Eliot had known as a child, became a convenient replacement. It is quite possible that Eliot taught Sassamon to read. At about the same time, Eliot was continuing to learn the Massachusetts language from Sassamon. Their personal relationship was in many important ways reciprocal, as syllable by syllable and word by word, each was mastering the other's language.[10]

Eliot established the first of his praying towns in nearby Natick in 1650. There, next to a large fort palisaded with trees, the Indians, with the help of an English carpenter, built a two-story house 50 feet long and 25 feet wide. The lower floor served as a church on Sunday and a schoolroom on weekdays. The upper floor served as a storeroom and Eliot's office. The General Court of Massachusetts appointed a Puritan magistrate over the town's Indians. Among his many duties was to provide a school so that Indian children would become literate and to collect 10 percent of the town's crops to pay the teachers and local administrators.[11]

Why was Indian literacy such an important part of Eliot's efforts to convert Indians? The answer lies in the traditional Puritan emphasis on providing a basic literacy education to purge the "natural" child and instill the teachings of Christianity through rigorous, disciplined training. Education in the praying towns stressed literacy above all.[12]

From Eliot's viewpoint the top priority was to enable the Indians to read the Bible. In 1663 Eliot published his first Indian-language Bible (see Figure 8.1). With the help of Indian translators, he had transcribed the entire Bible into the Massachusetts dialect of the Algonquian language. Eliot also had translated and written eight to ten additional educational and religious tracts, including *The Indian Primer, or the Way of Training Up of Our Indian Youth in the Good* s

Figure 8.1
John Eliot's Algonquian Language Indian Bible (1663)

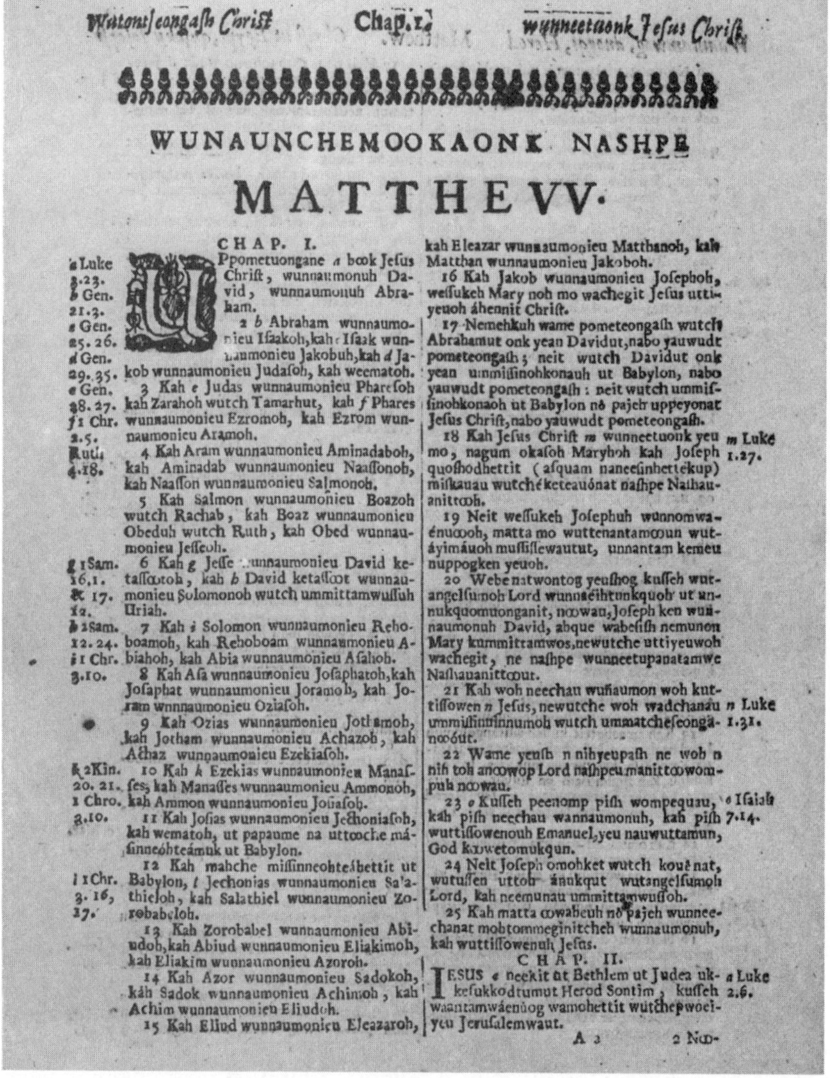
Wutonſeongaſh Chriſt Chap. I. wunneetuonk Jeſus Chriſt.

WUNAUNCHEMOOKAONK NASHPE

MATTHEVV.

CHAP. I.

a Luke 3.23. b Gen. 21.3. c Gen. 25.26. d Gen. 29.35. e Gen. 38.27. f 1 Chr. 2.5. Ruth 4.18.

Ppometuongane a book Jeſus Chriſt, wunnaumonuh David, wunnaumonuh Abraham.

2 b Abraham wunnaumonieu Iſaakoh, kah c Iſaak wunnaumonieu Jakobuh, kah d Jakob wunnaumonieu Judaſoh, kah weematoh.

3 Kah e Judas wunnaumonieu Pharesoh kah Zarahoh wutch Tamarhut, kah f Phares wunnaumonieu Ezromoh, kah Ezrom wunnaumonieu Aramoh.

4 Kah Aram wunnaumonieu Aminadaboh, kah Aminadab wunnaumonieu Naaſſonoh, kah Naaſſon wunnaumonieu Salmonoh.

5 Kah Salmon wunnaumonieu Boazoh wutch Rachab, kah Boaz wunnaumonieu Obeduh wutch Ruth, kah Obed wunnaumonieu Jeſſeoh.

g 1 Sam. 16.1. & 17. 12.

6 Kah g Jeſſe wunnaumonieu David ketaſſootoh, kah h David ketaſſoot wunnaumonieu Solomonoh wutch ummittamwuſſuh Uriah.

h 2 Sam. 12.24. i 1 Chr. 3.10.

7 Kah i Solomon wunnaumonieu Rehoboamoh, kah Rehoboam wunnaumonieu Abiahoh, kah Abia wunnaumonieu Aſahoh.

8 Kah Aſa wunnaumonieu Joſaphatoh, kah Joſaphat wunnaumonieu Joramoh, kah Joram wunnaumonieu Oziaſoh.

9 Kah Ozias wunnaumonieu Jothamoh, kah Jotham wunnaumonieu Achazoh, kah Achaz wunnaumonieu Ezekiaſoh.

k 2 Kin. 20.21. 1 Chro. 3.10.

10 Kah k Ezekias wunnaumonieu Manaſſes, kah Manaſſes wunnaumonieu Ammonoh, kah Ammon wunnaumonieu Joſiaſoh.

11 Kah Joſias wunnaumonieu Jechoniaſoh, kah wematoh, ut papaume na uttooche máſinneohteámuk ut Babylon.

l 1 Chr. 3.16, 17.

12 Kah mahche miſſinneohteáhettit ut Babylon, l Jechonias wunnaumonieu Salathieloh, kah Salathiel wunnaumonieu Zorobabeloh.

13 Kah Zorobabel wunnaumonieu Abiudoh, kah Abiud wunnaumonieu Eliakimoh, kah Eliakim wunnaumonieu Azoroh.

14 Kah Azor wunnaumonieu Sadokoh, kah Sadok wunnaumonieu Achimoh, kah Achim wunnaumonieu Eliudoh.

15 Kah Eliud wunnaumonieu Eleazaroh, kah Eleazar wunnaumonieu Matthanoh, kah Matthan wunnaumonieu Jakoboh.

16 Kah Jakob wunnaumonieu Joſephoh, weſſukeh Mary noh mo wachegit Jeſus uttiyeuoh áhennit Chriſt.

17 Nemehkuh wame pometeongaſh wutch Abrahamut onk yean Davidut, nabo yauwudt pometeongaſh; neit wutch Davidut onk yean ummiſſinohkonauh ut Babylon, nabo yauwudt pometeongaſh: neit wutch ummiſſinohkonaoh ut Babylon nô pajeh uppeyonat Jeſus Chriſt, nabo yauwudt pometeongaſh.

m Luke 1.27.

18 Kah Jeſus Chriſt m wunneetuonk yeu mo, nagum okaſoh Maryhoh kah Joſeph quoſhodhettit (aſquam naneeſinhettekup) miſkauau wutchéketeauónat naſhpe Naihauanittooh.

19 Neit weſſukeh Joſephuh wunnomwaénuooh, matta mo wuttenantamooun wutáyimáuoh muſſiſſewautut, unnantam kemeu nuppogken yeuoh.

20 Webe natwontog yeuſhog kuſſeh wutangelſumoh Lord wunnáeihtunkquoh ut unnukquomuonganit, noowau, Joſeph ken wunnaumonuh David, ahque wabeſiſh nemunon Mary kummittamwos, newutche uttiyeuwoh wachegit, ne naſhpe wunneetupanatamwe Naſhauanittoout.

n Luke 1.31.

21 Kah woh neechau wuſiaumon woh kuttiſſowen n Jeſus, newutche woh wadchanau ummiſſinninnumoh wutch ummatcheſeongánooóut.

22 Wame yeuſh n nihyeupaſh ne woh n nih toh anoowop Lord naſhpeu manittoowompuh noowau,

o Iſaiah 7.14.

23 o Kuſſeh peenomp piſh wompequau, kah piſh neechau wannaumonuh, kah piſh wuttiſſowenouh Emanuel, yeu nauwuttamun, God kuwetomukqun.

24 Neit Joſeph omohket wutch kouenat, wutuſſen uttoh ánukqut wutangelſumoh Lord, kah neemunau ummittamwuſſoh.

25 Kah matta oowaheuh nô pajeh wunneechanat mohtommeginitcheh wunnaumonuh, kah wuttiſſowenuh Jeſus.

CHAP. II.

a Luke 2.6.

JESUS a neekit ut Bethlem ut Judea ukkeſukkodtumut Herod Sontim, kuſſeh waantamwáenúog wamohettit wutchepwoeiyeu Jeruſalemwaut.

A 2 2 Noo-

Source: This item is reproduced by permission of *The Huntington Library, San Marino, California* (RB 18573).

Knowledge of God in Knowledge of the Scriptures and in an Ability to Read (1669). This oldest extant American primer played a dual role, as it was used in both reading and religious instruction.[13]

Indian teachers had to be trained by Eliot at Natick due to a lack of dedicated white instructors. For the same reason he also had to rely on native preachers who were trained at an Indian college established at Harvard in 1654. Only three to five Indians attended (including John Sassamon) during its brief existence. No student of the college lived long enough to preach. Two died of disease before or shortly after graduation. One dropped out early. Their Indian brethren murdered two others. Similar mortality rates plagued other Indian students placed under the instruction of English schoolmasters.[14]

Just south of Cape Cod, Thomas Mayhew, Jr., purchased the Elizabeth Islands, Nantucket, and Martha's Vineyard. By the fall of 1652, Mayhew, who had learned the local Indian language, opened a school for 30 of the Indian children on Martha's Vineyard. This began the work of five generations of Mayhews who sought to dominate Indian life on these islands from 1652 to the early nineteenth century.[15]

Missionaries like John Eliot, Thomas Mayhew, and others such as John Cotton and Richard Bourne were somewhat successful in helping some Indians become literate in their own language. By 1675 a chain of 14 "Praying Indian Towns" existed between northeastern Connecticut and the Merrimack River, with about 20 more on or near Cape Cod. However the total number of converted Indians never exceeded 2,500 out of a population of 10,000 Indians in southern New England. A 1664 survey by Eliot revealed rather low literacy rates for Indians living in the 14 praying towns. Among the 462 converted Indians, 142 could read the Massachusetts language, 72 could write, and only nine could read English. A similar survey taken by Mayhew on Martha's Vineyard shows that out of 128 Indian child and adult converts, only 60 were able to read and nine able to write.[16]

Puritan efforts at literacy and conversion were largely illusory. The focus of their literacy education program encouraged these Indians to reject their own culture and emulate the Puritans. At the same time it denied these Indians any possibility of either cultural assimilation or revitalization. The literate Indian converts were left caught between two cultures: resentful "wild" Indians whose chiefs and medicine men resisted literacy and conversion because it undermined their authority and their white neighbors who wanted the Indians' land and were suspicious of these Indian converts.[17]

Eliot's vision of using literacy to Christianize the Indians was shattered in 1675 with the outbreak of King Philip's War. The "wild" Indians were beginning to feel badly crowded with the steady advance of Puritan settlements. Sassamon had left Eliot about 1662 and became the interpreter and secretary of Metacon (called King Philip by the English), a chief sachem of the Wampanoag. Philip had a strong anti-Christian bias and an innate hostility to the encroaching whites. Sassamon, either as Philip's secretary or as a spy, tipped off Governor Winslow of Plymouth about his plans to attack the English settlements. Within a week, Sassamon was murdered by three of Philip's men. The three Indians were tried by a Plymouth court and executed. Just three days later King Philip's War began.[18]

The Puritans would suffer the destruction of 25 of their towns and the death of more than one in ten colonists. Before the war's conclusion almost the entire native population of southeastern New England was annihilated. In proportion to the small population involved, King Philip's War has the distinction of being the most fatal war in American history.[19]

A large number of the Praying Indians helped the colonists as scouts and fighters against their own people. However, the Puritans did not trust the Praying Indians and unjustly suspected them of being a "fifth column." For the war's duration they shipped over 500 Praying Indians to be miserably interned on Deer Island in Boston Harbor. Left there without adequate food or shelter, many of these Indians died from starvation or exposure during the bitter winter. White hoodlum vigilantes murdered many others.[20]

Few of the praying towns survived the war. Those that did quickly lost their religious focus and political autonomy and their ability to advance Native American literacy. Yet much of John Eliot's failure was of his own making. He insisted that Indians no longer be Indians. Most native and Puritan New Englanders understood that this was impossible and absurd. Eliot used literacy education and religion to provide the Puritan government with the means to wage cultural warfare on an often powerless minority. In no small way the literacy education of the Praying Indians, as well as their religious conversions, led to King Philip's War. This well-intentioned mixture of literacy and religion established a cultural precedent that would be tragically repeated over the next two hundred years of American Indian history.[21]

BILINGUAL INDIAN LITERACY

The German Moravians were a Protestant Saxon fellowship that began in the 1720s under the leadership of Count Nikolaus von Zinzendorf of Saxony, Germany. They lived simply, apart from their neighbors, in highly literate, independent economic and spiritual towns. Influenced by the evangelistic spirit, the Moravian church established missions in South Africa and the West Indies and in the 1740s among Mohicans, Delawares, and other New York, Connecticut, and Pennsylvania Indians.

Between 1765 and 1782 about 250 to 300 baptized Delawares lived in the Moravian Susquehanna and Ohio valley missions. These missions were most successful when the missionaries and Indians were in accord regarding literacy education for Indian children.[22]

The Moravians helped their Indian converts build schoolhouses for these literacy programs in the larger Indian mission towns. At Friedenshütten the schoolhouse became a public building second only in importance to the Versammlungs-Haus, or meetinghouse, in which religious services were held.

These Indians had become interested in literacy education because of their growing dependence on Moravian missionaries to read and compose letters for them to white officials. For example, in 1768 the Moravians helped the Mohicans in their written appeal to Sir William Johnson, the British Northern

Superintendent of Indian Affairs, after the murders of other Mohicans by white settlers.[23]

The Moravian Indian schools were for children of both sexes. The large number of students, often as many as a hundred at a time, demonstrated the Indians' enthusiasm for literacy instruction, as did the fact that the children rose before dawn to complete their chores so as to not miss school. One of their Moravian schoolmasters even commented that the children "would rather miss their meal than school."[24]

Using the Bible or hymn verses set to music, the Moravian schools emphasized English instruction as the most useful European language. However, the missionaries also incorporated Indian language into their teaching, thus ensuring that Indian children learned English while not relinquishing their own language. This bilingual approach to literacy held great appeal for Indian parents, for it helped children both to navigate in a white-dominated world and to maintain a strong bond with their native roots. In the years before the American Revolution (1776–1783), up to 250 to 300 Delawares attended the Moravian schools.[25] Unfortunately, during that conflict these mission Indians were trapped between conflicting British and American loyalties. By 1782, after being forcibly evicted from their homes by the British, some Indian converts returned, only to be ruthlessly killed by the local American Washington County militia.[26]

INDIANS AT WILLIAM AND MARY COLLEGE

Beginning in the 1720s, the Boyle Indian School was one of four educational institutions maintained by William and Mary College. Through seven and a half decades it offered Indian youth the most enduring literacy education program in the colonies. Housed in the Brafferton building and financed by the Boyle Fund, up to 20 Indian students studied reading, writing, arithmetic, and perhaps some Latin and Greek.[27]

During treaty negotiations with the Iroquois, Cherokee, and other tribes, the English offered gifts and other incentives such as an English education in exchange for Indian lands and tribal loyalty. The schoolmaster at the Boyle School offered his Indian students what was essentially a basic literacy education. However, though their studies differed from those of the other college students, their everyday life in Brafferton Hall was similar to that of their white counterparts. The Indian students ate the same food, were dressed like the white students, and were taught in English.

In theory the mission of the Boyle School was to train Indian missionaries. This never occurred, though some Indians became cultural brokers, such as John Montour, of mixed Indian and French Canadian ancestry, who was bilingual and participated in the American Revolution.[28] Most Indians, however, did not view an English education as an attraction.

In 1744 the Iroquois delegate, Canassatego, at the Lancaster treaty conference explained that "the Indians are not inclined to give their Children Learning." (The word "Learning" for the Iroquois meant English classroom schooling with books.) "We allow it to be good, but our Customs differing from yours, you will be so good as to excuse us."[29]

Benjamin Franklin was told by the Iroquois that students who had "been educated in that college ... were absolutely good for nothing ... for killing deer, catching beaver or surprising an enemy." For they had forgotten the "true methods" of the Indians. Instead Franklin tells us that the Iroquois proposed that English children be sent to them. The Iroquois, "would take care of their Education, bring them up ... and make men of them."[30]

By the time of the American Revolution (1776), Brafferton Hall still had some Indian residents, but in that year the funds were cut off and Boyle School was forced to close. Later after the Revolutionary War, the Boyle Fund was used to teach blacks in the British West Indies. Thomas Jefferson, the governor of Virginia in 1785, thought that "the purposes of the Brafferton would be better answered by maintaining a perpetual mission among the Indian tribes."[31] Perhaps Jefferson was influenced by the successes of the most renowned missionaries of eighteenth-century America such as Samson Occom, Eleazar Wheelock, and others, whose work we will now explore.

INDIAN LITERACY AND THE GREAT AWAKENING

Between 1726 to 1756 a series of religious revivals known as the "Great Awakening" had a major influence on American life and gave an impetus to Indian schools. In New England and the Middle Colonies Indian schools run by different denominations opened their doors. One of the most remarkable of these religious-literacy missionaries was the Mohican Indian, Samson Occom.[32]

Born in 1723 near Uncas Hill, Connecticut, Occom at age 16 became caught up in the emotional intensity of the Great Awakening revival. His religious conversion provided a brief interlude of hope for the future, with literacy serving as the first tool to take him in that direction.

After I was awakened and converted I went to all the meetings I could ... at which time I began to Learn the English letters; got me a Primer and used to go to my English Neighbors frequently for Assistance in Reading, but went to no School....Thus I continued till I was in my 19th year; by this time I could Read a bit in the Bible.[33]

Occom soon discovered that teaching himself was slow going. He endeavored to find a sympathetic tutor who would direct a more systematic study program. In 1743 Occom heard of Eleazar Wheelock, a popular itinerant New England preacher, who had a special interest in Indian education. His mother went to Lebanon and asked Wheelock "Whether he would take me a little while to Instruct me in Reading." Wheelock agreed. "So I went up thinking I should be back again in a few Days....I Spent 4 years with him."[34]

From 1743 to 1748 Occom studied English, Latin, Greek, and Hebrew with Wheelock and other teachers in that area. By age 25, he was as well educated as many other contemporary Congregationalist ministers. During these years of study Occom became an itinerant preacher to Indian people, serving informally as a minister for southern Connecticut Indian communities. Thus he established a pattern to be followed in future decades as a literacy educator.[35]

Severe eyestrain postponed indefinitely Occom's plans to attend Yale to prepare further for the ministry. He began to seek employment as a schoolmaster in nearby Indian communities. (Occom was finally ordained as a Presbyterian minister in 1759.) While on a fishing trip to Long Island, New York, Occom began preaching to the local Montauk Indians. He was so compelling that they asked him to remain as their schoolmaster. Occom remained with the Montauk as their literacy educator for the next 12 years. While there he married Mary Fowler, a young Montauk woman, and began raising six children.[36]

Because of Occom's astounding educational progress, Wheelock developed a plan for educating other Indian youth in order to employ them as instructors for other Indian children. Thus in 1754 Eleazar Wheelock founded Moor's School as a charity boarding institution for both Indian and white youth.[37] Wheelock's experiment in Indian education was also conceived as a potential remedy for mitigating fear of Indian frontier attacks during the French and Indian War (1754–1763).

For the next 16 years Wheelock supervised the school in Lebanon and engineered its transformation and relocation to Hanover, New Hampshire, where it formed the nucleus for Dartmouth College. He started with only two Delaware male pupils in 1754, but by the end of the decade he decided to add Indian girls as students. Between 1761 to 1769 about 16 Indian girls were enrolled at Moor's School. They received the rudiments of reading and writing literacy, but most of their education was training in housekeeping. The education of these Indian girls, according to Wheelock, was undertaken "to prepare them to accompany these [Indian] Boys, when they shall have Occasion for such Assistance in the Business of their Mission."[38]

This idyllic picture of future husband and wife Indian missionaries being educated together was often more illusory than real. The boys were subjected to a rigorous, daily routine of prayer, catechism, Latin, Greek, and sometimes Hebrew. Unfortunately, drunkenness, misbehavior, and runaways were also daily occurrences. The inclusion of girl students increased the school's chronic disciplinary problems with Indian boy and girl "frolics."[39]

Whatever its strengths or weaknesses, Wheelock's school served as a highly publicized hub for Indian literacy and encouraged other Indian schools to open during the mid-1700s. These included one founded by the Rev. John Sergeant and continued by Jonathan Edwards in Stockbridge, Massachusetts, the Moravian schools (already mentioned) in Pennsylvania and Ohio, and the literacy efforts of John Brainerd at Crossweeksung in New Jersey (see Figure 8.2).[40]

Figure 8.2
Colonial Indian Schools

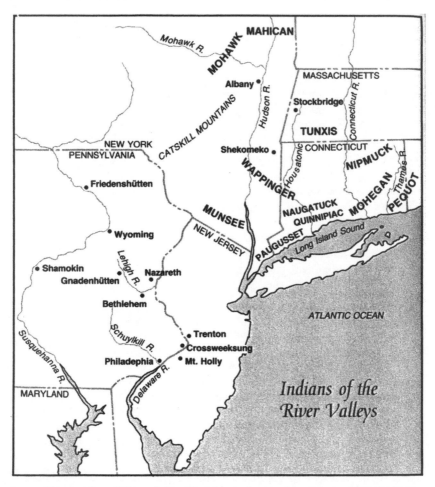

Source: Margaret Connell Szasz, *Indian Education in the American Colonies, 1607–1783* (Albuquerque: University of New Mexico Press, 1988).

Were these colonial Indian schools of the Great Awakening successful as literacy programs? Only to the extent that many of the better-educated Indians used their advanced literacy skills to act as cultural intermediaries between the Indian and American colonial worlds.

As we have seen, such Indians as John Sassamon, Cockenoe, and Samson Occom worked to establish peaceful relations and achieve a balance between these two cultural worlds. Many other Indians also made remarkable educational progress, including Joel Hiacoomes and Caleb Cheeshahteaumauk, Algonquian students at Harvard College, as well as Joseph Johnson, Hannah Garrett, and

David Fowler. Mary Musgrove, a Creek, helped James Oglethorpe negotiate peaceful relations with the Creek Nation. Joseph Brant, the half-Indian son of the British Indian Superintendent Sir William Johnson, was educated biculturally to become an Iroquois leader during the American Revolution.

Literacy empowered these individuals to at times become political, religious, and economic brokers between two rapidly changing worlds that were often in conflict. These early literacy achievements give us an important benchmark for comparing later ventures in Indian literacy over the next 100 years.[41]

LITERACY AND THE INDIAN QUESTION (1800–1860)

Following the American Revolution the fledgling United States government faced an unsolvable riddle often called the "Indian Question." "How do we humanely treat the Indian tribes, and at the same time, take their lands?" The concepts of human equality and civil rights were ignored. Instead white elitism and expansionism reduced the basic issue to "What do we do with the Indians?"[42]

Despite the limited success of literacy education during the colonial period, schooling was still viewed favorably by government leaders who had inherited the "Indian problem" from England. This positive motivation was based partly on the 1791 Seneca petition to President George Washington for teachers to instruct their children in basic literacy, agriculture, and cottage arts. Also two treaties, the first in 1794 with the Oneida, Tuscarora, and Stockbridge tribes, the second with the Kaskaskia in 1803, included government funds for literacy education. On the whole, however, until 1820 Indian literacy received haphazard support.[43]

Though the War Department since 1789 had responsibility for Indian affairs, including their education, it was again Christian missionaries who undertook "civilizing" the Indians by transforming them into farmers through the gospel and schooling. But in 1819 the Superintendent of Indian Trade found only four schools in Indian country and three outside it.[44] This motivated the U.S. Congress in that year to pass an act establishing the "civilization fund." Each year the President could expend $10,000 to employ "capable persons" in Indian literacy and agricultural education programs. These funds were to be used to fund existing missionary efforts rather than establishing new government schools.[45]

Stimulated by this literacy funding, a throng of Protestant groups threw themselves into the work among the Indians, including Quakers, Baptists, Congregationalists, Presbyterians, Episcopalians, Methodists, and Lutherans. By 1824 an estimated 24 to 32 literacy schools were in operation among the tribes, enrolling over 900 children. New treaties with individual tribes increasingly included provisions for additional literacy-education funds.[46]

The American Board for Commissioners for Foreign Missions (ABCFM) was a Protestant missionary society that figured prominently in these efforts. Beginning in 1815 the ABCFM provided funds for the construction of schools to be built among the Cherokees, Choctaws, Dakotas, Ojibways, and Tuscaroras.

Eight of these schools among the Cherokees were viewed as such paragons that they were visited by many dignitaries, including President James Monroe.[47] (The Cherokee literacy experience will be covered later in more detail.)

The Indian Removal Act (1830) signed by President Andrew Jackson caused great suffering and disruption to many tribes, as by 1838 almost all eastern Indians were forcibly evicted to lands west of the Mississippi River.[48] Though these migrations caused setbacks in literacy education programs, they proved only temporary. The Methodist boarding school established in 1839 for the Shawnees began a new phase in Indian education due to its heavy emphasis on manual labor. T. Hartley Crawford, the Commissioner of Indian Affairs in 1844, advocated using this model, stating, "The greatest good we can bestow upon them is education in its broadest sense—education in letters, education in labor and the mechanic arts, education in morals, and education in Christianity."[49] This would establish a fatal precedent for many Indian children.

Thus, the Bureau of Indian Affairs (transferred in 1849 to the new Department of Interior), allied with missionaries in the field, promoted the development of such boarding schools to increase significantly the number of Indian students receiving schooling. By 1849 Indian Commissioner Orlando Brown predicted that boarding schools would bring an ultimate and quick success by causing a "great moral and social revolution" that would spread to all the tribes.[50] These literacy efforts, which continued into the early twentieth century, were largely both educationally and socially disastrous for most Indian children.

THE FIVE CIVILIZED TRIBES

The Cherokee as part of the "Five Civilized Tribes" (the others being the Creek, Choctaw, Chickasaw, and Seminole) in the eastern United States, were known for their early pursuit of literacy. Between 1804 and 1810, Moravian and Presbyterian missionaries began operating a basic literacy school that also taught boys agriculture and girls sewing, knitting, and spinning. In May 1806 Thomas Jefferson encouraged a delegation of visiting Cherokees to continue in these literacy efforts.[51]

Several attempts also were made by the ABCFM to adopt Joseph Lancaster's monitorial system (discussed in Chapter 4) for Indian literacy education. On 45 acres near Lookout Mountain, Tennessee, Reverend Cyrus Kingsbury built such a school named the Brainerd School, after David Brainerd, an early missionary among the Delaware Indians. It opened in 1817 with 26 pupils, many of them Cherokees. Kingsbury initially used Lancaster's idea of employing older or more advanced student "monitors" as instructors for the other children. Soon this system was largely abandoned in favor of stressing manual labor training almost to the exclusion of literacy education. Whites of that time commonly believed that Indian children were incapable of becoming literate and that manual labor instruction better suited their limited aptitudes.[52]

In the early days of the American Republic, the Cherokee Nation east of the Mississippi by 1817 had established its own national council. Meeting annually, the Cherokees were governed by its acts. Written tribal laws first had been recorded in 1810. This national council divided the Cherokee territory into eight districts (parts of present-day Tennessee, Georgia, and North Carolina). It appointed circuit judges, sheriffs, constables, justices of the peace, and taxed the Cherokee people to build a courthouse in each district. The national council also elected John Ross its president; he served for many years in that office.[53]

The Cherokee prospered under their system of government, modeled on that of the United States. They built many roads, schools, and churches throughout their territory. By 1825 their census showed a tribal population of 15,160 people, over 7,000 horses, 46,000 pigs, 2,500 sheep, 10 sawmills, 31 gristmills, and 18 schools.[54] Caught between two worlds, on December 29, 1835, the Cherokee Nation petitioned the United States Congress to help them survive.

In truth, our cause is your own. It is the cause of liberty and of justice. It is based upon your own principles, which we have learned from yourselves; for we have gloried to count your Washington and your Jefferson our great teachers.... We have practised their precepts with success. And the result is manifest. The wilderness of forest has given place to comfortable dwellings and cultivated fields.... Mental culture, industrial habits, and domestic enjoyments, have succeeded the rudeness of the savage state. We have learned your religion also. We have read your sacred books. Hundred of our people have embraced their doctrines, practised the virtues they teach, cherished the hopes they awaken, ... we speak to the representatives of a Christian country; the friends of justice; the patrons of the oppressed. And our hopes revive, and our prospects brighten, as well indulge the thought. On your sentence our fate is suspended....On your kindness, on your humanity, on your compassion, on your benevolence, we rest our hopes.[55]

These successful social achievements were further highlighted by one of the most significant milestones in the history of Indian literacy. In 1821 Sequoya, a former Indian warrior, perfected a system of writing and teaching the Cherokee language. Born about 1760, Sequoya's mother was the sister of several Cherokee chiefs. His father was a white man. In 1813–14 Sequoya served in a Cherokee regiment in the U.S. Army. Later he was a hunter, fur trader, farmer, mechanic, silversmith, and painter. He had no education and neither spoke, read, or wrote English.

About 1809, after being wounded in a hunting accident, Sequoya devoted himself to inventing a written Cherokee language. Sequoya had become convinced that writing was a major source of white power, as it allowed for a greater accumulation of knowledge and the transmission of information over longer distances than did speech alone. Because he believed a written Cherokee language would greatly benefit his fellow tribe men, Sequoya persisted for 12 years in constructing a Cherokee alphabet.[56]

In 1821 he held a public demonstration during which he showed how messages could be transmitted by writing. Soon after, Sequoya taught his 86-symbol alphabet with relative ease to a group of men. Once these symbols were mastered, anyone could write messages in the Cherokee language. Cherokee leaders quickly recognized the powerful value of Sequoya's achievement. Within a matter of months thousands could read and write using the new alphabet. Within one to two years, many Cherokees were using it to communicate privately with each other. The missionary William Chamberlain in October 1824 wrote in awe how "A great part of the Cherokees can read and write in their own language. The knowledge of (Seqouya's) Alphabet is spreading through the nation like fire among the leaves."[57]

By 1828, after obtaining a printing press, the Cherokee began the publication of a weekly newspaper, the *Cherokee Phoenix*, in both Cherokee and English. This caused some Cherokees to feel they no longer needed as teachers white missionaries who, they felt, looked down upon their Cherokee culture. Almost overnight the Cherokees had miraculously moved from an illiterate to a literate people. But at the same time more than a fourth of the Cherokee nation became highly displeased with all these radical changes and migrated west of the Mississippi.[58]

This Emigration or Removal Party, which consisted of a small group of Cherokee chiefs, also had concluded by 1832 that there was no way of stopping President Andrew Jackson from implementing the Indian Removal Act (1830). Under its terms, all the tribes east of the Mississippi River were to cede their lands in exchange for territory in the West. Fewer than 500 tribesmen negotiated the land forfeiture affecting all 17,000 Cherokee.[59]

The Five Civilized Tribes—Cherokee, Creek, Choctaw, Chickasaw, and Seminole—numbered about eighty-four thousand at the beginning of their forced migration.[60] During the winter of 1831 this exodus was led by the Choctaw; the Chickasaw (from present-day Mississippi and Alabama) followed three years later. By 1835 the Creeks were driven off their lands in what are now Alabama and Georgia and were forcibly led west with their chiefs chained and handcuffed. Shortly after arriving in the new Indian Territory (present-day Oklahoma), 3,500 of the 15,000 forced emigrants had died from exposure and disease.[61]

Despite their petitions to the U.S. Congress, in May 1838 the Cherokees were divided into 13 separate detachments and sent out westward, guarded by U.S. troops on their "trail of tears." The people suffered the irreparable loss of 4,000 of the 13,000 emigrants, who perished during the indescribable hardships of this brutal exodus.[62]

But this great tragedy did not stifle the Cherokee quest for literacy. Many thousands of them could speak and write the English language with fluency and comparative accuracy. One of the first acts in 1839 of the new Cherokee National Council was to set up new schools throughout the Indian nation. By 1841 it had enacted an 11-school, eight-district system supported by the interest from the national school fund.[63]

The Choctaws also began building a school system. By 1836, with the help of missionaries of the ABCFM, they had opened 11 schools enrolling 228 Choctaw children. The nation by 1848 also was supporting nine boarding schools. Adults too were instructed through Sunday schools in arithmetic and basic literacy in the Choctaw language.[64]

Likewise, the Cherokee fostered literacy through an Indian-language printing press operated by Rev. Samuel A. Worcester at Park Hill. In 1843 he reported the following books and pamphlets published in Cherokee, Creek, and Choctaw:

In the Cherokee Language

Title	No. of Copies
Child's Book	200
Cherokee Primer (two editions)	4,500
Catechism (two editions)	3,000
Cherokee Hymns (48 pages)	5,000
Cherokee Hymns (68 pages)	5,000
Cherokee Almanac for 1830	450
Cherokee Almanac for 1838	500
Cherokee Almanac for 1839	2,000
Cherokee Almanac for 1840	1,800
Cherokee Almanac for 1842	1,000
Cherokee Almanac for 1843	1,000
Tract on Marriage	1,500
Tract on Temperence	1,500
Gospel of John (two editions)	6,500
Gospel of Matthew	3,000
Epistles of John (two editions)	8,000
Cherokee Laws	1,000
Methodist Discipline	1,000
Address on Intoxicating Drink	5,000
Message of Principal Chief (in Cherokee & English)	1,000
Special Message of Principal Chief (in Creek)	1,000
Child's Guide	
Muscogee Teacher	

In the Choctaw Language

Choctaw Friend	3,000
Choctaw Reader	2,000
Choctaw Constitution and Laws	
Methodist Discipline	
Epistles of John	1,000
Child's Book on the Soul	400
Child's Book on the Creation	400
Bible Stories	350
Choctaw Almanac for 1836	
Choctaw Almanac for 1837	
Choctaw Almanac for 1839	
Choctaw Almanac for 1843[65]	

From July 18, 1845, to August 18, 1846, Worcester printed 276,000 pages of Cherokee schoolbooks and tracts, 386,000 in Choctaw and 18,000 in Creek.[66]

A literacy event of even greater significance for the Indians was the resumption of their own weekly newspaper. The U.S. government as part of its program to break the Cherokees' spirit and drive them from their eastern homes in 1832 had seized and destroyed the original *Cherokee Phoenix* newspaper. But in September 1844, the *Cherokee Advocate* made its appearance as a paper printed in both English and Cherokee, and for many years it contributed much to the welfare and literacy of the Cherokee people.[67]

In his 1844 report, Pierce M. Butler, the Cherokee Indian agent, gave a very positive assessment of their literacy skills. He thought that the Cherokees were "exceedingly fond of reading and have a very inquisitive mind." They took "great delight ... in the manual process of writing," particularly "with the whites and agents of the government." Many had acquired "a taste for ... general literature."[68]

The overall literacy achievements of the Five Civilized Tribes in general and the Cherokee in particular are made even more impressive by their basic self-reliance inspired by the creative genius of Sequoya. It is a sad testament to the racism of the U.S. government and the American people that they failed so miserably to collaborate with and later build upon these Indian literacy achievements.

LITERACY AT THE MISSIONS

In the southern regions of seventeenth-century North America, small bands of Spanish missionaries fanned out across Florida, Texas, New Mexico, Arizona, and eventually California. They made rapid inroads, changing the daily lives of many Indians, with religion and the spread of literacy going hand in hand. As was the case with the Puritans in colonial New England, Christianity imbued the Spanish with a powerful sense of self-righteousness.[69]

This was made crystal clear in a document called the "requerimiento," which was read by the early Spanish conquistadors as a summons to countless native Americans. This proclamation commanded Indians to "acknowledge the [Catholic] Church as the ruler and superior of the whole world, and the high priest called Pope, and in his name the king and queen [of Spain]." Those Indians who obeyed would be well treated. Those who did not were told that, "with the help of God we shall forcefully ... make war against you ... take you and your wives and your children and make slaves of them ... and shall do to you all the harm and damage that we can." One soldier who fought in the conquest of Mexico explained this zealotry clearly: The Spanish had left Europe "to serve God and his Majesty, to give light to those who were in darkness and grow rich as all men desire to."[70]

Bands of Franciscan priests moved with a small military escort among the Indians of the four provinces of Spanish Florida and the native pueblos of New Mexico. These missionaries undertook the construction of a small, rectangular, fortress-like mission church. In an adjacent building the mission school taught both adults and children the basics of Catholic doctrine, formula prayers, and the catechism. As in early New England, religion provided the essential textbooks for literacy instruction.[71]

In 1565 Spain founded St. Augustine, Florida, the oldest settlement in North America. By the mid-1600s the city had several hundred residents, and the Franciscans had established a school for boys, a hospital, and a convent. This school seems to also have educated a number of Indian boys, a few of whom studied for the priesthood and were admitted.[72]

By the mid-seventeenth century each Franciscan mission community in New Mexico had a convent for the friars and a school in which the Indians were taught Christian doctrine and also basic reading, writing, and music. Some students learned so well that they in turn taught other Indians their catechism. In these earliest mission schools, some boys, girls, and even adults of both sexes were given basic literacy instruction. A few even became literate in Spanish as well as other languages. However, most Indians may have mastered the recitation of prayers, but they did not know how to read or write.

The Franciscans also attempted to "civilize" the Indians by altering their social customs. Vocational training in skilled crafts and various trades, such as cattle herding and sheep raising, was given to convert the Indians into living in a European manner.[73]

A bilingual catechism was commonly used in these literacy programs. Franciscans also produced religious primers in native languages, but few were printed. The wide variety of Indian languages and the relatively limited numbers of native speakers in any single language made their publication impractical. Some Franciscan priests failed to learn local native languages, a task that often seemed impossible because of the multitude of Indian languages in much of North America.[74]

In New Mexico widespread resentment of Spanish colonizing practices was fueled by the suppression of native religions and the regimentation of mission life. This sparked a widespread Indian revolt in 1680. The New Mexico missions were wiped out with the killing of 21 out of 32 Franciscans, who had been ministering to about 35,000 mission Indians. The missionaries slowly rebuilt. Only by 1750 were 22 missions again serving about 17,500 Indian converts.[75]

Within the framework of these Spanish missions the use of Indian "doctrinarios" was a key element in the literacy process. These young boys and girls were carefully selected from the upper classes of the New Mexican Indian pueblos. They were virtually raised by the friars while living inside the convents and learning reading, writing, and singing based on religious texts.

These young doctrinarios in turn taught other Indians in much the same way. They often read the catechism in village classrooms. In a sense the doctrinarios might be considered agents of literacy performing a function similar to that of student monitors (in the monitorial schools).[76]

By the mid-1700s there were very few literacy opportunities in New Mexico outside of the Indian pueblos. Only during the first decade of the following century were the first permanent schools established in Santa Fe. But these institutions were primarily for the children of the soldiers and officers of the Santa Fe presidio (fort). Many other non-Indian children were given basic literacy instruction at home by their parents.[77]

In California between 1769 and 1823 the Franciscans built an elaborate system of 21 Indian missions stretching 650 miles from San Diego in the south to Sonoma in the north. After discovering California in 1579, the Spanish largely ignored the area since it was remote from the bases of supply in New Spain. This attitude abruptly changed, because between 1740 and 1765 Russian fur traders and explorers sailed from their Alaskan bases as far south as present-day San Francisco looking for new trading opportunities with the Indians along the Pacific coast. The Russians eventually built Fort Ross in 1812 at Bodega Bay, California. These Russian trade activities motivated the Spanish to protect their original claim and dust off their colonizing plans for California.[78]

The first Spanish mission at San Diego was founded in 1768 by Father Junípero Serra. Until his death in 1784 Serra pioneered the building of a chain of missions covering much of today's California. By 1823 these 21 missions were located one day's travel from each other, connected by El Camino Real (The Royal Road) that stretched between San Diego in the south to Sonoma in the north.[79] (See Figure 8.3.)

The rise of this mission system in California and elsewhere in the two Americas was a practical solution to Spain's colonial policy. Her population in Europe was small, and few Spanish people were motivated to immigrate to the New World. Lacking colonists, Spain would colonize her New World possessions with Indians. The missions were much more than the adobe chapels and workshops preserved today throughout modern California (see Figure 8.4). Instead, these missions were designed to become self-supporting communities and later to serve as the core of a permanent settlement.

The Franciscan missionaries were not only preachers but also teachers and early social engineers. It was their long-term goal to people the Spanish frontier with civilized natives and thus supplement the few Spanish colonists. The mission properties were held in trust by the Franciscans for the Indians, to whom they were expected to revert when the Indians were sufficiently civilized to run them. Spain used this mission model repeatedly with varying degrees of success throughout its 250 years of colonial rule in South America, Central America, and the southwestern United States. In 1833 the Mexican independence movement resulted in a decree to secularize the California missions. However, the Indians at the 21 missions were not ready to take over their own affairs, though the Franciscans had settled many Indians on these mission lands. The resulting disintegration of the missions led to the Indians being swindled out of their land holdings by local Mexican ranchers.[80]

Literacy and vocational education were two of the mission's basic purposes. Some of the priests at the California missions believed they could overcome formidable obstacles in order to teach the Indians to read and write Spanish.

Figure 8.3
The Missions of Spanish California

Source: California Missions: A Pictoral Tour. Oakland: Mike Roberts Color Productions, 1979.

The generality of the Indians understand to a great extent the Spanish language, and they speak it with sufficient fluency, especially those who were born at the Mission. Those who have had opportunities to deal more with the Spaniards excel, of course.

In the boys born at the Mission and of better instruction, there is noticed much inclination to read and write in Spanish; but for reading and writing in their own idiom little or no inclination has been observed, but we doubt not that with facility they would acquit themselves in the one as in the other language were not paper, pen, etc., lacking. (Fr. Juan Bautista Sancho, Dr. Pedro Cabot, Mission San Antonio)[81]

Figure 8.4
A Typical California Mission

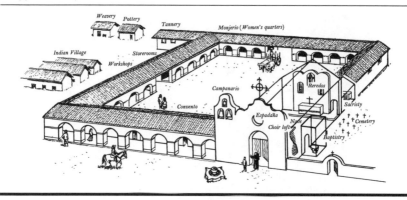

Source: *The California Missions: A Pictoral History.* Menlo Park, California: Sunset Publishing Company, 1979, p. 57.

Six different languages were spoken by Indians between San Diego and Sonoma, along with a babel of local dialects. "At the Mission five languages or idioms are spoken. Those who join at the age of thirty and over never learn another language than their own.... There is a good number that learn to speak Spanish" (Frs. Abella and Lucio, Mission San Francisco de Asis).[82]

A truly remarkable document relating to literacy is "The Conversion of the Luiseño Indians of California" written in 1835 by the Luiseño Indian Pablo Tac while residing in Rome. Pablo Tac was born at the California Mission of San Luis Rey de Francia in 1822. He died in Rome, Italy, in 1841. His was the first account of California mission life written by an Indian. It gives an interesting personal testimony of the impact of literacy education on some California Indians.[83]

Pablo was one of six children and was baptized shortly after his birth. In the mission school Pablo was a diligent student who by age 10 showed the capacity for more advanced work. Fr. Antonio Peyri, the administrator of the mission, chose Pablo and another boy to accompany him to the Franciscan College of San Fernando in Mexico City. He apparently had already decided to send these two Indian boys to Rome to complete their education. From 1832 to 1834 Pablo resided at the Franciscan College. Fr. Antonio then took the boys to Spain via New York and France.

By September, 1834 the Indian boys had arrived in Rome and were enrolled at the Urban College. One can only imagine the overwhelming culture shock for both boys as they began a four-year studies program in Latin. Unfortunately Agapito Amamix fell ill and died in 1837 at the college villa outside Rome. Pablo Tac completed his course in 1838, then went on to study rhetoric, humanities, and philosophy. In 1839 Pablo took his priestly vows to continue his preparation as a missionary.[84]

Pablo worked on a grammatical sketch of the Luiseño tongue with a dictionary of about 1,200 words. He was unable to finish this book because he died in

December 1841, a month short of his twentieth birthday. Fortunately he had already completed his "Conversion of the San Luiseños of California" at an earlier date. In it he described the local missionary work of the Franciscans among his Indian people. He also told of the customs, dances, and games of the Luiseños.[85] "What Is Done Each Day" related the daily work of each Indian family.

> ... and if these also have sons and daughters, they stay in the mission, the sons at school to learn the alphabet, and if they already know it, to learn the catechism, and if this also, to the choir of singers, and if he was a singer, to work, because all the musical singers work the day of work and Sunday to the choir to sing, but without a book, because the teacher teaches them by memory, holding the book.[86]

What makes this document even more remarkable is that the evidence suggests that this account was written by Pablo soon after his arrival at the Urban College in Rome at the age of 12 or 13. It is certainly the only written account of native life at that time by an Indian and is a testimonial both to Pablo's genius and the literacy-education efforts of the Franciscan missions.[87]

Much of what Tac wrote has been confirmed by other eyewitness accounts. At another California mission, several priests also tell us, "The little boys of the Mission in a few months learn anything, as reading in Spanish or Latin, and learn to read from manuscripts, to sing the plain as well as the figured music." (Fr. Juan Martin, Fr. Juan Cabot, Mission San Miguel)[88]

When Indians did not respond well to literacy education, they were directed instead toward vocational education. The missions developed into great vocational schools, soon dwarfing their literacy classes. The largest schools sometimes enrolled more than 2,000 Indians learning tanning, blacksmithing, wine making, stock tending, and the care of fields and crops. Women learned to cook, sew, spin, and weave. By 1834, on the eve of the termination of the missions, the California Indians at the 21 missions herded 396,000 cattle, 62,000 horses, and 321,000 hogs, sheep, and goats and harvested 123,000 bushels of grain. It is amazing to consider that 65 years earlier there had not existed a single horse, cow, sheep, goat, hog, or bushel of wheat in the whole of California. All this abundance was too tempting a target of wealth for Mexican officials and local landholders to resist. The Mexican Revolution swept Spain out of the region and with it the church's land-holding trust for the local Indians.[89]

It is important not to paint an idealistic picture of Indian life at the California missions. Once an Indian agreed to live at a mission community, he could not take his family and leave without permission. Indians were subjected to a rigid authoritarian discipline. Besides learning the externals of Catholic worship, they were expected to attend worship services several times a day. Everyone went to school to learn a basic trade so that each mission could be self-sufficient.

The Indians were well fed three times a day, freeing them from the perpetual search for food that had dominated their pre-mission days. The Spanish also observed almost every saint's feast day as a holiday of celebrations, processions, games, and fiestas. Many of the missions also gave Indians a two-week vacation every five weeks to visit their native village.

Though the majority of Indians seemed to be content with this new way of life, a large minority did not adjust to this regimented life and suppression of their prior customs. Runaway Indians were constantly being hunted down and punished. Near almost every mission there were unconverted Indians who harassed the mission Indians and encouraged escape and rebellion. In several instances there were large-scale Indian revolts resulting in the death of mission priests and the destruction of mission buildings (such as New Mexico in 1680 and San Diego in 1776). As a result of these problems a corporal's guard of five or six soldiers was assigned to each mission.[90]

The Indians of California were basically peace loving and lacked a strong warrior tradition, but they did resent the Spanish invasion and suppression of their way of life. Perhaps this is why only 300 Spanish soldiers scattered over 650 miles were able to keep in check an Indian population of about 100,000. Also, the devotion and skill of the 60 Franciscan missionaries is a tribute to their success in teaching literacy and the rudiments of Western civilization to about 31,000 Christianized Indians.

Critics of the mission system charge that it was a thinly disguised form of slavery and that the friars failed to Hispanicize the Indians. Besides suppressing native cultures, the mission system introduced diseases that devastated a population that had no immunity against the white man's ailments.

However, when California became a territory of the United States, the Indians were virtually eradicated by disease. The U.S. government drove them off their ancestral lands and herded the few survivors into arid reservations located on some of the most useless land in the state. In an ironic twist of fate it was the same federal government that finally, as a belated gesture for Indian welfare, adopted much of the same educational program as the early Spanish missionaries—the vocational boarding school.[91]

GOVERNMENT LITERACY: CONFORM OR BE CRUSHED

After the Civil War ended (1865), the federal government faced an accelerated conflict over Indian land as large numbers of new settlers migrated across the western plains and mountains. Under the peace policy of President Ulysses S. Grant, the government fell back upon its long tradition of enlisting church groups to "civilize" these new Indian tribes by appointing missionaries as agents and teachers among the western tribes.

Grant first invited the Quakers to teach the tribes. By 1870 other religious groups were also running schools, so that the Commissioner of Indian Affairs, Ely S. Parker, a Seneca Indian, declared that they had "proven such a success" that both Catholic and other Protestant denominations were invited to participate in the acculturation process. The goal was to fuse religion and education as the "means for their (Indians') moral and intellectual development." By 1872 Presbyterians had nine agencies overseeing 38,069 Indians, and Catholics at seven agencies guided 17,856 Indians. Education was the centerpiece of the Grant administration's "peace policy." The Board of Indian Commissioners stated that in order to civilize the Indians, "education must be regarded as a fundamental and indispensable factor."

But this mass outsourcing of Indian schooling did very little to improve either their education or the general peace on the western plains. The 1870s witnessed some of the worst violence of the Indian wars, including Custer's Last Stand (1876). By the early 1880s the federal government was ready to end this ambitious church-state experiment and take direct control.[92]

Beginning in the late 1870s, growing dissatisfaction with the results of the missions and day schools led the Bureau of Indian Affairs to establish boarding or industrial schools to acculturate the Indians. The general goals of these institutions were to teach Indian youths how to read and write, how to think, how to live, and how to work at becoming self-supporting. The final objective, however, was to end the enormous government financial outlays needed for maintaining large numbers of Indians on reservations.

The Bureau of Indian Affairs (BIA) proposed to reduce federal subsidies to the Indian population through a universal Indian common-school system. During the next 20 years a fierce policy struggle would occur within the BIA and American society, over the desirability of reservation schools versus boarding schools. If the Indians were to be made self-supporting, manual labor schools had to be boarding schools, argued many reformers. Although reservation day schools were important to introduce literacy education, only boarding schools could complete the process of the transformation of Indian children from their native ways to the ways of white civilization. Reformers argued that compared to boarding schools, day schools on reservations were a failure because the exposure of the children "to the demoralization and degradation of an Indian home neutralizes the efforts of the schoolteacher." In the boarding school the child could become properly acculturated, far removed from Indian language and his irregular life on the reservation.[93]

By 1876 the Secretary of the Interior, Zachariah Chandler, saw the education alternative as the only rational policy for solving the "Indian problem" other than the "gradual extinction of the race."[94] Appropriations rose rapidly from $20,000 in 1870 to almost $3 million by 1900 as the BIA set up its own schools and forced the church missionary groups to the sidelines. By 1877 over 3,000 Indian pupils were enrolled in 150 of these government schools. This increased to over 26,000 by 1900 at 307 schools, out of an estimated Indian school-age population of 40,000 children.[95]

The appearance in the 1870s of Richard Henry Pratt, a remarkable young army officer, offered a successful Indian boarding school model that he had pioneered in Florida. Pratt, a second lieutenant in the Tenth Cavalry, between 1868 and 1875 saw considerable military action on the southern plains against hostile Indians. As a commander of Indian scouts he acquired firsthand experience with Indian character and culture.

In 1875 Pratt was detailed to escort 72 Indian prisoners to Fort Marion at St. Augustine, Florida. Instead of imprisoning them in close confinement, he received permission to begin literacy classes for them and to find useful work for them in the St. Augustine area. Pratt interested white benefactors in his cause of educating Indians toward accepting white ways by treating them with dignity and providing opportunities to mix with whites. His school became a remarkable success.[96]

In fact, it attracted the attention of Harriet Beecher Stowe, who came for a visit in 1877. Stowe, the author of the world-famous *Uncle Tom's Cabin*, turned her attention to the "Indian problem" once slavery was abolished, as did a number of other prominent abolitionists. Stowe was very impressed with what she witnessed.

We found no savages.... The bell soon rang for school hours, and hurrying from all quarters came more dark men in the United States uniform, neat, compact, trim, with well-brushed boots and nicely kept clothing, and books in their hands.

... Large spelling cards adorned one side of the wall, containing various pictures and object-lessons adapted to the earliest stages of learning.

... When they read in concert, when they mastered perfectly the pronunciation of a difficult word, when they gave the right answer to a question they were evidently delighted.

They specially prided themselves in showing how plainly they could speak "th"— which embarrasses every foreigner in the English tongue—rendering it with an anxious and careful precision.

The lessons proceeded; reading, spelling explaining the meaning of each word, and when a meaning was made clear that had been obscure, the bright smile on the smart faces showed the joy of a new idea.

... We have tried fighting and killing the Indians and gained little by it.... Suppose we try education.... Might not the money now constantly spent on armies, forts and frontier be better invested in educating young men who shall return and teach their people to live like civilized beings?[97]

Pratt was successful in persuading Secretary Carl Schurz of the Interior Department to use the abandoned cavalry barracks at Carlisle, Pennsylvania, for Indian education. There, in 1879, 82 Sioux children were soon joined by 55 students from other tribes in the Indian Territory to inaugurate the Carlisle Indian Industrial School. As enrollment and facilities grew, the school's fame spread until it reached a maximum enrollment of about 1,200 students (1903). During Pratt's 24-year tenure as the school's superintendent, 4,903 Indian boys and girls from 77 tribes received schooling there.[98]

The school's curriculum included both academic and vocational education. Above all, Pratt sought to help every Indian child acquire fluency in speaking, reading, and writing the English language. He thought this the most vital requirement for any Indian to make a successful adjustment to the white man's world. The school also gave instruction in the usual elementary and high school subjects such as arithmetic, geography, and history. The boys learned a trade:

farming, carpentry, blacksmithing, tailoring, wagon-making, and many other vocations. The girls learned the domestic skills of the homemaker in the kitchen and sewing room.[99]

But dominating this entire educational program was Pratt's fundamental principle that the Indians must be completely integrated into white society. Anything that might isolate or segregate the Indians was anathema to him. The Indian reservations were "this whole segregatory and reservating process" and therefore an unmitigated evil promoting outmoded tribal ways and attitudes.

To promote this philosophy, the school's "Carlisle Outing" program placed Indian children with white farm families during the summer months for practical experience in civilization. This was certainly the most famous feature of the Carlisle curriculum, which won nearly universal acclaim.[100]

In Pratt's mind, African Americans had furnished the example of what could be done. Slavery had forced them from their tribal existence and placed them in a new environment where they had adopted new customs, dress, and language. As African Americans had been "civilized," so could American Indians. Pratt advocated the total eradication of their culture and complete assimilation of the Indian into general American society. He even suggested half jestingly that the 260,000 Indians (1879) could be sprinkled over the 2,700 existing counties, ninety-six to a county, across the United States. The keystone of Pratt's vision of Indian assimilation was the Carlisle literacy and vocational education program.

Throughout the 1880s and 1890s, using his abundant promotional skills, Pratt made the story of Carlisle widely known across the nation. It became a showcase, the prototype for an extensive system of government boarding schools designed for the mass acculturation of all Indian children. To that end Pratt lectured across the country, encouraged influential people to visit the school, and facilitated the appearance of the Carlisle band at numerous parades and social events. In the 1890s Pratt discovered that his Indian boys could play great college football. Though Carlisle did not graduate a class until 1889 and only later added the first two years of high school and some teacher training, its football teams competed with the best Ivy League schools, such as Harvard, Cornell, and Pennsylvania.[101]

Over Pratt's loud objections, off-reservation schools like Carlisle became the capstone for a system of Indian literacy that began with reservation day and boarding schools. They would, in turn, feed their best and brightest children into far more advanced studies at Carlisle and other similar institutions. Pratt saved his strongest denunciations for the Bureau of Indian Affairs because its educational policies favored reservation schooling. Finally, in 1904, Pratt's cantankerous attitudes resulted in his dismissal from his post at Carlisle.[102] Yet there were many others who shared his views on Indian assimilation.

Sheldon Jackson was a Presbyterian clergyman from upstate New York. He was rejected by his church's foreign mission board as too frail for mission work. Instead he was sent to minister to Indians and pioneer settlers in the Rocky Mountains. In 1877 he traveled from Seattle to start a mission school at Fort

Wrangell in the southern Alaskan panhandle. At that time there were few schools, let alone any education for the native Indians.

Between 1877 and 1884 Jackson made two trips to Alaska. He started five mission schools. Jackson wrote a book, *Alaska*, and gave about nine hundred speeches to church groups and politicians about conditions on America's last great frontier. He emerged as the country's foremost expert on the region. Unfortunately, *Alaska* was a lurid volume that portrayed the Indians as almost subhuman demons from hell, cannibals who ate corpses or dogs alive, killers of babies, torturers, enslavers, and even worse.[103]

This horrid book served Jackson's propaganda purposes of mobilizing public support for his educational policy of eliminating native ways, root and branch. His boarding school for Indian boys and girls in Sitka followed these practices to the letter. Parents were forced to sign a five-year contract stipulating that the child's family and tribe would not contact the student so as to prevent further contamination. Successful Indian education led itself to further controls. The brighter Indian girls who did well in Jackson's program were further institutionalized in a "home" where "they could be gathered and taken out from under control of their mothers."[104]

In 1880 Jackson succeeded in attracting other Protestant churches to establish missions with schools. Baptists, Episcopalians, Methodists, Moravians, and Congregationalists worked with Jackson in lobbying Congress to proclaim a District of Alaska in 1884 and create an agency for Alaskan education. (Alaska became a territory in 1912, and a state in 1959.) A year later Jackson was put in charge of the agency. However, a miserly U.S. Congress forced him to combine government-run Indian schools with mission schools that received only a pittance from the government.[105]

Into this Alaskan Indian school system stepped Hannah Breece in 1904. She was 45 years old when she came to teach Aleuts, Kenais, Athabaskans, and Eskimos. In her memoir, *The Story of Hannah Breece*, this middle-aged woman encumbered by long, voluminous skirts and petticoats traveled among hundreds of little Indian settlements without schools. Hannah scaled cliffs, fell through the ice, and even once outraced a galloping forest fire.[106]

She emerged from the charred wreckage to teach at an Indian summer encampment.

At the fishing camp I half expected the children to have forgotten all they had learned the summer before. Not so. Both they and their parents were proud to show me how much more they had learned over the winter. I had left books and writing materials in Zackar's care and he had seen to it they were used. Older children had taught younger ones as far as they could, and went on to read all the books I had left. They had done all the arithmetic problems as far as they had knowledge. So this summer we had a good foundation, and we all made the most of it.[107]

In the schools Hannah provided a basic literacy education and taught the girls the home arts; other teachers helped the boys learn carpentry and other trades.

During her 14 years teaching Alaskan Indian children, Hannah's sense of her personal mission never seemed to waver.

It was to furnish educational advantages to a people, large classes of whom too ignorant to appreciate them, and who require some form of pressure to oblige them to keep their children in school regularly. It was a system of schools among a people who, while in the main only partially civilized, yet have a future before them as American citizens.[108]

This statement echoes the viewpoint of Sheldon Jackson, who persisted in believing that only compulsion could guarantee Indian school attendance. For the 22 years he led Alaskan Indian education, he lobbied Congress to legislate compulsory attendance. But as in many other areas governing Indian life, Congress always balked since it did not want to spend the money in Alaska or the "lower 48."[109]

During the 1870s many eastern humanitarian groups had produced several powerful organizations that lobbied to secure justice for the Indians. Many white Americans came to see justice as the Indians' due. Civilization, education, and the integration of the Indian into greater American society was another matter that never appealed to any great number.[110]

By the standards of that time, however, considerable progress was made in the overall system of Indian education during the 25 years after the Civil War. The report of Secretary of the Interior Teller in 1884 enumerated 81 reservation boarding schools, 76 reservation day schools, six industrial or manual labor schools (such as Carlisle), another 14 boarding schools operated by religious denominations under government contract, and 23 other missionary schools run without any government support.[111] Three years later, 231 schools were enrolling over 10,000 students at a cost of almost $1,200,000.[112]

Although this seemed to show that more Indians were interested in education, the reality remained that only compulsory education would ever motivate all Indian children to attend school. The failure of the U.S. Congress ever to provide adequate funds to reach this goal made compulsion unfeasible. Also a general feeling persisted among reformers that a peaceable approach to Indian assimilation must rest on persuasion, not force.[113]

The appointment of Thomas Jefferson Morgan, a professional educator, as Commissioner of Indian Affairs (1889–1893) gave a powerful impetus to embarking the United States government upon a truly comprehensive system of Indian literacy education. Morgan believed that the Indians could not be maintained in their "anomalous position." The reservation system had to cease and Indians be absorbed into American life as citizens. "This civilization may not be the best possible, but it is the best the Indians can get. They cannot escape it, and must either conform to it or be crushed by it."[114]

With these brutal principles at the core of his educational philosophy, Morgan appeared at the Lake Mohonk Conference (1888) to present in detail his proposals for such an Indian educational system. At the heart of his proposal was the expansion of the Carlisle model into industrial-trade boarding schools that would remove all children from the reservations and the substitution of an Indian public-school system for the church-run contract mission schools.[115]

The rise of these federally controlled Indian schools saw the imposition of regimentation and discipline upon children. Morgan admitted that the Indian boarding facilities were modeled after the state reform schools in Michigan, Texas, and New Jersey. However, some of these schools were far more humane than others in the treatment of their Indian students. At the Rapid City, South Dakota, school administrators showed a genuine concern for the student's health, diet, sanitation, education, and employment opportunities. Conditions were far different at the Mount Pleasant Industrial School (Michigan), where children were physically abused and told that any misbehavior would result in permanent isolation from their parents. Students were outfitted in prison-like garb for easy identification and to make successful escape more difficult. It is understandable why Indian parents were not supportive of such schools.[116]

Little by little the Congress implemented this plan to do away with contract mission schools in favor of government-run schools designed to make Indians exemplary Americans. By 1900 the government ended all support of church-run schools. Though Morgan did bring a greater degree of coherence to Indian literacy education, he failed to provide uniformity throughout the haphazard collection of Indian schools dispersed across the entire country and serving such culturally diversified Indian peoples.

By 1900 the government had to concede that only about 26,000 out of an estimated Indian school-age population of 40,000 were even enrolled in these schools. Twenty-seven industrial schools had been created by 1910. Although this helped absenteeism to decline, serious overcrowding of available government classroom space meant, that as late as the 1920s, large numbers of Indian children did not attend any kind of school. Educational quality also suffered. The government's own official publications admitted in 1928 that few of its schools offered high school-level instruction.[117]

BETWEEN TWO WORLDS

Assimilation, disease, and oppression had by around 1900 reduced the number of Indians to about 250,000, or less than one-third of the estimated population in 1492. The United States government had made many repeated and rigorous attempts over many years to demolish tribal ties and structures, using literacy education as a means to that end. Indian children who grew up in this system of government boarding schools found themselves isolated in a social system that might educate them, clothe them, and even on occasion give them kind and courteous treatment. But assimilation foundered because few white families would accept an Indian as an equal member of their society.

When two cultures meet, one culture does not have to be totally assimilated into the other. But until quite recently in U.S. history, government policy largely sought the eradication of Indian culture and civilization. Unfortunately, literacy education often was a component of this process as it was used to teach Indian students to feel shame and contempt for their "blanket Indian" parents and their way of life.[118]

Considering all of these adversities, it is amazing how most Indian communities climbed out of a slough of despondency in the twentieth century. During World War II about 25,000 Indians served in the armed forces, about one-third of all adult Indian males. The military gave some GIs their first substantial literacy-education opportunities. For most it was their first real look at the outside world, and they returned home full of new ideas for the future. Making use of the GI Bill, a number of Indian men entered the professions, paving the way for the educational advancement of future generations.[119]

But at the beginning of the twenty-first century, reservation education is failing to meet the literacy needs of most Indian children. Much more must be done to help more Indian students prepare for meaningful participation in today's social and economic life. Many Indians today remain caught between two worlds.

NOTES

1. Scott Riney, *The Rapid City Indian School 1898–1933* (Norman: University of Oklahoma Press, 1999), 9.

2. Richard Henry Pratt, *Battlefield and Classroom: Four Decades with the American Indian, 1867–1904*, ed. Robert M. Utley (New Haven: Yale University Press, 1964), xiii; Dale Van Every, *Forth to the Wilderness: The First American Frontier* (New York: New American Library, 1961), 48, 51.

3. Neal Salisbury, "Red Puritans: The 'Praying Indians' of Massachusetts Bay and John Eliot," *William and Mary Quarterly*, 3rd Series, 31 (January 1974): 27–29.

4. Jill Lepore, "Dead Men Tell No Tales: John Sassamon and the Fatal Consequences of Literacy," *American Quarterly* 46 (December 1994): 486–487; Salisbury, "Red Puritans," 27–29. Samuel Eliot Morison, *The Oxford History of the American People* (New York: Oxford University Press, 1965), 108; Francis Russell, "Apostle to the Indians," in *Treasury of American Heritage* (New York: Simon & Schuster, 1959), 67.

5. Salisbury, "Red Puritans," 30–31; Russell, "Apostle," 68.

6. Margaret Connell Szasz, *Indian Education in the American Colonies, 1607–1783* (Albuquerque: University of New Mexico Press, 1980), 104.

7. Ibid., 110; Morison, *American People*, 108.

8. Szasz, *Indian Education*, 111; Salisbury, "Red Puritans," 32.

9. Cotton Mather, *The Life and Death of Renowned Mr. John Eliot* (London, 1691), 52; Lepore, "Literacy," 489; Russell, "Apostle," 68.

10. Lepore, "Literacy," 489–490.

11. Ibid., 490; Norman Earl Tanis, "Education in John Eliot's Indian Utopias 1646–1675," *History of Education Quarterly* 10 (Fall 1970): 313–316.

12. Salisbury, "Red Puritans," 42; Lepore, "Literacy," 492.

13. John Eliot, *The Indian Primer; or the Way of Training Up Our Indian Youth in the Good Knowledge of God, in the Knowledge of the Scriptures and in an Ability to Read* (Cambridge, Massachusetts, 1669); Salisbury, "Red Puritans," 42; Jennifer Monaghan, "Literacy Instruction and Gender in Colonial New England," *American Quarterly* 40 (March 1988): 20.

14. Salisbury, "Red Puritans," 46–47.

15. E. Jennifer Monaghan, "She Loved to Read in Good Books: Literacy and the Indians of Martha's Vineyard, 1643–1725," *History of Education Quarterly* 30 (Winter 1990): 493–521; Szasz, *Indian Education*, 120–123.

16. Morison, *American People*, 107–108. Eliot's survey can be found in a letter from Richard Bourne to Daniel Gookin, 1 September 1664, in Daniel Gookin, "An Historical Account of the Doings and Sufferings of the Christian Indians in New England in the Years 1675, 1676, 1677," *Collections of the American Antiquarian Society* 2 (1836): 197; Monaghan, "Martha's Vineyard," 502.

17. Salisbury, "Red Puritans," 46; Morison, *American People*, 108.

18. Lepore, "Literacy," 482–486; Russell, "Apostle," 72; Morison, *American People*, 108.

19. Lepore, "Literacy," 481.

20. Ibid., 499; Morison, *American People*, 109; Tanis, "Utopias," 320.

21. Lepore, "Literacy," 502; Salisbury, "Red Puritans," 54.

22. Elisabeth W. Sommer, *Serving Two Masters: Moravian Brethren in German and North Carolina 1727–1801* (Lexington: University Press of Kentucky, 2000); Amy C. Schutt, "What Will Become of Our Young People? Goals for Indian Children in Moravian Missions," *History of Education Quarterly* 38 (Fall 1998): 268–272.

23. Ibid., 283.

24. Ibid., 284.

25. Ibid., 284–285.

26. Ibid., 285; Christopher Ward, *The War of the Revolution*, vol. 2 (New York: Macmillan Company, 1952), 629, 863.

27. Szasz, *Indian Education*, 74.

28. Ibid., 74–76.

29. Ibid., 77.

30. Ibid.

31. Ibid., 76.

32. Richard Morris, ed., *Encyclopedia of American History* (New York: Harper & Row, 1970), 581; Szasz, *Indian Education*, 191–192.

33. Samson Occom, Samson Occom Diary, Vol. 1, Darmouth College Archives, 84.

34. Ibid.; Szasz, *Indian Education*, 195–196.

35. Szasz, *Indian Education*, 197.

36. Ibid., 198–199.

37. Ibid., 199–200.

38. Ibid., 218–223.

39. Ibid., 223.

40. Ibid., 200, 216–217.

41. Ibid., 262–263.

42. Michael C. Coleman, *American Indian Children at School 1850–1930* (Jackson: University Press of Mississippi, 1993), 38; Ronald Rayman, "Joseph Lancaster's Monito-

rial System of Instruction and American Indian Education 1918–1838," *History of Education Quarterly* 21 (Winter 1981): 395.

43. Rayman, "American Indian Education," 396.

44. Letter, Thomas L. McKenney to John C. Calhoun, August 14, 1819, in *Records of the Office of Indian Trade*, Letters Sent, National Archives Record Group 75, 298–302.

45. *United States Statutes at Large, III*, 516–517; Circular, September 3, 1819, American State Papers: Indian Affairs, Vol. 2 (Washington, D.C.: Gales and Seaton, 1832–1834), 201.

46. Reports of House Committee on Indian Affairs, U.S. Congress, Washington, D.C., March 23, 1824, 457–459; Alica C. Fletcher, *Indian Education and Civilization*, Senate Executive Document No. 95, 48 Congress, 2 session, serial 2264 (Washington, D.C., 1888), 197.

47. Rayman, "American Indian Education," 398; Coleman, *American Indian Children*, 40.

48. "Removal of Southern Indians to Indian Territory," extract from Andrew Jackson's Seventh Annual Message to Congress, December 7, 1835, *Messengers and Papers*, vol. 3 (National Archives, Washington, D.C.), 171.

49. Report of the Commissioner of Indian Affairs, 1844, Washington, D.C. in serial 449, 315; Report of the Commissioner of Indian Affairs, 1842, Washington, D.C., in serial 413, 386.

50. Report of the Commissioner of Indian Affairs, 1849, Washington, D.C., in serial 570, 956–957.

51. Grant Foreman, *The Five Civilized Tribes* (Norman: University of Oklahoma Press, 1934), 352–353; William G. McLoughlin, *Cherokees and Missionaries 1789–1839* (New Haven: Yale University Press, 1984), 63–65.

52. Rayman, "American Indian Education," 398–401; Coleman, *American Indian Children*, 40.

53. Foreman, *Tribes*, 355.

54. William Brandon, *The American Heritage Book of Indians* (New York: Simon & Schuster, 1961), 219; Foreman, *Tribes*, 356.

55. Brandon, *Indians*, 417.

56. "Sequoya," in *Biographical Dictionary of Indians of the Americas*, vol. 2 (Newport Beach, California: American Indian Publishers, 1991), 672; McLoughlin, *Cherokees*, 83–84.

57. "Sequoya," *Biographical Dictionary*, 673; McLoughlin, *Cherokees*, 85.

58. Brandon, *Indians*, 219; McLoughlin, *Cherokees*, 85; "Sequoya," *Biographical Dictionary*, 673.

59. McLoughlin, *Cherokees*, 307–308; Brandon, *Indians*, 235.

60. Robert M. Utley and Wilcomb E. Washburn, *The American Heritage History of Indian Wars* (New York: The American Heritage Publishing Co./Bonanza Books, 1977), 168.

61. Brandon, *Indians*, 235.

62. McLoughlin, *Cherokees*, 326; Brandon, *Indians*, 235.

63. Foreman, *Tribes*, 360, 364; *Report of Pierce M. Butler, September 30, 1843*, in Report of the Commissioner of Indian Affairs, 1843, Washington, D.C.

64. Joan K. Smith, Grayson Noley, Courtney Vaughn, and Mary Frances Smith, "From Majority to Minority: The Choctaw Society and the Wright Family in Oklahoma," *Midwest History of Education Journal* 25 (1998): 132–136.

65. Adapted from Foreman, *Tribes*, 365–366.

66. Ibid., 367.

67. Ibid.

68. *Report of Pierce M. Butler.*

69. David J. Weber, *The Spanish Frontier in North America* (New Haven: Yale University Press, 1992), 105; Bernardo P. Gallegos, *Literacy, Education and Society in New Mexico 1693–1821* (Albuquerque: University of New Mexico, 1992), 62–63.

70. Weber, *Spanish Frontier*, 22, 23.

71. Ibid., 105.

72. John Tracy Ellis, *Catholics in Colonial America* (Baltimore: Helicon Press, 1965), 40–42.

73. Ellis, *Colonial America*, 56–57; Weber, *Spanish Frontier*, 105.

74. Weber, *Spanish Frontier*, 110.

75. Ellis, *Colonial America*, 59.

76. Gallegos, *New Mexico*, 65–66.

77. Ibid., 30–39.

78. Dorothy Krell, ed., *The California Missions* (Menlo Park, California: Sunset Publishing Corporation, 1979), 37–39.

79. Ibid., 44–51, 85.

80. Ibid., 53–54, 63–66; Herbert Eugene Bolton, *Anza's California Expeditions*, 5 vols. (Berkeley: University of California Press, 1930); Juan Crespi, *Fray Juan Crispi, Missionary Explorer on the Pacific Coast 1769–1774* (Berkeley: University of California Press, 1927); Robert H. Jackson and Edward Castillo, *Indians, Franciscans and Spanish Colonization* (Albuquerque, University of New Mexico Press, 1995), 11–13, 32–36.

81. Edith Buckland Webb, *Indian Life at the Old Missions* (Los Angeles: W. F. Lewis, 1952; reprint, Lincoln: University of Nebraska Press, 1982), 47.

82. Ibid.

83. Minna Heves and Gordon Heves, trans. & eds., "Indian Life and Customs at Mission San Luis Rey," *The Americas* 9 (1952), 87.

84. Ibid., 88–90.

85. Ibid., 89–91.

86. Ibid., 92–106.

87. Ibid., 87, 91.

88. Webb, *Indian Life*, 47.

89. Krell, *California Missions*, 55–56.

90. Ibid., 58–59; Jackson, *Indians*, 76–83.

91. Krell, *California Missions*, 60–61; Weber, *Spanish Frontier*, 121.

92. Coleman, *American Indian Children*, 41; Francis P. Prucha, *American Indian Policy in Crisis* (Norman: University of Oklahoma, 1967), 268–269; Riney, *Rapid City Indian School*, 5–10; Report of the Secretary of the Interior, 1876, in serial 1749 (Washington, D.C.), iii–iv.

93. Prucha, *Indian Policy*, 269–270; Annual *Report of the Board of Indian Commissioners*, 1871, (Washington, D.C.: Government Printing Office, 1901), 11.

94. Prucha, *Indian Policy*, 269.

95. Coleman, *American Indian Children*, 41, 45.

96. Prucha, *Indian Policy*, 271–272.

97. Mrs. Harriet Beecher Stowe, "The Indians at St. Augustine," quoted in *Battlefield and Classroom*, 155–162.

98. Prucha, *Indian Policy*, 273–274; Pratt, *Classroom*, xiii.

99. Pratt, *Classroom*, xiii.

100. Prucha, *Indian Policy*, 274; Pratt, *Classroom*, xiii–xiv.

101. Prucha, *Indian Policy*, 276–277.

102. Ibid., 280–282.

103. Hannah Breece, *A Schoolteacher in Old Alaska: The Story of Hannah Breece*, ed. Jane Jacobs (New York: Random House, 1995), 198–200.

104. Ibid., 200–201.

105. Ibid., 201–203.

106. Ibid., 1, 203.

107. Ibid., 150.

108. Ibid., 198.

109. Ibid., 203.

110. Pratt, *Classroom*, xiii.

111. "Report of the Secretary of the Interior, 1884," in serial 2286, Washington, D.C., iii–v.

112. "Report of the Secretary of the Interior, 1887," in serial 2541, Washington, D.C., 29.

113. Prucha, *Indian Policy*, 289–290.

114. "Report of the Commissioner of Indian Affairs, 1889," in serial 2725, Washington, D.C., 3–4.

115. Prucha, *Indian Policy*, 297–304.

116. Riney, *Rapid City Indian School*, 200–250.

117. Coleman, *American Indian Children*, 45. Prucha, *Indian Policy*, 318, 319.

118. Brandon, *Indians*, 403–404; Peter Farb, *Man's Rise to Civilization as Shown by the Indians of North America from Primeval Times to the Coming of the Industrial State* (New York: Dutton, 1968), 264–265.

119. Brandon, *Indians*, 409–410.

Chapter 9

Contraband Education:
The Struggle for African-American Literacy

Much of the struggle for African-American literacy has been long and bitter, and it continues today. This literacy odyssey began almost from the moment the first African Americans were forcibly brought to America. Personal freedom became an important subtext in this search for literacy. Freedom has been achieved. For many the personal quest for an equal literacy education in the United States remains an illusive goal.

LITERACY AND RELIGION IN COLONIAL AMERICA

Because of their religious ideals the Puritans of New England believed in providing a literacy education for their slaves. The diversified economy of colonial New England also encouraged African-American literacy, which would turn an intelligent slave into a more valuable asset for his master. These social forces combined so that many slaves received a basic literacy education as well as craft training. This did not begin any enlightened general literacy movement, but was encouraged by various members of the clergy, religious organizations, and more progressive slaveowners.[1]

Literacy schools for blacks, who then comprised only about 3 percent of the population of New England, was encouraged by such prominent Puritans as John Eliot, who as we have seen also provided literacy education for the Indians. He formulated a plan for the instruction of slaves, but died before he could implement it. However, Cotton Mather carried out Eliot's intentions. He encouraged masters to educate their slaves as he personally did, and in 1717 he opened a charity school for blacks and Indians (for more details see Chapter 1). Even though this school was short-lived, Mather continued to express his determination to "revive the charity school for Negro's."[2]

Others followed Mather's lead. On April 8, 1728, the following announcement for a Boston school appeared in the *New England Weekly Journal*:

Mr. Nath Pigott intends to open a School on Monday, next, for the Instruction of Negro's in Reading, Catechizing & Writing if required, if any are so well inclined as to send their Servants to said school near Mr. Checkley's Meeting House care will be taken for their Instruction as aforesaid.[3]

For a few like Phillis Wheatley (c. 1753–84), education opened a new life. Born in Africa, possibly in Senegal, at the age of eight, Phillis was brought to Boston on a slave ship. There she was bought by John Wheatley, a prosperous tailor, as a servant for his wife. They sent her to school, where she soon mastered English and Latin. Phillis read widely, particularly contemporary poets and the classics. She became a recognized poet when her friends arranged for the publication of her *Poems on Various Subjects, Religious and Moral* (1773). In that same year she was sent to England because of poor health, accompanied by Wheatley's son Nathaniel. Phillis became a popular figure in London society. Unfortunately, upon her return to Boston the Wheatleys died. Without their support and after an unhappy marriage, Phillis died alone and in poverty at the age of 31.[4]

Other religious groups such as the Anglican missionaries for the Society for the Propagation of the Gospel in Foreign Parts (SPG) also established literacy schools for African Americans in colonial America.[5] About 1704, a French Huguenot convert, Elias Neau, was appointed an SPG catechist to the black population of New York City. He began with about 28 women and 18 men sent by slaveowners, who included both the governor of New York and the rector of Trinity Church. By the summer of 1705 he had over 100 catechumens meeting on Wednesdays, Fridays, and Saturdays at five o'clock and on Sunday evenings. These mostly adult slaves (though Indians and whites also attended) crowded into a second-story room in the house where he lodged, where before an audience of white onlookers a class of two or more hours was held. Neau lit candles when it grew too dark to read the words and sing notes from the English psalters or follow the lines of the catechisms.[6]

When not in class an untiring Neau went from house to house, catechizing, exhorting, and instructing his flock, comforting the sick or praying for their dead. All the time he pursued his broader goal, which was "to give them an idea altogether spiritual of a Being infinitely perfect."[7]

In spite of these laudable spiritual goals, Neau's school came under suspicion by the slaveowners after a 1712 slave uprising that included arson and murder. The school "was charged as the cause of the mischief, the place of conspiracy and that instruction [that] had made them cunning and insolent." However, a formal inquiry failed to implicate any of Neau's students in the uprising. Despite strong opposition the school was permitted to remain open with one important caveat. The Common Council ordered that blacks without lanterns were banned from the streets of New York after dark. White masters could thus thwart black literacy education by denying them illumination. Since most of Neau's students worked during the daylight hours, his school quickly reverted to its original modest size.[8] We will witness time and again the fear of slave insurrection as a powerful tool used by whites to deny African Americans even the most basic literacy instruction.

After Neau's death in 1722, William Huddleston, who directed the SPG charity school in the city, continued this ministry to the slave population. But after two years a series of assistant rectors of Trinity Church operated the school.[9]

Later in 1727 the head of the SPG, Bishop Gibson of London, sent out 10,000 circular letters to all his American missionaries as well as to the masters and mistresses of slaves. He called upon them, "as a religious duty to teach their slaves and domestics to read and write."[10] Despite the general unpopularity of the Episcopal Church in New England, SPG ministers furnished schoolmasters to teach slave children, sometimes in the same class with white pupils. In 1774 a Mr. Taylor taught 14 children, including one black student, in the SPG school at Providence, Rhode Island. Other slave schools existed at Narragansett and Newport. This latter institution had 30 black students in 1762. By 1773, however, this school was on the point of closing due to lack of financial support. Eleven years later the Rhode Island Emancipation Bill of 1784 made it compulsory that black children be taught to read and write. To what extent this was carried out is unknown.[11]

The Quakers had long been against slavery. Rhode Island Quakers at their Yearly Meeting (1760) forbade their members to engage in the slave trade.[12] Quaker educators such as Anthony Benezet and John Woolman surpassed William Penn in denouncing the unmitigated evil of slavery and calling for the manumission and education of all African Americans. However, there never was a large black population in Pennsylvania (est. 3,000 in 1750), given the nature of the economy and the traditional Quaker opposition to slavery.[13]

Many slaves were actually tutored in the homes of their masters, while some attended school with whites. In Philadelphia a separate black school was established in 1758 under the auspices of Thomas Bray's Associates, an English philanthropic society. A committee of the Society of Friends organized another school in 1770 to offer a basic literacy education of reading, writing, and arithmetic and useful domestic skills such as sewing and knitting. Attendance was free of any expense to the parents with operating funds raised by subscription among the Quakers. Between 1777 to 1782, 250 children and adults entered this school.[14]

Anthony Benezet, a French Huguenot, moved this school from its own building to his home. By 1784 about 100 students were enrolled, but only 15 to 35 pupils were usually in attendance. In 1786 a woman schoolmistress founded another school for blacks, which by the early 1790s had a regular attendance of 80 students. By the early 1790s this school could count 80 students regularly present each day. Though these numbers appear to be small, the Quakers can be credited with making a major contribution to black literacy in the northern colonies.[15]

By the time of the American Revolution (1776), over half of the population of the eastern seaboard resided in the southern colonies of Maryland, Virginia, the Carolinas, and Georgia. About 500,000 blacks lived throughout the 13 colonies, but most of these were southern slaves.

As in the North, African-American literacy opportunities in the colonial South were restricted mainly to one major source, denominational education. The SPG also spearheaded literacy for black children throughout the southern colonies. One notable success was an unusual plan developed by Commissary Alexander Garden for a school in Charleston, South Carolina. He purchased two young African Americans, Harry and Andrew, and trained them to become schoolmasters. They would teach black children from various parts of the colony to read so that they might in turn instruct other students. This monitorial school was opened in 1743 by subscription. The Charleston school enrolled between 50 to 70 pupils before it closed at the death of its black teacher in 1764. How well the other black monitorial schools functioned is unknown.[16]

Samuel Davies was a Presbyterian minister from frontier Hanover, Virginia, and president of the College of New Jersey from 1759 to 1761. Many today consider Davies a major leader of the Great Awakening in the American colonies since he was unsurpassed as a pulpit orator. He also made a major contribution to African-American literacy by encouraging reading and participation in church services.[17]

Davies adhered to the Presbyterian tradition that religion and education went hand in hand, and he promoted the literacy of blacks and Indians as well as whites. Davies occasionally took a young man into his home to prepare him personally for college or the ministry. However, he never established a formal school, probably because of the vast numbers under his pastoral care. Instead, he distributed large numbers of books donated from England.[18]

There is no evidence of any serious opposition to his efforts supporting African-American literacy. The people of colonial Virginia had not yet developed the abiding mistrust of educating blacks that was later linked to southern fears of slave rebellions. Davies wrote in March 1755, "Never have I been so struck with the appearance of an assembly as when I have glanced my eye to that part of the meeting house where they usually sit … with so many black countenances eagerly attentive to every word they hear, and frequently bathed in tears."[19]

Much of the time Davies used for black religious instruction was actually devoted to teaching them how to read. He was certainly one of the first Presbyterian leaders to actively devote himself to African-American literacy with significant success. As late as 1843 one witness stated that of the blacks taught to read by Davies, "A considerable number of them have given credible evidences, not only of their acquaintance with the important doctrines of the Christian religion, but also a deep sense of them upon their minds, attested by a life of strict piety and holiness."[20]

Davies was personally gratified that he met so little opposition. This may have been a function of the small number of black slaves involved and of Davies' basic intention, which was "not to make them dissenters, but good Christians and good servants."[21]

In his sermons Davies emphasized the necessity of humane treatment by echoing seventeenth-century admonitions to families regarding the training of apprentices in their homes. Here Davies linked children and slaves together by admonishing parents and masters to treat all those living in their households as members of their own family. He strongly encouraged masters to provide a literacy education and religious worship for their slaves, a progressive concept that actually benefited relatively few African Americans in the colonial South.[22]

THE "ARMOR" OF LITERACY:
THE ANTEBELLUM NORTH (1800–1860)

Literacy education opportunities expanded for African Americans in the North during the antebellum years, but remain difficult to measure. Much of what was available came from private religious sources or private schools, largely financed by blacks themselves. The vast majority of African Americans, whether slave or free, lived their whole lives with very little formal education or indeed any exposure to literacy education.

Most of the northern states before the Civil War offered limited and segregated black public education. In the border states and in cities like Cincinnati, blacks were barred from public education.[23]

There were notable exceptions. The public schools for black children in New York City were segregated and inferior to those for white students. However, they gradually improved after a publicity campaign organized by black leaders exposed the schools' most blatant problems. Some public elementary education in Philadelphia was offered to the African-American community. However, by 1860 the city could count 56 private black schools, with only 12 conducted by white educators.

In 1827 the *Freedom's Journal* survey of "African Free Schools" in the Northeast found:

Portland, Me. With a colored population of 900 provides one school under the care of a mistress.

Boston, Mass. With a colored population of 2000 provides three schools, two primary under the care of African female teachers, and a Grammar School under a master.

Salem, Mass. With a colored population of 400, put a school into operation last year, but it closed after six months.

New Haven, Conn. With a colored population of 800 two schools three months during the year.

Providence, R.I. With a colored population of 1500, and Hartford, Conn., with 500 provide none.

Philadelphia. With a colored population of 15,000 provides three schools.

New York. With a colored population of 15,000 provides two schools.[24]

Before the Civil War, in some northern states including Pennsylvania, Massachusetts, Connecticut, Rhode Island, New Jersey, and Ohio, either black or integrated schools made some gains. The overwhelming response from white northern society to literacy for blacks was at best indifference, bordering on open hostility. In addition, some of the same social attitudes that prevented an all-out effort to educate white children and adults only compounded the literacy problems of African Americans.

Beginning in the 1820s many northern states began to curtail the rights of free African Americans to vote, learn to read and write, emigrate, or even hear the word of God. Many whites disliked the idea of sharing their prosperity with freed northern blacks and tried to prevent it. They were afraid that the blacks would not remain content with their second-class social status. Many states disfranchised blacks by adopting white manhood suffrage laws. After 1819 new states admitted to the Union immediately restricted voting rights to white males. The majority of northern states limited or barred further black immigration. They qualified black participation in their state courts. Cities enacted codes segregating blacks from whites in schools, churches, public transportation, accommodations, and entertainment. Civil laws, popular opinion, and mob violence enforced these discriminatory practices. Black schools in particular became a favorite target for the mobs. Is it any wonder that thousands of blacks left the United States seeking better literacy opportunities and justice for their children and themselves in Canada?

Such was the experience of the Female Boarding School in Canterbury, Connecticut. In 1832 Sarah Harris, an African American, asked Prudence Crandall, a white teacher, if she might attend her school as a day student. After admitting her Crandall was warned by outsiders "that she must be removed, or my school would be greatly injured."

As Crandall refused to expel Sarah, the white pupils withdrew. Crandall then reorganized the school for "Young Ladies and Misses of Color." Even though the school was expensive by the standards of that day ($25 a quarter), by April 1833, 20 young African-American women had enrolled from New York, Boston, Providence, and nearby Connecticut towns. The people of Canterbury then began to harass Miss Crandall's pupils in school and out. Ministers barred them from church. Storekeepers refused to sell them food. Rotten eggs were thrown through the school's windows, and manure dumped in the well. Even the local doctor refused to provide medical treatment to them. When the students walked about the town, horns were blown and pistols fired.

The state legislature passed a new law that forbade the teaching of blacks from out of state without the permission of local authorities. Crandall was arrested for defying this law but later won the case on appeal. Yet, the school still was forced to close after Canterbury townspeople set the building on fire and smashed its walls and windows with heavy iron bars.[25]

Opposed to this rising tide of bigotry and fear throughout the Northwest, the Quakers established schools for blacks in their settlements and in communities of former slaves. Excluded from most sources of free schooling, African Americans rose to the challenge by operating their own Sunday schools or funding black relief societies that supported schools and tutors offering the rudiments of literacy. By 1817 in New York blacks constituted 25 percent of the students enrolled in the schools of the Sunday School Union Society. Similarly, by 1819 in the schools of the Philadelphia Sunday and Adult School Union, about two-thirds of the almost eleven hundred adult students were black. Whites were often astonished how ardently adult African Americans sought out these Sunday-school literacy opportunities and how they displayed a personal "disposition for receiving instruction and an intenseness of application." In most of these programs women outnumbered men.[26]

As forms of tax-supported public schools or subscription schools expanded, an unfortunate result for blacks was a diminished focus on literacy training by adult Sunday schools. As early as 1824 the Philadelphia Union Adult Society, which especially focused on basic literacy skills for blacks, closed two of its four schools for want of public financial support. By 1860 the Bethany Colored Mission was the only one of Philadelphia's 124 non–church-affiliated schools that taught reading to black students.[27]

Diminished white interest also coincided with the Nat Turner slave rebellion of 1831 in Virginia. One consequence was the mass exclusion of blacks from many white-run Sunday schools throughout the United States. But these events did not bring about the disappearance of black schools. Instead, some of this demand for literacy was met by blacks running their own schools. With the expulsion of their children from white-sponsored Sunday schools, blacks in Washington, D.C., began their own schools. In Baltimore, Maryland; Elizabeth, New Jersey; and throughout the North, black Sunday schools flourished and had plenty of teachers. Since enrollment information was not kept, there is no way to know how many African-American children acquired basic literacy at these schools.[28]

The literary societies established by free African-American women in cities throughout the North were another means of furthering black literacy. The Philadelphia Female Literary Society was the earliest such society, founded in 1831. Other similar institutions were established by black women in Boston (1832), Rochester (1833), New York City (1834), and Buffalo (1837). To advance the cause of the educated women, the Philadelphia Female Literary Society sponsored original member essays, some of which were later published in the *Liberator* (an abolitionist newspaper). In New York the Ladies Literary Society offered a public exhibition that featured the diversity of its members' achievements.[29]

Literacy for these black women became just as important as their individual freedom, as it constituted a collective act of resistance to their oppressors. Their literacy challenged "our enemies [who] rejoice and say, we do not believe they have any minds; if they have, they are unsusceptible of improvement." In joining these societies black women undermined this stereotype, "that by so doing, we may break down the strong barrier of prejudice."[30]

Sarah Mapps Douglass (1806–1882) and Margaretta Forten (1808–1875) exemplified these African-American women literacy activists. Sarah was born in Philadelphia, where her maternal grandfather, a Quaker, owned a bakery, operated a school, and was an early member of the Free African Society, the first U.S. African-American benevolent organization. Needless to say, Douglass received an unusually fine education for that time. For several years she was privately tutored before entering a school established in 1819 by her mother and the wealthy black shipbuilder James Forten.

During the 1820s Douglass established her own school for black children, later financially supported by the Philadelphia Female Anti-Slavery Society. Her work in this society led to a lifelong friendship with the Grimké sisters, Sarah and Angelina, prominent white abolitionists. She later continued her teaching career as head of the girls' primary department (1853) at the Institute of Colored Youth, where she remained until her retirement in 1877. She also devoted her time to antislavery activities. After the Civil War ended, Douglass became vice-chairman of the Woman's Pennsylvania Branch of the American Freedmen's Aid Commission.[31]

Margaretta Forten (1808–1875) was the eldest child of James Forten. He and his wife taught their six children the basics of literacy at home. Since there was no black school in Philadelphia that would offer their children a more advanced education, in 1819 the Fortens and the Douglasses hired Britton E. Chamberlain as a teacher in a school for their children and pupils from other wealthier families in the black community. Forten also hired private tutors for his daughters.

Later, as an adult, Margaretta ran a successful private school for 30 years. An antislavery activist, Forten joined the Female Anti-Slavery Society. She remained a dedicated teacher and successful advocate of social reform until her death.[32]

Northern black male leaders such as Frederick Douglass, Samuel Cornish, and Daniel Payne also became promoters of literacy opportunities for northern free blacks and southern black slaves and inspired more of them to send their children to school. African-American societies passed resolutions at their conventions encouraging blacks to pursue literacy. As we have seen, numerous benevolent associations throughout the North, such as the New York Phoenix Society, ran schools and urged parents to send their children for literacy instruction.[33]

As journalists, Douglass and Cornish praised the benefits of literacy in their respective journals. In 1859, the editor of *Anglo-African Magazine* deplored the low state of literacy among black people. "Instruction is the great want of the colored race; it needs the light, ideas, facts, principles of action, for its development and progress. In this armor alone can it fight its battles, and secure its rights, and protect its interests amid the focus of civilization."[34]

Northern abolitionist leaders understood the power of the black literacy issue. In his famous "Address to the Slaves," Henry Highland Garnet in 1843 at the National Negro Convention denounced the widespread state laws that prohibited black literacy. "Nearly three millions of your fellow-citizens are prohibited by law and public opinion from reading the Book of Life (the Bible)!" he declared.[35]

Daniel Payne, a prominent African Methodist Episcopal (A.M.E.) preacher and bishop, fought for a literate black people. He characterized this quest as "that struggle between darkness and light, between ignorance and knowledge, between baptized superstition and Christianity." Payne founded numerous Sunday schools and a church newspaper and led in the establishment of Wilberforce College. Since his A.M.E. church was a strong religious force throughout the border states, Payne's agitation for black literacy was felt there and throughout the North.[36]

"MY ESCAPE FROM THE GRAVEYARD OF THE MIND"— THE ANTEBELLUM SOUTH (1800–1860)

The frequent hearing of my mistress reading the Bible aloud, ... awakened my curiosity in respect to this *mystery* of reading, and roused in me the desire to learn. Up to this time I had known nothing whatever of this wonderful art, and my ignorance and inexperience of what it could do for me, as well as my confidence in my mistress, emboldened me to ask her to teach me to read. ... In an incredibly short time, by her kind assistance, I had mastered the alphabet and could spell words of three or four letters. ... [My master] forbade her to give me any further instruction ... [but] the determination which he expressed to keep me in ignorance only rendered me the more resolute to seek intelligence. In learning to read, therefore, I am not sure that I do not owe quite as much to the opposition of my master as to the kindly assistance of my amiable mistress.[37]

With these words Frederick Douglass began his odyssey to become literate and defeat the cruelties of brutal enslavement. It was a symbol of the liberating force of literacy that Douglass wrote at the end of his autobiography, "I subscribe myself. ... Frederick Douglass." Literacy had helped him become a thinking person, freed from ignorance, and it kindled a thirst to free others.[38]

Similar strong emotions regarding the liberating power of literacy were expressed by Henry Bibb.

I can truly say that I have been educated in the school of adversity, whips, and chains. Experience and observation have been my principal teachers, with the exception of three weeks schooling which I have had the good fortune to receive since my escape from the graveyard of the mind and the dark prison of human bondage.[39]

The brutal oppression of slavery could even be a powerful motivator for those African Americans who struggled to become literate and paid a terrible personal price. Papa Dallas, who lived to be 104, told his story to Tonea Stewart when she was a child.

He was blind and had these ugly scars around his eyes. One day [when she was 5 or 6 years old], I asked Papa Dallas what happened to his eyes.

Well daughter, he answered, when I was mighty young, just about your age, I used to steal away under a big oak tree, and I tried to learn my alphabets so that I could learn to read my Bible. But one day, the overseer caught me, and he drug me out on the plantation, and he called out for all the field hands. And he turned to 'em and said, "Let this be lesson to all of you darkies. You ain't got no right to learn to read!" And then he whooped me and he whooped me. And he whooped me. And, daughter, as if that wasn't enough, he turned around and burned my eyes out.

Papa Dallas implored Stewart to

Promise me that you gonna pick up every book you can and you gonna read it from cover to cover. . . . Promise me that you gonna go all the way through school, as far as you can. And one more thing, I want you to promise that you gonna tell all the children my story.

Stewart kept those vows. She became a professor and director of theater arts at Alabama State University.[40]

In the antebellum years, white southerners were in an awkward position. Mass literacy was being promoted in the northern United States as a positive social good necessary for educating the citizens of the republic and helping them cope with the early Industrial Revolution. However, the majority of white southerners were willing to go to great lengths to prevent their enslaved African Americans from learning to read. The general perception of being out of step with the rest of the country seemed to make white southerners even more adamant against general literacy, even for their own white children! (For more details see Chapter 5.)

In the minds of the slaveowners there seemed to be some valid justifications for fearing a literate black population. A small group of whites thought they could teach slaves "Bible literacy," thereby upholding the social order. But the vast majority of white southerners knew that the knowledge gained through literacy could cut the social fabric of slavery to shreds. The slaveowners had it right. Literate African-American slaves used their reading and writing skills to run away. But becoming literate signified something of even greater importance: the establishment of the black person's human identity. Black recognition of the significance of literacy helped to destabilize the southern slaveholder's dehumanizing economic system.[41]

Among those blacks who did somehow learn to read and write, the majority were house servants, city workers, or children who went to school as companions to their master's children. Since children often worked in the slaveholder's home before assuming other jobs, they had greater opportunities to acquire knowledge. The field slaves who did become literate mainly learned from black teachers. Others were taught to read in Sunday schools operated by either blacks or whites.[42]

A 1930s Federal Writers Project interviewed many former slaves and added to the scores of other narratives written by former slaves. According to their testimony and autobiographies it seems that a surprising number of methods for attaining literacy were pursued in almost every region and every state in the antebellum South. Some blacks and whites were willing to run the considerable risks of either legal prosecution and/or open brutality in order either to teach others or to become literate themselves. Black schools are known to have existed at different times before the Civil War in Savannah, Georgia; Charleston, South Carolina; Lexington and Louisville, Kentucky; Fredericksburg and Norfolk, Virginia; and Florida, Tennessee, and Louisiana.

The anti-literacy laws convinced both whites and blacks to keep quiet about learning to read. Fear drilled this lesson into the slave population: don't read, or if you do, do it with great stealth. A house servant in 1850s Alabama explained how many slaves could read but "de kep' daat up deir sleeve, dey played dumb lack dey couldn't read a bitt till after surrender." (Lee's surrender in 1865 at Appomattax that ended the Civil War).[43]

Slaves testified that the most common age to begin learning to read was between age six and eight. This was often the case since young children were usually given jobs in or around the plantation/farm house until they were strong enough for field work. White children taught their slave playmates secretly, but often black children who spent most of their time around the house could learn by listening as the white children learned.

Like any other American child of that time, slaves who somehow learned to read usually did so from the famous Noah Webster's "blue-back" speller. The Bible was their most important book. Among former slaves the motive given above all others for attaining literacy was the desire to read the Bible. The Bible and the black church gave most slaves a central identity in their communities and lives.[44]

During Booker T. Washington's childhood he accompanied his master's daughter to school. He witnessed how her classmates were busily learning how to read. "The picture of several dozen boys and girls in a schoolroom engaged in study made a deep impression," Washington later reflected. As a little boy who longed to learn how to read, he considered the luxury of going to school like "getting into paradise."[45]

Most slaves who received any literacy education had some relationship with whites who made it possible—frequently under adverse circumstances. Henry Bibb, whom we met earlier, explains the tenuous position of black literacy instruction in Kentucky of 1833.

There were quite a number of slaves in the neighborhood, who felt very desirous to be taught to read the bible. There was a Miss Davis, a poor white girl, who offered to teach a Sabbath school for the slaves, notwithstanding public opinion and the law was opposed to it. Books were furnished and she commenced the school; but the news soon got to our owners that she was teaching us to read. This caused quite an excitement in the neighborhood. Patrols were appointed to go and break it up the next Sabbath. They were determined that we should not have a Sabbath School in operation. For slaves this was called an incendiary movement.[46]

There were actually a wide variety of ways that African-American children could enter the literacy "paradise." In Virginia Nat Turner's family taught him to read. Thomas Pittus believed that his owner taught him to read so he might "be half way able to use tolerably good language around his grandchildren." There seemingly existed very little agreement among masters over the issue of black literacy, as a Kentucky slaveowner surprisingly wrote. "You colored boys and girls must learn to read and write, no matter what powers object ... your parents and your grandparents were taught to read and write when they belonged to my forefathers and you young negros have to learn as much." So he built them a school and hired a teacher![47]

The struggle for black literacy usually flowed from strong personal motivation. As Frederick Douglass explains, freeing the mind from ignorance was the first major step to somehow escaping physical bondage.

Very soon after I went to live with Mr. and Mrs. Auld, she very kindly commenced to teach me the A, B, C. After I had learned this, she assisted me in learning to spell words of three or four letters. Just at this point of my progress, Mr. Auld found out what was going on, and at once forbade Mrs. Auld to instruct me further, telling her, among other things, that it was unlawful, as well as unsafe, to teach a slave to read. To use his own words, further, he said, "if you give a nigger an inch, he will take an ell. A nigger should know nothing but to obey his master—to do as he is told to do. Learning would *spoil* the best nigger in the world. Now," said he, "if you teach that nigger (speaking of myself) how to read, there would be no keeping him. It would forever unfit him to be a slave."

Though conscious of the difficulty of learning without a teacher, I set out with high hope, and a fixed purpose, at whatever cost of trouble, to learn how to read. The very decided manner with which he spoke, and strove to impress his wife with the evil consequences of giving me instruction, served to convince me that he was deeply sensible of the truths he was uttering. It gave me the best assurance that I might rely with the utmost confidence on the results which, he said, would flow from teaching me to read. What he most dreaded, that I most desired. What he most loved, that I most hated. That which to him as a great evil, to be carefully shunned, was to me a great good, to be diligently sought; and the argument which he so warmly urged, against my learning to read, only served to inspire me with a desire and determination to learn. In learning to read, I owe almost as much to the bitter opposition of my master, as to the kindly aid of my mistress. I acknowledge the benefit of both.

The plan which I adopted, and the one by which I was most successful, was that of making friends with all the little white boys whom I met in the street. As many of these as I could, I converted into teachers. With their kindly aid, obtained at different times and in different places, I finally succeeded in learning to read. When I was sent of (sic) errands, I always took my book with me, and by going on part of my errand quickly, I found time to get a lesson before my return. I used also to carry bread with me, enough of which was always in the house, and to which I was always welcome; for I was much better off in this regard than many of the poor white children in our neighborhood. This bread I used to bestow upon the hungry little urchins, who, in return, would give me that more valuable bread of knowledge. I am strongly tempted to give the names of two or three of those little boys, as a testimonial of the gratitude and affection I bear them; but prudence forbids;—not that it would injure me, but it might embarrass them; for it is almost an unpardonable offence to teach slaves to read in this Christian country.

The idea as to how I might learn to write was suggested to me by being in Durgin and Bailey's shipyard, and frequently seeing the ship carpenters, after hewing, and getting a piece of timber ready for use, write on the timber the name of that part of the ship for which it was intended. When a piece of timber was intended for the larboard side, it would be marked thus—"L." When a piece was for the starboard side, it would be marked thus—"S." A piece for the larboard side forward, would be marked thus— "L.F." When a piece was for the starboard side forward, it would be marked thus— "S.F." For the larboard aft, it would be marked thus—"L.A." For starboard aft, it would be marked thus—"S.A." I soon learned the names of these letters, and for what they were intended when placed upon a piece of timber in the ship-yard. I immediately commenced copying them, and in a short time was able to make the four letters named. After that, when I met with any boy I knew could write, I would tell him I could write as well as he. The next word would be, "I don't believe you. Let me see you try it." I would then make the letters which I had been so fortunate as to learn, and ask him to beat that.

During this time my copy-book was the board fence, brick wall, and pavement; my pen and ink was a lump of chalk. With these, I learned mainly how to write. I then commenced and continued copying the Italics in Websters' Spelling Book, until I could make them all without looking on the book. By this time, my little Master Thomas had gone to school, and learned how to write, and had written over a number of copy-books. These had been brought home, and shown to some of our near neighbors, and then laid aside. My mistress used to go to class meeting at the Wilk Street meeting-house every Monday afternoon, and leave me to take care of the house. When left thus, I used to spend the time in writing in the spaces left in Master Thomas's copy-book, copying what he had written. I continued to do this until I could write a hand very similar to that of Master Thomas. Thus, after a long, tedious effort for years, I finally succeeded in learning how to write.[48]

Later, as a young adult, Douglass was a slave on Mr. Freeland's farm in St. Michael's, Maryland. There he began a Sabbath school, starting with his two fellow slaves at the farm. They mustered up some old spelling books, and soon neighboring slaves heard about the school and also wanted to learn how to read.

I held my Sabbath school at the house of a free colored man, whose name I deem it imprudent to mention; for should it be known, it might embarrass him greatly, though the crime of holding the school was committed ten years ago. I had at one time over forty scholars, and those of the right sort, ardently desiring to learn. They were of all ages, though mostly men and women. I look back to those Sundays with an amount of pleasure not [to] be expressed.

> These dear souls came not to Sabbath school because it was popular to do so, nor did I teach them because it was reputable to be thus engaged. Every moment they spent in that school, they were liable to be taken up, and given thirty-nine lashes. They came because they wished to learn. Their minds had been starved by their cruel masters. They had been shut up in mental darkness. I taught them, because it was the delight of my soul to be doing something that looked like bettering the condition of my race. I kept up my school nearly the whole year I lived with Mr. Freeland; and, beside my Sabbath school, I devoted three evenings in the week, during the winter, to teaching the slaves at home. And I have the happiness to know, that several of those who came to Sabbath school learned how to read; and that one, at least, is now free through my agency.

Douglass' school was finally broken up in a bloody manner by local whites who used sticks and stones on the slaves. But the desire to free their minds seemed stronger than any retribution.[49]

Even when the slaveowner was sympathetic to providing a black literacy education program, the realities of bondage intervened. In 1840 Louisa Cocke opened a slave school at her Hopewell, Alabama, plantation. Lucy Skipwith, herself a slave, operated the school. Lucy had been educated at a similar plantation school in Virginia. The daily routine of the Hopewell school troubled her. The problem was the boys' irregular attendance caused by their plantation work. Lucy sought her owner's permission to allow her students to miss work to attend school. This was not to be. During the cotton-picking season, the children's attendance further declined. To compensate, Lucy opened a night school, but this alternative superseded common sense and their ability to work all day and study at night. The children were just too tired, Lucy complained. "I can't keep their eyes open." Even if these students had not been slaves, child labor does not facilitate childhood literacy.[50]

It seems that many other southern whites also helped blacks to escape from the bondage of illiteracy. John Thompson was born a slave in Maryland in 1812. At the age of eight he learned to read when he was sent to carry the dinners of the white children to the local schoolhouse, about two miles distant. Thompson was taught by Henry Ashton, his owner's son, after he told Henry that he would like to know how to read. However, they made a mutual pact not to reveal this activity to anyone.

> He (Henry) commenced teaching me from his book my letters. We sometimes started an hour or two after school time, that we might have more leisure for our undertaking. We had a piece of woods to pass on our way, which also facilitated the practical operation of our plans, as we could, by going into them, escape the observation of the other school children or of passers by in the road....
>
>   I made such rapid progress that Henry was encouraged and delighted. When my father knew of the matter, he gave Henry some money with which to purchase me a book....[51]

For the next three years Thompson accompanied the children to school and continued to study at every convenient moment. He then became the body servant of John Wagar (Henry's cousin), although Henry continued to teach Thompson but with less frequency. "I soon got through my first book, *Webster's Spelling Book*, after which Henry bought me the *Introduction to the English Reader*. He also commenced setting me copies (making copies), as he thought it time I was commencing to write, though he still kept me at reading until I had nearly completed my second book."[52]

Fate now intervened. Henry's father died, leaving his family penniless and forcing Henry and his mother and sister to leave their uncle's plantation. Thompson was forever grateful to Henry for helping him become literate. "Through this I have been enabled to read the Word of God, and thereby learn the way of salvation; and though I could never repay these services, yet God has doubly paid him (Henry), for before I left Maryland (as a fugitive slave), his name ranked among the most respectable and wealthy of county merchants."

"After this I continued to read and write at every opportunity, often carrying my book in my hat, that I might lose no chance of using it." Later, in the south of Maryland, Thompson was taught in secret by an Englishman. This continued for about nine months until the Englishman and his whole family abruptly died from unknown causes. After escaping to the North, Thompson continued his education at an evening school in Philadelphia.[53]

Another unusual feature of the antebellum South was the fact that some plantation owners employed literate slaves in the position of plantation preacher. In the early part of the nineteenth century, Jack was kidnapped in Africa at the age of seven and brought to Nottoway County, Virginia. After his conversion to Christianity, he was tutored in reading by his owner's children. At the age of 40 he was licensed to preach to plantation slaves. However, Jack soon began preaching to white congregations that included "many of the most wealthy and refined people" of the county. This was not an isolated example. Elisha Green in Kentucky was a sexton in a white Baptist church for 16 years. By the 1850s he became the pastor of his own African Baptist Church, although only with the financial support and protection of Kentucky whites.[54]

In the peculiar mind of the white South, a gap yawned between a brutal society and its most thoughtful and devout Christian members. There was no overall ban on teaching slaves to read because white Christian southerners had been told for decades that all people should have access to the Bible. Earlier in the 1800s this concept had contributed to the establishment of separate black churches such as the African Methodist Episcopal (A.M.E.) Church and the A.M.E. Zion Church. These congregations counted thousands of members in the southern cities of Charleston and Baltimore as well as in northern cities.[55] The resulting efforts at "Bible literacy" was a primary motivator for many thoughtful Christian southerners, although these white teachers unrealistically believed that they could somehow control what the slaves read and how the slaves used their literacy skills. This was part of the slaveholders' basic belief that they could do whatever they wished with their slave property. Though "Bible literacy" influenced some whites, it appears that the majority of southerners were basically indifferent to literacy for African Americans, and a few were rabidly against it.[56]

Southern nervousness over the growth of black literacy and emancipation increased after the Nat Turner (1831) insurrection in Southampton, Virginia. Over 60 white men, women, and children died within 24 hours. Turner was literate and quoted the Old Testament in fomenting retribution against slaveholding families.

Before the Civil War, 75 percent of the southern white population owned no slaves and had no immediate economic interest in maintaining slavery or the plantation system. By 1860, 200,000 owners held five slaves or fewer and another 388,000 owners held fewer than 20 slaves. This represented 88 percent of all slaveholders. However, there still existed a general fear of the large African-American population held in bondage. In 1790 there had been fewer than 700,000 slaves in the United States. By 1860 this number had increased to almost four million persons. This compared to a white population of about five and a half million in the deep South and another 2.6 million in the border states (Delaware, Maryland, Kentucky, Missouri). In many regions of the deep South, African-American slaves certainly outnumbered their masters, which caused great unease among whites.

Further fanning the flames of brutal repression directed toward African Americans was the news from Jamaica. At about the same time as the Nat Turner incident, blacks had risen in a similar rebellion led by Sam Sharpe, a black Sunday-school teacher.[57]

As a result of the fear that swept the South, between 1829 and 1834 many state legislatures passed restrictive laws limiting the rights of slaves. Some states enacted laws against their instruction. However only four states—Virginia, Georgia, North Carolina, and South Carolina—passed prohibitions banning the teaching of slaves from the 1830s to 1865. Some states' restrictions appeared in the "slave code" or "black code" but not in the state legal code. Other states, such as Missouri and Maryland, banned the public assembly of blacks for educational or religious purposes. However, these states did not penalize anyone for personally instructing slaves or freed blacks in reading or writing.[58]

The impact of these slave laws was extremely variable from place to place even within any one state. In Kentucky both Henry Bibb and Elisha Green noted that slaveowner patrollers broke up slave Sunday schools and whipped all the adult students. However in other parts of the same state, slaveowners privately though quietly supported slave literacy. Throughout the deep South even as late as the 1850s, sympathetic slaveholders secretly taught African Americans how to read and write. But, as we have already noted, slaves caught reading did risk grim punishments.

In the 1830s a Georgia master told his slave to keep his reading to himself, because if the other white men of the community found out that he could write, they would cut the fingers off his hand.[59] Nevertheless, it has been estimated that before the Civil War about 5,000 of Georgia's 400,000 slaves overcame their personal fears of white retribution to become literate.

The Federal Writers Project in the 1930s gives us another measure of how widespread African-American literacy became in the antebellum South. About 5 percent of the former slaves interviewed claimed to have learned to read or to read and write before the Civil War. Further, studies of runaway slaves indicate that from about 9 to 20 percent were able to read.[60]

Surprisingly, freed African Americans also established private schools (both free and tuition-based) throughout the South. These black schools widely varied in number and accessibility from city to city. Washington, D.C., had the largest number of these schools in the South. All of these institutions increased the potential availability of literacy education to the black population.

Some African Americans used their literacy skills to gain their freedom. In 1848 William and Ellen Craft escaped their bondage in Macon, Georgia. In their book *Running a Thousand Miles for Freedom*, they tell how they travelled in first-class accommodations first on trains to the North and then on a steamer to England. Ellen was disguised as a young white southern planter's daughter and William as her slave and body servant. While they stayed in Philadephia, local whites aided them in improving their literacy skills. This helped them to reach their final destination—England. They were not safe in Pennsylvania because of the Federal Fugitive Slave Law (1850), as by its provisions they could be recaptured by federal marshals and returned to the South. "It was not until we stepped upon the shore at Liverpool that we were free from every slavish fear." Ellen and William both continued their education in England.[61]

In New Orleans J. B. Roudanez, a free mulatto-Creole engineer and mechanic employed on sugar plantations, believed that "generally upon every plantation there are at least one man who had somehow learned to read to the others." On the day after news of the dramatic raid by John Brown at Harpers Ferry, Virginia (1859), a slave 75 miles upriver, told Roudanez what had occurred. A newspaper was given to a slave to wipe down sugarhouse machinery. This slave hid that newspaper and later read it aloud to his plantation slave brothers and sisters. It was the story of John Brown's hanging, an event that soon after propelled the nation into civil war and ended American slavery forever.[62]

FROM "CONTRABANDS" TO CITIZENS:
THE CIVIL WAR AND RECONSTRUCTION (1861–1900)

The War Between the States (1861–1865) unleashed a tidal wave of literacy education for the nearly four million African-American slaves in the South. Early in the war a number of freedmen's aid associations and church mission societies began sending literacy educators into the southern areas occupied by Union troops and founded schools for blacks. By 1865 through their combined efforts more than 900 literacy instructors had given an estimated 200,000 free slaves the rudiments of literacy instruction.[63]

This significant black literacy revolution had its beginnings at Fortress Monroe, Virginia. Soon after the outbreak of the Civil War, Union troops launched an amphibious invasion that occupied Hampton, Virginia, and nearby Fortress Monroe. Federal troops offered their protection to thousands of "contrabands" (the wartime jargon that described confiscated rebel property), who fled nearby plantations and flocked to the Union lines.

The earliest, largest, and in the long term most effective of the northern freedmen's aid societies was the American Missionary Association. Founded in 1846 by abolitionists, the society began as a protest against the neutral stance toward slavery of many Protestant church bodies. The society saw this concentration of contrabands around Fortress Monroe as a golden opportunity to help slaves begin their transition to freedom.[64]

In September 1861, Lewis C. Lockwood arrived at Fortress Monroe as the association's first missionary to the freedmen. Some of these black children told Lockwood of a local black teacher, Mrs. Mary S. Peake (1823–1862). Her father was an Englishman and her mother a free African-American of Norfolk. When she was six, her mother sent her to school in Alexandria, Virginia, where she lived with her aunt for 10 years. Mary actually attended several different free black schools with different black or white teachers, her last instructor being Mr. Nuthall, an Englishman. This came to an abrupt halt when the U.S. Congress determined that laws of Virginia prohibiting free black education should also prevail in the federal District of Columbia. Mary was forced to leave school since she was a legal resident of the state of Virginia.

According to a fellow student from Rhode Island, Mary was a very amiable girl and a good student. As a result she acquired an excellent English education, which was among the chief reasons why Lockwood enthusiastically recruited her to begin the first day-school for contraband children.[65]

Mary's school started on September 17, 1861, with only about six students in the first-story front room of the Brown Cottage. Her own family's apartment was in the front room of the second story. After a few days Mary's class grew to between 50 to 60 pupils. Among these children was her own five-year-old daughter Hattie. A basic literacy curriculum included the use of a primer, a catechism, and other elementary religious books furnished by the American Missionary Association.

The response to literacy instruction was so positive among the local African-American community that other schools were soon established. Mary also began teaching a night school for adults with some success. Unfortunately she became ill with tuberculosis. Even when confined to her bed, Mary continued to teach her pupils until her death in February 1862. An interesting footnote to Mary Peake's school was the irony that it was located near the exact spot where the first cargo of African slaves landed in Virginia (1619). Today's Hampton Institute is the descendant of these first literacy schools established at Fortress Monroe during the war.[66]

The second, far larger experiment in Civil War African-American literacy education was headquartered at Beaufort, on Port Royal Island in the South Carolina Sea Islands. On November 7, 1861, seven months after the fall of Fort Sumter in Charleston, South Carolina, a fleet of the U.S. Navy under the command of Commodore S. F. DuPont sailed into Port Royal Sound. After a bombardment of the islands, Union troops occupied them on the following day. The entire white population fled to the mainland, leaving about ten thousand slaves behind. Something had to be done since the old slave regime had been so suddenly swept away, but no new authority was ready to take its place.[67]

Secretary of State William H. Seward and abolitionist Senator Charles Sumner authorized a young Boston attorney, Edward L. Pierce, to organize the private Port Royal Relief Committee. Their mission was to prevent the land from lying fallow, get out a future cotton crop, and thereby prevent "contrabands" from becoming dependent on government charity. Unless they succeeded, the opponents of emancipation would have a very good case for asserting that freed blacks could not become economically self-sufficient. An unofficial part of Pierce's original plan was sending ministers and teachers to open schools for black children. In a short time the committee officially broadened its purposes, intending to teach "the rudimentary arts of civilized life" and "to instruct them (Afro-Americans) in the elements of an English education."[68]

Into this island limbo sailed the first small band of 53 missionaries in March 1862. They would be followed by several hundred other mainly young antislavery people determined to help and guide the newly liberated into their new life. In general these literacy teachers were joyfully accepted everywhere. Because these remote islands were more isolated from the mainstream of American culture, the cotton plantations were worked by slaves who were considered by many to be hopelessly primitive and barbaric and who spoke a dialect that was unknown to most whites. However, the northern teachers were amazed by the eagerness among these African Americans to learn how to read.

The reason behind their great motivation to learn was that despite the antiblack literacy laws of South Carolina, it had been virtually impossible to exclude all African Americans from learning to read. As we have already witnessed in other southern states, many religious white people in South Carolina had protested against these laws on the grounds that it was just as necessary for a black Christian to learn to read the Bible as for a white one.

Despite the fact that the vast majority of slaves were illiterate, these northern teachers discovered a number of black plantation foremen who could read and write. It is clear that more than a few white masters taught their black foremen to the point that they were able to write intelligent reports on the condition of plantation crops. Others had also received secret instruction.[69]

Whatever the motivation, the island's literacy programs grew so quickly that by the end of 1862 over 1,700 students were enrolled in schools on Port Royal, Ladies, and St. Helena Islands. Various northern relief committees also provided literacy education in other parts of the South occupied by federal troops. There

were 400 students receiving instruction in Florida and around 500 on Paris and
Hilton Head Islands. Most of these were basic literacy programs offering rote-
memory instruction of letters and numbers. Some of these instructors found
that most pupils made better progress in spelling and writing than in reading,
until they discerned that these southern black children were totally unfamiliar
with most of the vocabulary used in the northern primers. Another major disadvantage was that nearly all these black students had to wedge their lessons
between chores and field work.[70]

One of these literacy instructors was Laura Towne representing the Philadelphia Port Royal Relief Committee. Although she was not a schoolteacher, she
espoused the root-and-branch abolitionism of New England. After her arrival,
Towne opened her Penn School on the Sea Islands little dreaming that she would
remain in South Carolina for the rest of her life.[71]

Towne had to cope with greatly overcrowded classrooms and petty rivalries
with other northern religious groups also on the islands. In her diary Towne responded to an inquiry from the Commission of Philadelphia whether there was
any need to build schoolhouses.

March 25, 1864
  We need a school-house for several reasons. We cannot make the school convenient
for writing, blackboards, etc. We have the noise of three large schools in one room and
it is trying to the voice and strength, and not conducive to good order.[72]

In October 1864, when Towne's school had an enrollment of 199 students, the
Freedman's Aid Society of Pennsylvania sent a small prefabricated schoolhouse,
"which looks exceedingly pretty, but has not half seats enough in it, and wants
other improvements."[73] By Christmas she had moved into her new school, which
was filled to overflowing with about 250 children. In early 1865 Towne further
petitioned the society to send a bell for its little tower to give the children for
miles around the classic American summons to school. However, she confirmed
in her diary that "Our children came from 5 and 6 miles, but I think no bell could
be heard so far."[74]

In 1865, after only three years of operation, the Penn School had become a
great success. Its students knew all the parts of speech and were even able to
write compositions. They also had read books on physiology and U.S. history.
Towne considered it a high school and began preparing black teachers to offer
instruction throughout the state of South Carolina. It attained the unique distinction of being the only school founded by northerners during the Civil War
that continues in operation today.[75]

In the turbulent years immediately after the war, Laura Towne and the other
teachers anxiously waited to see if the freed blacks would be given confiscated
farmland. Instead they were given permission to lease 20-acre lots with a six-
year option to buy. The federal Freedmen's Bureau did authorize five thousand
dollars for the restoration and repair of school buildings and hospitals. However,
the financial support of the teachers remained dependent on northern charity,

which was wearing thin. A lethargy regarding this cause was creeping over the northern contributors. The New England Freedmen's Aid Society did briefly rally and raised an all-time high sum of $76,000 in the year 1866–1867. But by 1868 contributions tumbled dramatically, to about $29,000. There existed a general feeling that northerners had given so much money over the past 10 years that the society should turn over as many of its schools as possible to the local authorities in the South.[76]

By 1870 Laura Towne clearly understood the consequences of these events. "Our school exists on charity, and charity that is weary. If turned over to the state, no Northern colored person has a chance of being appointed teacher of a state school." Since her brother liberally provided for her, Towne did not take a salary, "but reserved it for other teachers, so that the school may go on as it is for one or two years longer."[77]

The school struggled on, mainly through continued private donations that just barely covered the Penn School's operating costs. In 1877 Towne raised $200 for the school. This and other contributions would keep the classroom doors open for two more years, but only if Towne and another teacher forfeited any salary and her five assistants were paid no more than $10 a month.[78]

The enthusiam and talent of Laura Towne as a literacy missionary were matched by the ability and exertions of her pupils.

October 28, 1877
   Our school is a delight. It rained one day last week, but through the pelting showers came nearly every blessed child. Some of them walk six miles and back, besides doing their task of cotton-picking. Their steady eagerness to learn is just something amazing. To be deprived of a lesson is a severe punishment. "I got no reading today, or no writing, or no sums," is cause for bitter tears.[79]

Until 1884 Towne continued to make invaluable contributions to African-American literacy in the South.

Charlotte Forten Grimké (1837–1914) was the first African-American teacher on these islands. Her diary recorded what she experienced as the only literacy educator stationed on St. Helena Island. Born in Philadelphia, Charlotte represented the fourth generation of Fortens who were born free. Her uncle James Forten owned a prosperous shipyard that provided his family with a stately home and fine private tuition. Charlotte's father Robert Forten had been educated privately and was considered the most talented of his clan, as he was known in Philadelphia as a mathematician, poet, and orator. His dedication to antislavery and civil rights eventually led him to move first to Canada (1855) and then to England (1858).[80]

Much of what we know regarding Charlotte Forten comes from a journal she began keeping at the age of 16 (1854). She had just moved to Salem, Massachusetts, to complete her education. Prior to that time Charlotte had been privately tutored at home, since her father considered Philadelphia's racially segregated schools poorly equipped to educate his daughter. Salem offered an integrated school of sound reputation and was also the location of a fine teacher's academy (normal school) that could prepare Charlotte for a teaching career.[81] Between 1856 and 1868 she held several positions as a teacher in different Salem and Philadelphia schools and as a private tutor. On October 22, 1862, Charlotte left Philadelphia for Port Royal, South Carolina, to teach under the auspices of the Port Royal Relief Association.[82]

As a literacy educator to contraband children, Charlotte was placed in a one-room schoolhouse with children of all ages to teach them basic reading, writing, spelling, history, and math. Her first few months were socially difficult and un-doubtedly the most challenging period of her young life. As the first northern black teacher, Charlotte encountered the racist feelings of northern teachers and the Union military. She felt no "congeniality among those with whom she lived." This later changed with the arrival on the island of her old white aboli-tionist friends. The contraband slaves did not know how to treat her. At first they found it difficult to treat Charlotte as an equal to the other Anglo-American teachers. During her first year on St. Helena, the black domestic staff were sim-ply unprepared to wait on this young black woman.[83] But Charlotte found sol-ace in her teaching work.

I never before saw children so eager to learn, although I had had several years' experi-ence in New-England schools. Coming to school is a constant delight and recreation to them. They come here as other children go to play. The older ones, during the summer, work in the fields from early morning until eleven or twelve o'clock, and then come into school, after their hard toil in the hot sun, as bright and as anxious to learn as ever.[84]

The tiniest children are delighted to get a book in their hands. Many of them al-ready know their letters. The parents are eager to have them learn. ... They are willing to make many sacrifices that their children may attend school.[85]

Another teacher from the North teaching at nearby Beaufort recorded:

My school numbered about forty of the children. Most of them were very dirty and poorly dressed. ... A happier group of children I never expect to witness than those who composed my school: bright eyes, happy looks, kind and patient dispositions, made them look attractive to my eyes. ... But they were so innocent, so despised by others and withal so anxious to learn, that I felt a true sympathy for them. ...

They are very eager to learn. Every one wishes to be taught first; yet unlike some white children, they are patient and willing to wait. They do not easily tire of study but are very diligent in getting their lessons.[86]

This teacher was surprised to find the widespread practice of peer tutoring and even cross-age tutoring,

I have known them teach each other, or sit alone and drill over a lesson for two hours at a time. Let me relate to you a little incident that will illustrate what I have just said. One day, at Beaufort, soon after we landed, while walking through the upper portion of the town, I heard a little voice say the alphabet, while another wee voice, scarcely audible, was repeating it after the first. I looked quickly around to discover from whence the voice came; and what do you think I saw? Why, seated on the piazza of a large empty house were two little negro children, one about seven, the other not more than three years old. The elder had his arm thrown lovingly around the almost naked form of the other, and with an open primer in the lap of one, they were at their study. An hour after, I returned by the same spot, and was both pleased and surprised to find them still at it.[87]

Charlotte Forten was especially gratified by adults who came in the evening for reading lessons. "This eve Harry, one of the men on the place, came in for a lesson. He is most eager to learn, and is really a scholar to be proud of. He learns rapidly. I gave him his first lesson in writing to-night, and his progress was wonderful. He held his pen almost perfectly right the first time. He will very soon learn to write, I think."[88] These adults often sought literacy instruction so as not to be embarrassed by their own children who were in school. Many also understood the future life advantages they might derive from becoming a literate person.

While on St. Helena, Charlotte became a close friend of Colonel Wentworth Higginson, a dedicated white abolitionist from Massachusetts. Higginson was placed in command of the First South Carolina Volunteers, a regiment composed entirely of Sea Islands African Americans. The Colonel thought so highly of Charlotte that he tried to recruit her as a teacher for his regiment on their campaign to Florida in 1863. She was thrilled at this new literacy challenge. "If I can help them in any way I shall be glad to do so." However, Charlotte was never able to join the regiment on this expedition since the Union army in Florida was losing ground. Higginson and the First Carolina Volunteers were eventually evacuated and returned to Port Royal.[89]

Charlotte also met Colonel Robert Gould Shaw, the commander of the first all-black federal regiment, the 54th Massachusetts. She felt that he was "one of the most delightful persons I have ever met." Charlotte was so stunned by his death and that of most of his regiment at the bloody siege of Fort Wagner at nearby Morris Island, South Carolina (July 18, 1863), that Charlotte volunteered as a nurse to treat its wounded soldiers. Later in 1871 she returned to South Carolina as a teacher at the Shaw Memorial School in Charleston.[90]

Less than a year later Charlotte resigned her position as a teacher on St. Helena Island and returned home to Philadelphia. Shortly thereafter the *Atlantic Monthly* published her essays, "Life on the Sea Islands," recounting her experiences as a literacy instructor. Charlotte's personal experience as a teacher offers us intriguing glimpses of the frontline battle of literacy for African Americans in the South.[91]

Other blacks who struggled to become literate in the South during the Civil War were literally in the real front lines of battle. Such was the personal story of W. E. Northcross, a slave living in Alabama when he felt "that he had been called to preach."

At this time I did not know "A" from "B", but I met a man who could read a little. This man liked me and promised to teach me how to read, provided I would keep it secret. This I gladly promised to do. ... I secured a blue-back speller and went out on the mountain every Sunday to meet this gentleman, to be taught. I would stay on the mountain all day Sunday without food. I continued this way for a year and succeeded well.

Northcross worked as a blacksmith and then was captured by the Yankees. Caught in battle again, he escaped and was captured by the southern army, and finally made his way back to home in Colbert County, Alabama.

I went home and got another book—spelling book, although it was not allowed. Some of my own people told my master that I had a book trying to read. He sent for me to come to the house, I obeyed, thought I dreaded to meet him, not knowing what the consequence would be. But his heart had been touched by Divine power and he simply told me that he heard that I had a book, and if I was caught with it I would be hung.... Notwithstanding my master's counsel I thirsted for knowledge and got some old boards and carried them to my house to make a light by which I could see to read. I would shut the doors, put an end of a board into the fire, and proceed to study; but whenever I heard the dogs barking I would throw my book under the bed and peep and listen to see what was up.

   I like the Ethiopian, wanted a guide. I moved to Mrs. McReynold's. God bless her! She gave me a lesson every night for a period of four years. Then I went to my old master's brother, whose wife helped me every night as long as I would go to her for help. Rev. Shacklefard (white) greatly aided me for a period of three years.

   Northcross was ordained in 1867 and laid the foundation stones for African-American Baptist churches in several Alabama counties. He became the pastor of the First Baptist Church at Tuscumbia, Alabama.[92]

   In the midst of the violence and upheaval of the Civil War, the literacy-building work went forward through the efforts of thousands of men and women like Laura Towne and Charlotte Forten. They built a solid foundation that the various northern mission societies expanded after the war. By 1869 during the reconstruction of the South, the Federal Bureau of Refugees, Freedmen, and Abandoned Lands (commonly called the Freedmen's Bureau) had more than a thousand schools in operation across the region. From these basic educational institutions grew many of the future academies and colleges that ultimately provided most of the secondary education and nearly all of the college education available to southern African Americans for well into the twentieth century. This was one of the most important legacies of this part of America's literacy journey.[93]

   The history of the American Civil War and the Reconstruction Era is usually related as stories of battles, death, destruction, and political corruption. Yet heroic efforts were made to provide literacy to freed slaves during the war. Afterwards thousands of northern men and women took up the literacy challenge to build a new South on the basis of liberty and literacy.

After 1865, the response of African Americans across the South to the availability of literacy education "was virtually unparalleled in the history of emancipated peoples."[94] Former slaves of all ages stormed the new schoolhouses seeking a basic literacy education. Booker T. Washington, himself a former slave, best summarized this overwhelming thirst for education.

Few people who were not right in the midst of the scene can have any exact idea of the intense desire which the people of my race showed for education ... it was a whole race trying to go to school. Few were too young, and none too old, to make the attempt to learn. As fast as any kind of teacher could be secured, not only were day schools filled, but night-schools as well. The great ambition of the older people was to try to learn to read the Bible before they died. With this end in view, men and women who were fifty and seventy years old, would be found in the night schools. Sunday-school was formed soon after freedom, but the principal book studied in Sunday-school was always the speller. Day-school, night-school, and Sunday-school were always crowded, and often many had to be turned away for want of room.[95]

These newly freed African Americans gave of their own time and meager financial resources to the building of schools. Their own efforts helped to supplement the aid of the Freedmen's Bureau and the northern aid societies in the daunting tasks of recruiting thousands of literacy instructors, raising millions of dollars, establishing hundreds of schools, and distributing teaching materials in this new battle to bring literacy to four million former slaves.

This does not mean that all black children went to school or even received the rudiments of literacy. Their great need easily outstripped the capacity of volunteerism. But there was a zest for learning by both old and young southern blacks that was matched by the courageous efforts of their northern teachers to add the emancipation of literacy to the freedom they had won.[96]

In the early years after the war the local conditions that greeted these literacy educators were at the very least difficult, usually disquieting, and often dangerous. Local southern whites frequently did not share their zeal to educate former slaves. Teachers suffered the indignities of ostracism and bitter hatred from white society. Outside interference and violence against teachers by individuals and groups, including the Ku Klux Klan, was not uncommon. This opposition from whites stemmed from their continued desire to deny equal rights to African Americans. Despite their reactionary campaign of intimidation, blacks flocked to the first postwar primitive schools in cabins, tents, church basements, and converted military barracks. Usually there were no student desks, insufficient and mismatched books, and few other educational supplies.[97]

In Alabama after the war Charles Hayes attended a school for "slave children" on the plantation grounds. His grandmother taught them from the Bible, because this was the text her former mistress in Virginia had used to teach her to read and write. Debbie Lewis, an Alabama house servant before 1865, was taught to read by "the white folks." She and her brother were taught to read using a blue-back speller.

Nettie Henry of Mississippi had been the slave of Mr. and Mrs. John C. Higgins. After the war they had moved to Meridian.

Mr. Higgins he died pretty soon an' Miss Lizzie went to teaching school. Her chillun—Miss Annie an' dem—would try to teach us. Den us carried Blue Black Spellers to Sund'y school an' a old Baptist cullud preacher would teach us out o' it. He say, "de same words is in dis book what's in de Bible. You chillun learn 'em de way dey is fixed for you to learn 'em in dis here Blue Black Speller, den de first thing you know you can read de Bible."[98]

Many of these first southern schools were taught by black and white young women from the North. Some were motivated by the crusader spirit built up by four years of war. For others it offered a degree of autonomy, independence, mobility, and authority far above what women of that time could expect in northern classrooms or city life. Moving south certainly required a great deal of courage.[99]

Viola Knapp was among these young women, the schoolteacher daughter of a Vermont cabinetmaker. When she arrived in West Virginia to teach blacks at the rough, improvised little school, Viola was treated as a social outcast by all the white people in the town. No one spoke to her. No one would even look at her. Viola even had great difficulty in finding a place to live.

The town's ostracism was complete. People refused to walk down the same side of the street. When Knapp entered a shop, every white person would immediately leave. The clerk served her in silence and avoided eye contact. However, being a New Englander who believed in the righteousness of her cause, Viola found great personal satisfaction in undergoing this martyrdom for a cause she considered good.[100] She also met another outcast.

Stationed there was a young Lieutenant Ruffner of the U.S. Army assigned to supervise the care of the local federal cemetery for soldiers killed in a nearby battle. It did not take long for these two northern outsiders to meet and marry. They then settled down and raised a family, as the young lieutenant rose in the army to become a major and finally a general. Little did Viola know she was destined to help educate one of the most famous African Americans of that post-Civil War era—Booker T. Washington.[101]

After the Civil War (1865) Washington's family left Virginia and moved to Malden, West Virginia, where the primary industry was processing salt.

From the time that I can remember having any thoughts about anything, I recall that I had an intense longing to learn to read. I determined when quite a small child that, if I accomplished nothing else in life, I would in some way get enough education to enable me to read common books and newspapers.[102]

His mother somehow got him a copy of Webster's blue-back speller. "I began at once to devour this book, and I think that it was the first one I ever had in my hands." Washington tried to teach himself, since "I could find no one to teach me." At that time there were no other blacks living nearby who could read. "In some way within a few weeks, I mastered the greater portion of the alphabet."[103]

Since there was no free school for blacks in the area, a subscription school was started by these families. The teacher was a black army veteran from Ohio. Unfortunately for Washington, his stepfather would not let him leave work at the salt factory to go to this day school. However, he made an arrangement with the instructor to be taught at night. "My own experience in the night-school gave me faith in the night-school idea, with which, in after years, I had to do both at Hampton and Tuskegee (Institutes)."[104]

About that time I heard two pieces of news which were like very distant, very faint glimmers in the blackness of the coal mine in which nearly all my working hours were spent. One was about a school for colored students—Hampton Institute it was—where they could learn more than their letters. The other was that the wife of General Ruffner was from Vermont, that before her marriage she had been a teacher in one of the first schools for Negroes, and that she took an interest in education of the colored people who worked for her.[105]

Washington secured a position paying $5 a month working for the wife of General Ruffner, the owner of the salt factory and coal mine. Washington claimed, "She opened the door through which I took my first step towards civilized standards of living."[106]

Mrs. Ruffner always encouraged and sympathized with all Washington's efforts to get an education. She gave him the opportunity to go to school for an hour a day during the winter months. In 1872, when he was 14, she helped him start out for the Hampton Institute. Washington worked in Richmond for a time unloading a boat to get enough food and money to get to the school. He worked as a janitor in order to earn the tuition and eventually graduated from the institute. Washington's determination to "secure an education at any cost" is probably the most fitting tribute to the self-determination of so many African Americans to achieve personal literacy and to all the teachers who supported them along the way.[107]

While attending the Hampton Institute, Washington became the protegé of Samuel C. Armstrong, its founder. A colonel of a Civil War African-American regiment, Armstrong had been an agent for the Freedman's Bureau. Under his influence, Washington adopted much of the same northern white abolitionist educational philosophy. Their "scientific" ideas about black education led to education wrapped around submission to white authority and culture. Basic literacy and industrial education were at the core of this program. The striking similarity of this movement to contemporary American Indian literary/cultural assimilation programs was no accident. Both were spearheaded by northern abolitionist religious groups.[108]

It should not come as a surprise that when Washington established his Tuskegee Institute in 1881, he emphasized the same values.[109] Over the next 20 years this Hampton-Tuskegee model of basic literacy would be repeated in numerous local African-American schools across the southern states. One such effort was the Calhoun Colored School in Alabama.[110]

In 1891 Washington met with a group of African Americans at the Ramah Baptist Church in Lowndes County, Alabama, a poor, rural economically isolated area in which public funding for African-American schooling was meager or nonexistent. They sought his help in establishing an independent community school, for which they pledged to raise the needed funds. Shortly afterwards, when Washington spoke about this project at the Hampton Institute, two white northern teachers there, Charlotte Thorn and Mabel Dillingham, volunteered their help in founding such a school. They became its co-principals and for the next 40 years they and their successors solicited financial support and donations in the form of books and clothing by publishing letters in *The Southern Workman* and other northeastern newspapers.

When the Calhoun Colored School opened its doors in October 1892, the extent of the local black community's desire for literacy education was demonstrated by the 300 men, women, and children who arrived on the first day of school and the fact that $360 in tuition fees and $536 in donations were raised "out of a poverty beyond description."[111] The Calhoun Colored School offered a basic literacy education and vocational training. Most of the boys were taught farming. The girls received training to become dressmakers, cooks, or laundresses. Literacy instruction was centered on oral reading and memorization, but also had some progressive features. The school required students to buy their textbooks rather than use discards from other schools. School literary societies were formed. Community outreach was encouraged. Students read voluntarily to the elderly. The teachers invited parents and others in the community to attend school plays, socials, and student debates.

The Calhoun Colored School also offered a free night school. It was established so that the parents of children in the day school could learn to read, write, and perform simple arithmetic. In 1896, Susan Showers, the head of the school's Academic Department, began requiring classroom teachers to visit each child's home. She sought to have teachers gain a better understanding of each student's family life, so that they could shape their instruction to help overcome difficulties in each pupil's daily environment.

A most important part of the Calhoun literacy program was employing donated materials to establish a "reading room," which became the nucleus of a library for the school and the local community. By 1902 the school library contained 1,660 books, 800 reference books, and bound periodicals and had a card catalog. The library also received two daily newspapers and monthly magazines.[112]

By 1898 the curriculum of the Calhoun Colored School included a free kindergarten completed over two years. This was followed by three years of primary education and three years of intermediate work. Another four years were then required in the "grammar school." Thus, twelve years were required to complete a standard eighth-grade education. The reasoning behind this departure from a standard curriculum is unknown.

In spite of the success of the Calhoun Colored School, by the beginning of the twentieth century, only one in four African-American children in Lowndes County was receiving even basic literacy instruction. Over the next 30 years this school's basic literacy programs of recitation, rote memorization, spelling, and penmanship would evolve with national literacy trends. More college-educated faculty would introduce phonics, popular basal readers, good literature, math, and science. The Calhoun Colored School is but one example of "possibly thousands of local struggles for access to literacy" across the South after the Civil War.[113]

FROM SLAVERY TO FREEDOM

Literacy for African Americans was far more important than just learning to read, write and cipher. It was a critical personal step on an individual's road to freedom. In general a white world tried to enslave both the bodies and the minds of African Americans. Their quest for literacy became a communal act of political resistance to oppression and of self-determination for the black community.

The denominational literacy efforts of the Puritans, Episcopalians, Quakers, and others show us that not all whites were totally blind to the harsh injustice of slavery. But a rising tide of bigotry and fear in the antebellum North negated much of these efforts.

Nor could the "Bible literacy" of the antebellum South start to meet the literacy needs of their black slaves or begin to morally justify the abomination of bondage in America. It is a true irony that because of their own racial fears of literate slaves, white southerners before the Civil War would deny many of their own children the means to achieve literacy.

Frederick Douglass, Booker T. Washington, Laura Towne, Charlotte Forten, Reverend W. E. Northcross, and countless other individuals served in this struggle to free minds, hearts, and bodies. Their incredible determination and self-sacrifice to achieve personal literacy and to teach others will serve forever as stark testimony of an important chapter in the struggle to overcome political oppression and gain freedom for all African-Americans.

NOTES

1. Lorenzo Johnston Greene, *The Negro in Colonial New England* (Port Washington, New York: Kennikat Press, 1966), 237.

2. Another factor that seemed to encourage slave literacy among the Puritans was the limited number of slaves in the area, which meant that fears of a slave uprising were never present. Margaret Connell Szasz, *Indian Education in the American Colonies, 1607–1783* (Albuquerque: University of New Mexico Press, 1988), 37–38; Greene, *Colonial New England*, 237–238.

3. Greene, *Colonial New England*, 238.

4. *The International Dictionary of Women's Biography*, s.v. "Phillis Wheatley" (New York: Continuum, 1982), 495.

5. Szasz, *American Colonies*, 38.

6. John Hellawell Calam, "Parsons and Pedagogues: The SPG Adventure in American Education" (Ph.D. diss., University of Michigan, 1969), 86–87.

7. Lawrence A. Cremin, *American Education: The Colonial Experience 1607–1786* (New York: Harper & Row, 1970), 351.

8. Calam, "Parsons," 88.

9. Cremin, *Colonial Experience*, 351.

10. Greene, *Colonial New England*, 240.

11. Ibid., 239–241.

12. Ibid., 239.

13. Cremin, *Colonial Experience*, 308.

14. Thomas Woody, *Early Quaker Education in Pennsylvania* (New York: Teacher's College, Columbia University, 1920; reprint, New York: Arno Press, 1969), 240–241.

15. Woody, *Education in Pennsylvania*, 242–244.

16. Szasz, *American Colonies*, 41; Cremin, *Colonial Experience*, 351.

17. George William Pilcher, *Samuel Davies: Apostle of Dissent in Colonial Virginia* (Knoxville: University of Tennessee Press, 1971), vii–ix; Szasz, *American Colonies*, 41–42.

18. Pilcher, *Samuel Davies*, 101–102, 106.

19. Ibid., 107–108.

20. Ibid., 108.

21. Ibid., 111.

22. Ibid., 113–114.

23. Janet Duitsman Cornelius, *"When I Can Read My Title Clear": Literacy, Slavery, and Religion in the Antebellum South* (Columbia: University of South Carolina Press, 1991), 82; a very important published source of information on many aspects of African-American literacy. Winthrop D. Jordan, *White over Black: American Attitudes Toward the Negro* (Baltimore, Maryland: Penguin Books, 1968), 133.

24. "Survey of American Free Schools," *Freedom's Journal*, 1827, as quoted in *We Are Your Sisters: Black Women in the Nineteenth Century*, ed. Dorothy Sterling (New York: W.W. Norton, 1984), 180.

25. Cornelius, *Literacy*, 82; Sterling, *We Are Your Sisters*, 180–182. The infamous U.S. Supreme Court "Dred Scott" decision in 1857 also motivated many blacks who had escaped from slavery to flee to Canada, fearing being forced to return to their Southern masters.

26. Cornelius, *Literacy*, 82; Anne M. Boylan, *Sunday School: The Formation of an American Institution, 1790–1880* (New Haven: Yale University Press, 1988), 23.

27. Boylan, *Sunday School*, 24–25.

28. Ibid., 27–28. In 1831 the so-called rebellion of Nat Turner, a slave insurrection, occurred in Virginia. Over 50 whites died before it ended.

29. Mary Kelley, "Reading Women/Women Reading: The Making of Learned Women in Antebellum America," *Journal of American History* 83 (September 1996): 421–422.

30. Ibid., 422.

31. Jessie Carney Smith, "Sarah Mapps Douglass," in *Notable Black American Women*, ed. Jessie Carney Smith (Detroit: Gale Research, 1992), 354–358.

32. Julie Winch, "Margaretta Forten," in *Notable Black American Women*, 288–289.

33. Frederick Douglass, *My Bondage and My Freedom* (New York: Miller, Orton and Mulligan, 1855), 123; Cornelius, *Literacy*, 82–83.

34. *Anglo-African Magazine* 1 (July 1859): 339, as quoted in Cornelius, *Literacy*, 83.

35. Cornelius, *Literacy*, 83.

36. Ibid.

37. Frederick Douglass, *The Life and Times of Frederick Douglass.* (Hartford: Park Publishing Company, 1881), 69–71.

38. Cornelius, *Literacy*, 1–2.

39. Henry Bibb, *Narrative of the Life and Adventures of Henry Bibb. An American Slave* (New York: The Author, 1849; reprint, New York: Negro Universities Press, 1969), xi.

40. Vicki Moeser, "Radio Documentary Brings to Life Stories and Voice of Former Slaves," *Smithsonian Institution Research Reports*, No. 95 (Winter 1999): 6.

41. Cornelius, *Literacy*, 6, 16.

42. Wilma King, *Stolen Childhood: Slave Youth in Nineteenth Century America* (Bloomington: Indiana University Press, 1995), 74; Cornelius, *Literacy*, 61.

43. Cornelius, *Literacy*, 63, 67; John Hope Franklin, *From Slavery to Freedom: A History of Negro Americans*, 3rd ed. (New York: Vintage Books, 1969), 202.

44. Ibid., 69–70.

45. Booker T. Washington, *Up from Slavery: An Autobiography* (Williamstown, Massachusetts: Corner House Publishers, 1978), 10.

46. Bibb, *American Slave*, 21.

47. King, *Stolen Childhood*, 75–76.

48. Frederick Douglass, *Narrative of the Life of Frederick Douglass, an American Slave* (Boston: Antislavery Office, 1845), 33–34, 38, 43–44.

49. Ibid., 81–82.

50. King, *Stolen Childhood*, 75–76.

51. John Thompson, *The Life of John Thompson: A Fugitive Slave* (Worcester, Massachusetts: John Thompson, 1856), 103–104.

52. Ibid., 105.

53. Ibid., 106–107.

54. Cornelius, *Literacy*, 100, 102; Elisha Green, *Life of the Rev Elisha W. Green* (Maysville, Kentucky: Republican Printing Office, 1888), 15–21.

55. Cornelius, *Literacy*, 32.

56. Ibid., 4.

57. Franklin, *Freedom*, 185–186, 212–213; Samuel Eliot Morison, *The Oxford History of the American People* (New York: Oxford University Press, 1965), 615.

58. King, *Stolen Childhood*, 78–79; Cornelius, *Literacy*, 33–34.

59. Bibb, *An American Slave*, 21; Green, *Life*, 15; *The American Slave: A Composite Autobiography*, George L. Rawick, ed., vol. 13. *Georgia Narratives* (Westport, Connecticut: Greenwood Publishing, 1972–76), 201; Franklin, *Freedom*, 203; Cornelius, *Literacy*, 65.

60. Ibid., 9, 63.

61. Ibid., 79; William Craft and Ellen Craft, *Running a Thousand Miles for Freedom* (London: Tweedie, 1860; reprint Boston: Beacon Press, 1964), 84–109.

62. James McKaye, *Mastership and Its Fruits: The Emancipated Slave Face to Face with His Old Master* (New York: Loyal Publication Society, 1864), 7.

63. Lewis C. Lockwood, *Mary S. Peake: The Colored Teacher at Fortress Monroe* (Boston: American Tract Society, 1863; reprint, *Two Black Teachers During the Civil War*, New York: Arno Press, 1969), i.

64. Ibid., i–ii.

65. Ibid., 6–7.

66. Ibid., ii–iii, 31–32, 34–35.

67. Willie Lee Rose, *Rehearsal for Reconstruction* (Indianapolis: The Bobbs-Merrill Company, 1964), xv–xvi.

68. Ibid., 21, 29–30, 76.

69. Ibid., xvi, 85–87.

70. Ibid., 230–231.

71. Ibid., 77–78; Laura M. Towne, *The Letters and Diary of Laura M. Towne Written from the Sea Islands of South Carolina 1862–1884*, ed. Rupert Sargen Holland (Cambridge: Riverside Press, 1912; reprint, New York: Negro University Press, 1969).

72. Towne, *Letters*, 104–105, 134–135.

73. Ibid., 140.

74. Ibid., 140, 145, 148.

75. Ibid., 163.

76. Rose, *Rehearsal*, 374–376, 388.

77. Towne, *Letters*, 220.

78. Ibid., 249.

79. Ibid., 275, 281, 301.

80. Charlotte L. Forten, *The Letters of Charlotte Forten Grimké*, ed. Brenda Stevenson (New York: Oxford University Press, 1988), 3–5, 13, 38.

81. Ibid., 17.

82. Ibid., xxxiv–xxxvi.

83. Ibid., 39–40.

84. Charlotte Forten, "Life in the Sea Islands," in Lockwood, *Two Black Teachers*, 71.

85. Ibid., 77.

86. Lockwood, *Two Black Teachers*, 58.

87. Ibid., 59.

88. Forten, *Letters*, 398.

89. Ibid., 40–42.

90. Ibid., 42–43, xxxvii.

91. Ibid., xxxvii.

92. *The American Slave*, vol. 6: *Alabama and Indiana Narratives*, 300–302.

93. Lockwood, *Two Black Teachers*, i–ii.

94. Ronald E. Butchart. "Perspectives on Gender, Race, Calling, and Commitment in Nineteenth-Century America: A Collective Biography of the Teachers of the Freed People, 1862–1875," *Vitae Scholasticae* 13 (Spring 1994): 16.

95. Washington, *Up from Slavery*, 30.

96. Butchart, "Perspectives," 17; King, *Stolen Childhood*, 162.

97. King, *Stolen Childhood*, 163–164; Butchart, "Perspectives," 18.

98. *The American Slave: A Composite Autobiography*, ed. George P. Rawick, Supplement, series 1, vol. 1. *Alabama Narratives* (Westport, Connecticut: Greenwood Publishing Co., 1977), 175, 257; *The American Slave*, Supplement, series 1, vol. 9. *Mississippi Narratives*, 61–67.

99. Dorothy Canfield Fisher, "The Washed Window" in *A Treasury of American Heritage* (New York: Simon & Schuster, 1959), 148; Butchart, "Perspectives," 23.

100. Fisher, "The Washed Window," 149.

101. Ibid.

102. Washington, *Up from Slavery*, 27.

103. Ibid., 28.

104. Ibid., 31.

105. Fisher, "The Washed Window," 150.

106. Ibid., 151.

107. Washington, *Up from Slavery*, 45.

108. Arlette Ingram Willis, "Literacy at Calhoun Colored School 1892–1945," *Reading Research Quarterly* 37 (January-March 2002): 15.

109. Franklin, *From Slavery to Freedom*, 370.

110. Willis, "Calhoun Colored School," 15–16. For a detailed history of African-American literacy education in the South, consult J. Anderson, *The Education of Blacks in the South, 1860–1935* (Chapel Hill: University of North Carolina Press, 1988); and by the same author, "Literacy and Education in the African-American Experience," in *Literacy among African-American Youth* (Cresskill, New Jersey: Hampton Press, 1995).

111. Charlotte Thorn and Mabel Dillingham, *Report of the Work of the Calhoun Colored School, Calhoun, Alabama, for October, 1892 to May, 1894*, as quoted in Willis, "Calhoun Colored School," 19.

112. Willis, "Calhoun Colored School," 25.

113. Ibid., 17–39.

Part V

Literacy in the Modern Age (1870–)

Chapter 10

Literacy for Everyone?

ENACTING LITERACY

As the last decades of the nineteenth century merged with the twentieth, the majority of Americans began to see personal literacy as a necessity for everyday life. This social phenomenon was driven mainly by the twin forces of an acceleration in industrialization and the migration of more people into America's cities. This support for increasing literacy became linked to a growing public demand for more access to schooling.

Between 1870 and 1920, for the nation as a whole, there were profound disparities in the schooling that was actually available to any given American. As already shown, there were significant regional differences in attitudes toward literacy education and establishing schools. Further, there were major racial, ethnic, and religious disparities in access to literacy and schooling and in what the schools were designed to accomplish for their students. Finally, there were major variations in teacher training qualifications, the length of the school year, and the optional age range of student attendance.[1]

Even so, before 1900 the courts had helped to clarify what was meant by a "free public school." A Massachusetts court in 1866 had defined the term "public" or "common" school as an institution:

1. "supported by general taxation"
2. "open to all free of expense"
3. "under the immediate control and superintendence of agents appointed by the voters of each town and city."[2]

This has become with some variations the standard definition of a "public school" that has become the chief institution of modern American literacy.

The cornerstone of U.S. public schooling rests on the enactment by each individual state of mandatory, tax-supported, compulsory education laws. Today when we consider "compulsory school attendance," it rests on the following components:

1. Funding: Public funding for all children
2. Age: From 6/7 to 16/18
3. School year: About 180 days
4. Grades: K/1 to 12
5. Attendance: Enforceable truancy laws with legal/financial penalties for non-compliance by parents or guardians

Between 1852 and 1918, all the states passed compulsory education laws. And passed them, and repassed them again and again (see Table 10.1). Massachusetts

Table 10.1
Dates of Enactment of District of Columbia and Forty-Eight States' First Compulsory Education Laws in the United States, 1852–1918

Massachusetts	1852	Rhode Island	1883	Iowa	1902
District of Columbia	1864	Illinois	1883	Maryland	1902
Vermont	1867	North Dakota	1883	Missouri	1905
New Hampshire	1871	South Dakota	1883	Tennessee	1905
Michigan	1871	Montana	1883	Delaware	1907
Washington	1871	Minnesota	1885	North Carolina	1907
Connecticut	1872	Nebraska	1887	Oklahoma	1907
Nevada	1873	Idaho	1887	Virginia	1908
New York	1874	Colorado	1889	Arkansas	1909
Kansas	1874	Oregon	1889	Louisiana	1910
California	1874	Utah	1890	Alabama	1915
Maine	1875	New Mexico	1891	Florida	1915
New Jersey	1875	Pennsylvania	1895	South Carolina	1915
Wyoming	1876	Kentucky	1896	Texas	1915
Ohio	1877	West Virginia	1897	Georgia	1916
Wisconsin	1879	Indiana	1897	Mississippi	1918
		Arizona	1899		

Source: Walter S. Defenbaugh and Ward W. Keesecker, "Compulsory School Attendance Laws and Their Administration," *United States Office of Education Bulletin,* no. 4 (Washington, D.C.: U.S. Government Printing Office, 1935), p. 8.

has the distinction of being the first state to successfully pass a compulsory education law statewide. Its 1852 law required children to attend school from 8 to 14 years of age and for only 12 weeks each year, of which only six weeks needed to be consecutive. Also, parents were excused from compliance if they could prove extreme poverty. Little enforcement of this law was attempted by the state. The penalty seldom used for noncompliance was only $20. In a modern sense these and numerous other loopholes in the 1852 law rendered it largely ineffective in guaranteeing school attendance by every child.[3]

It appears that before 1880 those states that passed these early compulsory school laws saw no increase in actual school attendance. Between 1880 and 1890 those states that enacted new laws found that only small increases in enrollments resulted. However, with each passing decade it became more obvious that enacting mandatory education clearly influenced the overall level of American literacy across the entire society. The better these laws were enforced, the higher their requirements, the better the final results.[4] This trend can be seen in the 1870 to 1900 data from the U.S. Census Bureau and the U.S. Office of Education. In 1870 illiteracy stood at 20 percent of the population. There were 6,871,000 students enrolled, or about 57 percent of the school age population (see Table 10.2). However, by 1920 illiteracy had shrunk to 6 percent, but now over 21,000,000 students, or 78 percent of eligible children, were now in school.[5]

What had started in colonial America as a desire for basic literacy education through the family now emerged into a demand for universal literacy education. The continued educational demands of the Industrial Revolution and the growth of America's cities required schools to meet the social needs of the children. This included not only literacy but also manners, morals, health, recreational, vocational, and citizenship education.[6]

Literacy through compulsory schooling also assumed a new role as a panacea for other late-nineteenth-century social ills. At that time many adults consid-

Table 10.2
Literacy and Schooling in America, 1870–1920

	1870	1880	1890	1900	1910	1920
Total population	38,558,371	50,155,783	62,622,250	75,602,515	91,972,266	105,710,620
Population 5-17 years, inclusive	12,055,443	15,065,767	18,543,201	21,404,322	24,239,948	27,728,788
Pupils enrolled in public schools	6,871,522	9,867,767	12,722,581	15,503,110	17,813,852	21,578,316
Percent of population 5-17, inclusive	57.00	65.50	68.61	72.43	73.49	77.8
Number of teachers	200,515	286,593	363,922	423,062	523,210	679,533
Total expenditure for education (thousands of dollars)	63,397	78,095	140,507	214,965	426,250	1,036,151
Percent of population illiterate 10 years and over	20.00	17.0	13.3	10.7	7.7	6.0

Sources: U.S. Department of Education and U.S. Census Bureau.

ered child labor, both on the farm and in the factory, as essential to keep a family fed and the factory running. Literacy laws requiring school attendance permanently changed public attitudes by removing children from unsuitable labor conditions and ending their competition for jobs with adults. Beginning in the 1880s, organized labor began supporting compulsory education as a means of removing children from the labor pool because they displaced adult workers from their jobs.[7]

This policy had significant economic ramifications across American society and was only achieved by stages. Only gradually between 1887 and 1915 did most of the states adopt child-labor laws that supported schooling through adolescence (see Table 10.3).[8] Only later did the other western European industrial countries adopt a policy similar to America's in requiring school attendance for everyone.[9]

Immigrant assimilation in America became another major social force behind this drive for literacy. A tidal wave of over 28,000,000 immigrants came to America's shores between 1880 and 1930:

Decade	Number of Immigrants
1880–1890	5,703,870
1891–1900	3,687,564
1901–1910	8,795,386
1911–1920	5,735,811
1921–1930	4,107,209[10]

Literacy education was seen by many political, educational, social, and business leaders as an important means, "to assimilate and amalgamate these people as a part of our American race."[11] The public schools became the institution of choice to transform the immigrants through basic literacy. But that transformation went far beyond literacy. The teachers of New York City found themselves giving baths to hundreds of students. Others provided training in manners, cleanliness, dress, citizenship, and "ethical character." Literacy education became a means to an end in the transformation of foreign children, who in some schoolrooms spoke a half-dozen different languages, none of them English. A massive study in 1909 by the U.S. Immigration Commission showed that children of foreign-born parentage comprised significant majorities of the students in 37 of America's largest cities, with percentages as high as 71.5 in New York, 67.3 in Chicago, 63.5 in Boston, and 74.1 in Duluth, Minnesota. Literacy and "Americanization" were linked together as a venture in social education that went far beyond mere book learning.[12]

Literacy was also used in negative ways to shut off the flow of immigrants. In six of the ten years between 1905 and 1914 a million people a year streamed into the United States. This helped keep wages very low and also hampered labor unions' efforts to organize more workers. As a result, in 1913, 1915, and 1917 attempts were made by the U.S. Congress to exclude illiterate immigrants. President Howard Taft vetoed the 1913 bill. President Woodrow Wilson vetoed the 1915 and 1917 bills. However, anti-immigration sentiments were so strong that the 1917 bill was passed over Wilson's veto. The 1917 bill featured a literacy test in English applying the reasoning that a lack of literacy was a negative character trait. Taft and Wilson both had argued that the reason for immigrant illiter-

Table 10.3

Compulsory School Attendance Age Limits: 50 States, the District of Columbia, and Puerto Rico, for Selected Years from 1887 to 1965

STATE	1887	1915	1935	1959	1965
Alabama	–	–	7-16	7-16	7-16
Alaska	–	–	7-16	7-16	7-16
Arizona	–	8-16	8-16	8-16	8-16
California	8-14	7-15	8-16	8-16	8-16
Colorado	–	8-16	8-16	8-16	7-16
Connecticut	8-16	7-16	7-16	7-16	7-16
Delaware	–	7-14	7-17	7-16	7-16
District of Columbia	8-14	8-14	7-16	7-16	7-16
Florida	–	–	7-16	7-16	7-16
Georgia	–	–	8-14	7-16	7-16
Hawaii	–	6-15	6-14	6-16	6-16
Idaho	8-14	8-18	8-18	7-16	7-16
Illinois	7-14	7-16	7-16	7-16	7-16
Indiana	–	7-16	7-16	7-16	7-16
Iowa	–	7-16	7-16	7-16	7-16
Kansas	8-14	8-15	7-16	7-16	7-16
Kentucky	–	7-16	7-16	7-16	7-16
Louisiana	–	8-16	7-14	7-16	7-16
Maine	8-15	7-15	7-16	7-16	7-17
Maryland	–	8-16	7-16	7-16	7-16
Massachusetts	8-14	7-16	7-16	7-16	7-16
Michigan	8-14	7-16	7-16	6-16	6-16
Minnesota	8-16	8-16	8-16	7-16	7-16
Mississippi	–	–	7-17	–	–
Missouri	–	8-16	7-16	7-16	7-16
Montana	8-14	8-16	8-16	7-16	7-16
Nebraska	8-14	7-15	7-16	7-16	7-16
Nevada	8-14	8-16	7-18	7-17	7-17
New Hampshire	6-16	8-16	8-16	6-16	6-16

Table 10.3 *(Continued)*

New Jersey	7-16	7-16	7-16	7-16	6-16
New Mexico	–	7-14	6-17	6-17	6-17
New York	8-14	8-16	7-16	7-16	7-16
North Carolina	–	8-12	7-14	7-16	7-16
North Dakota	10-14	8-15	7-17	7-16	7-16
Ohio	8-16	8-16	6-18	6-18	6-18
Oklahoma	–	8-16	8-18	7-18	7-18
Oregon	–	9-15	8-16	7-18	7-18
Pennsylvania	–	8-16	8-16	8-17	8-17
Puerto Rico	–	8-14	8-14	8-14	8-16
Rhode Island	7-15	7-15	7-16	7-16	7-16
South Carolina	–	–	8-14	–	–
South Dakota	10-14	8-14	8-17	7-16	7-16
Tennessee	–	8-16	7-17	7-17	7-17
Texas	–	–	7-16	7-16	7-17
Utah	–	8-16	8-18	6-18	6-18
Vermont	8-14	8-16	8-16	7-16	7-16
Virginia	–	8-12	7-15	7-16	7-16
Washington	8-18	8-16	8-16	8-16	8-16
West Virginia	–	8-15	7-16	7-16	7-16
Wisconsin	7-15	7-16	7-16	7-16	7-16
Wyoming	7-16	7-14	7-16	7-16	7-17

Note: Where there is no entry, a State had no compulsory attendance law for the year reported. The laws typically permit exemptions for children within the age ranges for several reasons, such as completion of certain grades or under certain conditions of employment.

Source: U.S. Department of Health Education and Welfare, *State Law on Compulsory Attendance,* by August W. Steinhilber and Carl J. Sokolowski (Washington, D.C.: U.S. Government Printing Office, 1966), p. 3, Table 2.

acy was a lack of educational opportunity. The later Immigration Acts of 1921, 1924, and 1929 further restricted immigration to the United States. They helped labor to hold the wage gains workers had made during World War I (1914–1918). Immigration after 1930 was slowed to less than 100,000 persons each year, a trend that did not change until after World War II (1946).[13]

Between the passage of the first statewide compulsory attendance law (1852) in Massachusetts and the last in Mississippi (1918), literacy educators learned many painful lessons (see Table 10.4). You can pass laws requiring attendance, but you must have the means to enforce them. You can offer literacy education for everyone, but you must have the funds needed for an adequately long school year. You may want everyone to learn how to read, but you must have a large

Table 10.4
Literacy's Long March Through Compulsory Education

STATE	Date of Enactment of First Compulsory Attendance Law	Date of Enactment of Present or Amended Law
Alabama	1915	1915
Arizona	1899	1912
Arkansas	1909	1917
California	1874	1911
Colorado	1889	1911
Connecticut	1650	1911
Delaware	1907	1909
District of Columbia	1864	1906
Florida	1915	1915
Georgia	1916	1916
Idaho	1887	1917
Illinois	1883	1909
Indiana	1897	1915
Iowa	1902	1913
Kansas	1874	1907
Kentucky	1893	1918
Louisiana	1916	1916
Maine	1875	1913
Maryland	1902	1916
Massachusetts	1852	1913
Michigan	1871	1917
Minnesota	1885	1911
Mississippi	1918	1918
Missouri	1905	1905
Montana	1883	1913
Nebraska	1887	1913
Nevada	1873	1913

Table 10.4 *(Continued)*

New Hampshire	1871	1917
New Jersey	1875	1914
New Mexico	1872	1915
New York	1853	1917
North Carolina	1907	1913
North Dakota	1882	1917
Ohio	1877	1913
Oklahoma	1907	1913
Oregon	1889	1911
Pennsylvania	1895	1911
Rhode Island	1883	1917
South Carolina	1915	1915
South Dakota	1883	1915
Tennessee	1905	1913
Texas	1915	1915
Utah	1890	1905
Vermont	1867	1915
Virginia	1908	1918
Washington	1871	1909
West Virginia	1897	1915
Wisconsin	1879	1907
Wyoming	1876	1909

Source: H. R. Bonner, "Compulsory Attendance Laws," *The American School Board Journal* 60 (February 1920): 46.

enough number of properly educated teachers to accommodate these growing numbers of children, as well as the children of immigrants and many other students with special educational needs. You may want to offer every child at least a basic literacy education, but without laws regulating child labor, compulsory attendance becomes a sham that is unenforceable and ultimately meaningless.

If it had not been for the Progressive Movement (1890–1920), which swept through many other aspects of American life, such as the pure food and drug laws, utility/railroad regulations, and antitrust business laws, to mention a few, literacy through compulsory school attendance would have taken even longer to accomplish. It is not an accident that the final enactment of these state laws (1905–1918) occurred at the height of the political power of the Progressive Movement. This was a watershed era that helped transform the rural thinly populated United States of the nineteenth century into a twentieth-century world industrial power. Can there remain any doubt that from the very beginning of that transformation, literacy for the masses was its essential component?[14]

During the Progressive Era, from about 1890 to 1920, the business and political leaders' linkage of schooling with social progress was a force behind the continued universal growth of literacy. The world of economic and political theory represented by John Locke and Adam Smith was now joined by Samuel Gompers of the AFL, industrialist Henry Ford, scientist Thomas Edison, "robber baron" Andrew Carnegie, and politicians such as Theodore Roosevelt and Woodrow Wilson. They saw literacy and education as fostering a better American society. Their view was that education helped create useful, productive members of society. A new relationship existed between the social and economic forces spawned by nineteenth-century industrialization in the United States. Instead of home crafts and agricultural industries, a worker's production was now set by a clock and an imposed production schedule. Literacy through schooling was one of the best means discovered by business to perpetuate productive worker values that included punctuality, respect for authority, producing quality work, and self-discipline. These were the essential work-ethic demands of a new mass-production urban society.[15]

The impetus for the Industrial Revolution in America first began in the textile industry (1790–1830), as a response to a severe shortage of unskilled labor. This necessitated the introduction of labor-saving devices. However, this new technology relied on sophisticated gauging techniques, variable speed control, automatic stop-motion mechanisms, and advanced cutting tools. A severe shortage of machinists developed as industry expanded. As the eighteenth century advanced, even the available machinists proved to be increasingly incapable of operating more complex technology. Most machinists until then had relied upon "rule of thumb" methods, and had neither the mathematical nor technical knowledge required to mass produce precision parts.

Industry and the skilled trades responded by establishing "mechanics' institutes," voluntary organizations that promoted the learning of practical and scientific knowledge. However, the reading and math used by most of these institutes far exceeded the prior school preparation of many workers. In many trade journals proposals began to appear by mid-century calling for educational reform to bring this instruction into the common school. The *Scientific American* noted in 1859, "We cannot help reflecting, as we write, how many thousands of dollars, and how much wasted brainwork would have been saved to the inventors of this country, if our common schools had paid more attention to the physical and mathematical science than they have hitherto done." These "old" ideas sound strikingly familiar to a twenty-first-century audience.

Moreover, it is interesting to note that education for industrial utility was not enthusiastically shared by all. Many argued that literate workers would place too much pressure on the social system. A well-educated worker might become not only unhappy with his/her job and social standing, but also politically critical and restive. Literacy only alienated people from manual labor. The natural social order would be undermined, social mobility overpromoted. Why should business have to pay to educate its workers? This debate went on throughout the nineteenth century and still continues today. The American public school won out.

Good, free public schools emerged victorious through an alliance among educators, social reformers, and workers' associations. These diverse groups all agreed that America's multiplying skilled-machine factories needed workers with greater literacy and technical skills. Public education they saw as largely industrial education. It would provide functional literacy by teaching the elements of the mechanical arts and natural sciences needed to work in industry or agriculture. (These were the two chief occupations for most Americans of the time.)

Horace Mann, America's most famous advocate of free public education, had often based his arguments on the schools' role in industrializing America. Mann was from Massachusetts, which might help explain, in part, why it was the state that not only led in industrial production but also in the establishment of a public education system. Mann praised the improvements that manufacturing was bringing to his state. He argued that better-educated working men and women would bring greater prosperity for all.

In other states such as Connecticut, companies responded to this broad appeal by building large halls for workers' lectures, concerts, and political meetings. Some industries even built schools. Business began the introduction of "scientific management," and industrial psychologists arose to formulate aptitude and performance ratings for workers. By 1910, 29 states provided some form of functional-context, industrial education. Ten states opened technical high schools. Eighteen offered basic manual skill training, and 11 states included skilled trade or industrial courses in public school requirements.

The effort to provide schooling and literacy in America supported an age of unprecedented social change and economic expansion. Literacy contributed to the establishment and growth of middle-class America. It created better occupations at higher pay. Literacy enhanced individual abilities and skills. It helped American culture flourish. Universal literacy became a cornerstone for modernization, democracy, and the American consumer economy.[16]

LITERACY'S CHANGING DEFINITION

What it means to be a "literate person" in America has changed greatly over the past hundred years. Beginning with the 1840 U.S. Census, literacy data was based on asking heads of families how many persons in the family over age 20 had the ability to read and write. However, this form of "self-reported literacy" contained many accuracy problems. Sometimes illiterate adults reported themselves as being illiterate in writing, but not reading (thinking this was the lesser evil), thereby further distorting the census numbers reported at the time.

These problems were partially corrected by the 1870 U.S. Census. For the first time, literacy information was gathered on children between the ages of 10 and 19. More important, for the first time a distinction was made between reading literacy and writing literacy. As a result, the 1870 census showed a significant decline in U.S. literacy since 1860 (Table 10.5). By 1900 the U.S. Census Bureau defined an "illiterate" as a person 10 years of age or older unable to read and write in a native language (see Figure 10.1).[17]

By 1918, all 48 states had enacted compulsory school attendance laws that supported the expansion of literacy. But the task was far from complete. With America's entry into World War I (1917), the U.S. Army administered literacy tests to all recruits. Twenty-five percent of all draftees were found to be illiterate. Ten million men registered for the draft. Approximately 700,000 were totally illiterate. It was not uncommon for federal officers to arrest illiterate "draft dodgers" who did not know of the draft or that the country was even at war.

During the 1920s and 1930s America's public schools continued to provide training in functional, basic literacy skills to the greater population. At this level

Table 10.5
U.S. Illiteracy Rates, 1860–1959

| Year | Whites | | | | Blacks |
	All U.S.	Native-Born	Foreign-Born	All Whites	
1860	8.3	-	-	-	-
1870	20.0	-	-	11.5	81.4
1880	17.0	8.7	11.8	9.4	-
1890	13.3	6.2	13.1	7.7	57.1
1900	10.7	4.6	12.9	6.2	44.5
1910	7.7	3.0	12.7	5.0	30.4
1920	6.0	2.0	13.1	4.0	22.9
1930	4.3	1.5	9.9	-	17.5
1940	2.9	1.1	9.0	-	11.5
1952	2.5	-	-	1.8	10.2
1959	2.2	-	-	1.6	7.5

Source: 1988 U.S. Census Bureau.

Figure 10.1
What Does It Mean to Be a "Literate Person" in America?
(1900–21st Century)

1900:	Able to write your own name
1930s:	Three or more years of schooling *(Civilian Conservation Corps)*
WWII:	Fourth-grade education *(U.S. Army)*
1947:	Five or more years of school *(Census Bureau)*
1952:	Six or more years of school *(Census Bureau)*
1970:	Ninth-grade education *(U.S. Office of Education)*
21st Century:	High-school education plus *(U.S. Department of Education and the Conference Board)*

Source: U.S. Department of Education, National Center for Education Statistics, *National Adult Literacy Survey,* September 1993.

they were highly successful. The 1940 U.S. Census considered the completion of the fourth grade as evidence of literacy. Only 2.9 percent of all Americans failed to meet this 1940 standard. However, by the end of World War II (1941–1945), the military had rejected nearly 750,000 potential draftees because of educational deficiencies.

By 1950 there remained over ten million Americans who had never attended school or who had completed less than five years of education. During the Korean War (1950–1953), approximately 300,000 men were rejected for illiteracy. Ten to 15 percent of those enlisted had less than a fourth-grade education. During the 1950s the Bureau of the Census reported that 6.8 percent of the entire U.S. workforce had less than five years of schooling and were considered functionally illiterate. Of that group, 2 percent were totally unable to read or write.

By the 1970s, at least a ninth-grade level came closer to defining the functional reading needs of late twentieth-century adults. Driver's license applications, banking forms, and insurance claims require a tenth-grade reading level or higher. IRS tax forms have a readability level at or above twelfth grade. In its 1969 population survey, the U.S. Census Bureau reported that approximately 39 million people lacked a ninth-grade education. Throughout the entire twentieth century, millions of Americans remained functionally illiterate by choice or public neglect. Their children grew up assimilating the same indifference. They remain an integral part of the workforce of twenty-first-century America.[18]

LITERACY IN TRANSITION

From the mid-nineteenth century forward, literacy became an important element in the social transformation of American society.[19] During this watershed era, the education of children shifted from the family to the school. In part this can be traced to socioeconomic changes such as the fact that work was no longer "home based" and the waning of the apprenticeship system of the pre-industrial era. During and after World War II, more mothers worked outside the home. Most parents relinquished to the schools the responsibility for teaching the importance of literacy and how it meshed with social norms and future economic attainments.[20]

The twin obstacles to mass literacy in America, sparsely populated regions and poor urban school attendance, were successfully overcome only after a long protracted struggle in each of the 48 states.[21] The basic right of all children to obtain effective literacy education may have been legally established by 1920; however, other important social issues have continued to muddle the national literacy picture to our present time. Beginning in the nineteenth century, many advocated literacy instruction as part of a "shop culture" rather than a "school culture." As we have seen, in many cities institutes were opened that sought to integrate manual training and basic literacy from elementary to high school. This conflict was sharp and not easily reconciled. By the early twentieth century these manual training schools were assimilated into the vocational education movement of the Progressive Era.[22]

The rise of high schools also paralleled these literacy developments. School attendance for these "new" institutions rose from 202,963 students attending 2,526 public high schools in 1890 to 3,389,878 students in about 22,500 public institutions by 1923–1924.[23] The national development of a public "classical" high school in which the liberal arts, mathematics, and the natural sciences were taught had to overcome strong opposition. Only in 1874 did the Michigan Supreme Court confirm that all boys and girls had a basic right to a comprehensive and advanced education. It helped establish that the United States would not have, as was the case in much of contemporary Europe, two secondary school systems, one for manual, practical education and another teaching liberal arts. Instead there would be one high school offering advanced literacy education for all. These comprehensive high schools by the 1920s offered general, college preparatory, and specific career-education courses.[24]

The segregation of African-American children into separate, inferior schools largely ignored this public common-school literacy formula throughout the twentieth century. Large numbers of African-American children did not attend school in certain regions of the nation. Many others sat in grossly underfunded or in other ways inferior literacy education programs. It is amazing that out of this confused pattern of literacy education, there did emerge by the 1950s a body of highly educated African-American men and women in both the professions and the skilled trades.[25]

Significant numbers of other American children voluntarily opted out of public common-school literacy programs. Many Protestants and Roman Catholics choose to have their children attend parochial schools, particularly in urban areas. In 1884 the American Catholic hierarchy decreed at its Third Plenary Council in Baltimore that a parochial school should be built near every Catholic church. They went even further by obligating every Catholic family to send their children to these Catholic schools.[26]

These parochial schools were staffed by religious communities such as the Sisters of Mercy or School Sisters of Notre Dame. German and later Polish parish schools taught immigrant students in their native language as well as English. By 1910 the Poles alone had established more than 350 parish schools in over a dozen states. Four nuns from Cracow, Poland, established the Felician congregation in Detroit as the first order of Polish-American teaching nuns. This was soon followed by other orders, as the demand for Polish teaching sisters increased. By 1914, over 2,200 Polish-American nuns were teaching in parish schools in two dozen states. The continuing literacy education contributions made by these teaching orders was considerable, reaching a peak of 5.6 million children (1965) attending parochial schools throughout America (see Figure 10.2).[27]

Catholics were joined by other religious denominations in the development of alternative schools to meet the literacy needs of their children. The Presbyterian Church established a substantial system of parochial schooling in the nineteenth century. This system waned as the public schools expanded, though this was not always the case with other Protestant groups. The Evangelical Lutheran Synod formulated an early policy (1847) of establishing a parochial school for every congregation. The curriculum was rooted in their religion's sacred books to help children retain a specific religious-cultural-linguistic tradition. We have abundantly illustrated that throughout America's historical development religion and literacy have been closely linked. Throughout the twentieth century public tax-supported compulsory education would always provide literacy education for the majority of students. However, without question private religious and nonreligious schools had a considerable influence, with a peak enrollment of 6.4 million (1965), in raising literacy standards across American society (see Figure 10.3).[28]

The nation's tradition for personal self-improvement also became a powerful and pervasive force that reduced illiteracy between 1890 and 1920. This was highlighted by the beginning of mass-market fiction through the production of cheap book reprints and dime novels. They became important catalysts for the

Figure 10.2
Trends in Catholic and Other Private School Enrollment, 1929–30 to 1985–86

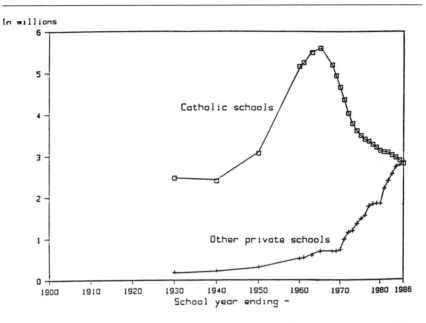

Source: U.S. Department of Education, Center for Statistics, *Digest of Educational Statistics, 1985–86.*

growth of popular literacy in America. Countless works of fiction taught the masses the virtues of self-education. Nowhere is this genre more evident than in the 108 novels of the New England minister-author Horatio Alger. In the *Ragged Dick* series, thrift, industry, sobriety, and self-education are central, illustrated by the rise of Dick, the boy hero, from rags to riches. Dick attended Sunday-school classes. He was tutored in his boardinghouse room. Later a portion of every evening was spent by Dick and his tutor-benefactor conversing in French and studying mathematics and, of course, scripture. From the beginning of the *Ragged Dick* series in 1867 until after World War I (1914–1918), these novels sold over one hundred million copies.[29]

The public's access to books and other reading materials was greatly increased by the development of public libraries in the United States. In 1848 Boston was the first city to appropriate funds for a public library. Nearly two hundred were established by 1875, and by the beginning of the twentieth century the number of public libraries in the United States had increased to over one thousand.[30] This growth was particularly fueled by philanthropic foundations and the growth of voluntary associations devoted to promoting self-improvement through education.

Figure 10.3
Trends in Public and Private School Enrollment, Grades K–12, 1899–1900 to 1985–86

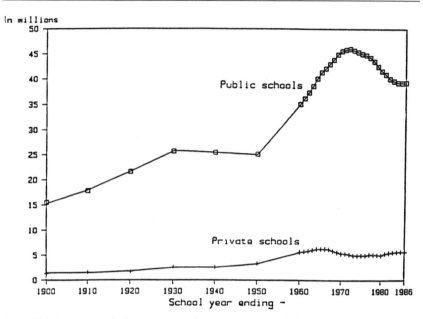

Source: U.S. Department of Education, Center for Statistics, *Digest of Educational Statistics, 1985–86.*

One of the most successful self-improvement groups was the Chautauqua Literary and Scientific Circle. Begun by John Vincent in 1878, it promoted habits of reading, study, and thinking for the general adult population. Eight thousand men and women enrolled in the Chautauqua Program during its first year. Diplomas were awarded four years later to 1,718 persons. By the early 1890s, enrollment rose to almost 200,000 and by 1918 to 300,000. During the Chautauqua movement's first two decades, an estimated 10,000 local circles sprang up across the nation, many in rural America. Half of these programs were held in towns with populations of 500 to 3,500, a quarter in villages with populations fewer than 500 persons. Its popularity peaked in 1920, when 21 Chautauqua tent companies were operating 93 circuits through the United States and Canada. These programs were presented in 8,580 towns to 35,449,750 people. Chautauqua exercised enormous educational influence, with Theodore Roosevelt calling it "the most American thing about America." It undoubtedly had a positive impact on the pursuit of literacy for many adult Americans and reinforced their support of local rural one-room schooling.[31]

LITTLE SCHOOLS ON THE PRAIRIE

In 1870 only 57 percent of the nation's children between five and 18 years of age had been enrolled in elementary schools at some point. We have reviewed how, after a major national struggle to pass comprehensive compulsory school legislation, this figure increased to 75 percent by 1918. Moreover, children also spent much more time attending school. Average daily personal attendance rose from 45 days per year in 1870 to over 90 in 1918. Though all the states finally had embraced mandatory public education, none of these statutes specified the means of student instruction.[32]

In most rural American communities a single teacher taught children from ages six through 14–16 in one-room schools. By 1916 over 200,000 of these little schools were scattered like stars in the night sky across America (see Table 10.6). Montana by the end of World War I (1918) still used 229 mine claim shacks and 54 ranch houses as "schools." Eastern Washington State had 144 school districts with fewer than four students enrolled in each one (1922). Even by 1930 the majority of children were still receiving their literacy education in these one-room public schools. This included 94 percent of all schools in the iso-

Table 10.6
One-Room Schools in the United States, 1916-1991

Year	One-Room Schools	Total Schools	% of Total
1916	200,100	NA	NA
1920	190,700	NA	NA
1930	149,282	247,769	54%
1940	113,600	238,169	48%
1950	61,247	166,473	37%
1956	34,964	146,732	24%
1960	23,695	NA	NA
1970	1,800	NA	NA
1985	800	NA	NA
1991	640	NA	NA

Sources: Historical Statistics of the United States, Part 1 (Washington, D.C.: Bureau of the Census, 1975), 368. The Statistical History of the United States from Colonial Times to the Present (Stamford, Conn.: Fairfield Publishers, 1965), 208.

lated rural communities of North Dakota, 63 percent of all the schools in the state of New York, 69 percent in Michigan, and 70 percent in Illinois.[33]

These schools offered very little beyond a basic literacy education, yet in most schools no subject was as important as reading. One-room schools were organized around a rough three-grade-division system offering beginning, intermediate, and advanced instruction. This approach addressed both the curriculum and the sporadic attendance patterns of surprisingly large numbers of children.

The beginning grade stressed reading, writing, spelling, and arithmetic. Geography and nature study were added in the intermediate grade. The advanced grade completed the one-room-school curriculum with history and grammar.

The flexibility of this three-grade system made it possible for children to drop out, to help on the farm, and to reenter without the personal embarrassment of having to start over in a beginner's class. Country one-room schools daily practiced "take the student where he is" long before modern educators invented "individualized instruction."[34]

Such was the experience of Bess Corey, who taught the immigrants flooding into South Dakota from 1909 to 1950. In her first school she taught 9–20 pupils in a two-room schoolhouse that was 8 feet wide by 16 feet long. "My school will begin Sept. 6th and close Dec. 26th for eight weeks vacation during the bad part of the winter. It begins again Feb. 21st and closes June 10th."[35] When not called in groups to the teacher's desk to read or recite, individual students did slate work at their desks. Others would memorize their lessons, diagram sentences, work arithmetic problems, or draw maps at the blackboard. These tiny schoolrooms hummed with activity.

Beneath the steady drone of the recitations going on at the front of the room, there was the subdued whispering of students working together at their big double desks. Since the children in these one-room schoolhouses were all at such different educational levels and ages, teachers found they could not do the entire instructional job alone. The teachers designated older students as tutors to help younger children or their own peers. The consensus among these educators and parents was that this method helped the younger child's education and simultaneously strengthened the learning and self-image of the older peer tutor.[36]

Many of these one-room-school teachers recorded their impressions as to how and why they used peer-tutoring to facilitate literacy instruction.

I don't believe any rural school teacher ever taught without help from older students. That's the truth of it! I don't believe you could handle that many grades without a cooperative effort from everybody.

If they got their own work and were making good enough grades, the older children always helped the small ones. I used them that way all the time when I taught.

They [the peer tutors] would try to imitate the teacher. I had children I couldn't, like, teach long division. So I said, "Well ... I'm going to let some [of] these children try it." And they did a pretty good job of it ... all of them would want to do that, some of them that couldn't even do it. They'd want to help this child when they couldn't even help themselves.[37]

Many of the one-room schools were successful at literacy education because of this tutorial atmosphere. Teachers felt an increased responsibility for each child's learning. Using peer tutors gave teachers the time to work with students individually and obtain a detailed understanding of each student's personality and degree of subject mastery. The effective use of peer tutoring created a familiar classroom atmosphere and acted as an instructional secret weapon that helped many teachers get through the day.

Recitation periods in the country school were not primarily for learning but for displays of learning already mastered. Older students listened to younger ones recite. In turn if younger students heard their older brothers' and sisters' recitations, this did them no harm. Repetition was a key to basic literacy learning, and still is. This "over-learning" activity paved the way for better student understanding in the future. At times it worked so well that individual younger students absorbed so much that they were able to skip a grade or two.[38]

McGuffey's Eclectic Readers were still in common use in these one-room schools as the most common texts to be memorized and recited. Between 1836 and 1922 about 122 million copies of these readers were sold.[39] But this massive use of one text did not slow down the teacher's effort to individualize her pupils' instruction.

Bess Corey also used applied learning activities with her students. As a South Dakota homesteader, she used situations from the pupils' lives to help them master more difficult lessons.

September 26, 1909

 My small pupils made strenuous objections to number work so I changed my desk into Fort Pierre [the local town], cut out money and with marbles, dominoes and pasteboard shacks I started each holding a [homesteader] claim on his desk top. One day I heard angry whispers and went to investigate—one younger said the other was "too high" and the other said "I ain't either. One dollar's enough for the pigs but he ought to give me two dollars for the old sow."[40]

Ethel Schnaufer, like Beth Corey, was a homesteader, and in 1916 she became a teacher in Trinidad, Colorado. The Federal Homestead Act (1862) sold 40 acres at a very low price to any farmer. The law required the homesteader to live on the land for three years, plow the 40 acres, build a house, and drill a well. After the three years the homesteader could either sell the land or live on it. Throughout the nineteenth century and the first decades of the twentieth century much of the West's useable farm land was divided into these homesteader plots. This resulted in a diffusion of the population over vast areas and helps explain the demand for so many one-room schoolhouses.

Ethel's schoolhouse was about 10 miles from her homestead. She taught students in a local family's house. Many had never been to school before.

I had some that were 16 or 17 years old and were in the first grade. . . . We did a lot of discussion and never got through with studies until the end of the day. . . . I started every one off in the same books and they worked at their own speed. In many schools today they think that is a new idea, of letting youngsters work at their own speed. Also, some of the children couldn't speak English. They were Mexican and of European family's.[41]

Bess Corey also had to cope with the scattered homestead population. During the 1913 school year she used Fort Pierre, South Dakota, as a base of operation and began driving out to distant ranches, including the "Donahue School . . . [that] have only the three little rusty headed Donahue girls for pupils."[42] Like Callie Wright on the 1860 Texas frontier (see Chapter 7), Bess traveled a circuit teaching in one-room schools and also doing private tutoring at remote ranches and farmhouses.

September 21, 1914
   This is my third week of school. I'm very busy and will be all year. Have pupils from three different schools and two counties.[43]
   . . . Myrtle went home with me. Mae has been wanting me to help her with her arithmetic so there would be more chance of her making her grade next year.[44]

One-room schools had a tendency to appear in the unlikeliest of places, wherever a cluster of homesteading families wanted a school of their own to help their children become literate. Bess Corey's life in South Dakota was devoted to being a one-room schoolmarm. She renewed her teaching certificate in 1938, again in 1941, and every third year thereafter until 1950. She, as well as tens of thousands of other one-room-school teachers acted as the mainstays of American public education and important agents of rural literacy for a good part of the twentieth century.[45]

By 1991 only 640 one-room public schools were left in the United States. About 350 were in Nebraska. The remaining ones were scattered across Wyoming, South Dakota, North Dakota, Washington State, California, Alaska, Vermont, and several other states that still have thinly populated remote regions. Since most Americans live in urban areas with schools serving thousands of students, these remaining one-room schools might seem like an anachronism.[46]

Yet think about it again. Imagine a public school with few discipline problems, no drugs, violence, or bad language. Students work by themselves, tutor one another and have a strong sense of community. Are there such schools left in America? At Pine Grove Elementary in Jordan, Montana, a school of nine students in eight grades, the standard one-room school formula still works. Montana still has about a hundred of these schools and ranked third nationally in achievement tests (1991).[47] But Pine Grove is not an exception.

Sand Hill School is 50 miles from the town of Valentine in Cherry County, Nebraska. Larger than Connecticut, the county has fewer than 7,000 residents. Yet the students do well academically. Nebraska has the greatest number of one-room schools. It ranks fourth on standardized achievement tests when compared with other states (1985). The local high school in Valentine draws about 25 percent of its students from one-room schools. It ranks above average within Nebraska. Each year about 70 percent of its graduates go on to college.[48]

What then is its secret to higher levels of literacy? The teachers in Nebraska's one- or two-room schools use the same curriculum and texts as the larger town schools. They have the same teaching credentials, but are paid less. "The key is the teacher," says Bruce Barker, a professor of rural education at Texas Tech University in Lubbock. "If she loves young people and is well prepared, she has a unique opportunity."[49]

There is no place for a student or teacher to hide in a schoolroom little bigger than a good-sized living room. "Basically, we're like one big school here, with a lot of space between the classrooms," explains County Superintendent John Carr. "I don't think you could find a better education unless you went back to Plato and Socrates and the days when you had tutors."[50]

Those who want to close one-room schools argue that these rural students are disadvantaged. That position now seems a moot point. The other argument for consolidation is that one-room schools are too expensive. But the cost discrepancy is usually not an insurmountable problem. Taxpayers will pay the additional cost when they think it's money well spent.

"Studies show that small schools exist where people can afford them," concludes Faith Dunne from Dartmouth College, New Hampshire. After conducting a comprehensive survey of small rural schools in America she found that "Where there is a choice, people choose to keep the small schools."[51]

At the Cherry Hill School in Nebraska, all the students are working ahead of their grade level. When the teacher Marilyn Graham teaches the children individually, they sit together on a couch under the windows where the afternoon light comes in behind them. "It's almost like tutoring," explains Michigan teacher Alta Munson. "It's more like home schooling than a classroom where you only have one student working on a certain subject."

At the beginning of the twenty-first century, six hundred schools were still in active use; community groups all over America have been organized to restore one-room schoolhouses and open them as museums. Some one-room schools have been preserved on their original sites. Others have been moved and reconstructed board by board at a new location, adding modern heating, cooling, and plumbing systems to help them last another hundred years. One-room-school conferences have been held by universities and other institutions to encourage this activity, raise private donations, and organize local community support. Many previously unknown teacher diaries and journals are presented at these conferences. They are part of the powerful testimony by many Americans to the unique contributions that these small learning outposts made in the cause of American literacy.[52]

THE HOME SCHOOL EVOLUTION

Until the second half of the nineteenth century domestic education remained a necessity for at least part of many children's literacy education. This only altered with the success of compulsory education through the growth of one-room schools and the urban public/private school systems.

Except for children living in the remotest rural areas, home schooling in-creasingly became the exclusive educational enclave of the privileged few. Among them was Theodore Roosevelt (1858–1919), the twenty-sixth president of the United States, who never attended a primary or secondary school. Roo-sevelt was taught at home by a succession of tutors until he enrolled at Harvard (1876) at age 16.[53] His fifth cousin Franklin Delano Roosevelt, thirty-second president (1882–1945), also was educated by eight governesses and tutors until age 14, when he entered Groton, an English prep school.[54]

Though attending school at home is hardly a new concept, home schooling was virtually unheard of in twentieth-century America until the 1970s. Then the number of home schoolers increased rapidly, from about 15,000 to estimates that range from 120,000 to 200,000 by 1987. At first, Christian home-school in-struction groups predominated in this movement. Fundamentalist religious groups objected to the secular nature of public and even some private schools.[55]

This had dramatically changed by the early 1990s, as the world of home schooling became more vigorous and diverse. Families are keeping their chil-dren at home as a matter of choice, often a "value-laden choice." Some parents object to political or cultural values taught at schools. Others do not like the in-structional methods. Many parents want to spend more time with their chil-dren. Precocious children are recognized by their parents as needing highly individualized programs. Even disabled children often respond well to individ-ualized home tutoring by their parents. By the 1990–91 school year, the U.S. Department of Education estimated the home-schooled population at between 248,500 and 353,500.[56]

By 1999 a study by the National Center for Educational Statistics showed that at least 850,000 (or 1.7 percent of the school-age population) children are part of domestic education programs. However, this figure overlooked many home schoolers whose parents would not answer a survey for philosophical reasons. Also uncounted are thousands of home-schooling families whose states legally require them to operate as "private schools." If these two groups are included, at least one million students were studying at home.

When parents are asked why they do it, almost half think they can give their child a better education at home. After decades of falling literacy attainments recorded by national school-test scores, many parents once again see basic lit-eracy as a primary family responsibility.[57]

Between 1980 and 2000 the public education agencies in all 50 states began to permit home schooling. However, only 37 states have home-schooling standards. Laws vary from state to state and fall into four distinct categories: home-school statute states, private-school states, approval instruction states, and equivalent instruction states.[58] Currently about half of the 37 states with home-schooling standards mandate annual testing. Only in the state of Oklahoma does the constitution guarantee parents' the right to home school their children. For the right child and parent, home schooling may work as a literacy alternative to regular schooling.[59]

An important corollary of America's contemporary home schooling movement is that more parents than ever before are turning to tutors for help in overcoming a variety of literacy issues, including underachievement, slow learners, attention deficient disorder, dyslexia, and other learning issues.[60]

From what we have seen throughout America's history, tutoring as a form of literacy education has a long and venerable history. It is as old as civilization. There is much evidence that a sizable amount of literacy education took place in the home using one-to-one instruction from a parent, relative, tutor, or governess.[61]

At the beginning of the twenty-first century there is no doubt that tutoring has again emerged as a prominent literacy-education phenomenon throughout American society. A 2000 *Newsweek* poll found that 42 percent of Americans believe there is a "great need" for children to receive private, outside tutoring. The marketing analysts at Bear-Stearns now estimate that the parents of students in the top 5 percent and the bottom 15 percent of their classes are likely to seek tutoring. This translates into almost seven million elementary school students. Current estimates of annual tutoring expenditures show that tutoring has grown to an over $5–$8 billion professional-service industry.[62]

Tutors today come in all shapes and sizes. Adult volunteers, homework hotlines, peer tutors, individual teachers, franchised learning centers, university clinics, and private professional agencies are among the different types of tutoring services. They vary in quality and cost.[63]

Private tutoring practices are the most commonly found tutoring options across America. Hundreds of thousands of teachers annually tutor millions of students for a fee in their own home, the child's residence, or local public libraries. Most of these tutors are classroom teachers who also work after school, on weekends, or in the summer tutoring local children. One such tutor is Opal McAlister, who started teaching in Ohio in 1923. For the next 52 years she was a dedicated public school teacher, but she also tutored children who needed her help. When her supervisors chastised her for wasting time with low-performing students by tutoring them at home or before or after school, she grew more determined to help them. "You help a child when they need the help and are asking for it," she says. At age 95 she gave a talk to high school students about World War II on a recent Memorial Day. "When I saw those kids, they were so thoughtful. They didn't push to get out of the room, but they stopped to thank me," Opal says. "I'll never forget those kids. That's when I think, if I were just in that classroom ... or tutoring somebody again?"[64]

LITERACY TODAY

By the 1980s nearly all young adults (ages 18–35) are considered to be literate by the U.S. Census standard of the last century. Of those with a college degree, 80 percent read at an eleventh-grade level. However, numerous studies indicate a disturbing inability among young adults, when working on complex tasks, to use information effectively above a literal, concrete level. Only a small percentage, using their literacy skills, can carry out moderately complex tasks. Many have great difficulty synthesizing the main argument from a newspaper article, computing the cost of a meal in a restaurant, or determining correct change from a stated amount. Only about 40 percent of all white students, 10 percent of black students and 20 percent of Hispanic students were found to be successful at these activities.[65]

Fluency, not illiteracy, has become the number one issue for contemporary America. In the 1980s the U.S. Department of Education defined fluency for a literate adult as "the ability to read, write and compute ... the ability to hold a decent job to support self and family, to lead a life of dignity and pride." But at what literacy level can an adult hold a "decent" job?[66]

At the lowest literacy standard, an employable adult can read street signs, simple texts, or possibly parts of the daily newspaper with difficulty. This represents about the fourth- to sixth-grade level of fluency. Sixteen to 27 million adults are considered to be at this level of limited fluency (see Table 10.7).

A higher fluency standard at the eighth-grade level requires the ability to read a driver's license manual, fill out a job application, read short digest articles or newspapers, and compute change when making a purchase. Forty-five million Americans do not have these abilities.

The highest literacy standard at the high school level (10th to 12th grade) includes the ability to read technical manuals, magazines such as *Time* and *Sports*

Table 10.7
Skills of Adults at Level 1

Can Usually Perform	Cannot Usually Perform
Sign one's name	Locate eligibility from a table of employee benefits
Identify a country in a short article	Locate intersection on a street map
Locate one piece of information in a sports article	Locate two pieces of information in a sports article
Locate the expiration date information on a driver's license	Identify and enter background information on a social security card application
Total a bank deposit entry	Calculate total costs of purchase from an order form

Illustrated, read and compute an IRS tax return, or write a simple letter. In the 1980s between 44 and 82 million adults lacked these simple skills.[67]

Business communication and manufacturing modes are changing at an ever-increasing pace. Computerization of the office and shop means that the great majority of future workers must learn to integrate and coordinate different reading, math, and thinking abilities to perform most jobs. This requires a far higher level of fluency for the average worker in the 1990s than it did for workers in 1900, 1950, or even as late as 1970.

According to a 1994 estimate of the U.S. education and labor departments, 80 percent of all jobs in the high-tech workplace minimally require fluency at 12th-grade levels in reading, math, comprehension, and application skills. Unfortunately, the National Adult Literacy Survey (NALS) reported (1998) that 48 percent of the U.S. adult population who are at level one and level two of literacy fail to meet this criteria (see Figure 10.4). This means that at least half of the current workforce is not able to adequately perform the range of complex job tasks considered important for the United States to compete successfully in a

Figure 10.4
Literacy Levels of Adult Americans

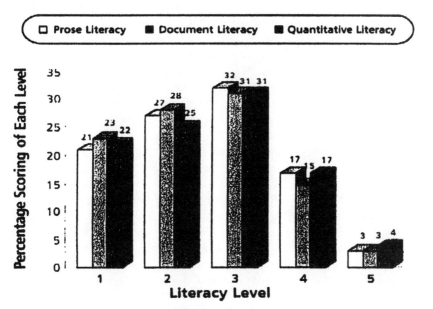

1 represents the lowest level of proficiency; 5 the highest.

Source: U.S. Department of Education, National Center for Education Statistics, *National Adult Literacy Survey*, September 1993.

global economy. Unless this trend is somehow changed, many Americans are doomed to join the ranks of a new techno-peasant underclass.[68]

During the 1990s study after study has confirmed that many businesses see the low literacy level of their workers as the principal threat to their success. The American Management Association (AMA) in a national survey of major U.S. companies reported (1998, 2000) that 40 percent of the job applicants failed basic math tests and 32 percent lacked the reading skills required for the jobs they sought. The National Association of Manufacturers (NAM) also reported (2000) similar results from its members. In Detroit, Michigan, only one out of four applicants at the city's Daimler-Chrysler car plants can pass a test requiring 10th-grade skills. Motorola reports that 80 percent of all applicants screened nationally failed a test of seventh-grade English and fifth-grade math. Other premier U.S. Fortune 500 companies, such as Intel, Boeing, and IBM and many others, all report the same dismal picture of a workforce barely literate for today's jobs.

Since 1950 millions of manual-labor jobs have been replaced by technology. Yet over the same period the number of jobs has grown almost continuously, and with it the real incomes of most people in the United States. America is now entering a new, watershed era. We are leaving the age of the wrench and entering the age of the robot and the advanced computer. This rapid rate of technological change increases the need for almost all new entry-level workers to be better educated. There is also a growing demand for the continuous educational improvement of the current workforce, which will have an impact on personal performance and the productivity of almost every organization.[69]

It should come than as no surprise that the International Organization for Economic Cooperation and Development (OECD) in 2000 ranked the United States 18th out of 19 major industrial nations on its international literacy standard (see Figure 10.5). Put in even a broader world context, of the 158 member nations in the United Nations, the United States ranks 49th in overall literacy. This stems from the fact that about half of the United States population reads below the eighth-grade level, with many other Americans below even the sixth-grade level. From all this mountain of data, the New York Conference Board concluded that more than 40 percent of the U.S. workforce, over 50 percent of high school graduates, and even 16 percent of college graduates have inadequate fluency skills for today's workplace. Sixty percent of our adult population has never read any kind of book since leaving school, and only 30 percent of all adults now even read a daily newspaper. Is it a surprise that a Roper Survey (1996) reported that 58 percent of American high school seniors could not understand a newspaper editorial in any newspaper?[70]

We must resist the notion that the United States is experiencing an "unprecedented literacy tailspin." Americans are not less literate today than they were in 1900. In many ways, the overall population is more literate. However, we have forever thrown away our old "yardsticks" and today demand a much higher level of personal education and/or technical skills. Even if our public/private

Figure 10.5
U.S. High-School Graduate Lag in Literacy (Percentage below an International Literacy Standard)

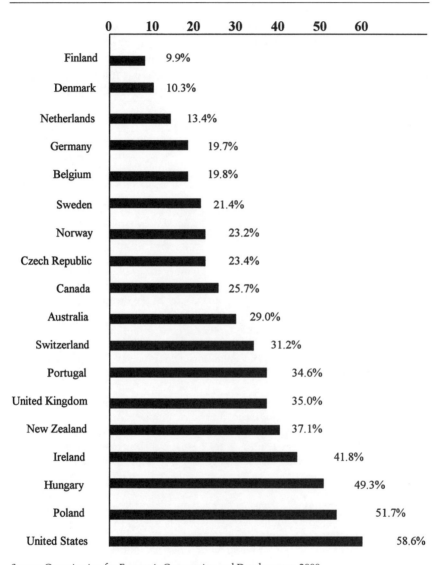

Source: Organization for Economic Cooperation and Development, 2000.

schools are performing at about the same levels as in the 1950s and 1960s, a literacy crisis exists because the needs of a proportionally larger group for increased fluency have outpaced the public school system's ability to educate or train.[71]

Meeting the demands of literacy for late twentieth- and early twenty-first-century America has become increasingly difficult with each passing decade. Every American child and adult now needs a much higher level of reading fluency to attain personal success and help preserve our republic. America's great relative decline in personal educational attainments, as documented in many international comparisons and studies, must act as a wake–up call to ensure higher levels of literacy for more Americans.[72]

NOTES

1. Lawrence A. Cremin, *American Education: The National Experience 1783–1876* (New York: Harper & Row, 1980), 180.

2. *Merrick vs. Amherst*, 94 Massachusetts (12 Allen), 509.

3. Ronald Richard Mrozinski, "Compulsory Education: A Historical Review of Origins, Growth, and Challenges" (Ph.D. diss, University of Michigan, 1977), 34–35, 94–95.

4. Ibid., 106, 132.

5. Samuel Eliot Morison and Henry Steele Commager, *The Growth of the American Republic*, Vol. 2 (New York: Oxford University Press, 1960), 306–307, 919; *The Statistical History of the United States from Colonial Times to the Present* (Stamford, Connecticut: Fairfield Publisher, 1965), 214.

6. Mrozinski, "Compulsory Education," 40.

7. Ibid., 39, 107, 128.

8. Moses Stambler, "The Effect of Compulsory Education and Child Labor Laws on High School Attendance in New York City," *History of Education Quarterly*, 8 (Summer 1968): 190–191.

9. Mrozinski, "Compulsory Education," 40. August W. Steinhilber and Carl J. Sokolowski, *State Law on Compulsory Attendance*, U.S. Department of Health, Education and Welfare (Washington, D.C.: U.S. Government Printing Office, 1966), 3.

10. *Statistical History of the United States*, 56–57; Department of Justice, Immigration and Naturalization Service releases; Morison, *American Republic*, 910.

11. Ellwood P. Cubberley, *Changing Conceptions of Education* (Boston: Houghton Mifflin, 1909), 15–16.

12. Lawrence A. Cremin, *The Transformation of the School* (New York: Vintage Books, 1964), 72–75; United States Immigration Commission, *Abstract of the Report on the Children of Immigrants in Schools* (Washington, D.C., 1911), 18–19.

13. "Taft Veto of Literacy Test for Immigrants" February 14, 1913, *Supplement to the Messages and Papers of the Presidents Covering the Administration of William Howard Taft*, National Archives of the United States, Washington, D.C., p. 8228; "Wilson Veto of Literacy Test for Immigration," *Congressional Record*, 63rd Congress, 3rd session, 52 (January 28, 1915): 2481–2482; Samuel Eliot Morison, *The Oxford History of the American People* (New York: Oxford University Press, 1965), 813–814, 897.

14. Cremin, *Transformation*, 125–126.

15. Geraldine Joncich Clifford, "Buch und Lesen: Historical Perspectives on Literacy and Schooling," *Review of Educational Research* 54 (Winter 1984): 472–500; Marie Costa, *Adult Literacy/Illiteracy in the United States: A Handbook for Reference and Research* (Santa Barbara: ABC-Clio, 1988), 4–7; Carl F. Kaestle, "Introduction to Special Issue on the History of Literacy," *History of Education Quarterly* 30 (Winter 1990): 487–491.

16. Edward W. Stevens, Jr., "Technology Literacy, and Early Industrial Expansion in the United States," *History of Education Quarterly* 30 (Winter 1990): 523–544; Nell P. Eurich, *Corporate Classrooms* (Princeton, New Jersey: Carnegie Foundation, 1985), 30–36.

17. Harvey J. Graff, *The Legacies of Literacy* (Bloomington: Indiana University Press, 1987), 163–165, 173–174, 179, 260–262, 343–344, 351, 375; Cremin, *National Experience*, 491; Carl F. Kaestle, "Literacy and Diversity: Themes from a Social History of the American Reading Public," *History of Education Quarterly* 28 (Winter 1988): 523–549.

18. Wanda Cook, *Adult Literacy Education in the United States* (Newark, Delaware: International Reading Association, 1977), 11, 58, 64, 72, 105.

19. Lee Soltow and Edward Stevens, *The Rise of Literacy and the Common School in the United States: A Socioeconomic Analysis to 1870* (Chicago: University of Chicago Press, 1981), 20.

20. Antoine Prost and Gerard Vincent, eds., *A History of Private Life, Vol 5, Riddles of Identity in Modern Times* (London: Belknap Press of Harvard University, 1991), 71–72, 77.

21. Soltow, *Rise of Literacy*, 94.

22. Andrew Dawson, "The Workshop and the Classroom: Philadelphia Engineering, the Decline of Apprenticeship and the Rise of Industrial Training 1878–1900," *History of Education Quarterly* 39 (Summer 1999), 152–160; Cremin, *National Experience*, 364–365.

23. Edward A. Krug, *The Shaping of the American High School* (New York: Harper & Row, 1964), 439; *Annual Report of the U.S. Commissioner of Education for the Year 1890–91*. vol. 2 (Washington, D.C.: Government Printing Office), 790. *Report of the U.S. Commissioner of Education for the Year Ended June 30, 1926* Washington, D.C.: Government Printing Office), 2–3.

24. Cremin, *National Experience*, 163; *Charles E. Stuart and others vs. School District No. 1 of the Village of Kalamazoo and others*, 30 Michigan (1874), 84; Thomas J. Schlereth, *Victorian America: Transformations in Everyday Life 1876–1915* (New York: HarperCollins, 1991), 247–248.

25. John Hope Franklin, *From Slavery to Freedom: A History of Negro Americans*, 3rd ed. (New York: Vintage Books, 1969), 546–559.

26. Cremin, *National Experience*, 169; Neil G. McCluskey, ed., *Catholic Education in America: A Documentary History* (New York: Teachers College, Columbia University, 1964), 94.

27. Schlereth, *Victorian America*, 246; Timothy Walch, *Parish School: American Catholic Parochial Education from Colonial Times to the Present* (New York: Crossroad Publishing Co., 1995), 79–80.

28. Cremin, *National Experience*, 170–171.

29. Carl F. Kaestle et al., *Literacy in the United States: Readers and Reading since 1880* (New Haven: Yale University Press, 1991), 65, 70; Cremin, *National Experience*, 260.

30. Jane Aiken Rosenberg, *The Nation's Great Library* (Urbana: University of Illinois Press, 1992), 7.

31. Schlereth, *Victorian America*, 253–255; Theodore Morrison, *Chautauqua: A Center for Education, Religion, and the Arts in America* (Chicago: University of Chicago Press, 1974).

32. Schlereth, *Victorian America*, 244.

33. *Historical Statistics of the United States*, Part I, (Washington, D.C.: Bureau of the Census, 1975), 368; *Statistical History of the United States*, 208; Elliott West, *Growing Up with the Country: Childhood on the Western Frontier* (Albuquerque: University of New Mexico Press, 1989), 208; Kate V. Wofford, *Modern Education in the Small Rural School* (New York: Macmillan, 1938), 329.

34. Schlereth, *Victorian America*, 244; Wayne E. Fuller, *One Room Schools of the Middle West: An Illustrated History* (Lawrence: University Press of Kansas, 1994), 46, 54–55, 65–66.

35. Elizabeth Corey, *Bachelor Bess: The Homesteading Letters of Elizabeth Corey, 1909–1919*, Philip L. Gerber, ed. (Iowa City: University of Iowa Press, 1990), 27.

36. West, *Growing Up*, 46.

37. Thad Sitton and Milan C. Rowold, *Ringing the Children In: Texas Country Schools* (College Station: Texas A&M University Press, 1987), 85–86; Wayne E. Fuller, *The Old County School* (Chicago: University of Chicago Press, 1982), 14, 195.

38. Sitton, *Ringing the Children In*, 207–208; West, *Growing Up*, 47; Bill Broz, "Tutoring: Lessons from the Country School," *English Journal* 73 (December 1984): 36; Sophie Bloom, *Peer and Cross-Age Tutoring in the Schools* (Washington, D.C.: U.S. Department of Health, Education and Welfare, National Institute of Education, 1976), 3.

39. Corey, *Homesteading Letters*, 39.

40. Schlereth, *Victorian America*, 244.

41. Interview with Ethel Schnaufer, April 1974, by Leslie Schnaufer, Texas Panhandle–Plains Museum Archives, Canyon, Texas.

42. Corey, *Homesteading Letters*, 230.

43. Ibid., 266.

44. Ibid., 297.

45. Ibid., 385.

46. Mark M. Kindley, "Little Schools on the Prairie Still Teach a Big Lesson," *Smithsonian* 16 (October 1985): 119; Sam Allis, "Little Schoolhouse on the Prairie," *Time*, February 4, 1991, 64.

47. Allis, *Schoolhouse*, 64.

48. Kindley, "Big Lesson," 119, 122.

49. Eileen Ogintz, "One Room School Running Out of Pupils," *Chicago Tribune*, October 20, 1985, sec. 1, p. 3.

50. As quoted in Kindley, "Big Lesson," 122.

51. As quoted in Kindley, "Big Lesson," 126.

52. Ibid., 128; Tom Dammann, "One Room Schoolhouse Economics Lesson," *Chicago Tribune*, March 12, 1991, Sec. 5; One-Room School Conference, Northern Illinois University, DeKalb, Illinois, June 21–23, 2001.

53. Nathan Miller, *Theodore Roosevelt: A Life* (New York: William Morrow, 1992), 19, 26, 37, 45, 62, 63–64, 73.

54. Geoffrey C. Ward, *Before the Trumpet: Young Franklin Roosevelt, 1882–1905* (New York: Harper & Row, 1985), 150–153, 173–174.

55. Patricia Lines, "An Overview of Home Instruction," *Phi Delta Kappan* 68 (March 1987): 512.

56. Patricia M. Lines, *Estimating the Home Schooled Population,* Office of Research, U.S. Department of Education, Working Paper, 1991. James C. Carper, "Home Schooling in the United States: An Historical Reflection," unpublished paper, University of South Carolina, Columbia, 1990.

57. Catherine Gevertz, "Study Estimates 850,000 U.S. Children Schooled at Home," *Education Week,* August 8, 2001, 12.

58. Patricia M. Lines, *Homeschooling: Private Choices and Public Obligations,* Office of Research, Office of Educational Research and Improvement, U.S. Department of Education, Working Paper, 1993.

59. Steve Stecklow, "Fed Up with Schools, More Parents Turn to Teaching at Home," *Wall Street Journal,* May 10, 1994, A1, A12.

60. Edward E. Gordon, *Tutor Quest: Finding Effective Education for Children and Adults* (Bloomington, Indiana: Phi Delta Kappa Educational Foundation, 2002) 11-16, 41-65.

61. Edward E. Gordon and Elaine H. Gordon, *Centuries of Tutoring: A History of Alternative Education in America and Western Europe* (Lanham, Maryland: University Press of America, 1990).

62. Gordon, *Tutor Quest,* 21-22.

63. Ibid. 23–37.

64. Robert C. Johnston, "A Teaching Gem," *Education Week,* September 15, 1999, 40–45.

65. Marie Costa, *Adult Literacy/Illiteracy in the United States: A Handbook for Reference and Research* (Santa Barbara: ABC-Clio, 1988), 64–65.

66. Geraldine Joncich Clifford, "Buch und Lesen: Historical Perspectives," 472–500.

67. J. S. Chall, E. Heron, and A. Hilferty, "Adult Literacy: New and Enduring Problems," *Phi Delta Kappan* 69 (November 1987), 190–196; Costa, *Literacy,* 75.

68. U.S. Department of Education, National Center for Educational Statistics, *National Adult Literacy Survey* (Washington, D.C., 1993, 1998).

69. Edward E. Gordon, *Skill Wars: Winning the Battle for Productivity and Profit* (Boston: Butterworth-Heinemann, 2000), 9, 139–141.

70. Edward E. Gordon, *America's Meltdown: Why We Are Losing the Skill Wars and What We Can Do About It,* White Paper presented at the U.S. Chamber of Commerce, Washington, D.C., November 13, 2001, 3–4.

71. Edward E. Gordon, Judith A. Ponticell, and Ronald R. Morgan, *Closing the Literacy Gap in American Business* (New York: Quorum Books, 1991), 28.

72. Lawrence C. Stedman and Carl F. Kaestle, "Literacy and Reading Performance in the United States from 1880 to the Present" in *Literacy in the United States* (New Haven: Yale University Press, 1991), 128.

Conclusion: The Lessons of Literacy
for Today and Tomorrow

At the start of the twenty-first century the United States is almost in the same position in regard to literacy as it was at the beginning of the twentieth century. In 1901 Americans gradually began to understand that fundamental change was occurring across the nation and world. Many recent immigrants had come to America to get ahead. The United States was conceived on the ideal of personal progress. More and more people were coming to see that literacy education was good, even necessary, for our democracy to succeed.

The United States was locked in fierce international competition with Great Britain and Germany, then the industrial greats of the world. Technology was rapidly spreading across the entire workplace. Automobiles, motion pictures, telephones, radio, x-rays, electric lights—all of them milestone technologies— excited the minds of Americans a hundred years ago. Yet the United States would not compete effectively unless the average American worker was literate. Between 1890 and 1920, the United States embarked on the difficult task of introducing a sweeping literacy education revolution—schooling for everyone. Business leaders supported this literacy revolution because they recognized that a literate workforce had become a requirement to make and export quality goods and to capture a larger share of the growing domestic consumer market. Union leaders supported this literacy-education revolution because it would ultimately give their members better jobs at higher wages. Politicians and community leaders embraced this literacy revolution because the average parent realized that it would lead to a better life for their children. Education for democracy became the American way of life.

The twentieth-century American educational system was organized on the premise that we needed to educate only 20–25 percent of the entire population to the highest levels of fluency necessary for professional/managerial careers. Though almost everyone went to school, many received at best a minimal literacy education.

For most of the twentieth century, through two world wars, the rise of the American middle class, and the collapse of the Soviet Union that ended the Cold War, this literacy arrangement worked very well. It transformed America from a rural, agricultural nation, into the world's number-one political/economic superpower. Here is how it worked: 25 percent of the population graduated from college; another 40 percent graduated from high school; some got additional technical or post-secondary education; the bottom 35 percent had a hard time in school, and more dropped out with each passing decade.

Because this U.S. literacy game plan worked for so long, for so many, most Americans (particularly future managers and professionals) came to believe that only a fraction of the population was capable of really benefiting from advanced literacy education. Why spend more money on the rest?[1]

In the twenty-first century contemporary public apathy still abounds over these literacy issues. In Kentucky only 33 percent of residents over the age of 25 have high school diplomas. The state ranks last in the nation, yet the magistrates of Grayson County unanimously rejected a proposal to build the county's first library with a 6 percent property-tax increase. County Magistrate Carlos Wells said residents pay plenty of taxes already. "I'm not anti-libraries. After several weeks of study, I didn't find facts indicating that we needed a public library." As many as 44 percent of Kentucky residents are functionally illiterate, according to a 1996 survey by the University of Kentucky. There is often a failure of local community leadership across the United States to recognize and address these fundamental literacy educational issues.[2]

These literacy trends have even begun to change the face of higher education. A rising tide of freshman college students at public and private institutions need basic literacy education. This included (2000) 35 percent of freshmen at private Columbia College in Chicago and even 7.4 percent of first-year students at DePaul University. This raises serious questions about whether the mission of higher education is to train society's best minds or to take over the functional literacy jobs that elementary and high schools have failed to complete.[3]

Carl F. Kaestle, a prominent literacy historian, believes that "literacy has leveled off and even declined in some ways during the past ten to twenty years (1970–1990) due to various social factors and to the expansion of the electronic media."[4] He also focuses on data from the U.S. Bureau of the Census showing that by 1980 20 to 30 percent of the U.S. population was considered to be functionally illiterate.[5] Since that time the fluency rates for functional literacy have only become worse.

Without constant practice, an individual's ability to read, write, or calculate will atrophy and decay. This has long been recognized as a basic condition for foreign language fluency or for playing a musical instrument well. The modern intrusions of first the telephone, then radio and television, and now the computer place basic reading, writing, and calculating skills at greater risk. Personal fluency is declining for too many Americans. Daily newspaper readership has been in a steady decline since the 1950s. Reading as a leisure activity may even be decreasing. Popular culture has seemingly adopted the attitude, "Who has time for reading? I'm only into scanning."

Today and into the foreseeable future, because of the historic rate of human technological progress, our modern society is becoming more and more dependent upon jobs that call for the majority of all employees to exercise their brains rather than their brawn. Between 1750 and 1900 human knowledge doubled. In the first 50 years of the twentieth century it doubled again. Since 1960 each decade has seen a further acceleration in the pace of change. This continued explosion of raw data means that people need to learn how to better understand and judge the value of all this information.[6] Some have called this learning process "critical thinking." Kaestle agrees that "We shall need much better reading skills across the entire population if we are to survive and improve as a democratic society in an increasingly complex age, quite apart from workplace demands for more literacy."[7]

Other researchers on school reform, such as Martin Haberman at the University of Wisconsin, believe that many need to reconsider their basic assumptions about what a school is and what the participants do there. In too many schools "teaching" and literacy no longer seem to be the primary focus of schooling. In fact, far too often, "learning is not used as the primary criterion for judging teachers. ... If [they] can keep a lid on the classroom, that [teacher] is considered successful regardless of how much or how little is being taught or learned in his or her classroom."[8]

For this reason Haberman makes this startling comparison. "Successful urban schools appear to have many of the qualities of successful day camps. Attendees are cared for and treated well while they go through a schedule of daily activities. ... Staff members in these day camps are sophisticated enough to realize that life will be more pleasant for everyone if the campers are kept mollified and busy."[9]

Many drop-outs or even graduates of such schools who develop only basic literacy skills later discover "that they cannot meet employers' expectations." Those that try to go to college or post-secondary institutions often "realize that they lack the most basic prerequisite knowledge for benefitting from the courses."[10]

Case studies of literacy's failed school infrastructure seem to surface all too readily. The valedictorian of an inner-city Chicago high school was discovered to be functionally illiterate after being tested by a local community college. The experience of Diana Strzalka, a Chicago freelance reporter, was a personal struggle to become literate despite her public schooling.

As a child growing up in a poor neighborhood I was robbed of an education. . . .
   Tough-talking kids ran the halls and teachers, afraid of their cars being vandalized, wouldn't stand up to them. . . .

It was a mistake, I know. But teachers seemed to be more like baby-sitters or security guards to me.[11]

After she worked in a series of low-paying jobs, Diana was persuaded to take the GED test by Lettie King, a social worker. She then earned her bachelor's degree in journalism from Columbia College after eight years of working at night and on weekends. "It took a long time and I still can't think kindly about the process of public education and what it represents for me. Education should be the same for everybody. . . . It shouldn't matter what neighborhood you live in. When you go to school your only worry should be learning."[12]

Diane Ravitch agrees with Strzalka. In *A Century of Failed School Reform* (2000), she asks the question, What should schools focus on? "They cannot be successful as schools unless nearly all their pupils gain literacy, and numeracy, as well as a good understanding of history and the sciences, literature, and a foreign language. They cannot be successful unless they teach children the importance of honesty, personal responsibility, intellectual curiosity, industry, empathy, and courage."[13]

The prominent African-American W. E. B. DuBois once told his audiences that there was only one way for schools to cure society's problems, and that was by making more people literate. Schools had to teach people how to read, write, and count well. If a school fails to do this and substitutes something for which a school is not adapted, it will fail in its primary function a well as all other attempted functions.[14]

Unlike the last 50 or even 70 years, during which the U.S. workplace had an almost unquenchable thirst for men and women with minimal literacy, twenty-first-century technology has less and less use for them. In every type of business there is a demand for "knowledge workers," that is, persons with certain amounts of specialized training, based on an advanced literacy education. With job content changing so often in every field, higher reading-comprehension abilities paired with constant education updates are necessities for almost every American.

The "catch-22" is that the United States has outstripped both the supply of adults with these advanced literacy skills and the capacity of local public/private schools to make the next generation more fluent. We simply lack enough well-educated literate people who have developed the successful critical thinking and technical skills required by a worldwide, high-performance workplace.[15] "Have society's demands for literacy skills overwhelmed the school's ability to produce readers who can be effective workers and citizens?" asks Carl Kaestle.[16]

We don't want to go back to those good old days of one-room schoolhouses. We want to edit them. Our current educational system did not suddenly spring up at the beginning of the twentieth century as a natural process of an enlightened America. Then, business people overall were no less greedy, or union leaders less truculent, or politicians any less corrupt than today. This "First American Literacy Revolution" took place very gradually. As we have seen, it was punctuated in each individual state by long and bitter arguments among politicians, unions, businesses, and the general public.

There are important differences at the dawn of the twenty-first century from the beginning of the last century. During the early 1900s, 85 percent of Americans were farmers. Today agricultural employees make up less than 3 percent of the U.S. workforce. In 1950, 73 percent of employees worked in production and manufacturing. The number now hovers around 15 percent. In the year 2001, no industrialized country has more than one-sixth or one-eighth of its workforce making or moving goods. Two-thirds of U.S. workers are employed in the service sector. Knowledge has become their most important product. The U.S. Department of Labor estimates that at least 44 percent of all workers are in data-service businesses—gathering, processing, retrieving, or analyzing information. Becoming a highly literate person is no longer just another option for an elite few; instead, it is now a necessity of life for almost anyone who wishes to be part of middle-class America.[17]

As the United States begins a new century, we need a "Second American Literacy Revolution." Workers and students need higher levels of academic, technical, communication, and information-processing literacy skills in order to function effectively in society. Our institutions, including government, business, and health care need updating for the twenty-first century. Why should literacy education be any different? How we support literacy education needs to be reinvented rather than just reformed.

As you read this, the public's call for a Second American Literacy Revolution is gathering momentum across the nation. Much of what will drive this new literacy revolution is the growing dissatisfaction of more parents with the sad fact that too many schools are failing to produce graduates who meet the levels of literacy fluency needed in today's global society. For the first time in several generations, parents are beginning to understand that because of inadequate fluency their children might achieve less, rather than more, in their lifetime.[18] This may help account for the current rise in home schooling and increases in student tutoring programs.

Family life in America is very different today than it was even 20 years ago. As a social institution the family is most resistant to change. Yet it is just as deeply attached to the historical forces of change as any other institution.

As we have seen in our review of the history of literacy in America, 300 years ago the family was the bedrock of education, religion, politics, and the economy of colonial America. During that era the family performed many basic social functions that have since been delegated to other institutions. For example, the Puritan family was the primary educational and religious unit of New England society. We have noted that basic literacy was so important to the people of that time and place that laws were even enacted (as early as 1642) that required parents to teach their children and even servants how to read. This was unprecedented for that era. Few other societies outside of colonial America even considered enlisting families in the pursuit of literacy.[19]

Thereafter, throughout the history of the United States the family has remained a primary agent in the search for individual literacy. We have also witnessed the personal struggles of individuals who assumed a responsibility for
their own literacy education in the antebellum North and South, on the Western frontier, or among African-American or Native-American groups. Both famous and obscure women and men, such as Frederick Douglass, Callie Wright,
Sequoya, Cotton Mather, Margaretta Forten, Laura Towne, and countless others, became champions of literacy as well as community leaders. At times they
had to overcome tremendous barriers or pay a tremendous personal price to obtain literacy all by themselves or with the help of a diverse mixture of literacy
agents. They helped make the notion of personal self-education an important
core cultural concept in the United States.

What then for families are the practical differences between yesterday and
today in this quest for an appropriate literacy education? Yesterday in American literacy education (that is, before 1920), parents enlisted a wide variety of
alternatives, such as dame schools, common schools, subscription schools, private academics, domestic education, sectarian schools, one-room schools, grammar schools, and numerous other literacy-education variations that we have
explored. Yet parents remained the primary agents in supporting and choosing
their children's literacy alternatives. Throughout the history of America, we
have seen how that combination of parental love and sense of duty provided
powerful support for literacy education.

Today in America mandatory, tax-supported, compulsory education has assumed the primary societal responsibility of providing literacy for all. The state
is expected to provide a level literacy playing field through its public schools.
The relative contributions of schooling and the family to literacy are near impossible to estimate.[20] Balancing this family-versus-state responsibility for societal literacy may seem for many an internal contradiction that has no practical
resolution.

Perhaps a 1926 U.S. Supreme Court ruling can be of assistance in helping us
strike the right balance. The case dealt with an Oregon State referendum that
threatened to close all private schools in the state so that all children would attend only public schools. The U.S. Supreme Court ruled conclusively regarding
the primary rights and responsibilities of parents to direct and control their children's education: "The child is not a mere creature of the state; those who nurture him and direct his destiny have the right, coupled with the high duty, to
recognize and prepare him for additional obligations."[21]

We cannot precisely measure the support that so many families over the past
300 years have willingly given in their fulfillment of this "high duty." But we
certainly have witnessed how so many families struggled to provide their children with a literacy education appropriate to meeting the needs of that day's society. Nor can the success of the local schools they established and controlled be
determined with any degree of accuracy. These are historical intangibles. Yet we
have seen, time and time again, how important these literacy programs were to

the families who took great personal pride in giving their children the legacy of literacy. The U.S. Commissioner of Education acknowledged this when he wrote in 1890, "In education as in other departments of human activity it is self-help that stimulates the healthiest and most vigorous growth and leads to the most enduring results. ... History shows conclusively that popular education has flourished most in those states where government is most democratic."[22]

Many of the social building blocks of America were founded upon family self-help and democracy. These themes need a revival if America is to rebuild popular literacy to a higher, world-class standard. We need to put on a new mind-set of schools without walls that allies parents and teachers in the quest for daily literacy education. Literacy is not something external that can be applied to people like bandages or tattoos. Enacting new governmental literacy programs will fail if they don't mobilize more direct family participation. Literacy education is an internal developmental process that occurs slowly over a lifetime. We need literacy programs that will motivate more families to support child or adult daily reading and learning activities in their own homes.

One such contemporary self-help literacy project was a North Central Association of Colleges and Schools (NCA) tutorial school that for 33 years (1968–2001) brought subject-certified teachers, retrained as tutors, into the homes of more than 12,000 children (K-12) and adults. These students represented every socioeconomic group and were tutored in their own homes across the six-county Chicago metropolitan area. The majority of students were tutored in basic reading and math areas, though high school and even college subjects were also tutored.

These tutoring programs were usually the parents' first experience of a teacher regularly visiting their home. By involving the parents in an ongoing literacy conversation over a typical 10-to 13-week tutoring program, many families came to a better understanding of their child's literacy needs and learning abilities. For the first time many parents came to see that becoming literate takes time. Successful learning is an everyday activity involving the time of both parent and child.

A provocative poll by Public Agenda (1999) confirmed that many parents have a difficult time dealing with these home literacy issues. They found that seven in 10 families say they are more involved in their child's education than were their own parents, but most believe they are not doing enough. The same poll reported that only one in 10 teachers finds that parents regularly check to make sure that their child's homework is done and done correctly.

In the NCA-accredited tutoring program it was found that these literacy support issues could be more effectively addressed by tutoring a child in his/her own home rather than at school or in a library or community center. The tutor was able to meet with the parent after every tutoring class, review results, give homework assignments, and establish a dialogue on progress. They coached parents on how to provide a quiet, comfortable, well-lighted place that is equipped with all the necessary learning supplies for the child. Parents needed to become literacy role models. The tutor's day-to-day coaching showed parents how to become more personally involved through reviewing the student's work and engaging in personal drill and practice or reading activities.

They also found that the first principle of successful personal literacy was that a student must first "learn how to learn" at home coached by a supportive family environment, before he/she can successfully learn every day in a school classroom. This professional tutoring program often overcame a literacy roadblock for a child. But of equal importance was the tutor acting as a literacy coach to establish a supportive learning environment, improve study habits, and motivate the child to learn by enhancing self-discipline. However, parents remained the primary motivators of their children. For the long term, only they can set the right literacy example by personally demonstrating that they value literacy education as the key element in all children's preparation for life.[23]

Contemporary research supports parents becoming involved in these literacy activities, from establishing daily homework routines, to teaching for understanding, to even developing basic student learning strategies.[24] Even though younger children have shorter attention spans, the link between homework each night and student achievement grows progressively stronger as they age.[25]

The ideal of achieving general societal literacy through the establishment of compulsory schooling is as valid today as it was in the early twentieth century. There is wide agreement even on what constitutes the acceptable level of literacy fluency in an abstract sense, but the devil is in the details. Why is it so hard to create good schools for more students?[26]

The authors and other educational researchers believe that home background and parental support are more powerful influences than schooling in determining personal literacy achievement. Schools can reinforce and develop personal literacy, but the family must plant the seed and nurture its young sprouts before the first bloom of knowledge.[27]

This takes personal motivation and a lifetime dream. Some people have it. George Dawson published his first book at age 102. He learned to read at age 100. Dawson was born in 1898 in Marshall, Texas, the grandson of slaves. Despite his family's hardships, Dawson's father always trained his son to see the richness of life. "Life is so good father said, I do believe it's getting better."

As the eldest son in a poor African-American family, George went to work at the age of four, while his younger brothers and sisters attended a local school for black children. All his life he was just too busy working to go to school.

Dawson outlived four wives and raised seven children. All seven graduated from both high school and college. In 1996 he learned about an adult basic education class at a local Dallas high school. At age 98, George, with the help of Mr. Henry, a retired schoolteacher, gradually learned how to read.

A local newspaper ran a story about Dawson's struggle to become literate. The Associated Press ran the story nationwide. An elementary teacher, Richard Glaubman from Washington State, was so inspired by George's story that he flew to Dallas to visit him. Together they collaborated to write *Life Is So Good*, which has sold more than 100,000 copies.

Dawson became a celebrity, appearing on Oprah Winfrey's television show, where he explained his lifetime's basic motivation. "I always had a dream that I would learn how to read."[28]

The ability to read remains only a dream for many of the world's citizens. According to the United Nations Human Development Report (1999), 850 million of the planet's six billion people are totally illiterate and the lack of appropriate reading fluency is far higher.

Hamidullah is a freckle-faced 15-year-old Afghan boy who can expertly fire a rifle, but he cannot read or write. To identify himself, he uses a thumb-print.

Most of the men and boys in the warlord armies of Afghanistan are like Hamidullah. They have never spent a day in school. Repairing their weapons is difficult because they can't read directions. The constant wars in Afghanistan have robbed them of the barest essential literacy education and many alternatives for learning of the world around them. These victims of ignorance are easily manipulated by demagogues.

There is hope. Hamidullah says that he has never been inside a schoolhouse and that has left him with a sad feeling. But he has a dream. "I would like to write a letter. I would like to read a letter. I would also like to sign my name."[29] It is now time to make it possible for this dream to become reality for Hamidullah and so many people like him all over the world. Reading is for life!

NOTES

1. Edward E. Gordon, *Skill Wars: Winning the Battle for Productivity and Profit* (Boston: Butterworth/Heinemann, 2000), 14–16, 32–37.

2. Roger Alford, "No Library and Kentucky County Likes It That Way," *Chicago Tribune*, November 24, 2000, sec. 1, p. 20.

3. J. Linn Allen, "Colleges Take Up Burden of Remedial Instruction," *Chicago Tribune*, December 26, 2000, sec. 1, p. 2.

4. Carl F. Kaestle et al., *Literacy in the United States: Readers and Reading Since 1880* (New Haven: Yale University Press, 1991), 52.

5. Lawrence C. Stedman and Carl F. Kaestle, "Literacy and Reading Performance in the United States, from 1880 to the Present," *Reading Research Quarterly* 22 (Winter 1987): 11, 42.

6. Edward E. Gordon, Ronald R. Morgan, and Judith A. Ponticell, *Future Work: The Revolution Reshaping American Business* (Westport, Connecticut: Praeger, 1994), 1.

7. Kaestle, *Literacy in the United States*, 128.

8. Martin Haberman, "Urban Schools: Day Camps or Custodial Centers?" *Phi Delta Kappan* 82 (November 2000): 206.

9. Ibid.

10. Ibid., 208.

11. Diana Strzalka, "When Education Becomes a Struggle," *Chicago Tribune*, August 21, 2000, sec. 2, p. 5.

12. Ibid.

13. Diane Ravitch, *A Century of Failed School Reforms* (New York: Simon and Schuster, 2000), 212.

14. "Across the Nation," *Education Week*, September 13, 2000, p. 7.

15. Gordon, *Skill Wars*, 15.

16. Kaestle, *Literacy in the United States*, 91.

17. Gordon, *Skill Wars*, 14–16.

18. Ibid., 280.

19. Steven Mintz and Susan Kellogg, *Domestic Revolutions: A Social History of American Family Life* (New York: Free Press, 1908), xiv, 6–7.

20. Kaestle, *Literacy in the United States*, 31; Irwin S. Kirsch and Ann Jungeblut, *Literacy: Profiles of America's Young Adults: Final Report* (Princeton, New Jersey: National Assessment of Education Programs, Educational Testing Service, 1986), Chapter 7.

21. *Pierce vs. Society of the Sisters*, 268 U.S. 510, 45 Sup. Ct. Rep. 571, 69 L. Ed 1070 (1926), p. 1078; *Pierce vs. Hill Military Academy*, 268, U.S. 510, 45 Sup. Ct. Rep. 571, 69 L. Ed. 1070 (1926), p. 1078.

22. Wayne Fuller, *One-Room Schools of the Middle West* (Lawrence: University Press of Kansas, 1994), 78.

23. Edward E. Gordon and Elaine H. Gordon, *Centuries of Tutoring: A History of Alternative Education in America and Western Europe* (Lanham, Maryland: University Press of America, 1990), 317; Edward E. Gordon, *Educators' Consumer Guide to Private Tutoring Services* (Bloomington, Indiana: Phi Delta Kappa Educational Foundation, 1989); Edward E. Gordon, *Tutor Quest: Finding Effective Education for Children* (Bloomington, Indiana: Phi Delta Kappa Educational Foundation, 2002); Edward E. Gordon, "Home Tutoring Programs Gain Respectability," *Phi Delta Kappan* 64 (February 1983): 398. Imperial Tutoring and Educational Services in Chicago is administered by the author. Imperial trains school-district teaching personnel in its diagnostic/developmental tutoring programs for home outreach or in-school programs. It also supports private-practice community tutoring programs run by professional educators across the nation.

24. Kathleen C. Hoover-Dempsey et al., "Parental Involvement in Homework," *Educational Psychologist* 36 (Summer 2001): 195–209.

25. Harris Cooper and Jeffrey C. Valentine, "Using Research to Answer Practical Questions About Homework," *Educational Psychologist* 36 (Summer 2001): 143–153.

26. Henry M. Levin, review of *Reconstructing the Common Good in Education: Coping with Intractable American Dilemmas*, ed. Larry Cuban and Dorothy Shipps, *Educational Researcher* 30 (August/September 2001): 32–33.

27. James S. Coleman, "Methods and Results in the IEA Studies of Effects of School on Learning," *Review of Educational Research* 45 (Summer 1975): 355–386.

28. "Life Is So Good," *Reading Today* 18 (February/March 2001): 44.

29. Stephen Franklin, "For Boys, Learning Comes on Battlefield," *Chicago Tribune*, November 1, 2002, sec. 1, p. 1.

Bibliography

MANUSCRIPT COLLECTIONS

Henry E. Huntington Library, San Marino, California
Nebraska State Historical Society, Lincoln, Nebraska
Northwest Museum of Arts and Culture/Eastern Washington State Historical Society,
   Spokane, Washington
Panhandle Plains Museum Library, Canyon, Texas
Rutgers University Library, New Brunswick, New Jersey
University of North Carolina Library, Chapel Hill, North Carolina
University of Texas Library, Austin, Texas

BOOKS

Adams, Abigail. *Letters of Mrs. Adams.* 2 vols. Boston: Charles C. Little and James Brown,
   1841.
Adams, Hannah. *A Memoir of Miss Hannah Adams with Additional Notices.* Boston:
   Gray & Bowen, 1832.
Adams, John. *Adams Family Correspondence.* 4 vols. Edited by L. H. Butterfield. Cam-
   bridge: Harvard University, The Belknap Press, 1963.
Adams, John. *Letters of John Adams Addressed to His Wife.* 2 vols. Edited by C. F. Adams.
   Boston: C. C. Little and J. Brown, 1841.
Alcott, Louisa May. *Her Life, Letters and Journals.* Edited by Ednah D. Cheney. Boston:
   Little, Brown & Company, 1928.
———. *Work.* New York: Schocken Books, 1977.
Allen, Vernon L., ed. *Children As Teachers.* New York: Academic Press, 1976.
Anthony, Katharine. *First Lady of the Revolution: The Life of Mercy Otis Warren.* Gar-
   den City, New York: Doubleday & Co., 1958.

Aries, Philippe, and Georges Duby. *A History of Private Life*. Vol. 3. *Passions of the Renaissance*. Cambridge: Harvard University Press, 1989.

Arksey, Laura, Nancy Pries, and Marcia Reed. *American Diaries: An Annotated Bibliography of Published American Diaries and Journals*. Vol. 1. *Diaries Written from 1492 to 1844*, Detroit, Michigan: Gale Research Co., 1983.

Arnold, Lois Barber. *Four Lives in Science: Women's Education in the Nineteenth Century*. New York: Schocken Books, 1984.

Axtell, James. *The Educational Writings of John Locke*. Cambridge: Cambridge University Press, 1968.

———. *The School upon a Hill: Education and Society in Colonial New England*. New Haven: Yale University Press, 1974.

Bailyn, Bernard. *Education in the Forming of American Society*. Chapel Hill: University of North Carolina Press, 1960.

Beatty, Barbara. *Preschool Education in America: The Culture of Young Children from the Colonial Era to the Present*. New Haven: Yale University Press, 1995.

Bedell, Madelon. *The Alcotts: Biography of a Family*. New York: Clarkson N. Potter, 1980.

Bellows, Barbara L. *Benevolence Among Slaveholders: Assisting the Poor in Charleston 1670–1860*. Baton Rouge: Louisiana State University Press, 1993.

Benson, Mary Sumner. *Women in Eighteenth Century America*. New York: Columbia University Press, 1935.

Betts, Edwin Morris, and James Adam Bear, eds. *The Family Letters of Thomas Jefferson*. Columbia: University of Missouri Press, 1966.

Bibb, Henry. *Narrative of the Life and Adventures of Henry Bibb. An American Slave*. New York: The Author, 1849. Reprint. New York: Negro Universities Press, 1969.

Biddle, Henry D. *Extracts from the Journal of Elizabeth Drinker from 1759 to 1807*. Philadelphia: J.B. Lippincott Co., 1889.

Birney, Catherine H. *The Grimké Sisters; Sarah and Angelina Grimké, The First American Women Advocates of Abolition and Woman's Rights*. Reprint 1885 ed. Westport, Connecticut: Greenwood, 1969.

Bloom, Sophie. *Peer and Cross-Age Tutoring in the Schools*. Washington, D.C.: U.S. Department of Health, Education and Welfare, National Institute of Education, 1976.

Bourne, Eulalia. *Ranch Schoolteacher*. Tucson: University of Arizona Press, 1974.

Bourne, William Oland. *History of the Public School Society of the City of New York*, New York: W. Wood and Company, 1870.

Boylan, Anne M. *Sunday School: The Formation of an American Institution, 1790–1880*. New Haven: Yale University Press, 1988.

Brant, Irving. *James Madison*. New York: Bobbs-Merrill, 1941.

Breece, Hannah. *A Schoolteacher in Old Alaska: The Story of Hannah Breece*. Edited by Jane Jacobs. New York: Random House, 1995.

Bremner, Robert H., ed. *Children and Youth in America: A Documentary History*. 3 vols. Cambridge: Harvard University Press, 1970.

Bridenbaugh, Carl, and Jessica Bridenbaugh. *Rebels and Gentlemen: Philadelphia in the Age of Franklin*. New York: Oxford University Press, 1962.

Brink, J. R., ed. *Female Scholars: A Tradition of Learned Women before 1800*. Montreal: Eden Press, 1980.

Brown, Robert E., and B. Katherine Brown. *Virginia 1705–1786: Democracy or Aristocracy?* East Lansing: Michigan State University Press, 1964.

Brumbaugh, Martin G. *The Life and Works of Christopher Dock.* Philadelphia: J. B. Lippincott, 1908. Reprint. New York: Arno Press, 1969.

Burton, Warren. *The District School as It Was.* New York: T.Y. Crowell Company, 1928. Reprint. New York: Arno Press, 1969.

Button, H. Warren, and Eugene F. Provenzo, Jr. *History of Education and Cultures in America.* Englewood Cliffs: Prentice-Hall, 1983.

Cabot, Elizabeth Rogers Mason. *More Than Common Powers of Perception: The Diary of Elizabeth Rogers Mason Cabot.* Boston: Beacon, 1991.

Calhoun, Arthur W. *A Social History of the American Family from Colonial Times to the Present.* 3 vols. New York: Barnes & Noble, 1945.

Chace, Elizabeth Buffum, and Lucy Buffum Lovell. *Two Quaker Sisters: From the Original Diaries of Elizabeth Buffum Chace and Lucy Buffum Lovell.* New York: Liveright Publishing Corporation, 1937.

Clayton, John. *The Illinois Fact Book and Historical Almanac.* Carbondale: Southern Illinois University Press, 1970.

Clifford, Deborah Pickman. *Crusader for Freedom: A Life of Lydia Maria Child.* Boston: Beacon Press, 1992.

Cohen, Sheldon S. *A History of Colonial Education, 1607–1776.* New York: Wiley, 1974.

Coleman, Michael C. *American Indian Children at School, 1850–1930.* Jackson: University Press of Mississippi, 1993.

Commager, Henry Steele, ed. *Noah Webster's American Spelling Book.* New York: Teachers College Press, Columbia University, 1962.

Cook, Wanda. *Adult Literacy Education in the United States.* Newark, Delaware: International Reading Association, 1977.

Cordier, Mary Hurlbut. *Schoolwomen of the Prairies and Plains: Personal Narratives from Iowa, Kansas, and Nebraska, 1860s to 1920s.* Albuquerque: University of New Mexico Press, 1992.

Corey, Elizabeth. *Bachelor Bess: The Homesteading Letters of Elizabeth Corey, 1909–1919.* Edited by Philip L. Gerber. Iowa City: University of Iowa Press, 1990.

Cornelius, Janet Duitsman. *"When I Can Read My Title Clear": Literacy, Slavery, and Religion in the Antebellum South.* Columbia: University of South Carolina Press, 1991.

Costa, Marie. *Adult Literacy/Illiteracy in the United States: A Handbook for Reference and Research.* Santa Barbara, California: ABC-Clio, 1988.

Cott, Nancy F. *The Bonds of Womanhood: Women's Sphere in New England, 1780–1835.* New Haven: Yale University Press, 1977.

Craft, William, and Ellen Craft. *Running a Thousand Miles for Freedom.* London: Tweedie, 1860. Reprint. Boston: Beacon Press, 1964.

Cremin, Lawrence A. *American Education: The Colonial Experience, 1607–1786.* New York: Harper & Row, 1970.

———. *American Education: The National Experience, 1783–1876.* New York: Harper & Row, 1980.

———. *The Transformation of the School.* New York: Vintage Books, 1964.

Cubberley, Ellwood P. *Changing Conceptions of Education.* Boston: Houghton Mifflin, 1909.

Davis, James Edward. *Frontier Illinois.* Bloomington: Indiana University Press, 1998.

Davis, John. *Travels of Four Years and a Half in the United States of America during 1798, 1799, 1800, 1801 and 1802.* New York: Holt, 1909.

Demos, John, and Sarane Spence Boocock. *Turning Points: Historical and Sociological Essays on the Family*. Chicago: University of Chicago Press, 1978.

Derr, Mark. *The Frontiersman*. New York: William Morrow and Company, 1993.

Douglass, Frederick. *The Life and Times of Frederick Douglass*. Hartford: Park Publishing Co., 1881.

———. *My Bondage and My Freedom*. New York: Miller, Orton, & Mulligan, 1885.

———. *Narrative of the Life of Frederick Douglass, an American Slave*. Boston: Anti-Slavery Society, 1845.

Dowdey, Clifford. *The Great Plantation*. Charles City, Virginia: Berkeley Plantation, 1957.

Earle, Alice Morse. *Child Life in Colonial Days*. New York: Macmillan, 1899. Reprint Stockbridge, Massachusetts: Berkshire House Publishers, 1993.

Edgeworth, Maria. *Maria Edgeworth: Chosen Letters*. Edited by F. V. Barry. New York: Houghton Mifflin, 1931.

Ellis, John Tracy. *Catholics in Colonial America*. Baltimore: Helicon Press, 1965.

Emerson, Ralph Waldo. *The Journals of Ralph Waldo Emerson, 1820–1872*. 10 vols. Edited by Edward Waldo Emerson and Waldo Emerson Forbes. Cambridge: Riverside Press, 1909–1914.

Eurich, Nell P. *Corporate Classrooms*. Princeton, New Jersey: Carnegie Foundation, 1985.

Fischer, Christiane, ed. *Let Them Speak for Themselves: Women in the American West, 1849–1900*. Hamden, Connecticut: Archon Books, 1977.

Ford, Paul Leicester, ed. *The New England Primer*. New York: Teachers College Press, 1962.

Foreman, Grant. *The Five Civilized Tribes*. Norman: University of Oklahoma Press, 1934.

Forten, Charlotte L. *The Letters of Charlotte Forten Grimké*. Edited by Brenda Stevenson. New York: Oxford University Press, 1988.

Franklin, Benjamin. *The Works of Benjamin Franklin*. 10 vols. Edited by Jared Sparks. Boston: Hillard, Gray, 1840.

Franklin, John Hope. *From Slavery to Freedom: A History of Negro Americans*. 3rd ed. New York: Vintage Books, 1969.

———. *A Southern Odyssey: Travelers in the Antebellum North*. Baton Rouge: Louisiana State University Press, 1976.

Frost, J. William. *The Quaker Family in Colonial America*. New York: St. Martin's Press, 1973.

Fuller, Wayne E. *The Old Country School: The Story of Rural Education in the Middle West*. Chicago: University of Chicago Press, 1982.

———. *One-Room Schools of the Middle West: An Illustrated History*. Lawrence, Kansas: University Press of Kansas, 1994.

Gallegos, Bernardo P. *Literacy Education and Society in New Mexico 1693–1821*. Albuquerque: University of New Mexico, 1992.

Garland, Hamlin. *A Son of the Middle Border*. New York: Macmillan, 1917.

Giles, Chauncy. *The Life of Chauncy Giles as Told in His Diary and Correspondence*. Compiled and edited by Carrie Giles Carter. Boston: New-Church Union, 1920.

Gilmore, William J. *Elementary Literacy on the Eve of the Industrial Revolution: Trends in Rural New England, 1760–1830*. Charlottesville: University of Virginia Press, 1983.

———. *Reading Becomes a Necessity of Life: Material and Cultural Life in Rural New England 1780–1835*. Knoxville: University of Tennessee Press, 1989.

Gordon, Edward E. *Skill Wars: Winning the Battle for Productivity and Profit*. Boston: Butterworth/Heinemann, 2000.

————. *Tutor Quest: Finding Effective Education for Children and Adults*. Blooming-ton, Indiana: Phi Delta Kappa Educational Foundation, 2002.

Gordon, Edward E., and Elaine H. Gordon. *Centuries of Tutoring: A History of Alternative Education in America and Western Europe*. Lanham, Maryland: University Press of America, 1990.

Gordon, Edward E., Judith A. Ponticell, and Ronald R. Morgan. *Closing the Literacy Gap in American Business*. New York: Quorum Books, 1991.

————. *FutureWork: The Revolution Reshaping American Business*. Westport, Connecticut: Praeger, 1994.

Graff, Harvey J. *The Legacies of Literacy*. Bloomington: Indiana University Press, 1987.

Grant, Anne MacVicar. *Memoir of an American Lady*. New York: Dodd, Mead, 1901.

Green, Elisha. *Life of the Rev. Elisha W. Green*. Maysville, Kentucky: Republican Printing Office, 1888.

Greene, Lorenzo Johnston. *The Negro in Colonial New England*. Port Washington, New York: Kennikat Press, 1966.

Gulliford, Andrew. *America's Country Schools*. Washington, D.C.: The Preservation Press, 1984.

Gutek, Gerald Lee. *Education and Schooling in America*. Boston: Allyn and Bacon, 1992.

————. *Joseph Neef: The Americanication of Pestalozzianism*. University, Alabama: University of Alabama Press, 1976.

————. *Pestalozzi and Education*. New York: Random House, 1968.

Haefner, George E. *A Critical Estimate of the Educational Theories and Practices of A. Bronson Alcott*. New York: Columbia University Press, 1937. Reprint. Westport, Connecticut: Greenwood Press, 1970.

Hamilton, Stanislaus Murray ed. *Letters to Washington and Accompanying Papers*. 5 vols. Boston: Houghton Mifflin, 1898–1902.

Hampsten, Elizabeth. *Settler's Children: Growing Up on the Great Plains*. Norman: University of Oklahoma Press, 1991.

Harden, Elizabeth. *Maria Edgeworth*. Boston: Twayne Publishers, 1984.

Harrower, John. *The Journal of John Harrower*. Williamsburg, Virginia: Colonial Williamsburg, 1963.

Heaney, Sister Jane Frances. *A Century of Pioneering: A History of the Ursuline Nuns in New Orleans (1727–1827)*. New Orleans: Ursuline Sisters of New Orleans, Louisiana, 1993.

Houston, R. A. *Literacy in Early Modern Europe: Culture and Education, 1500–1800*. New York: Longman, 1988.

Howe, Bea. *A Galaxy of Governesses*. London: Derek Verschoyle, 1954.

Hunt, Harriot. *Glances and Glimpses*. Boston: J. P. Jewett & Co., 1856.

Jackson, Robert H., and Edward Castillo. *Indians, Franciscans and Spanish Civilization*. Albuquerque: University of New Mexico Press, 1995.

Jacobs, Harriet. *Incidents in the Life of a Slave Girl Written by Herself*. Boston: Published by the author, 1862.

Inglis-Jones, Elizabeth. *The Great Maria: Portrait of Maria Edgeworth*. Westport, Connecticut: Greenwood Press, 1959.

Jarratt, Devereux. *The Life of the Reverend Devereux Jarratt, Rector of Bath Parish, Dinwiddie County, Virginia*. Baltimore: Warner & Hanna, 1806.

Jedrey, Christopher M. *The World of John Cleaveland: Family and Community in Eighteenth Century New England*. New York: Norton, 1979.

Jefferson, Thomas. *The Writings of Thomas Jefferson*. 9 vols. Edited by H. A. Washington. Washington, D.C.: Taylor and Maury, 1853–1854.

Jeffrey, Julie Roy. *Frontier Women: The Trans-Mississippi West 1840–1880*. New York: Hill and Wang, 1979.

Jernegan, Marcus W. *Laboring and Dependent Classes in Colonial America, 1607–1783*. Chicago: University of Chicago Press, 1931.

Jordon, Winthrop D. *White over Black: American Attitudes toward the Negro*. Baltimore: Penguin Books, 1969.

Jorgenson, Lloyd P. *The State and the Non-Public School, 1825–1925*. Columbia: University of Missouri Press, 1987.

Kaestle, Carl F. *The Evolution of an Urban School System, New York City, 1750–1850*. Cambridge: Harvard University Press, 1973.

———, ed. *Joseph Lancaster and the Monitorial School Movement: A Documentary History*. New York: Teachers College Press, 1973.

———. *Pillars of the Republic*. New York: Hill and Wang, 1983.

Kaestle, Carl F., Helen Damon-Moore, Lawrence C. Stedman, Katherine Tinsley, & William Vance Trollinger, Jr. *Literacy in the United States: Readers and Reading since 1880*. New Haven: Yale University Press, 1991.

Kammen, Michael. *Colonial New York, A History*. New York: Scribner, 1975.

Kaufman, Polly Welts. *Women Teachers on the Frontier*. New Haven: Yale University Press, 1984.

Keller, Robert H., Jr. *American Protestantism and United States Indian Policy 1869–82*. Lincoln: University of Nebraska Press, 1983.

Kendall, Amos. *The Autobiography of Amos Kendall*. Boston: Lee & Shepard, 1872.

Kennedy, Millard Fillmore. *Schoolmaster of Yesterday: A Three-Generation Story*. New York: McGraw-Hill, 1940.

Kilpatrick, William Heard. *The Dutch Schools of New Netherland and Colonial New York*. United States Bureau of Education. *Bulletin*. 12 (1912). Reprint. New York: Arno Press, 1969.

King, Wilma. *Stolen Childhood: Slave Youth in Nineteenth Century America*. Bloomington: Indiana University Press, 1995.

Kirsch, Irwin S., and Ann Jungeblut. *Literacy: Profiles of America's Young Adults: Final Report*. Princeton, New Jersey: National Assessment of Education Programs, Educational Testing Service, 1986.

Knight, Edgar W., ed. *A Documentary History of Education in the South before 1860*. 5 vols. Chapel Hill: University of North Carolina Press, 1949–1953.

———. *Public School Education in North Carolina*. Boston: Houghton Mifflin, 1916. Reprint. New York: Negro University Press, 1969.

Kuhn, Anne L. *The Mother's Role in Childhood Education: New England Concepts 1830–1860*. New Haven: Yale University Press, 1947.

Lancaster, Joseph. *Improvements in Education As It Respects the Industrious Classes of the Community*. London: Darton and Harvey, 1803.

Larcum, Lucy. *Lucy Larcum: Life, Letters and Diary*. Boston: Houghton, Mifflin, 1894. Reprint. New York: Gale Research, 1970.

———. *A New England Girlhood*. Boston: Northeastern University Press, 1986.

Lee, Agnes. *Growing Up in the 1850's: The Journal of Agnes Lee*. Edited by Mary Custis Lee de Butts. Chapel Hill: University of North Carolina Press, 1984.

Lerner, Gerda. *The Grimké Sisters from South Carolina*. New York: Schocken Books, 1967.

Lines, Amelia Akehurst. *To Raise Myself a Little: The Diaries and Letters of Jennie, a Georgia Teacher 1851–1886*. Edited by Thomas Dyer. Athens: University of Georgia Press, 1982.

Lockridge, Kenneth A. *Literacy in Colonial New England: An Enquiry into the Social Context of Literacy in the Early Modern West*. New York: W.W. Norton & Company, 1974.

Lockwood, John H. *Westfield and Its Historic Influences 1669–1919*. Springfield, Massachusetts: Printed by the author, 1922.

Lockwood, Lewis C. *Mary S. Peake, the Colored Teacher at Fortess Monroe*. Boston: American Tract Society, 1863. Reprint. *Two Black Teachers during the Civil War*. New York: Arno Press, 1969.

Ludlow, Fitz Hugh. *The Heart of the Continent: A Record of Travel Across the Plains and in Oregon*. New York: Hurd and Houghton, 1870.

Maddox, William Arthur. *The Free School Idea in Virginia Before the Civil War*. New York: Columbia University, 1918.

Mathews, Mitford. *Teaching to Read, Historically Considered*. Chicago: University of Chicago Press, 1966.

McCluskey, Neil G., ed. *Catholic Education in America: A Documentary History*. New York: Teachers College Columbia University, 1964.

McFarland, Gerald W. *A Scattered People: An American Family Moves West*. New York: Pantheon Books, 1985.

McLoughlin, William G. *Cherokees and Missionaries 1789–1839*. New Haven: Yale University Press, 1984.

Miller, Donald L. *City of the Century: The Epic of Chicago and the Making of America*. New York: Simon & Schuster, 1996.

Miller, Nathan. *Theodore Roosevelt: A Life*. New York: William Morrow, 1992.

Mintz, Steven, and Susan Kellogg. *Domestic Revolutions: A Social History of American Family Life*. New York: Free Press, 1988.

Monaghan, E. Jennifer. *A Common Heritage: Noah Webster's Blue-Back Speller*. Hamden, Connecticut: Archon Books, 1983.

Moran, Gerald F., and Maris A. Vinovskis, eds. *Religion, Family and the Life Course*. Ann Arbor: University of Michigan Press, 1992.

Morgan, Edmund S. *The Puritan Family: Religion and Domestic Relations in Seventeenth Century New England*. Rev. ed. New York: Harper & Row, 1966.

———. *Virginians at Home: Family Life in the Eighteenth Century*. Williamsburg, Virginia: Colonial Williamsburg, Inc., 1952.

Morison, Samuel Eliot. *The Oxford History of the American People*. New York: Oxford University Press, 1965.

Morris, Robert C. *Reading, Riting and Reconstruction: The Education of Freedmen in the South, 1861–1870*. Chicago: University of Chicago Press, 1981.

Morrison, Theodore. *Chautauqua: A Center for Education, Religion, and the Arts in America*. Chicago: University of Chicago Press, 1974.

Morton, Louis. *Robert Carter of Nomini Hall*. Williamsburg, Virginia: Colonial Williamsburg, 1941.

Neef, Joseph. *The Method of Instructing Children Rationally in the Arts of Reading and Writing*. Philadelphia: Printed for the Author, 1813.

Newcomer, James. *Maria Edgeworth*. Lewisburg: Bucknell University Press, 1973.

O'Brien, Michael, ed. *An Evening When Alone: Four Journals of Single Women in the South, 1827–67*. Charlottesville: University of Virginia Press, 1993.

Peabody, Elizabeth Palmer. *Letters of Elizabeth Palmer Peabody: American Renaissance Woman*. Edited and with an introduction by Bruce A. Ronda. Middletown, Connecticut: Wesleyan University Press, 1984.

———. *Record of Mr. Alcott's School*. 3rd ed. rev. Boston: Roberts Brothers, 1874.

Pease, Jane H., and William H. Pease. *Ladies, Women and Wenches: Choice & Constraint in Antebellum Charleston & Boston*. Chapel Hill: University of North Carolina Press, 1990.

Peavy, Linda, and Ursula Smith. *Women in Waiting in the Westward Movement: Life on the Home Frontier*. Norman: University of Oklahoma Press, 1994.

Perko, F. Michael, ed. *Enlightening the Next Generation: Catholics and Their Schools, 1830–1980*. New York: Garland, 1988.

Pilcher, George William. *Samuel Davies, Apostle of Dissent in Colonial Virginia*. Knoxville: University of Tennessee Press, 1971.

Pratt, Richard Henry. *Battlefield and Classroom: Four Decades with the American Indian, 1867–1904*. Edited and with an introduction by Robert M. Utley. New Haven: Yale University Press, 1964.

Prost, Antoine, and Gerard Vincent, eds. *A History of Private Life*. Vol 5. *Riddles of Identity in Modern Times*. Cambridge: Belknap Press, Harvard University, 1991.

Prucha, Francis P. *American Indian Policy in Crisis: Christian Reformers and the Indian, 1865–1900*. Norman: University of Oklahoma Press, 1976.

Quick, Herbert. *One Man's Life: An Autobiography*. Indianapolis: Bobbs-Merrill, 1925.

Ramsay, David. *Memoirs of the Life of Martha Laurens Ramsay*. 2nd ed. Charlestown Mass: Samuel Etheridge, 1812.

Randolph, Sarah N., ed. *The Domestic Life of Thomas Jefferson*. New York: Doubleday, 1939.

Ravitch, Diane. *A Century of Failed School Reforms*. New York: Simon and Schuster, 2000.

Rawick, George P., ed. *The American Slave: A Composite Autobiography*. 19 vols.; Supplement, Series 1, 12 vols.; Supplement, Series 2, 10 vols. Westport, Connecticut: Greenwood, 1972–1976.

Reigart, John Franklin. *The Lancasterian System of Instruction in the Schools of New York City*. New York: Teachers College, Columbia University, 1916. Reprint New York: Arno Press, 1969.

Rice, Edwin W. *The Sunday-School Movement, 1780–1917, and the American Sunday School Union, 1817–1917*. Philadelphia: American Sunday School Union, 1917. Reprint. New York: Arno Press, 1971.

Riley, Glenda. *The Female Frontier: A Comparative View of Women on the Prairie and the Plains*. Lawrence, Kansas: University of Kansas, 1988.

Robinson, H. Alan, Vincent Faraone, Daniel R. Hittleman, and Elizabeth Unruh. *Reading Comprehension Instruction, 1783–1987: A Review of Research and Trends*. Newark, Delaware: International Reading Association, 1990.

Rose, Willie Lee. *Rehearsal for Reconstruction*. Indianapolis: The Bobbs-Merrill Company, 1964.

Rush, Benjamin. *Thoughts upon Female Education*. Philadelphia: Richard and Hall, 1787.

Salmon, David, ed. *The Practical Parts of Lancaster's Improvements and Bell's Experiment*. Cambridge: Cambridge University Press, 1932.

Sandburg, Carl. *Abraham Lincoln*. Vol. 1. *The Prairie Years*. New York: Harcourt, Brace, 1926.

Schlereth, Thomas J. *Victorian America: Transformations in Everyday Life 1876–1915*. New York: HarperCollins, 1991.

Schultz, Stanley K. *The Culture Factory: Boston Public Schools, 1789–1860*. New York: Oxford University Press, 1973.

Seybolt, Robert Francis. *The Evening School in Colonial America*. Urbana: University of Illinois Press, 1925. Reprint. New York: Arno Press, 1971.

———. *The Private Schools of Colonial Boston*. Cambridge: Harvard University Press, 1935.

———. *Some Schoolmasters of Colonial New York*. Albany: The University of the State of New York, 1921.

———. *Source Studies in American Colonial Education: The Private School*. Urbana: University of Illinois Press, 1925.

Shurtleff, Nathaniel B., ed. *Records of the Governor and Company of the Massachusetts Bay in New England*. 5 vols. Boston: William White, 1853–1854.

Sitton, Thad, and Milan C. Rowold. *Ringing the Children In: Texas Country Schools*. College Station: Texas A&M University Press, 1987.

Small, Walter. H. *Early New England Schools*. Boston: Ginn, 1914. Reprint. New York: Arno Press, 1969.

Smith, Daniel Blake. *Inside the Great House: Planter Life in Eighteenth Century Chesapeake Society*. Ithaca, New York: Cornell University Press, 1980.

Smith, Jessie Carney, ed. *Notable Black American Women*. Detroit: Gale Research, 1992.

Smith, Nila Banton. *American Reading Instruction*. Newark, Delaware: International Reading Association, 1986.

Soltow, Lee, and Edward Stevens. *The Rise of Literacy and the Common School in the United States: A Socioeconomic Analysis to 1870*. Chicago: University of Chicago Press, 1981.

Steinhilber, August W., and Carl J. Sokolowski. *State Law on Compulsory Attendance*. U.S. Department of Health, Education and Welfare. Washington, D.C.: U.S. Government Printing Office, 1966.

Sterkx, H. E. *The Free Negro in Ante-Bellum Louisiana*. Rutherford, New Jersey: Fairleigh Dickinson University Press, 1972.

Sterling, Dorothy, ed. *We Are Your Sisters: Black Women in the Nineteenth Century*. New York: W. W. Norton, 1984.

Stern, Madeleine B. *Louisa May Alcott*. Norman: University of Oklahoma Press, 1950.

Stratton, Joanna L. *Pioneer Women: Voices from the Kansas Frontier*. New York: Simon & Schuster, 1981.

Sutherland, Daniel E. *The Expansion of Everyday Life 1860–1876*. New York: Perennial Library, 1990.

Szasz, Margaret Connell. *Indian Education in the American Colonies, 1607–1783*. Albuquerque: University of New Mexico Press, 1988.

Tevis, Julia Ann. *Sixty Years in a School Room*. Cincinnati: Western Methodist Book Concern, 1878.

Thompson, John. *The Life of John Thompson: A Fugitive Slave*. Worcester, Massachusetts: John Thompson, 1856.

Towne, Laura M. *The Letters and Diary of Laura M. Towne Written from the Sea Islands of South Carolina 1862–1884*. Edited by Rupert Sargen Holland.

Cambridge: Riverside Press, 1912. Reprint. New York: Negro University Press, 1969.

Trinterud, Leonard J. *The Forming of an American Tradition: A Reexamination of Colonial Presbyterianism.* Freeport, New York: Books for Libraries Press, 1949. Reprinted 1970.

Turner, James. *The Liberal Education of Charles Eliot Norton.* Baltimore: The Johns Hopkins University Press, 1999.

Turner, Justin G., and Linda Levitt Turner. *Mary Todd Lincoln.* New York: Alfred A. Knopf, 1972.

Tyack, David, and Elizabeth Hansot. *Learning Together: A History of Coeducation in American Schools.* New Haven: Yale University Press, 1990.

Tyler, Alice Felt. *Freedom's Ferment.* New York: Harper & Row, 1962.

Ulrich, Laurel Thatcher. *Good Wives: Image and Reality in the Lives of Women of Northern New England, 1650–1750.* New York: Knopf, 1982.

Updegraff, Harlan. *The Origin of the Moving School in Massachusetts.* New York: Teachers College, Columbia University, 1908.

Vinovskis, Maris A. *Education, Society and Economic Opportunity: A Historical Perspective on Persistent Issues.* New Haven: Yale University Press, 1995.

Wagner, Lilya. *Peer Teaching: Historical Perspective.* Westport, Connecticut: Greenwood Press, 1982.

Walch, Timothy. *Parish School: American Catholic Parochial Education from Colonial Times to the Present.* New York: Crossroad Publishing Co., 1996.

Walsh, James J. *Education of the Founding Fathers of the Republic.* New York: Fordham University Press, 1935.

Ward, Geoffrey C. *Before the Trumpet: Young Franklin Roosevelt, 1882–1905.* New York: Harper & Row, 1985.

Washington, Booker T. *Up from Slavery: An Autobiography.* Williamstown, Massachusetts: Corner House Publishers, 1978.

Washington, George. *The Writings of George Washington.* 14 vols. Edited by W. C. Ford. New York: G. P. Putnam's Sons, 1889–1893.

Webb, Edith Buckland. *Indian Life at the Old Missions.* Los Angeles: W. F. Lewis, 1952. Reprint. Lincoln: University of Nebraska Press, 1982.

Weber, David J. *The Spanish Frontier in North America.* New Haven: Yale University Press, 1992.

West, Elliott. *Growing Up with the Country: Childhood on the Western Frontier.* Albuquerque: University of New Mexico Press, 1989.

West, Roscoe L. *Elementary Education in New Jersey: A History.* Princeton, New Jersey: D. Van Nostrand, 1964.

Westerhoff, John H. *McGuffey and His Readers: Piety, Morality, and Education in Nineteenth Century America.* Nashville: Abington Press, 1978.

Wikersham, James Pyle. *A History of Education in Pennsylvania.* Lancaster, Pennsylvania: Inquirer Publishing Company, 1886.

Willard, Emma. *A Plan for Improving Female Education.* Middlebury, Vermont: Middlebury College, 1918.

Willard, Frances. E. *Glimpses of Fifty Years.* Chicago: H. J. Smith & Co., 1889.

———. *Writing Out My Heart: Selections from the Journal of Frances E. Willard, 1855–96.* Edited by Carolyn Gifford. Urbana: University of Illinois Press, 1995.

Woody, Thomas. *Early Quaker Education in Pennsylvania.* New York: Teachers College, Columbia University, 1920. Reprint. New York: Arno Press, 1969.

———. *Quaker Education in the Colony and State of New Jersey.* Philadelphia: University of Pennsylvania, 1923. Reprint. New York: Arno Press, 1969.

———. *A History of Women's Education in the United States.* 2 vols. New York: Science Press, 1929.

Youcha, Geraldine. *Minding the Children: Child Care in America from Colonial Times to the Present,* New York: Scribner, 1995.

DISSERTATIONS

Barth, Pius Joseph. "Franciscan Education and Social Order in Spanish North America." Ph.D. diss., University of Chicago, 1945.

Calam, John Hellawell. "Parsons and Pedagogues: The SPG Adventure in American Education." Ph.D. diss., University of Michigan, 1969.

Fisher, Hersha Sue. "The Education of Elizabeth Peabody." Ed.D. thesis, Harvard University, 1980.

Mrozinski, Ronald Richard. "Compulsory Education: An Historical Review of Its Origins, Growth and Challenges." Ph.D. diss., University of Michigan, 1977.

Murphy, Geraldine. "Massachusetts Bay Colony: The Role of Government in Education." Ph.D. diss., Radcliffe College, 1960.

JOURNAL ARTICLES AND PARTS OF BOOKS

Auwers, Linda. "Reading the Marks of the Past: Exploring Female Literacy in Colonial Windsor, Conn." *Historical Methods* 13 (Fall 1980): 204–214.

Baumgarten, Nikola. "Education and Democracy in Frontier St. Louis: The Society of the Sacred Heart." *History of Education Quarterly* 31 (Summer 1994): 171–192.

Beall, Loulie Ayer. "A Webster County School." *Nebraska History* 23 (July–Sept. 1942): 195–204.

Bernard, Richard M., and Maris A. Vinovskis. "The Female School Teacher in Ante-Bellum Massachusetts." *Journal of Social History* 10 (March 1977): 332–345.

Brubb, F. W. "Growth of Literacy in Colonial America: Longitudinal Patterns, Economic Models, and the Direction of Future Research." *Social Science History* 14 (Winter 1990): 451–482.

Butchart, Ronald E. "Perspective on Gender, Race, Calling, and Commitment in Nineteenth-Century America: A Collective Biography of the Teachers of the Freedpeople, 1862–1875." *Vitae Scholasticae* 13 (Spring 1994): 15–32.

Chall, J. S., E. Heron, and A. Hilferty. "Adult Literacy: New and Enduring Problems." *Phi Delta Kappan* 69 (November 1987): 190–196.

Clifford, Geraldine Joncich. "Buch und Lesen: Historical Perspectives of Literacy and Schooling." *Review of Educational Research* 54 (Winter 1984): 472–500.

———. "Home and School in Nineteenth Century America: Some Personal-History Reports from the United States." *History of Education Quarterly* 18 (Spring 1978): 3–35.

———. "Saints, Sinners, and People." *History of Education Quarterly* 15 (Fall 1975): 257–272.

Coleman, James S. "Methods and Results in the IEA Studies of Effects of School on Learning." *Review of Educational Research* 45 (Summer 1975): 355–386.

Cooper, Harris, and Jeffrey C. Valentine. "Using Research to Answer Practical Questions About Homework." *Educational Psychologist* 36 (Summer 2001): 143–153.

Cotton, Joseph. "Extracts from the Diary of Josiah Cotton." *Publications of the Colonial Society of Massachusetts* 26 (1924–26): 277–280.

Cutler, Anna Bemis. "The First School at Sutton." *Nebraska History* 23 (July-Sept. 1942): 210–218.

Dawson, Andrew. "The Workshop and the Classroom: Philadelphia Engineering, the Decline of Apprenticeship and the Rise of Industrial Training 1878–1900." *History of Education Quarterly* 39 (Summer 1999): 152–160.

Emhoff, Floyd L., ed. "A Pioneer School Teacher in Central Iowa: Alice Money Lawrence." *Iowa Journal of History and Politics* 33 (October 1935): 376–395.

Everett, Dianna. "The Public School Debate in New Mexico, 1850–1891." *Arizona and the West* 26 (Summer 1984): 107–134.

Fisher, Dorothy Canfield. "The Washed Window." In *A Treasury of American Heritage*. New York: Simon & Schuster, 1959.

Gordon, Edward E. "Home Tutoring Programs Gain Respectability." *Phi Delta Kappan* 64 (February 1983): 398–399.

Haberman, Martin. "Urban Schools: Day Camps or Custodial Centers?" *Phi Delta Kappan* 82 (November 2000): 203–208.

Hall, D. D. "A Yankee Tutor in the Old South." *New England Quarterly* 33 (1960): 82–91.

Hall, M. G., ed. "The Autobiography of Increase Mather." *Proceedings of the American Antiquarian Society* 71 (1961): 260–289.

Hewes, Minna, and Gordon Hewes, trans. & eds. "Indian Life and Customs at Mission San Luis Rey." *The Americas* 9 (1952): 87–106.

Hinde, Helen. "The Early Days of the Ladies Education Society of Jacksonville, Illinois." *Illinois Heritage* 2 (Fall-Winter 1999): 23–27.

Hoover-Dempsey, Kathleen C., et al. "Parental Involvement in Homework." *Educational Psychologist* 36 (Summer 2001): 195–209.

Hotze, W. H. "Pioneer School Days in Southwest Nebraska: A Reminiscence." *Nebraska History* 33 (March 1952): 41–53.

Johnson, Anna. "Recollections of a Country School Teacher." *Annals of Iowa* 42 (Winter 1975): 485–505.

Kaestle, Carl F. "The History of Literacy and the History of Readers." *Review of Research in Education* 12 (1985): 11–53.

———. "Literacy and Diversity: Themes from a Social History of the American Reading Public." *History of Education Quarterly* 28 (Winter 1988): 523–549.

Kaestle, Carl F., and Maris A. Vinovskis. "From Apron Strings to ABCs: Parents, Children, and Schooling in Nineteenth-Century Massachusetts." *American Journal of Sociology* 84 (Supplement 1978): 539–580.

Kelley, Mary. "Reading Women/Women Reading: The Making of Learned Women in Antebellum America." *Journal of American History* 83 (September 1996): 401–424.

Kindley, Mark M. "Little Schools on the Prairie Still Teach a Big Lesson." *Smithsonian* 16 (October 1985): 118–128.

Lepore, Jill. "Dead Men Tell No Tales: John Sassamon and the Fatal Consequences of Literacy." *American Quarterly* 46 (December 1994): 479–512.

Long, Huey B. "Adult Basic Education in Colonial America." *Adult Literacy and Basic Education* 7 (1983): 55–68.

Lynott, Patricia A. "The Education of the Thirteenth Apostle: Susa Young Gates, 1856–1933." *Vitae Scholasticae* 16 (Fall 1997): 71–93.

Marshall, Megan. "The Sisters Who Showed the Way." *American Heritage* 38 (September-October 1987): 58–66.

May, Susan Short. "The Story of Her Ancestry and of Her Early Life in Illinois. *Journal of the Illinois State Historical Society* 6 (April 1913): 119–128.

Monaghan, E. Jennifer. "Family Literacy in Early Eighteenth-Century Boston: Cotton Mather and His Children." *Reading Research Quarterly* 26 (October–December 1991): 342–370.

———. "Literacy Instruction and Gender in Colonial New England." *American Quarterly* 40 (March 1988): 18–41.

———. "She Loved to Read in Good Books: Literacy and the Indians of Martha's Vineyard, 1643–1725." *History of Education Quarterly* 30 (Winter 1990): 493–521.

Moore, David W., E. Jennifer Monaghan, and Douglas K. Hartman. "Conversations: Values of Literacy History." *Reading Research Quarterly* 32 (January–March 1997): 90–102.

Murphy, Anna Marie, and Cullen Murphy. "Onward, Upward with McGuffey and Those Readers." *Smithsonian* 15 (November 1984): 182–208.

Nackman, Mark E., and Darryl K. Paton. "Recollections of an Illinois Woman." *Western Illinois Regional Studies* 1 (1978): 27–44.

Norse, Clifford C. "School Life of Amanda Worthington of Washington County, 1857–1862." *Journal of Mississippi History* 34 (May 1972): 107–116.

Perlman, Joel, and Dennis Shirley. "When Did New England Women Acquire Literacy?" *William and Mary Quarterly* (3rd series) 48 (January 1991): 50–67.

Perlman, Joel, Silvana R. Siddali, and Keith Whitescarver. "Literacy, Schooling, and Teaching among New England Women, 1730–1820." *History of Education Quarterly* 37 (Summer 1997): 117–139.

Porter, Kenneth Wiggins, ed. "Country Schoolteachers, 1898–1902, Rice Country, Kansas." *Kansas Magazine* (1961): 18–44.

Rayman, Ronald. "Joseph Lancaster's Monitorial System of Instruction and American Indian Education, 1815–1838." *History of Education Quarterly* 21 (Winter 1981): 395–409.

Resnick, Daniel P., and Lauren B. Resnick. "The Nature of Literacy: An Historical Exploration." *Harvard Educational Review* 47 (Fall 1977): 370–385.

Robenstine, Clark. "French Colonial Policy and the Education of Women and Minorities: Louisiana in the Early Eighteenth Century." *History of Education Quarterly* 32 (Summer 1992): 193–211.

Salisbury, Neal. "Red Puritans: 'The Praying Indians' of Massachusetts Bay and John Eliot." *William and Mary Quarterly* (3rd Series) 31 (January 1974): 27–54.

Schrimsher, Lila Gravatt, ed. "The Diary of Anna Webber: Early Day Teacher of Mitchell County." *Kansas Historical Quarterly* 38 (Autumn 1970): 320–337.

Schutt, Amy C. "'What Will Become of Our Young People?' Goals for Indian Children in Moravian Missions." *History of Education Quarterly* 38 (Fall 1998): 268–286.

Sklar, Kathryn Kish. "The Schooling of Girls and Changing Community Values in Massachusetts Towns, 1750–1820." *History of Education Quarterly* 33 (Winter 1993): 511–542.

Smith, Joan K., Grayson Noley, Courtney Vaughn, and Mary Frances Smith. "From Majority to Minority: The Chocktaw Society and the Wright Family in Oklahoma." *Midwest History of Education Journal* 25 (1998): 132–136.

Smith, Timothy. "Protestant Schooling and American Nationality, 1800–1850." *Journal of American History* 53 (March 1967): 679–695.

Stambler, Moses. "The Effect of Compulsory Education and Child Labor Laws on High School Attendance in New York City." *History of Education Quarterly* 8 (Summer 1968): 189–214.

Stedman, Lawrence C., and Carl F. Kaestle. "Literacy and Reading Performance in the United States, from 1880 to the Present." *Reading Research Quarterly* 22 (Winter 1987): 8–46.

Stevens, Edward W., Jr. "Technology Literacy, and Early Industrial Expansion in the United States." *History of Education Quarterly* 30 (Winter 1990): 523–544.

Tanis, Norman Earl. "Education in John Eliot's Indian Utopias, 1646–1675." *History of Education Quarterly* 10 (Fall 1970): 308–323.

Taylor, Brian W. "The Edgeworths' Influence on the Warrenton Female Academy." *Vitae Scholasticae* 14 (Spring 1995): 61–72.

Teaford, Jon. "The Transformation of Massachusetts Education, 1670–1780." *History of Education Quarterly* 10 (Fall 1970): 287–307.

Tully, Alan. "Literacy Levels and Educational Development in Rural Pennsylvania, 1729–1775." *Pennsylvania History* 39 (April 1972): 301–312.

Tyack, David. "The Kingdom of God and the Common School." *Harvard Educational Review* 36 (Fall 1966): 447–469.

Vinovskis, Maris A. "Family and Schooling in Colonial Nineteenth Century America." *Journal of Family History* 12 (1987): 19–37.

———. "Trends in Massachusetts Education." *History of Education Quarterly* 12 (Winter 1972): 501–529.

Watkinson, James D. "Reluctant Scholars: Apprentices and the Petersburg (Virginia) Benevolent Mechanic's Association School." *History of Education Quarterly* 36 (Winter 1996): 429–448.

Wecter, Dixon. "Literary Culture on the Frontier." In *A Literary History of the United States*. Rev. ed. Edited by Robert E. Spiller et al. New York: Macmillan, 1953.

Willis, Arlette Ingram. "Literacy at Calhoun Colored School 1892–1945." *Reading Research Quarterly* 37 (January-March 2002): 8–44.

Wright, Mary Byram. "Personal Recollections of the Early Settlement of Carlinville, Illinois." *Journal of the Illinois State Historical Society* 18 (1925–26): 668–685.

Index

ABCFM (American Board for Commissioners for Foreign Missions), 203–4
Adams, Abigail, 17–19, 21
Adams, Hannah, 16–17
Adams, John, 17–18
adult night schools, 16, 41, 45, 121, 122
advertisements, private tutor, 15–16, 41, 59, 73
African American education, 227–59;
    antebellum North, 231–35; antebellum South, 149, 235–43; assimilation programs, 253–55; Bible literacy, 236, 237, 241; black leaders promote, antebellum period, 233–35; Calhoun Colored School (Ala.), 253–55; during Civil War, in the South, 243–50; colonial period opportunities, 10, 44, 45, 72, 227–31; Female Boarding School (Conn.), 232–33; Hampton Institute (Va.), 244, 253; legislation against, 232, 242; literacy rates, antebellum period, 243; Penn School (S.C.), 246–47; plantation preachers, 241; Reconstruction era, in the South, 250–55; segregated schools, 275–76; slaves' methods of obtaining, 236–37, 238–40; through white aid, antebellum South, 236, 237, 238, 240–41;

white fear of, 232–33, 242–43, 251; women's literary societies, 233–34
African Methodist Episcopal (A.M.E.) Church, 235, 241
agents of literacy. *See* home education, family; religious agents
Alabama, 240
Alaska, 218–19
Alcott, Bronson, 97–99
Alcott, Louisa May, 98
Alger, Horatio, 277
alphabet method, 106
American Board for Commissioners for Foreign Missions (ABCFM), 203–4
American Home Missionary Society (AHMS), 89, 145, 181–82
The American Instructor, 16
American Literacy Revolutions, First and Second, 298–99
American Missionary Association, 244
The American Spelling Book (Webster), 106–7, 154
American Sunday School Union, 90, 166
Anderson Seminary (Va.), 121
Anglican schools, 40, 42, 45, 48, 56, 228–29, 230
apprenticeship, 24–25, 41, 56, 57, 104, 122

women teachers: of African Americans, Reconstruction era, 252; dame schools, 11, 12–14, 15, 22, 40; early nineteenth century, 108; financial independence, desire for, 23, 169; governesses, 73; haphazardness of careers, 147; summer schools, 22;

wages, 108. *See also* home education, family
world literacy, 303
Wright, Caledonia, 169–70

Young, Brigham, 183, 184

About the Authors

EDWARD E. GORDON is President of the Imperial Consulting Corporation. Through its two divisions, Imperial Tutoring and Educational Services (a North Central Accredited Tutoring School), and Imperial Corporate Training and Development, he has directed over the course of thirty years the development of education and training programs for tens of thousands of children and adults. Gordon has also taught for twenty years at three Chicago-area universities: DePaul, Loyola, and Northwestern. He is the author of twelve other books, including *Closing the Literacy Gap* (1991), *Futurework* (1994), *Enhancing Learning* (1998), and *Skills Wars* (2000). He is also author of over 200 articles on aspects of learning for children and adults. He earned his B.A. and M.A. degrees in history at DePaul University and his Ph.D. in history of education and educational psychology at Loyola University.

ELAINE H. GORDON is the Vice-President for Research of the Imperial Consulting Corporation. She was a reference librarian at the University of Illinois at Chicago for five years and then for fourteen years was the Instruction Librarian at DePaul University. She is the co-author with Edward E. Gordon of *Centuries of Tutoring: A History of Alternative Education in Western Europe and America* (1990). She earned her B.A. in Political Science at Manhattanville College, Purchase, New York; an M.A. in political science at Georgetown University; a M.L.S. from Dominican University, Oak Park, Illinois; and also pursued graduate studies in political science at the University of Wisconsin, Madison.